Oriental Enlightenment

In spite of growing fascination in the West in recent years for Oriental traditions such as Buddhism, Confucianism, Hinduism, and Taoism, there remain entrenched Eurocentric attitudes which tend to marginalise the influence of Eastern thought on the West.

Oriental Enlightenment: The Encounter Between Asian and Western Thought challenges such attitudes by exploring the role of 'orientalism' within the broad sweep of the modern Western intellectual tradition, and by demonstrating in detail how Eastern ideas have woven their way through debates in such fields as philosophy, religion, and psychology. In attempting to understand the deeper significance of this remarkable, if not always adequately acknowledged, strand in the history of Western ideas, *Oriental Enlightenment* explores some of the cultural, political, and intellectual factors that have helped to shape orientalist interests. J. J. Clarke offers a fresh evaluation of orientalist perspectives ranging from ecstatic romanticisation to condescending racism, and engages with recent arguments which see orientalism as simply an expression of Western imperial power. At the same time the author offers a sympathetic understanding of the positive role that the East has played in the intellectual and spiritual life of the West.

Covering the period from the ages of Enlightenment and Romanticism to the present, as well as engaging with contemporary postcolonial and postmodern debates, this highly accessible introduction will be of interest to students of history, philosophy, psychology and comparative religion, and anyone seeking an understanding of the development of modern Western thought.

J. J. Clarke is Head of History of Ideas at Kingston University, UK. He has also taught at the University of Singapore and is the author of *Jung and Eastern Thought* (Routledge). He recently edited the collection *Jung and the East* (Routledge).

Oriental Enlightenment

The encounter between Asian and Western thought

J. J. Clarke

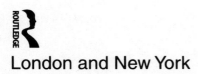

London and New York

First published 1997
by Routledge
11 New Fetter Lane, London EC4P 4EE

Simultaneously published in the USA and Canada
by Routledge
29 West 35th Street, New York, NY 10001

Reprinted 1997

Typeset in Baskerville by Routledge
Printed and bound in Great Britain by
T. J. International Ltd, Padstow, Cornwall

British Library Cataloguing in Publication Data
A catalogue record for this book is available from the British Library

Library of Congress Cataloguing in Publication Data
Clarke, J. J. (John James), 1937–
Oriental enlightenment: the encounter between Asian and Western
thought / J. J. Clarke.
p. cm.
Includes bibliographical references and index.
1. Philosophy, Oriental. 2. Civilization, Oriental.
3. East and West. I. Title.
B5010.C57 1997
950'.07'01821—dc20

96–41067
CIP

ISBN 0–415–13375–0 (hbk)
ISBN 0–415–13376–9 (pbk)

Contents

Acknowledgements

I am very grateful to many friends and colleagues who have given me invaluable encouragement and criticisms in the writing of this book. Special thanks are due to Nicholas Battye, Ray Billington, Jill Boezalt, Andrew Burniston, Ann Cartland, Barry Cavell, Peter Conradi, Chris Hughes, John Mepham, Mary Anne Perkins, Jonathan Rée, and Daphne Turner. I also wish to thank the Faculty of Human Sciences at Kingston University for giving me relief from teaching in order to complete this work.

Part I

Introduction

Chapter 1

Orientations
The issues

THE EAST: EUROPE'S 'OTHER'

He who knows himself and other,

Will also recognise that East and

West cannot be separated.

(Goethe)

Oh, East is East, and West is West,

and never the twain shall meet.

Till Earth and Sky stand presently,

at God's great Judgement Seat.

(Kipling)

The contradiction between these two opinions points to an age-old ambivalence in the West's attitude towards the East. On the one hand it has been a source of inspiration, fount of an ancient wisdom, a culturally rich civilisation which is far superior to, and can be used to reflect on the inadequacies of, our own. On the other, it is an alien region of looming threat and impenetrable mystery, long locked in its stagnant past until rudely awakened by the modernising impact of the West. It is a place which invites imaginative flights and exaggerations of all kinds. On the one hand, according to Voltaire, the East is the civilisation 'to which the West owes everything', and for Arnold Toynbee the West's encounter with the East is one of the most significant world events of our time. Others have been less enthusiastic: C. S. Peirce spoke contemptuously of 'the monstrous mysticism of the East', and Arthur Koestler dismissed its religions as 'a web of solemn absurdities'. For some, like Goethe, the relationship is deep and significant and, according to the sinologist Joseph Needham, there has been a dialogue going on for 3,000 years between 'the two ends of the Old World' in which East and West have greatly influenced each other. For others the relationship is peripheral and ephemeral, only really conspicuous in the brief neo-Romantic movement of the 1960s when young men and women went Eastwards in search of 'pop nirvana'.

This ambivalence is evident in a whole range of familiar stereotypes and myths which serve to place East and West in a variety of opposing or complementary relationships with each other. Some of these are tied to popular attitudes and prejudices, some to religious and political propaganda, and some originate from more scholarly sources and serve serious intellectual purposes. Oriental 'splendour', 'sensuality', 'cunning', and 'cruelty' are well-known examples of this genre. The East has often been perceived as colourful and alluring, summed up in the word 'exotic', or by contrast as sinister and threatening, as in such evocative phrases as 'yellow peril', 'Asiatic hordes', 'Oriental despotism'. Also familiar is the set of attitudes summed up in phrases like 'the mystical Orient' which carry the alluring appeal of spiritual sublimity and also of benighted obscurantism.[1] Broadening out from such stereotypes we can discern a perplexing variety of attitudes, ranging from the eulogistic to the defamatory. Needham expresses the former attitude in his remark that 'Chinese civilisation has the overpowering beauty of the wholly other, and only the wholly other can inspire the deepest love and the profoundest desire to learn' (1969a: 176).

However, even where there was respect for the East, often to the point of elevating it to a position high above the 'decadent' West, the otherness, even the strangeness, of the East has been emphasised; thus C. G. Jung, who was as sympathetic as any in the twentieth century towards the East, spoke of 'the strangeness, one might almost say . . . incomprehensibility, of the Eastern psyche' (1978: 187). And the Buddhist writer Stephen Batchelor has argued that for Europeans 'Asia came to stand for something both unknown and distant yet also to be feared', in psychological terms 'a cipher for the Western unconscious, the repository of all that is dark, unacknowledged, feminine, sensual, repressed and liable to eruption' (1994: 234).

The idea of the East as some shadowy, threatening 'other' with which the West is in sharp conflict, and the essentialising of East and West into two simple and contrastive categories, has a long history and can be traced back to the time of Herodotus and to the epic conflict between Hellenes and Persians, giving rise to the mythical contrast between the heroic, liberty-loving and dynamic West and the despotic, stagnant and passive East. This idea has taken various forms in more recent times. The historian Raghavan Iyer, for example, has spoken of a 'glass curtain' that the West has created between itself and the lands and cultures of the East, and has drawn attention to what he describes as 'an eternal schism' between Asians and Europeans which is backed by 'the dubious notion of an eternal East–West conflict, the extravagant assumption of a basic dichotomy in modes of thought and ways of life' (1965: 5 and 7). And the political theorist Samuel Huntington has recently argued that the conflict between East and West is part of a wider 'clash of civilisations', involving a fundamental cultural cleavage between Western and other civilisations which goes deeper than national or ideological differences (see Huntington 1993). Such polarities have sometimes taken less obviously conflictual form and been manifested in the archetypal myth of East and West as mutually complementary opposites, a view which has often encouraged the elevation of the East to sublime heights, though it has also at times sanctioned less flattering attitudes. In the hands of some thinkers this duality carries the Romantic message of the 'marriage of East and West' and the pursuit of the ultimate unity of the human spirit which has had the misfortune to become bifurcated in the modern age, the West's 'rationalistic and ethical, positivistic and practical' mind needing to be supplemented by 'the Eastern mind [which] is more inclined to inward life and intuitive thinking' (Radhakrishnan 1939: 48). For some it signifies the possibility of a more harmonious and complete mental life that encourages the integration of opposite yet complementary psychic factors such as introverted and extraverted tendencies, or which brings into balance the 'feminine' qualities of the East and the 'masculine' qualities of the West. And for yet others it has powerful political implications, addressing the modern dilemma of a world which is converging socially and economically, yet which at the same time is riven with mutual enmity and strife, and which needs the complementary qualities of both East and West. On the other side of the coin, such polarities have at times betokened fundamentally oppressive attitudes whereby, whether consciously or otherwise, the East is seen as the negative complement of the West, a passive inferior consort to the controlling masculine West, a culture characterised by emotional, feminine weakness, contrasted with the rational, male strength of its Western other.[2]

Equivocal attitudes such as these go some way to explain why there is still a reluctance in the academic world to take traditional Asian thought seriously. Even in times characterised by the globalisation of culture there still remains an endemic Eurocentrism, a persistent reluctance to accept that the West could ever have borrowed anything of significance from the East, or to see the place of Eastern thought within the Western tradition as much more than a recent manifestation, evanescent and intellectually lightweight, at best only a trivial part of a wider reaction against the modern world. For some the Orient is still associated with shady occultist flirtations, the unconscious rumblings of the repressed irrational urges of a culture that has put its faith in scientific rationalism. For others Eastern interests remain little more than the manifestation of the exotic but inconsequential extravagances of New Age mysticism. Many academics continue to feel a certain embarrassment about the whole subject of the East, and not only have histories of philosophy tended to exclude Eastern thought – 'Philosophy speaks Greek and only Greek' as Simon Critchley ironically put it (1995: 18) – but the role of Eastern thought within the broad Western intellectual tradition has largely been ignored by historians of ideas.[3] My aim in this book is to try to alter such perceptions and to show that throughout the modern period from the time of the Renaissance onwards, the East has exercised a strong fascination over Western minds, and has entered into Western cultural and intellectual life in ways which are of considerably more than passing significance within the history of Western ideas. I shall draw attention to the long tradition of orientalist research and intellectual curiosity in Europe and America which has helped to place religious and philosophical ideas of India, China, and Japan within the mainstream of Western thought, indicating how in the Enlightenment and Romantic periods the 'East' was a central theme of intellectual debates, and that in the nineteenth and twentieth centuries ideas from the Orient have played an increasingly serious role in a wide variety of contexts. Moreover, I shall suggest that the information flowing Westwards from these cultures has provided not merely entertainment and distraction, a sort of exotic time out, as is often supposed, but also an instrument of serious self-questioning and self-renewal, whether for good or ill, an external reference point from which to direct the light of critical inquiry into Western traditions and belief systems, and with which to inspire new possibilities.

The aim of this book, then, is to present a challenge to this myth, not only by displaying the Eurocentric narrowness of intellectual historiography, but also by bringing into sharp relief the momentous intellectual encounter that has indeed taken place between 'the two ends of the Old World'. This encounter of ideas between East and West over a considerable historical period is surprising enough in itself. What is all the more paradoxical is that it has occurred in the period of the rapid extension of Western military and economic power over the nations of South and East Asia, a period in which Western global superiority was being exerted and celebrated in so many fields of cultural endeavour. On the face of it, there is something deeply puzzling about the fact that the West, in a manner which is almost unique amongst major imperial powers, while exerting its hegemony over the East, has simultaneously admired it, elevated it, and held it up as a model, an ideal to be aspired to and emulated, going Eastwards as a 'pilgrim in sackcloth and ashes, anxious to prostrate himself at the guru's feet' (Koestler 1960: 11). Much of the West's perception of the East may have been clouded by fantasy and wishful thinking; as we shall see, the representations of the East by Western thinkers often tell us more about the minds of the latter than of the former. Nonetheless, it remains a matter of astonishment that generations of intellectuals and scholars, followed by an ever-growing sample of the educated public, have sought insight and inspiration in far-off lands in the East, and have endeavoured to incorporate the Orient into their own thinking. As the Indologist Wilhelm Halbfass observes, by contrast with the civilisations of Asia which have not spontaneously reached out towards Europe, the East has been 'the goal and referent of Utopian projections, of searching for the identity and the origins of Europe, of European self-questioning and self-criticism' (1988: 369).

There is, of course, another side to this story. The peoples and cultures of Asia have also been the objects of political and economic domination, and of arrogant, racist opprobrium in the West. The story of the relationship between the Western colonial powers and the nations of the East is not only one of enlightened intellectual and cultural exploration, but is often a shameful one of colonial exploitation and expropriation in which the peoples of Asia have been perceived as the inferior complement to the West, its opposite 'other', the bearer of negative qualities whereby the West's own superiority is by contrast underscored and its rule legitimised. It is painfully evident that the West has approached Asia 'armed with gun-and-gospel truth' (Koestler 1960: 11), systematically imposing its religions, its values, and its legal and political systems on Eastern nations, frequently careless of local sensitivities and indifferent to indigenous traditions. Moreover, recent postcolonial studies have drawn attention to the way in which oppressive and racist attitudes not only are to be found in the historical reality of empire, but also have become firmly inscribed in Western discourse at many levels, even at a time when the official apparatus of colonial rule has been all but dismantled. Colonialism survives in postcolonial minds and societies, for as one recent book in this field puts it: 'The hegemony of Europe did not end with the raising of a hundred national flags [for] its legacy of division and racism are alive and well in political, media, and legal domains' (Tiffin and Lawson 1994: 9). As I have already indicated, and as we shall discover in greater detail in the course of this work, there is indeed something deeply ambivalent about the West's attitude towards the East. Even where the conscious intentions and attitudes of Westerners have appeared most benign and reverential towards the East, it is difficult to escape the suspicion that the 'Light of Asia' has been exploited for Western purposes with as much ruthlessness as more tangible substances. There are those who would argue that, even where Western interests have been hallmarked with the purest of scientific intentions, Asian philosophical and religious ideas have been commodified and expropriated in ways that reflect and reinforce the more overt manifestations of imperialist expansion. Some would go so far as to claim that the relationship between West and East in the modern period, however spiritual and lofty it may appear, must necessarily be understood in the final analysis as 'a relationship of power, domination, of varying degrees of complex hegemony' (Said 1985: 5).

ORIENTALISM: TERMS AND THEMES

In this book, then, I shall seek to recover and re-examine the serious intellectual involvement – with all its incongruities and contrarieties – of the West with Eastern ideas. For the sake of convenience I shall employ the word *orientalism* to refer to the range of attitudes that have been evinced in the West towards the traditional religious and philosophical ideas and systems of South and East Asia. This is a debatable choice. 'Orientalism' has become a highly problematic term, one which is difficult to use in a neutral sense, and which according to the Islamicist Bernard Lewis 'is by now . . . polluted beyond salvation' (1993: 103). Moreover, it is a word which in recent years has been more typically associated with attitudes towards the cultures of the Middle East than with those of South and East Asia which are the concern of the present study.[4] The term first appeared in France in the 1830s, and has been employed since then in a variety of different ways: to refer to Oriental scholarship, to characterise a certain genre of romantic-fantasy literature, to describe a genre of painting, and – most significantly in recent times – to mark out a certain kind of ideological purview of the East which was a product of Western imperialism. The latter connotation is famously associated with Edward Said whose ideas are seminal to any debate on the subject matter of this book, as well as in the broad domain of postcolonial theory. A Palestinian who since 1963 has taught English and Comparative Literature at Columbia University, Said drew the concept into the centre of contention in the 1970s with his book *Orientalism*. There he used the term to launch a powerful critique of Western representations of the East, arguing that the 'Orient' is a Western construct, 'a system of ideological fictions', whose purpose is to reinforce and justify Western power over the Orient, and that Western knowledge of the Orient 'has generally proceeded not only from dominion and confrontation but also from cultural antipathy' (1985: 321 and 155).[5] To be sure, Said's concern in that book was, for the most part, with the Islamic world of the Middle East. Our concern in the present book, by contrast, will be with the philosophical/religious systems associated with the countries of South and East Asia, and which are usually known under such names as Hinduism, Buddhism, Confucianism, and Taoism.[6] Nevertheless, as a consequence of Said's writings the whole debate about Europe's relationship with its 'other' has been refigured, and has extended its terms of reference outwards to engage with a whole range of contemporary intellectual debates, into issues concerning, for example, multiculturalism, postcolonialism, subaltern studies, discourse theory, and postmodernism, one consequence of which is that any study of the West's relationship with Eastern thought must be contextualised within the debate which Said's work helped to initiate.

However, while the present work is indebted to Said, it will follow a path which is in certain important respects different from his own. Where Said painted orientalism in sombre hues, using it as the basis for a powerful ideological critique of Western liberalism, I shall use it to uncover a wider range of attitudes, both dark and light, and to recover a richer and often more affirmative orientalism, seeking to show that the West has endeavoured to integrate Eastern thought into its own intellectual concerns in a manner which, on the face of it, cannot be fully understood in terms of 'power' and 'domination'. Where Said, drawing on Michel Foucault's work concerning the relationship between knowledge and power, saw orientalism as a 'master narrative' of Western imperialism which constructs and controls its subjugated other, I shall portray it as tending to confront the structures of Western knowledge and power and to engage with Eastern ideas in ways which are more creative, more open-textured, and more reciprocal than are allowed for in Said's critique. This does not by any means imply a total rejection of Said's attitude of suspicion towards orientalism or his attempts to politicise it. Western representations of the East have certainly been shaped to some extent by colonial preoccupations and ethnocentric biases, and, following Said, a number of recent studies have documented and discussed the repressive and discriminative nature of much Western discourse about non-European peoples and cultures. However, while recognising that orientalism can only be understood adequately within the framework of colonialism and the imperialist expansion of the West, I wish to avoid seeing it as simply a mask for racism or as a purely Western construct which serves as a rationalisation of colonial domination. European hegemony over Asia represents a necessary but not a sufficient condition for orientalism. Power has been wielded over the Orient by superior guns and commercial muscle, as well as by the application of organising and classifying schemes which 'place' the East within a Western intellectual structure. On the face of it this is not essentially different from the way in which any expansionist nation or tribe seeks to dominate and control the resources and minds of its neighbours, but what is peculiar in the case of orientalism is the degree to which the colonised ideas have been elevated above those of the coloniser, and have been used to challenge and disrupt the master narratives of the colonising powers. Orientalism, I shall argue, cannot simply be identified with the ruling imperialist ideology, for in the Western context it represents a counter-movement, a subversive entelechy, albeit not a unified or consciously organised one, which in various ways has often tended to subvert rather than to confirm the discursive structures of imperial power.

In order to make this case adequately I shall examine a wide range of orientalist texts and debates from the seventeenth century up to the present time. There have been many admirable studies of the relationship between Eastern and Western thought in specific periods and from different perspectives, studies which have focused for example on the the Enlightenment or the Romantic periods, or which have examined particular themes, concepts, or controversies; I shall be making use of these studies in the chapters that follow. What has not yet been attempted, to my knowledge, is an overview which seeks to link these together in a way which, both historically and critically, locates orientalism within the broad sweep of the modern Western intellectual tradition.

This is an ambitious undertaking which requires some justification, especially in the light of current disfavour bestowed on the writing of 'linear' histories, and doubts about the possibility of treating the 'Western tradition' – let alone the 'Eastern' – in a coherent way. An obvious question is: why construe orientalism as just *one* story, as a *single* narrative? Certainly Edward Said believed that there is a discernible coherent history of European representation and intellectual appropriation of the Orient, 'a remarkably persistent framework of analysis which [is] expressed through theology, literature, philosophy, and sociology' (Turner 1994: 21). However, this view has been challenged in recent years in the service of a more pluralistic, heterogeneous approach, for example by the literary historian Lisa Lowe who queries 'the assumption that orientalism *monolithically* constructs the Orient as the Other of the Occident' (Lowe 1991: ix–x), and by the historian Rosanne Rocher who criticises Said for creating 'a single discourse, undifferentiated in space and time and across political, social, and intellectual identities' (in Breckenridge and van der Veer 1993: 215). In broader terms it might well be disputed by those who see it as an example of the essentialising and totalising strategies of traditional historiography in which differences are flattened out in pursuit of some transhistorical perspective. To be sure orientalism does not constitute a fixed, simple, or unified subject, and it does not manifest the self-conscious distinctiveness of, say, Catholicism, or science, or Marxism. I will be at pains to underline the historical discontinuities and changes in the focus of the West's attitude towards Asian thought that have occurred over the past few centuries, and to stress the diversity of ends and purposes that is to be found amongst orientalists, ranging from the religious and spiritual to the political and scientific. Nevertheless there is, I believe, an identifiable family of intellectual attitudes and practices for which this term provides a useful label, a recognisable style of thinking, responding, and evaluating that invites articulated historical and critical investigation.

This approach does not rest on any assumption about the East as a unified cultural object. I shall argue that the identity of orientalism, and hence the distinctiveness of this book's subject matter, lies not in the supposed unity of the object it has sought to represent, but rather in a characteristic family of attitudes and approaches that Europeans have taken to it, namely the manner in which, from the seventeenth to the twentieth centuries, Western thinkers have drawn Eastern ideas into the orbit of their intellectual and cultural interests, constructing a set of representations of it in pursuit of Western goals and aspirations. In the final analysis, though, the 'orientalism' narrated and dissected in this book is itself a construct, a story about stories, and hence only one of many possible ways of giving sense to the world, one of many possible versions of intellectual history. I want to avoid the assumption that there is some 'real' or 'essential' orientalism out there, a 'natural kind' to which my own narrative corresponds. Nevertheless, just as feminist, working-class, and black historians have remapped traditional historiography by drawing into the foreground historical perspectives previously occluded by dominant interests, so too the present book is an attempt to rethink modern Western intellectual history by highlighting a still too neglected and marginalised aspect. In one sense this procedure is indeed arbitrary, for it constitutes only one of many logically possible ways of ordering historical experience, yet at the same time I believe that historians of ideas, as well as those of other kinds, have an obligation to 'make sense' of the world, even while admitting that this sense is as much made as found.

A closely related question concerns the dangers of treating the Orient itself as a single undifferentiated entity. Crucial terms such as 'East', 'Orient', and 'West' become devices for reducing endless complexities and diversities into manageable and falsifying unities, a semantic artifice which has encouraged us to think in terms of the contrasting of East and West in some eternal transcendent opposition. For the sake of expository convenience and economy terms like 'East' and 'the Orient' will be used throughout the book to refer to the cultural and intellectual traditions of South and East Asia *tout court*. Also, for stylistic reasons they will be used interchangeably, without any intended semantic shift, to encompass the religious and philosophical legacies of Japan, China, Tibet, India, and Sri Lanka. However, they are used 'under erasure' (in Derrida's sense), and it will be made explicit in a number of places in this book that these terms are to be looked upon with scepticism, as indicative of an endemic inclination to stereotype and manipulate the cultures of Asia, and it is my hope that the variety of examples, cases, and texts cited will counter any tendency to fuse either the Orient or orientalism into an undifferentiated blur.

I need also to make it clear that orientalism will not be treated as an *isolated* phenomenon, a closed monolith, but will be shown to be bound up with and to intertwine with a number of other, wider intellectual and historical processes. These include in the first place the broad set of concerns associated with the traditional business of such disciplines as philosophy, theology, psychology, and the natural sciences, along with the historical factors that have underpinned these over the past few hundred years, and my account of orientalism will be designed to highlight the relationship between orientalism and some of the central themes and debates of the modern Western intellectual tradition. Other factors include a number of concepts and issues that have come sharply into focus in recent years, such as multiculturalism, ethnic identity, race, and gender, and the West's relationship with Islam, Africa, and other areas of one-time colonisation. This will involve invading a variety of discipline areas, a risky enterprise in an age of strict specialisms, but the subject matter of this book demands that the historian of ideas be prepared to make unusually wide connections. It is impossible now to reflect on the West's fascination with the Orient without linking it to the issue of globalisation of European culture with all its consequential social and intellectual problems, and we shall see not only how orientalism has played a role in the historical unfolding of these issues and conflicts, particularly in the context of imperialism and colonialism, but also how it continues to have relevance to contemporary debates concerning modernity and postmodernity.

HISTORY OF IDEAS: METHODS AND MEANS

This historically nuanced approach is typical of the discipline of the history of ideas as it is currently practised. In the past the historical study of ideas has often taken what can best be described as an 'idealist' form, in the sense that it has tended to treat the historical unfolding of ideas as if they existed in a dimension of reality detached from the rest of history, an approach which has drawn upon the heads of historians of ideas the contempt of those historians who claim to be concerned with the 'real' world.[7] There has certainly been a tendency towards a form of idealism in dealing with the East itself, to treat it as if it were composed of timeless, historically-neutered texts and ideas, 'dirt-free and smelling of sandalwood', as one writer ironically expressed it (Hillman 1975: 67). The history of ideas approach adopted here involves, in the first place, dealing with ideas and thinkers in their historical context, trying to make sense of them within the framework of social, political, and economic developments, rather than within an enclosed intellectual world. It also means that, while we will be concerned mainly with the Western *intellectual* tradition rather than with the broader domain of cultural and popular history, that is to say with matters which in a broad and non-technical sense could be described as 'philosophical', my approach will nevertheless place this tradition within a wider frame that includes literature, religion, and political attitudes. Furthermore, while we will spend a lot of time in the company of 'serious' thinkers ranging from Leibniz and Voltaire to Jung and Buber, it will situate these alongside more fashionable 'popular' writers such as Alan Watts and Arthur Koestler, and semi-popular movements such as theosophy and beat Zen. By the same token, this book is not a history of oriental scholarship, but of a form of discourse – orientalism – which both draws on and goes well beyond this academic discipline, drawing on, for example, the work of philosophers, theologians, and psychologists, and extending outwards to a broad cultural field which in recent orientalist debates has encompassed some of the main intellectual concerns of the late twentieth century. Nor, plainly, is this a history of Eastern, but rather of Western, ideas, and hence it will not seek any systematic or detailed elucidation of Oriental systems except where this is necessary for purposes of clarification, though I hope that the limitations of the term 'Western' in this context will become plain as the argument unfolds. This means that I shall not be directly concerned with the question of the adequacy of Western perceptions of the Orient, or of the correctness of orientalist interpretations, though I shall indicate where and how distortions and misrepresentations have arisen, and in what ways these cast light on the orientalist phenomenon.

The focus on orientalism as a peculiarly Western discourse also means that I shall not be addressing directly the question of the influence of Western thought in general on the East, nor more specifically will I be concerned with the impact of orientalist discourse on the consciousness. of colonial and postcolonial Asian societies. Nevertheless, it is important to bear in mind the richness and complexity of the cultural interchange involved, and hence the impossibility of drawing precise boundaries or of completely separating out the vectors of interest and influence. Many Asian thinkers over the past 200 years have been drawn into Western philosophical debates and movements such as Kantianism, existentialism, and logical positivism, and a number of Eastern thinkers have been influential in the formulation of orientalist outlooks. These inter-cultural cross-currents, involving figures such as Vivekananda, Radhakrishnan, and Suzuki who have spent time teaching in the West, will be of special interest to us in so far as they indicate that Eastern and Western traditions have been more intimately symbiotic than is often supposed.[8]

In seeking to understand the relationships between the Western and Oriental intellectual traditions I have found useful the *hermeneutical* philosophy of Hans-Georg Gadamer. Although, as I shall argue later, his way of thinking is insufficiently sensitive to the power structures that underlie discursive practices, it does offer a useful way to conceptualise the inter-textual encounters that take place within and across intellectual traditions, and helps to draw out some of the problems and limitations that beset orientalist enterprises. Adopting this approach is also especially appropriate here since increasingly in recent years thinkers from various disciplines have made explicit use of hermeneutics as a way of conceptualising Western engagement with Eastern ideas and traditions.[9] What is particularly useful is Gadamer's notion that all human understanding has to be construed as a kind of *dialogue*, an encounter in which a text or tradition is addressed and which answers questions, or itself questions the interpreter. This 'dialogue' involves 'the interplay of the movement of tradition and the move-ment of the interpreter' (1975: 261), a continuing exchange in which the sense of a text is sought by reiterative interplay of meaning between interpreter and interpreted. One of the consequences of this approach, according to Gadamer, is that we must avoid any supposition that we can enter into and fully recover the meanings and mentalities of past ages and their symbolic products. All knowing is historically grounded, which means that, though I can become aware of, and even critical of, this fact, I can never escape the historical conditions in which I think and write. The prejudices which beset the historical conditions of the inter-pretative process are, then, inescapable, but far from seeing this as a block to communication, he regards it as a necessary condition thereof. The 'prejudice of the Enlightenment against prejudice itself', as Gadamer calls it (1975: 329–40), arose from the illusion that the quest for knowledge could aspire to a place beyond history where the world could be viewed with total objectivity. But once this is seen as a logical impossibility, we can come to terms with the fact that all knowledge is invested with pre-judgements, with what Heidegger called 'fore-understandings', and that without preconceptions and anticipations knowledge would be impossible. Thus, attempts at understanding the past or another cul-ture must involve not an obliteration of difference, but a rapprochement which Gadamer calls a 'fusion' of conceptual horizons, involving the self-awareness of difference, the recognition of the otherness of the other, even the alienness of the other, for the truth 'becomes visible to me only through the "Thou", and only by letting myself be told something by it' (ibid.: xxiii).

What then of my own prejudices and fore-understandings? Clearly I cannot avoid beginning with the categories of my own tradition, and from the questions and assumptions arising from within it. In this sense I am aware that I approach orientalism, a subject which stands precariously between East and West, from a Western standpoint and from within a Western institutionalised context, and to that degree am complicit in what Heidegger described as 'the Europeanization of the earth'. From a more personal point of view I have not sought in this study to disguise my humanistic ideals or my enthusiasm for the orientalist project as tracing out, however imperfectly, an emancipatory trajectory for 'the two ends of the Old World'. At the same time, in seeking to construct a pathway through this complex and much-disputed territory, I have drawn into my discussion the major controversies that have enlivened it in recent years, giving voice to criticisms which would paint orientalism in more negative and even sinister hues, and drawing attention to regions where oriental enlightenment has yielded to palpa-ble evil. It is not my aim, then, to produce a feel-good history which will confirm that the story of orientalism is one of pure sweetness and light, nor on the other hand to brand orientalism as a mere annex to oppressive colonial policy, but rather to present a balanced account, a middle way which will bring out more clearly than is often the case the importance of orientalist debates in the West's intellectual history. There are those who, following Said's work, would argue that the whole historical relationship between East and West is so encumbered with the baggage of colonialism that a Westerner is incapable of dealing with the Orient in anything but a distorting and demeaning way. However, as Said himself points out, 'there is no vantage point *outside* the actuality of relations between cultures' (1989: 216), and so too for Gadamer all viewpoints are historically embedded. The best that authors can do in these circumstances is to alert readers to the position from which they are interpreting, rather than pretend they are in possession of what Richard Rorty has called 'sky hooks' whereby they can swing clear of history.

The structure of the book corresponds to my intention of not only 'telling the story' but of reflecting critically on it, and of rethinking and reconceptualising it in relation to contemporary frames of reference and debate. In the outer sections, therefore, a number of related issues are raised and discussed. Chapter 2 begins by posing the central question of the book: why has the East been an object of such interest and fascination in the West? After reviewing several possible and prevailing theories, it offers a conjecture which becomes a theoretical framework for the rest of the book. The middle two sections could be seen as a way of elaborating and testing this conjecture by narrating in broad outline the history of orientalism from about 1600 to the present, selecting representative samples of the most important streams of thought, debates, texts, and figures in this domain. The second section, and to some extent the third, makes use of and to a large extent summarises the growing body of scholarship which has been devoted to the different periods, and hence much of this will be familiar to specialists working in the field, but it will also provide a bibliographical resource for further research. The survey offered in Parts II and III together will also provide an overview for the general reader who may be surprised at the extent of the proliferation of orientalist activity and influence over the past few centuries. The final section of the book reflects both back and forward on the whole orientalist enterprise. It begins with a chapter which draws out some of the philosophical and ideological issues that have dogged the narrative sections of the book, issues such as relativism, inter-cultural interpretation and translation, and confronts a range of moral and political issues which have sometimes given rise to the claim that orientalism is profoundly misconceived, flawed, and even dangerous. The concluding chapter focuses attention on the present moment, questioning the subject matter of this book in the light of postmodernist attitudes and concerns and in the context of a supposedly postcolonial phase of the West's history, and suggesting ways of understanding the scope and relevance of orientalism at the present time.

I hope that the book will appeal to several categories of reader. In the first place it may appeal to the ever-growing number of people who continue to feel that the traditional philosophies of the East have much to teach us (whether or not we think of ourselves as orientals or occidentals, or neither), and wish to reinforce their interest by engaging with the historical richness of the East–West encounter of ideas. I hope that the book will also be read by scholars and specialists in those humanities and social science disciplines which, in spite of important historical and conceptual links with the East, have often been reluctant to extend their own conceptual horizons in an easterly direction, and that it may thereby provide a stimulus to further research in this area. One of the central claims of this work is that a purely occidental approach to intellectual history, and to the study of certain contemporary issues in such fields as psychology, theology, and sociology, must now be deemed to be inadequate. There remains a persistent insularity in Western intellectual life in spite of world-wide interests and traditions of scholarship in the West, and while many educationists have acknowledged the importance of a global outlook, our school and university curricula have often been slow to respond in practice.[10]

Kipling's verse quoted above may seem dated to many potential readers of this book, but no-one can doubt that we are still constrained within our cultural categories which often project an image of the East as remote and mysterious, and are all too prone to retreat into our ethnic and nationalistic enclaves. An element of pathology has always pervaded attitudes to foreigners, to the 'other', but in an imploding world, beset with global tensions and crises that threaten to engulf us, there is an urgent need to look beyond the simplistic attitudes that gave rise to Kipling's sentiment, and to seek a more ample and inclusive world view, a truly global hermeneutic. In this book we shall be examining the ideas of many bold thinkers who have sought to build bridges between East and West and thereby to further the cause of understanding between peoples of diverse cultural, religious, and intellectual backgrounds. One such bridge-builder was the Cistercian monk Thomas Merton, who left his monastery in America to engage in dialogue with his Hindu and Buddhist counterparts in South-East Asia, and who wrote that

> it is no longer sufficient merely to go back over the Christian and European cultural traditions. The horizons of the world are no longer confined to Europe and America. We have to gain new perspectives, and on this our spiritual and even our physical survival depends.
>
> (Merton 1961: 80)

The pages that follow represent a small contribution to this task.

Chapter 2

Orientalism
Some conjectures

THE ALLURES OF THE EAST

Why has the West been so fascinated by the East? Why, over many centuries, have so many Western thinkers, writers, and intellectuals of all sorts, along with a wide cross-section of the educated public, become infatuated with a culture so remote and so different from their own? In Ancient Greece the East was viewed as a place of wonder, and the naked philosophers of India – the 'gymnosophists' – were objects of considerable interest in the Hellenic world. Marco Polo's expedition to China in the thirteenth century is perhaps the best-known prologue to the long story of the imaginative construction of Asian cultures in the minds of Europeans. But it was the voyages of discovery of the sixteenth century, and the consequent expansion of European consciousness, interest and power, that constituted the first of the central acts of this drama. Where hitherto the Orient beyond the Middle East had been to all intents and purposes a blank sheet on which all kinds of fantasies could be inscribed, now information began to pour back into Europe, initially from the reports of Jesuit missionaries, but later from travellers of all kinds, from traders, colonial administrators, and finally from scholars and seekers of wisdom. It is no exaggeration to say that this information, albeit often distorted and tinged with fantasy and wishful thinking, exercised a magnetic attraction on the European mind. In the eighteenth century it was China that was the object of fascination, Confucius being elevated to almost cult status by European intellectuals such as Voltaire. In the Romantic period attention switched to India, where mystical visions of the unity of the Soul with the All, of Atman with Brahman, and the image of an ancient bond between East and West resonated powerfully with the interests and passions of leading European thinkers. In the nineteenth century it was the turn of Buddhism, with its powerful spiritual message combined with an outlook that appeared to be remarkably in tune with empirical science, which proved an attractive proposition to a number of Western intellectuals. The twentieth century has witnessed an extraordinary proliferation of orientalist interests, ranging from the well-known impact of Zen on the beat and hippie generations, and the dispersal of esoteric Buddhist wisdom from Tibet amongst eager recipients in the West, to the less-well-publicised interests of the academic world which has engaged with the East in dialogue across a whole range of disciplines including theology, philosophy, psychology, and psychotherapy.

This luxuriating fascination for the East, which for convenience I shall call *orientalism*, is on the face of it perplexing and cries out for some kind of historical explanation. As an American philosopher recently put it:

> Among all the surprising transformations of the contemporary world, none is stranger than the way the most industrialized nations of the West are ingesting with the air they breathe some of the oldest perspectives of the oldest systematic philosophy on the planet.
>
> (Jacobson 1981: 3)

What especially stands in need of explanation is the sheer one-sidedness of the West's interest in the East, at any rate until relatively recently. For hundreds, perhaps thousands, of years Western explorers and thinkers have sought out the East, explored and provoked encounters with it, studied and assimilated it, and have alternately enthroned it upon and deposed it from the inmost seats of the West's religious and cultural imagination. By contrast the East has not reached out to the West in the same way, has not actively sought either to conquer it, learn from it, or to bow down before it. To be sure the countries and cultures of Asia have in recent times acceded to the fascination of Western technology and its accompanying cult of consumption, to its political ideologies as well as to its popular cults and idols, and even to its philosophies, but it must be remembered that this process of 'modernisation' is one which did not flower spontaneously from oriental cultural roots, but which was in effect the outcome of Western intrusions and demands.

Also puzzling is the fact that much of the historical background against which the unfolding of orientalism took place was, on the face of it, hostile to the development of any sort of love affair with the East. While on the one hand European intellectuals were going to great literary lengths to elevate India and China to sublime heights of moral and philosophical perfection, the general attitude of the public, of traders, politicians, and colonial administrators was often a mixture of patronising chauvinism and racist contempt. The colonial rulers of British India, for example, saw themselves as a caste above the rest, and for the most part treated the sensibilities, beliefs, and religious practices of their subject peoples with indifference or scorn. China, though never colonised in the full sense, became in the period of Western imperial expansion a standard object of ethnocentric bias, ridiculed for its backwardness and moral vileness. Scholars often gave their support to such attitudes. The nineteenth-century sinologist S. Wells Williams, for example, condemned China as a country which manifested 'a kind and degree of moral degradation of which an excessive statement can scarcely be made, or an adequate conception hardly be formed' (1883: I, 836). Equally, those who were concerned with religious rather than commercial or political conquest often (there were, as we shall see, conspicuous exceptions) looked upon the beliefs and practices of the Asian peoples with horror and disdain. The belief in the Europeans' God-given right to civilise these peoples was indeed a particularly powerful driving force behind the activities of Christian missionaries, especially in the nineteenth century when even a liberal-minded Baptist missionary such as William Carey could maintain that without a Christianising influence Asian nations would relapse into 'rapine, plunder, bloodshed, and violence' (quoted in Kiernan 1972: 40).

What further demands explanation is the modern Western attitude of partial amnesia to the whole complex set of phenomena associated with orientalism. The exploits of Marco Polo have certainly been imprinted on the race-memory of Europeans, but many who pride themselves on a reasonably adequate knowledge of European history will be surprised to learn of the extent of Eastern penetration of the West since that date, and the degree to which that penetration has been the result of active importation. Many people are still under the impression that the fascination with the cultural products of India and China, and the active endeavour to acquire and adopt them, is, leaving aside a few isolated and marginal episodes, of relatively recent date. Art historians do indeed note the influence of Chinese painting on landscape garden and domestic product design in the eighteenth century, and the impact of Japanese prints on late-nineteenth-century European painting is well known. Philosophers occasionally recall that Schopenhauer – a figure not until recently accorded a central place in the philosophical canon – compared his own philosophy with that of the Hindus and Buddhists. The Theosophical Society is often mentioned by cultural historians, though usually in connection with the revival of occultism, or as an example of cultish fraudulence. Recently the work of Joseph Needham has drawn to our attention the possibility that many of the scientific and technical achievements attributed to Europe in the age of the scientific revolution were actually influenced by Chinese precedents, and that these constituted 'important influences upon nascent modern science during the Renaissance period' (1969a: 57). But such voices remain muted, and on the whole the Western self-image, both as popularly conceived and as intellectually constructed, has found little place for the idea that the East has played anything more than a negligible part in its cultural and intellectual formation.

By way of contrast, the influence of West on East has been readily acknowledged. The transformation and modernisation of Asia through the varied instruments of Christianity, science, technology, capitalism, socialism, and democracy have become the objects of extensive study. The Europeanisation of the globe, culturally, politically, intellectually, has become too considerable to be ignored, and along with it has come its inevitable portion of guilt and self-recrimination on the part of Europeans. The comparison between this degree of attention and the restricted perception of both scholars and the public at large of the degree of penetration of the East into the Western consciousness is instructive, and one of the purposes of this study will be to seek to rectify this imbalance and to show that the East has had a noteworthy role to play in the formation and transformation of European thought and culture from the eighteenth century onwards. To quote the Dutch theologian, Hendrik Kraemer, in addition to the West's invasion of the East, 'There is also an Eastern invasion of the West, more hidden and less spectacular than the Western invasion, but truly significant' (1960: 228).[1]

ORIENTAL ENCHANTMENT

One of the most common explanations for the West's persistent enchantment with the East can be summed up in the word *romanticisation*. According to this view, the West's interest in the Orient has been guided for the most part by the desire to escape into some remote and fantastic 'other', and to find there a lofty yet illusory means of uplift, or the material for dreams of lost wisdom or golden ages. Radhakrishnan, for example, speaks of the West's attraction towards 'the glamour of the exotic', and points to the fact that 'The East has ever been a romantic puzzle to the West, the home of adventures like those of the *Arabian Nights*, the abode of magic, the land of heart's desire' (1939: 251). Michel Le Bris, in his study of Romanticism, sees the East from the Westerner's viewpoint as

> That Elsewhere, that yearned-for realm where it was supposed that a man might get rid of the burden of self, that land outside space and time, thought of as being at once a place of wandering and a place of homecoming.
>
> (Le Bris 1981: 161)

The East, from this perspective, represents a tendency in the West to escape from its current ills, and to seek solace, however unrealistic and evanescent, in imaginary worlds elsewhere, a longing for a timeless state of being that transcends the painful divisions of this world. In brief it is Europe's collective day-dream, symptomatic of a certain weariness that from time to time besets European culture.

There is some truth in this hypothesis. In the first place much of the literature concerning the East has had, and indeed continues to have, an exaggerated, inflated tendency, a sublimated quality which offers the European an image of magic and mystery, something at once more wise, more exotic, and more thrilling than homespun urbanities. This is evident not only in the more popular genre of orientalist literature, such as the widely read fantasy tales and travelogues that proliferated from the seventeenth century onwards, perhaps the most famous image being that of Shangri-La, the fictitious Buddhist lama paradise described in James Hilton's *Lost Horizon* (1933), but it is a persistent feature, too, in the more 'serious' writings which will occupy our main attention in this book. For example, in the eighteenth century writers of the calibre of Voltaire were not content to write of the perceived virtues of Confucianism, but described it in exaggerated and emotionally charged terms which inevitably attract the epithet 'Romantic'. More recently the object of the West's romanticising tendencies has been Tibet, whose relative isolation, as Peter Bishop points out, 'has given permission for the West to use it as an imaginative escape, a sort of time-out, a relaxation', a place which 'has been described with all the qualities of a dream, a collective hallucination' (1993: 16). Furthermore, as we shall see in detail later, this romanticising tendency has often led to a systematic misrepresentation and oversimplification of the Orient, not only with regard to its ideas and its philosophies, but also with respect to its social and political realities. Nevertheless, while this tendency is clearly present within orientalist discourse throughout its whole history, it does not provide us with a fully satisfying explanation. The hypothesis that orientalism is fundamentally an escapist strategy ignores a number of important factors that will emerge from our historical survey which will underline the extent to which orientalist activities have been closely integrated within central Western intellectual concerns in the modern period, and which will imply that orientalism is to be seen not as an escape, an avoidance, but as a means of *confronting* some of the West's most pressing and immediate problems.[2]

Closely allied to this hypothesis is the belief that the West's fascination with the East represents a retreat from the modern world into *irrationalism*. Orientalism, especially in its more popular embodiments, has frequently been associated with the so-called 'flight from reason', an amorphous tendency of Europe's cultural history which is often seen as originating with the Romantic movement, receiving its philosophical blessing from Schopenhauer, Kierkegaard, and Nietzsche, and manifesting itself in a series of cultural and intellectual movements and fashions from the growth of occultism in the nineteenth century to the New Age movement in the late twentieth. There is no doubt that at various times the interest of Europeans in the Orient has been motivated by a reaction against what is perceived as the strong and central bias within modern Western culture towards what may loosely be described as 'reason', 'logic', 'the rational', indeed towards the whole ethos of science and technology, against what is often summed up as 'the Enlightenment project'. This view is reinforced, for example, by the deep interest shown by Arthur Schopenhauer – who has often been perceived as the arch- or proto-irrationalist – in the philosophies of the East, by the association of Eastern interests with the occult, by the more recent tendency to identify Eastern thought with esotericism and mysticism, and by the Oriental predilections of the beat and hippie generation.

We will need to examine in more detail in a later chapter the 'charge' of irrationalism; apart from any other considerations, this latter term is perhaps too imprecise and has too many complex philosophical ramifications to serve as a key with which to unlock orientalism. It is certainly the case that enthusiasm for Oriental ideas has at times been generated by a mood of disillusionment with what can broadly be termed 'scientific rationalism', and with the materialist and mechanistic philosophies that came to prominence in the wake of the Enlightenment, but as we shall see this by no means gives us an adequate account of orientalism. To take one obvious example, the orientalism of the eighteenth and the nineteenth centuries was often associated, not with irrationalism, but rather with the affirmation of reason and of science by very *contrast* with the perceived irrationalism of European ideologies and institutions, and much of the excitement at the 'discovery' of Buddhism in the Victorian period resulted from the belief that it represented, by contrast with superstitious Christianity, a religion compatible with the basic assumptions of science. It also needs to be emphasised that irrationalism in this context is not necessarily equivalent to a full-frontal assault on accepted methods of rational inquiry, but is often more to do with the recognition of the need to expand and enrich our concept of rationality. A number of twentieth-century thinkers who have taken an interest in Eastern ideas have drawn on Eastern models, not in order to subvert the methods of scientific rationalism as such, but rather to urge that the scope of these methods be broadened, and have seen 'irrationalist' elements in Eastern thought not in terms of replacing but of complementing and counterbalancing what has been seen as the excessive emphasis in the West on a narrowly conceived reasoning function.

If orientalism does not represent, fundamentally, the West's tendency to want to escape into unreality, or into a world where reason and logic no longer weigh down the human spirit, perhaps it arises out of another supposedly supremely European quality, namely *curiosity*. Perhaps, in the words of a Protestant theologian, it is a consequence of a 'Western quest for truth and knowledge, which is such an outstanding characteristic of Western culture' (Kraemer 1960: 18). According to this view, orientalism, whatever its exaggerations or however bizarre its rhetoric, was essentially driven by the desire to know, and was a product of that peculiarly Western invention, empirical science, and more broadly of what Joseph Needham ironically referred to as 'the aspirations of [Europe's] never-satisfied Faustian soul' (1969a: 120). This hypothesis has at times been used by those who claim to perceive fundamental differences between the psychological make-up of the peoples of East and West respectively, and has been invoked by those who are eager to emphasise the West's dynamic, thrusting, enterprising qualities by contrast with the self-satisfied lassitude of the East which, it is claimed, has shown little reciprocal curiosity about the West. For example, M. Collis speaks of Europe as being 'full of intellectual curiosity', and of being 'intelligent enough to see that she had much to learn from China', a quality which, by contrast with China, 'demonstrated her vitality' (1941: 43). And, in a spasm of unconscious self-parody, Denis de Rougemont proclaimed that 'Western man is the man who always goes further, beyond the limits set by nature, beyond traditions fixed by his ancestors, even beyond himself – *on to adventures!*' (1963: 25).[3]

Once again this factor represents part, but by no means the whole, of the story. The history of European culture from the sixteenth century onwards gives ample evidence of a growing awareness of new – and renewed – knowledge, an awareness which was closely tied to the economic and political transformations that were taking place at that time, and which both motivated and was stimulated by the voyages of global exploration in that period. Old ways of thinking about the world, society, values and human destiny were undergoing radical overhaul in the centuries immediately following the Renaissance. According to this perspective, orientalism is an unsurprising accompaniment to the ever-expanding quest for knowledge that is such a characteristic feature of the modern Western era, and which therefore requires no special explanation beyond that which might be offered for the expansion of the scientific spirit as a whole. The emergence of orientalism in the nineteenth century as a scholarly discipline, pursued with scientific rigor, could be cited as evidence in support of this general viewpoint, for here we might imagine that we can see a clear case of a programme of research which arose from the newly emerging scientific ethos of that age which in turn had roots that stretch back to the truth-seekers of Ancient Greece.

As in the case of the previous hypotheses, however, the 'curiosity' theory is too simple and does not fully explain the phenomena in question. When reviewing the history of orientalism we will find again and again that, while a desire for 'scientific' knowledge plays a part, it is usually tied closely in with other more complex factors. We will find that orientalist discourse is inextricably linked into agendas which are much wider than those associated with demands of Oriental scholarship as such, and that fascination with the East arises, not out of purely theoretical concern, even less from popular curiosity for foreign cultures, but rather out of interests which are closely connected to pragmatic concerns which are deeply rooted in Europe's own intellectual, cultural, and political history. These concerns, and the orientalist responses to them, may, as we shall see later, vary from one epoch to another, and it remains to be seen exactly what role they have played within modern Western discourse as a whole, but one of the main arguments of this book will be that orientalism, even in its most academic guise, is inextricably bound up with Western concerns and problems, and only to a limited extent can be thought of in terms of a disinterested quest for knowledge.

EDWARD SAID: THE QUESTION OF POWER

The most consistent and influential attack on the 'pure knowledge' interpretation of orientalism has come from Edward Said. Making use of Michel Foucault's 'power/knowledge' theory, Said argues that orientalism, whatever its explicit claims, offers us, not a 'true' picture of the Orient but a representation, a *re*-presentation of it, a reconstruction, in effect a 'colonising' knowledge, created by the conqueror to comprehend the conquered, and designed to confirm the West's own distinctive identity, and to enhance the West's political and cultural hegemony over Asian peoples. Orientalism, in Said's view, 'is a structure erected in the thick of an imperial contest whose dominant wing it represented and elaborated not only as scholarship but as partisan ideology . . . [which] hid the contest beneath its scholarly and aesthetic idioms' (1989: 211). On this account, therefore, it is a mistake to construe orientalism as a form of objective, disinterested knowledge, and an even greater mistake to think of it in terms of self-indulgent romancing. Nor is it even just a systematic misconception or racist distortion of Eastern traditions, for in Said's view it represents nothing less than the expression and justification of the global authority of the modern West.

Said's account of orientalism has, variously extended and modified, become almost a fashionable orthodoxy amongst scholars and provoked widespread debate in recent years, so it will be necessary to examine it in some detail. First we need to be clear about its scope. On the face of it the 'Orient' that Said is concerned with is not that of China, Japan, or India but rather the Middle East, and the orientalism that is the subject matter of the book of that name (first published in 1978) is concerned with Western intellectual treatment of the Arab/Islamic world over which the European powers, especially Britain and France, have wielded influence in one form or another for the past 200 years. In one sense this clearly excludes the Orient that lies beyond the Levant, and Said alludes to the obvious differences in the historical ties that link West Asia on the one hand and East and South Asia on the other to Europe (see 1985: 17). For example, by contrast with Islam, neither India nor China has been a military threat to Europe in the modern period, nor has Christianity been theologically intertwined with the religions of East and South Asia. In a word, the whole history of the Middle East has been bound up with that of Europe, politically, religiously, and intellectually, in ways that sharply contrast with the rest of Asia. Nevertheless, Said makes it clear that he wishes to see the implications of his argument extending beyond the Middle East to all those areas of the Orient which in one way or another have been brought under the influence of the European powers, an implication contained in his remark that 'The scope of Orientalism exactly matched the scope of empire' (ibid.: 104). Furthermore, while Said's remarks with regard to East and South Asia were tentative and spasmodic, other orientalist scholars have picked up the proffered baton and run with it. Bernard Faure, for example, in his investigation into Chan Buddhism, asserts that Said's argument 'remains valid in the case of the "Far East": India and China in particular had become objects of a similar Oriental discourse' (1993: 5–6). Colin Mackerras makes extensive use of a Saidian model in his study of Western images of China, arguing that 'Although designed specifically as a critique of the Western study of West Asian civilizations, its main points are equally applicable to the study of China' (1989: 3). Similarly, in his analysis of the role of Buddhist ideas in nineteenth-century Britain, Philip Almond starts out from the assumption 'that Victorian discourse about Buddhism is part of a broader discourse about the Orient such as has been brought to light by Edward Said in his book *Orientalism*' (1988: 5). A number of other scholars have come to similar conclusions quite independently of Said. René Guénon, for example, speaks of the German orientalist Hermann Oldenberg as being 'an instrument in the service of [German] national ambition', and sees the reason for the West's interest in Eastern philosophies as 'not to learn from them . . . but to strive, by brutal or insidious means, to convert them to her own way of thinking, and to preach to them' (1941: 156 and 135); and Ernest Gellner dismisses orientalism as 'an image of the East which is at once a travesty, an imposition, and a means of subjugation and domination' (1992: 39).

What, then, is 'orientalism' as Said conceives it? At its very minimum, orientalism is a field of learned study, surrounded by a hinterland of literary expression, amateur enthusiasm, and popular mythology. It is 'the discipline by which the Orient was (and is) approached systematically, as a topic of learning, discovery, and practice', but at the same time it embraces 'that collection of dreams, images, and vocabularies available to anyone who has tried to talk about [the Orient]' (1985: 73). Though informed by travel and fed with information relayed to Europe by missionaries, traders, and administrators, it is essentially a 'textual universe', a construction which has little to do with the current situation of the peoples of Asia, a 'European invention' which has been created to serve the needs of a specifically European agenda. The purpose of constructing such an image and of articulating such a frame of discourse is to establish a 'significant other' by means of which to define Europe's (or the West's) own self-identity, and to establish thereby Europe's superiority and right to rule. Of course, Said admits, 'all cultures impose corrections upon raw reality' and transform information about other cultures 'for the benefit of the receiver' (ibid.: 67). In this way, all knowledge is schematised and reduced to something manageable and assimilable. But as far as knowledge of the Orient is concerned, it is important to recognise that the element of *power* enters deeply into the process. We are not dealing here with a species of pure knowledge, even assuming such a thing actually exists, for however much orientalists may imagine that they are engaged in pure scholarship, standing apart from and untainted by political events, their discourse is inevitably caught up in the whole historical process that is summed up in the term 'Western imperialism'. In its most general form this argument concerns power in its broadest sense, and has roots that go back at least as far as Nietzsche. Its best-known contemporary form is Foucault's argument that knowledge is in effect a function of power, namely that 'power and knowledge directly imply one another . . . there is no power relation without the correlative constitution of a field of knowledge, nor any knowledge that does not presuppose and constitute at the same time power relations' (Foucault 1977: 27).

Thus Said argues that, in general, 'no production of knowledge in the human sciences can ever ignore or disclaim its author's involvement as a human subject in his own circumstances' (1985: 11), and hence, specifically, in the political circumstances of the West's historical relationship with the East.

A number of issues are cast up by this argument, both of a specific nature with regard to the historical validity of Said's case, and of a general epistemological nature. In the former category, some have argued that Said has given a distorted picture of the work of orientalists and has greatly exaggerated the extent to which their work was driven by hostility to Islam, but since these issues are concerned with the Middle East we can leave them on one side.[4] The epistemological issues are more relevant to our present concerns. Here it is not always clear what Said understands by the relationship between knowledge and power. On the one hand he states uncompromisingly that all knowledge about the Orient is shaped in the final analysis by overarching imperialist motivations, however sincere and detached the orientalist might claim to be; how else is one to construe statements like 'all academic knowledge about India and Egypt is somehow tinged and impressed with, violated by, the gross political fact [of empire]' (1985: 11)? Representations of the Orient are, he insists, systematic 'misrepresentations', 'deformations' (ibid.: 272–3). On the other hand he wants to avoid the implication that orientalism is a 'mere collection of lies' (ibid.: 6), and at several points he goes out of his way to disclaim any reductionist intentions, insisting that 'Orientalism is not a mere political subject matter or field that is reflected passively by culture, scholarship, or institutions' (ibid.: 12), and that 'unlike Foucault . . . I do believe in the determining imprint of individual writers upon the otherwise anonymous collective body of texts' (ibid.: 23). At a deeper level there lurks the age-old question of self-referentiality, an issue which haunts any fundamentally relativistic or sceptical position. As Christopher Norris has recently noted, one of the problems with using Foucault's understanding of power/knowledge is that if all truth-claims are bound up with the drive for mastery and control, then the very thesis itself is undermined. On this view, Norris argues, the most liberal and enlightened strategies that are associated with orientalism are epistemically indistinguishable from the most benighted forms of oppression and exploitation (1993: Chapter 5). In a similar vein, Bernard Faure has argued that Said's critique fails to be explicit about the author's own ideological underpinnings, and falls into the trap of 'methodological scapegoatism' whereby criticism of the faults of orientalists tends to overlook 'epistemological constraints' which beset all forms of discourse. Furthermore, Faure argues, Said does not allow adequately for the fact that orientalism has yielded a number of valuable insights, the latter being systematically discounted by the assumption that Western philosophers and scholars are the unconscious agents of Western imperialism (1993: 5–7). At its most trenchant, then, this criticism of Said would amount to the claim that the thesis of *Orientalism* must inevitably lead to a sterile scepticism, even to the point at which no adequate or just representation can conceivably be made of another culture.[5]

An alternative, more liberal, interpretation of Said's argument, according to which power would constitute only one of a number of factors in the East–West equation, might appear more intrinsically plausible. Phrases like 'the sheer knitted-together strength of Orientalist discourse, its very close ties to the enabling socio-economic and political institutions' (Said 1985: 6) suggest that the imperial domination of the East by the West is indeed only one factor, albeit an important one, in trying to make historical sense of orientalism. The strength of Said's case, it seems to me, lies in its power to force orientalism to reveal its suppressed historical origins and its hidden ideological agendas, whatever the specific nature of these origins and agendas is. It will become abundantly evident in the middle sections of this book that the West's love affair with China and India involved no 'dry white light', to use Francis Bacon's phrase, and was certainly not motivated for the most part by a disinterested desire for truth, but was compounded of a variety of motivational factors which were linked in their turn with the West's growing political and commercial interest in the East. The history of the cultural and intellectual relationship between Europe and Asia over the past four centuries must inevitably be viewed in the light of the growth of Western military and economic power. Some have gone so far as to suggest that orientalism, in its study of religious and philosophical traditions of Asia, was merely the intellectual wing of the whole co-ordinated strategy of mapping, measuring, and classifying the peoples of Asia for the purpose of more efficient control, and that the role of orientalists was little different from that of the geographers and surveyors who were part of the colonial retinue.[6] Thus the fascination with Indian religions which began in the late eighteenth century is seen not only as coinciding with the period of European colonial expansion in that sub-continent, but as intimately bound up with the desire to gain control, in all senses, over the newly acquired dominions. To cite just one example, E. J. Sharpe notes in his study of the Western images of the *Bhagavad Gītā* that

> The reason why the East India Company in London had been prepared to fund the first translation of the Gītā was partly that they had allowed themselves to be persuaded that it might prove politically expedient for them to do so. . . . Max Müller's text of the *Rig Veda* was funded by the same commercial company on the same grounds.
>
> (Sharpe 1985: 45)

But while the historical evidence to be adduced later points to the conclusion that what Foucault calls 'régimes of truth', whether in political, commercial, or religious guise, were either implicitly or explicitly at work in the orientalist enterprise, it also points to the conclusion that this cannot be offered as a completely satisfactory explanation of orientalism. As the Islamicist Albert Hourani expresses it, while Said

> is right to say that 'orientalism' is a typically 'occidental' mode of thought . . . he makes the matter too simple when he implies that this style of thought is inextricably bound up with the fact of domination, and indeed is derived from it.
>
> (Hourani 1991: 63)

The view I wish to put forward, therefore, is that while Said is right in his claim that no human knowledge is apolitical, the association of orientalism with colonising power can represent only one part of the story. To see what further needs to be told in elaborating this story, we must now look at some further criticisms of Said's work in this field.

The Saidian mode of explanation, even treated in its most liberal form, is at once too broad and too narrow for our present purposes. It is too broad because, even if we allow for its cogency within the 'high' colonial period of roughly 1800 to 1950, it becomes fragile when stretched beyond those limits. As one scholar puts it: 'There was an orientalism before the empires' (Rodinson 1988: 131). Thus, it is implausible to suggest that the interest of the Enlightenment *philosophes* in Confucianism was motivated, even unconsciously, by the desire to dominate China in anything but the most attenuated meaning of that term.

Furthermore, even within the period 1800–1950 there are some obvious and oft-cited exceptions to a Saidian thesis. The first is Germany. From the early nineteenth century German scholars played a central, sometimes even a leading, role in translating and commenting on the texts of ancient India which were being filtered through into Europe via British colonial employees, yet of course in that period Germany had virtually no colonial interests in India or China.[7] The second exception concerns Japan, which never became a European colony, was never subject to the kind of commercial manipulations that were inflicted on China in the nineteenth century, and from the early seventeenth century was not systematically proselytised by Christian missionaries, yet which also became an object of orientalist attentions.[8]

The narrowness of the Saidian explanation, on the other hand, arises from its inclination towards reductionism, and its tendency to ignore much of the richness and complexity of orientalism and of its accompanying motivations and impulsions, or else to constrain these to fit into an overly simple mould. While accepting the importance of factors associated with the endorsement of colonial power, we will see that one of the pervasive features of orientalism which prevailed right throughout the modern period is the way in which, though perceived as 'other', Eastern ideas have been used in the West as an agency for self-criticism and self-renewal, whether in the political, moral, or religious spheres. The perceived otherness of the Orient is not exclusively one of mutual antipathy, nor just a means of affirming Europe's triumphant superiority, but also provides a conceptual framework that allows much fertile cross-referencing, the discovery of similarities, analogies, and models; in other words, the underpinning of a productive hermeneutical relationship. It is not simply that the East has frequently been elevated to exalted heights of perfection and sublimity in European eyes – the 'romanticisation' hypothesis would serve to explain as much – but rather that this elevated status has then been a source of creative tension between East and West, and has been exploited as a position from which to reappraise and reform the institutions and thought systems indigenous to the West. We will find that again and again European intellectuals have over the centuries explicitly called into question the West's own indigenous traditions, its own uniqueness, even its self-respect – Confucius is the equal of Aristotle, the *Bhagavad Gītā* on a par with the Bible, the Upanishads comparable to Kant, Buddha to Christ, Taoist naturalism to Greek science. Inflated enthusiasm for Oriental ideas and practices has often been associated with the counter-culture movement of the 1960s with its youthful rebellion against the orthodoxies of modern bourgeois life, but what will become clear is that orientalism has for three centuries assumed a counter-cultural, counter-hegemonic role, and become in various ways a gadfly plaguing all kinds of orthodoxies, and an energiser of radical protest, and in doing so it has often been in the business not of reinforcing Europe's established role and identity, but rather of undermining it.[9] It must be added that this counter-cultural role is not necessarily one which should automatically demand our approval. Some would dispute the moral and social merits of the movement of the 1960s just referred to and argue that its aims and consequences were, by any account, pernicious. Controversial, too, is the attraction of some Oriental enthusiasts to fascist ideas, and beyond any dispute is the shameful involvement of certain orientalists in supporting the Nazi revolt against liberal democracy. We will return to these and other contentious examples later.

ORIENTALISM AS CORRECTIVE MIRROR

In the meantime, let us look more closely at this self-questioning strategy. This is a recognisable factor in the West's intellectual history which has emerged over the past few centuries and acquired a distinctive pattern, one which the historian of religions, Mircea Eliade, has spoken of as a 'hermeneutical' engagement with the East and as a 'confrontation with "the others" [which] helps Western man better to understand himself' (1960: 10–11). At one level it appears quite simply as a means whereby thinkers could stand back from Europe and view it as if from the outside, a mirror in which to scrutinise the assumptions and prejudices of their own traditions. This strategy is, of course, by no means confined to Europe's relationship with the East. During the Enlightenment period, for example, representations of foreign societies and tribes of all kinds, real and imaginary, were commonly deployed to criticise the follies and inadequacies of European civilisation; the myth of the Noble Savage is a well-known example of this genre. Thus Amy Glassner Gordon, in a discussion of French Enlightenment attitudes towards other cultures in general, points out that the *philosophes* 'believed that a wider perspective, a more thorough understanding of non-European societies, would enable them better to understand themselves and the world in which they lived' (in Pullapilly and Van Kley 1986: 75–6). As we shall see later, China offered the Enlightenment *philosophes* precisely the 'wider perspective' they needed. For the Romantics it was India that furnished the mirror in which to reveal the inadequacies of their times, and later Buddhism and Taoism have been pressed into similar service. The strategy is still very much in evidence today across a number of intellectual and cultural fields where, to quote Richard Bernstein at a recent East–West Philosophers' Conference, 'it is only through an engaged encounter with the Other, with the otherness of the Other, that one comes to a more informed, textured understanding of the traditions to which "we" belong' (in Deutsch 1991: 93).

Going more deeply, at the centre of this pattern lies what can best be described as a pervasive cultural disquietude, an uneasy awareness of fault lines running deep into the strata of European cultural life, down through the levels of politics, religion, and philosophy, giving rise to a sense of some fundamental breakdown at the heart of the West's intellectual, spiritual, and moral being. According to the historian William Haas, the West's interest in the East from the sixteenth century onwards reveals 'a deep uncertainty', and points to the fact that in the modern period 'Western civilization has become increasingly enigmatic with regard to itself – doubtful as to its essence and value – uneasy as to road and objective' (1956: 42–3). From a more philosophical point of view, Richard Bernstein speaks of a 'Cartesian anxiety' which continues to plague an intellectual tradition whose very foundations have become a persistent problem to itself (see Bernstein 1983: 16–25). Medical and psychoanalytic terms are frequently used in this context. It is not just that, in the words of the philosopher of religion Ninian Smart, East and West each constitute 'a useful critique of the other tradition [whereby] each will challenge the other and stand as a corrective to the other' (1992: 99 and 111). In a more radically subversive vein, we find again and again in orientalist literature talk of a 'crisis' or a 'sickness' of one form or another that is seen as besetting Western civilisation, and of the need to turn Eastwards for therapy and for cure. In the early 1930s, for example, C. G. Jung warned that 'We are living undeniably in a period of the greatest restlessness, nervous tension, confusion and disorientation of outlook' (1961: 266), and some decades later the philosopher Troy Wilson Organ commented that, in the face of the current crisis, 'we need to look beyond the West for therapy' (1975: 7). The 'therapy' which the Orient has enabled the West to prescribe for itself has varied with changing circumstances and demands over the past four centuries. It has become a commonplace that the recent 'resurgence of interest in Eastern religions coincides with a loss of confidence by the West in its own cultural values and with the diminishing place of Christianity in Western society and culture' (Davis 1971: 17), but it is the claim of this book that the search for diagnoses and cures through engagement with the East is by no means a recent phenomenon but can be traced back as a consistent theme, albeit with many variations, running through modern Western intellectual history.

Historical parallels in the East for this outward turn in search of spiritual and cultural therapy are difficult to come by in the modern period. There are of course many examples of interest in Western ideas amongst educated Chinese and Indians. A number of literati in Manchu China were eager to learn from and debate with the early Jesuit missionaries, and the court of the sixteenth-century Mogul emperor Akbar listened avidly to new ideas coming from Europe, but these interests were strictly limited in their cultural implications and cannot be viewed as manifestions of deep cultural unease. On the whole the East has not approached the West with enthusiasm and curiosity, has not of its own accord welcomed Western ideas, nor used the latter to undermine its own. To be sure there have been important reform movements in the East in recent times: in the nineteenth century Western ideas were deliberately assimilated by the Hindu reform movement, by Japan during the Meiji period (1868–1913), and by the Chinese Westernisation movement of the 1860s. And in the twentieth century India and China have assimilated and responded creatively to Western ideas in various ways, and have undergone as a consequence a period of anguished self-reappraisal and painful revolution. But, as Halbfass points out, this process 'was not the result of developments initiated and carried out within [the East] itself, but of changes and breaks imposed from the outside' (1988: 380). Indeed, according to Heinrich Kraemer, 'The self-questioning and inner crisis in the great Eastern civilizations of today . . . is thrown upon them like a bomb from outside' (1960: 230). Moreover, when we look to China at the height of its imperial power and influence in the fifteenth century, when many nations on the borders of China paid tribute to the Son of Heaven and were in effect subject to his overall suzerainty, we find no significant growth in curiosity concerning these subject nations, and little if any desire to learn from them. For nearly thirty years between 1405 and 1433 huge naval expeditions were dispatched from China under Cheng Ho, involving hundreds of ships – many of which were considerably larger than any built in Europe until the nineteenth century – whose purpose appears to have been to assert China's imperial hegemony in the China Sea and the Indian Ocean, yet neither then nor at any other period did any cultural phenomenon parallel to orientalism occur in China.[10]

How are we to explain this discrepancy? Some might urge that the lack of symmetry between East and West in this regard is simply the consequence of some deep underlying psychological difference between the two, and that the tendency of the West towards a somewhat pathological self-analysis is 'a law built into the very fibre of its being', and a consequence of its 'specific spiritual type and its inherent dynamism' (Kraemer 1960: 229–30). Some commentators, as we noted earlier in the chapter, have seen evidence in this of the West's 'Faustian' curiosity, and its inherent 'dynamism', and indeed, as we saw, it has been almost a cliché since the seventeenth century that Asian cultures are endemically static and intensely conservative by comparison with Europe. Perhaps, then, the West's tendency towards self-criticism is the manifestation of a kind of divine dissatisfaction, an inescapable desire to question and probe, tendencies which all emerged first with the Greek philosophers and which have been an essential feature of the European psyche ever since.

This sort of explanation would be an easy way out of our difficulties and would explain orientalism at a stroke. Yet would it be an explanation at all, rather than a piece of Western ideology, of racism masquerading as science? To find a more adequate explanation we need to broaden the focus of our discussion and to take into our purview the wider spectrum of modern Western cultural history.[11]

NIHILISM AND THE WEST

It is generally acknowledged by historians that during and following the Renaissance, at the very beginning of the modern period, at all levels from the intellectual and cultural to the political and economic, Europe underwent a profound transformation amounting to a radical discontinuity with its past. This transformation has often been painted in heroic colours, representing the overthrow of the feudal restrictions and intellectual repressions of the mediaeval period, and heralding the birth of the modern world with its discovery of individual freedom, its release of the powers of human reason, and its emancipation from the bonds of nature. But as a profound rupture with the past, with long-satisfying traditions of thought, belief and practice, and as a dismemberment of the theological and political syntheses that had painfully, if often inadequately, been wrought in the Middle Ages, the transformation can also be viewed as profoundly traumatic. It is this trauma, combined with the global expansion of European commercial and political interests, that, I shall argue, provides us with the best clue to the emergence of orientalism in the modern period, and is indeed a factor that remains in play to this day. This view is summed up by Joseph Needham who saw in 'the combined transfigurations of the Renaissance, the scientific revolution, the Reformation, and the rise of capitalism' historical factors which helped to generate a kind of cultural instability and 'schizophrenia of the soul' which led to a frenetic search for alternative paradigms (see Needham 1969a: 117–22).

Let us look at these transformations more closely. The fifteenth and sixteenth centuries, with the influx of ideas from classical Greece and Rome and from esoteric Jewish and Hermetic traditions, are usually seen as marking the fulcrum on which modern Western thought hinges. As the historian V. G. Kiernan puts it:

> In a couple of centuries after 1450 Europe underwent a thorough stirring and shaking up, as if being plunged for rejuvenation into a cauldron of Medea. It was again a more radical transformation than any of the other big regions [of the globe] ever experienced, the stormy passage, full of changes good and ill, from mediaeval to modern.
>
> (Kiernan 1972: 12)

At first, daring figures such as Marsilio Ficino and Pico della Mirandola, and later Robert Fludd and Giordano Bruno, sought to draw together and integrate these ideas within a new syncretic unity, and to re-establish the mediaeval synthesis on a new and more universal basis, a hermeneutical project which, as we shall see, was revived and re-embodied at various points down the centuries within orientalist discourse. In reaction against this syncretistic tendency the Protestant Reformation, perhaps the most profound and far-reaching metamorphosis in the West's intellectual life, effectively put an end to the universalist projects both of mediaeval Christendom and of the Renaissance, and opened up the exciting yet alarming prospect of theological and philosophical pluralism. The rediscovery of sceptical and atomistic philosophies from Ancient Greece ran sharply counter to well-established orthodoxy, and, in conjunction with the confusion generated by religious conflict, begat a new, more open and conflictual style of thinking, one which is best summed up in Descartes' commitment in the *Meditations* to the demolition of his hitherto established opinions, and to their reconstruction on new and firmer foundations. Furthermore, the scientific revolution not only transformed our understanding of nature, but at a deeper level helped to generate a new and more open spirit of inquiry and a sceptical attitude to received knowledge. And running like a vivid coloured thread through all of this was a conflict which in the seventeenth century became known as the 'Battle of the Ancients and the Moderns', the dispute over whether to stay with traditional and tried wisdom or – following the inspiration of pioneers such as Bacon, Descartes, and Galileo – to strike out in new uncharted directions.[12]

The paradoxical nature of orientalism, which displays in so singular a way an ambivalent self-image on the part of Europeans, can now to some extent be fathomed in terms of the ambivalences inherent in European history in the early modern period, and the internal tensions within Europe's cultural and intellectual life at that time. After all, this was the age in which the European nations began to emerge as self-consciously identifiable entities, when Europe began, after the long mediaeval period of defensive introversion, to turn outwards with renewed confidence and energy, when it became convinced of its superiority and its global mission. It was also a period which encouraged the efflorescence of a new humanist and scientific curiosity, and which stimulated the development of a new range of scholarly methods and disciplines. Yet at the same time it was an epoch which, by very dint of these profound changes, generated an unprecedented degree of anxiety and self-doubt, and indeed it is by no means an exaggeration to claim that 'the seeds of nihilism were there in the Enlightenment from the very beginning' (Giddens 1991: 48). The very rationalism which was so characteristic of the Enlightenment period, which promised to sweep away all ancient superstitions, helped to create an environment in which Asian traditions, inter alia, could become objects of reasoned analysis and study, thereby creating an intellectual counterpoint which would eventually be used to challenge the Enlightenment concept of reason itself. The irony of this situation is summed up by Hannah Arendt in her observation that 'When Europe in all earnest began to prescribe its laws to all other continents, it so happened that she herself had already lost her belief' (1955: 82).

The theoretical conception of this process of destabilisation and its accompanying anxieties has its locus classicus in Nietzsche's concept of nihilism, the notion that in the modern world all traditional values and beliefs have been discounted, that 'the highest values devaluate themselves. The aim is lacking; "why?" finds no answer' (1968b: 9). His analysis of nihilism goes well beyond the sceptical doubts about human knowledge that have preoccupied philosophers, and seeks to identify it as a crisis at the heart of Western civilisation, for nihilism has its roots in the very foundations of modernity. In his view, it is an historical condition which is peculiar to modern Europe, and which has been brought about by factors within Europe's own cultural history, factors which can be traced back to the Western philosophical tradition, to the rise of modern science, and even to Christianity itself. 'Complete nihilism', Nietzsche argues, 'is the necessary consequence of the ideals entertained hitherto', even of 'faith in the categories of reason' itself (ibid.: 19 and 13).

Themes similar to that of Nietzsche are evident in the writings of a number of twentieth-century sociologists. Émile Durkheim, in his analysis of the social revolution that accompanied the move from traditional to modern forms of human association, characterised it in terms of 'anomie', an excessive individualism which gave rise to uncertainty, unpredictability, and a catastrophic weakening of traditional norms of conduct. More recently Peter Berger has characterised modernity in terms of 'homelessness', a condition in which 'the individual literally no longer knows who he is', and 'reality becomes uncertain and threatened with meaninglessness' (1974: 137). This condition is engendered by a loss of encompassing traditional beliefs and by the emergence of a 'plurality of life-worlds' which 'confronts the individual with an ever-changing kaleidoscope of social experiences and meanings [forcing] him to make decisions and plans', and in which 'not only the world but the self becomes an object of . . . anguished scrutiny' (ibid.: 74–5). More recently still, sociologists such as Ulrich Beck and Anthony Giddens have seen modernity in terms of risk, hazard, and uncertainty, a situation which can be traced back to the growth of unregulated international trade in the seventeenth century, and which can be witnessed in the contemporary phenomenon of cultural globalisation which engenders in individuals and groups a tendency towards self-questioning anxiety.[13] In parallel with this is the history of modern philosophy. Here we see not only a field of conflict between rival schools – rationalism and empiricism, idealism and realism, monism and pluralism, to name some of the most pivotal – but a sphere in which the cultural anxieties just outlined come into intellectual focus. In this domain the threat of nihilism has always been at or just below the surface, from Descartes' struggle with scepticism, through Kant's response to Hume's doubts about human knowledge, to a range of twentieth-century philosophers from Russell to Rorty who have contended with the elusiveness of firm epistemological foundations.[14]

Orientalism, it should be emphasised, cannot be seen merely as a symptom or consequence of this state of cultural and intellectual perturbation, for it has also helped to sustain and exacerbate it. The discovery of ancient and sophisticated civilisations in the East simply added to the insecurity of a culture which had begun seriously to doubt the validity of its own. In this period European intellectuals began to articulate the idea of its uniqueness, indeed its inherent superiority to other cultures and races, yet the encounter with China, then with India, exerted a force which acted in an equal and opposite direction. As the French orientalist scholar Raymond Schwab has pointed out, 'the West perceived it was not the sole possessor of an admirable intellectual past', a realisation which occurred 'during a period when everything else was likewise new, unprecedented, extraordinary' (1984: xxiii). Furthermore the new discoveries provoked a whole host of awkward questions about the origins and uniqueness of Christianity, the origins of the human race, the historical sources of European languages, and the universality of religious and moral beliefs. In a period when the human sciences were beginning to be formulated, it is not surprising to discover thinkers searching for data beyond the confines both of Europe and of Biblical history, and in this context the existence of non-European civilisations with advanced yet radically different beliefs and manners provided important and at times disturbing information.

What of comparisons with Asia? There have certainly been great revolutions and upheavals in Asian societies, both in the political and the intellectual spheres, but these have not had the profound consequences that launched the modern period in European history, and which in a relatively short space of time gave rise to a global culture. To take the case of China, while rejecting simplistic explanations concerning China's supposed 'stagnation', the Chinese scholar Wen-yuan Qian accepts that in the period following the Cheng Ho expeditions in the early fifteenth century, China lacked the 'propitious politico-social conditions to produce, sustain, and promote . . . a series of totally new intellectual elements, new attitudes, new ways of thinking' such as emerged in Europe from the Renaissance onwards (1985: 31–2). Needham supports this judgement: 'Europe had a Renaissance, a Reformation, and a great commitment to economic change, which China did not have' (1956: 294), for China was caught in the grip of a stifling bureaucratic system, and did not undergo the radical transformation to modernity until impelled thereto by the West. An interesting counter-example might be mooted in the case of the social and political upheavals in China in the period following the collapse of the Han dynasty in 220 CE. These led to the subversion and overthrow of the ruling Confucian ideology and to a long period of cultural and intellectual turbulence, and paved the way for the rise to dominance of a foreign religion, Buddhism, and ultimately to the great cultural revival of the Sung dynasty. In this period, as the historian Arthur Wright comments, 'one sees an iconoclastic attitude toward ancient traditions, a restless, often passionate search for something new', which involved 'the reworking, then the appropriation, of what had been taken from an alien religion' (1971: 124). Nevertheless, in spite of superficial comparisons with the early modern period in Europe, it must be emphasised that this era in China's history was not characterised by any outward commercial or imperialistic expansion beyond its traditional sphere of influence, nor by anything like the rise of capitalist-inspired free enterprise or by the emergence of nation states, and hence nothing that in the final analysis compares with the transformations that occurred in Europe.

We are left, then, with the strong presumption that the rise and development of orientalism in the West was closely tied to conditions that were unique to Europe in the modern period – those of cultural revolution and global expansion – and that these conditions helped, first, to create a painful void in the spiritual and intellectual heart of Europe, and, second, to beget geopolitical conditions which facilitated the passage of alternative world views from the East. In the next two sections of the book these conjectures will be amplified and tested by tracing the whole historical development of orientalism over the past four centuries.

Part II

The making of the 'Orient'

Chapter 3

China cult
The age of Enlightenment

FROM THE ANCIENT TO THE MEDIAEVAL WORLD

Before attempting to narrate the history of the intellectual encounters between East and West in the Enlightenment period, we need to look back briefly to earlier cultural exchanges between East and West in the ancient world. The presence of Islam astride the Middle East from the seventh century CE onwards, looming as a seemingly impenetrable mental and physical barrier in the Middle Ages between the Mediterranean cultures and those of South and East Asia, has tended to obscure the fact that in the ancient world commercial and cultural intercourse between East and West was well established at the time when the philosophical foundations of Western thought were being laid in Greece, and continued to flourish right through the period of Roman hegemony and the founding of Christendom. The sophisticated infrastructure of highways and a common currency that had been developed from the sixth to the fourth centuries BCE by the Achaemenid empire of Persia, which extended as far as the Indus valley, helped to facilitate trade not only between India and the Euphrates but also along the famous Silk Routes between the Mediterranean and the East. In the Roman period there is plenty of evidence of a flourishing trade in which silk and spices were exchanged for wool, silver, and gold, and it was in that period too that Alexandria, which, from its foundation in 332 BCE, had rapidly displaced Athens as the centre of Hellenic intellectual life, acted as a cross-roads of commercial and cultural exchange between East and West.

In this context it would hardly be surprising if commodities more abstract than spices or gold were to be carried along the caravan and sea routes, and there are some indications of cultural transmission between East and West. Pythagoras, who had a profound influence on Plato, is believed to have spent some time in Egypt where he learned about Indian philosophy; the gymnosophists were objects of considerable curiosity to thinkers in the ancient Greek and Roman worlds; and Buddhist monks were known in the Hellenic world. Admittedly much of this is speculative and based on flimsy evidence, though we do know that the Indian Emperor Asoka (d. 228 BCE) propagated Buddhist teachings beyond his borders, sending monks Westwards with the Buddha's message, and translating some of his Buddhist-inspired edicts into Greek and Aramaic. The invasion of India by Alexander of Macedon in 327 BCE, however, marks the most dramatic and historically best-documented inception of a dialogue between East and West. Alexander, who it must be remembered had been tutored by Aristotle, was concerned not only with military conquest and political expansion, but appears to have held as an ideal the 'marriage' of Europe and Asia (see Halbfass 1988: 7). There is no doubt that Alexander and his companions already had some knowledge of India, fed by stories told by the Greek historian Ctesias of Cnidus (fl. 400 BCE), and he took with him on his expedition several philosophers, including Pyrrho, the founder of the school of Sceptics, and appears to have made an effort to acquaint himself with the religious and philosophical ideas of the lands he conquered. It is intriguing to speculate about the extent to which this brought about a real exchange of ideas. There are certainly some remarkable parallels between the outlook of Indian 'renouncers' such as Gautama Buddha on the one hand and the ideas of the Sceptics on the other: both are concerned with the painfulness of the human condition and with the attainment of a state of imperturbability through mental discipline. Another philosopher who accompanied Alexander on his expedition was Onesicritus, who was not only impressed by the self-discipline of the gymnosophists with their capacity to bear extreme forms of pain without complaint, but also saw their nudity as an expression of the 'natural attitude', of their adherence to the precepts of nature, a factor used by the Cynics as a critique of Greek customs.

When we come to the possible influence of Indian thought on Christianity we return once more to the realms of speculation and thought-provoking coincidences. Since the middle of the nineteenth century there have been conjectures about the possibility of historical connections between Christianity and Buddhism, and there are indeed some remarkable similarities between the two mythologies that cry out for explanation. We will return to examine these speculations in more detail in Chapter 5, but in the meantime it must be emphasised that the transmission of ideas from India to the West at the start of the Common Era is, from a purely historical standpoint, by no means improbable. We have already noted the Westward dispersion of Asoka's missionaries, and the openness of the Greeks to Eastern influence. In addition to this the cults of Orpheus, Dionysus, and Mithras, which flourished throughout the Graeco-Roman world, and which may have provided a model for many aspects of Christian doctrine and worship as they evolved in the early centuries after Christ, in all probability shared a common inheritance with the religions of India. Much of this is again speculative, and questions of priority here are difficult to decide, but what remains certain is that any attempt to separate out Western from Eastern traditions is highly artificial. Even though direct lines of influence are difficult to trace, it is possible to make much better sense of emergent Christianity, especially its concern with the soul and its tendency towards mysticism, if we view its origins within a wider context, and see it as part of a much wider set of traditions than that provided by standard accounts.[1]

Furthermore, there are clear indications that the Gnostic ideas, which played an important part in the early development of Christian doctrine, were influenced by Buddhist and Hindu thought. Clement (d. 220 CE) and Origen (186–253 CE), both citizens of Alexandria, were familiar with aspects of Indian philosophy, and there are a number of suggestive parallels between the ideas of the Gnostics, such as their concern with the soul, its inner life and its destiny, and ideas familiar in the East.[2] Furthermore the great Roman philosopher, Plotinus (205–70 CE), educated in Alexandria and subsequently to become so important in the formation of the Christian Neoplatonic and mystical traditions, was sufficiently interested in Eastern thought to travel to Persia in search of it. Even more than in the case of the Gnostics there are striking parallels between his thought and that of certain philosophical traditions of India.[3]

The dialogue between Europe and the East was curtailed by the sudden irruption of Islam in the seventh century CE, but was resumed with the epic journeys to China during the thirteenth century of the Franciscan Friars Plano Carpini and William Rubrock, and more famously those of Nicolo and Marco Polo. The tenuous nature of these contacts, added to the closed world view of the Christian Middle Ages, did not permit any real intellectual encounter between East and West, but in the event these travellers had the effect of stimulating once again the interest of the West in the mysterious and fabled lands of the East. For the Mediaeval West, the East was 'still a land of one-footed and dog-headed men, of unicorns and griffins, of winged scorpions and gold-digging ants, of the Paradise of the Genesis account, of the people of Gog and Magog' (Almond 1986: 85), but these expeditions saw the tentative beginnings of the formation of a whole new range of interests and beliefs concerning the Orient that were subsequently to play such an important role in the imaginative and intellectual constructs of the European mind.[4]

THE JESUITS AND THE NEW VISION OF CATHAY

Our story of the Enlightenment's encounter with ideas from the East, especially from China, begins with the voyages of global exploration and the subsequent expansion of European economic and political power in the fifteenth and sixteenth centuries, and any attempt to make sense of the meeting of the minds of Europe and Asia must be viewed in this context. These exploits heralded the beginning of an intensive period of exploration of the maritime regions of southern and eastern Asia, and paved the way for a rapid expansion in trade and commerce, an expansion which was both generated by and which served to facilitate the revolutionary economic and political changes which were taking place in Europe.[5]

The motivations which fuelled this dramatic and fateful European expansion Eastwards are complex, and embrace factors which range from the new intellectual openness and curiosity engendered by the Renaissance to the need to extend markets and to outflank Islam in the search for trade routes to the East. The religious motive was perhaps of equal importance to these, however, and indeed this remained an important factor in much of the work of studying, classifying, and interpreting Oriental ideas over the following centuries. Whatever the underlying long-term commercial or political impulsions, it was through the desire to convert the souls of unbelievers in Asia to the true faith that the real business of opening up and exploring the mind of the East began, and it was through the missionary work of the Jesuits, the shock-troops of the Catholic Counter-Reformation, who penetrated India, China, and Japan in the sixteenth and seventeenth centuries, that the first detailed understanding of the thought and culture of the East was brought home to Europe. Though their aim was certainly the conversion of 'heathens' to the Catholic faith, it must be remembered that the priests of the Society of Jesus were no bigoted, narrow-minded evangelists but highly educated and cultured men who had absorbed the mind-broadening ideals of Renaissance humanism. They developed an especially high regard for the Chinese civilisation, its Confucian philosophy, its literature and its institutions, sending back to Europe detailed and sympathetic accounts of the beliefs and practices of the people they sought to convert. They also translated some of the classical texts of Confucianism into Latin, first published in 1687 in Paris under the title *Confucius Sinarum Philosophus*. These reports and translations were widely read in Europe in the latter part of the seventeenth century, and the ideas they transmitted to the West were to have a profound influence on the European mind of that era, entering deeply into the ideological debates of the Enlightenment period, and playing a part in the formation of some of the major ideas of the time in ways which are often not adequately acknowledged.

As far as the Jesuits themselves were concerned, they had their own agenda which was, of course, the conversion of the Chinese, but in order to achieve this objective they recognised the necessity to understand the world view of the Chinese and to engage in some sort of dialogue with it, and in this sense they were the first orientalist scholars and the first to transmit a picture of Confucian philosophy and the Chinese world view to the West. As the historian Colin Mackerras puts it: 'The net result was that eighteenth-century Europe knew quite a lot about China' (1989: 37), and though in the end they failed to convert the Chinese to Christianity, the Jesuits 'were brilliantly successful in interpreting China to the West' (ibid.: 30). This interpretation inevitably betrayed their missionary agenda. They believed that by drawing close comparisons between the underlying philosophical assumptions of China and Christendom they would be able to demonstrate that the Chinese were sufficiently enlightened to be receptive to the Christian message.[6] One of the consequences of this was that they tended to portray the Chinese as a morally and politically sophisticated people, governed by wise and educated rulers who had established basic philosophical principles concerning morality and society on the basis of universal human reason. There were elements of truth in this account, for undoubtedly China at that time displayed qualities of political, social, and economic wisdom which were enviable from a European standpoint at that time, but at the same time it contained a strong dose of exaggeration and idealisation which served the purposes of their own agenda. Furthermore, the Chinese philosopher-rulers were construed by the Jesuits as having established belief in God by the natural light of reason, a supposition which rendered the Chinese easier to convert, but which was subsequently disputed by polemicists such as Bayle who, with an agenda quite different from that of the Jesuits, argued that the Chinese literati were in fact atheists.

In addition to the transmission of reports and texts, the Jesuits embarked on their own unique form of hermeneutical engagement with the religious ideas and practices of China, one which in many ways foreshadowed the East–West dialogue that was to come. The early missionaries, such as Matteo Ricci, soon realised on arriving in China that they were dealing not with a primitive culture, but with a civilisation as old as, indeed perhaps even older than, that of Europe, and whose people inherited a language, a literature, and a belief system that were as complex and as sophisticated as those of Western Christendom. It was pointless therefore to seek simply to strip away the old Confucian beliefs and terminology, and to replace them with those of the Christian faith. Some sort of accommodation was necessary, some compromise, at least in terms of the exterior rituals. What Ricci and his successors sought to do, therefore, was 'to interpret this cult rather than to suppress it' (Guy 1963: 45), to act not as outsiders seeking to impose on the native Chinese a totally alien set of doctrines and practices, but to infiltrate the very heart and soul of China by first adopting the learning and the habits of a scholar-bureaucrat, or mandarin, and then subtly adapting the Catholic rituals to Confucian customs and practices. This strategy ranged from relatively superficial matters such as the use of Confucian garments during the celebration of Mass, to the more contentious matter of adapting Confucian notions, such as ancestor worship, to Christian theology. As time went on even bolder spirits, such as Father Nobili in India, sought a linguistic/hermeneutic accommodation between Eastern and Christian scriptures, which inevitably transgressed the bounds of orthodoxy. The custodians of orthodoxy in Rome did not always sympathise with these efforts, seeing them as a dangerous dilution of the purity of the Catholic faith, and eventually, in 1742, this bold experiment in inter-cultural dialogue was brought to an end on the orders of the Pope.[7]

The reports of the Jesuits were soon followed by those of other travellers, and by the middle of the eighteenth century a considerable body of literature on the great civilisations of Asia had been built up, evoking widespread enthusiasm and debate amongst Europe's educated classes who became, in the words of one historian, 'infatuated with a vision of Cathay' (Edwardes 1971: 103). Indeed, in 1553, even before the Jesuit reports came flooding into Europe, the Frenchman Guillaume Postel had published a book entitled *Des merveilles du monde* in which he set out to demonstrate the superiority of the East over the West, and went so far as to claim that Christianity had no monopoly of divinely revealed truth. He maintained that 'the Oriental understanding is the best in the world', and envisioned Japan as a kind of utopia of natural reason (quoted in Bouwsma 1957:

208). Early Oriental enthusiasts such as Postel had to rely on fragmentary and unreliable information, but by the time of Voltaire and the Encyclopaedists there was available a number of systematic studies on Asia, the most famous of which was a four-volume historical account of China by Jean-Baptiste Du Halde entitled in its 1736 English translation *The General History of China*, and first published in France a year earlier. Like so many of the Jesuit writings of the period, this work was extremely complimentary towards China, praising every aspect of its social and intellectual life, and frequently drawing comparisons with Europe that were unfavourable towards the latter.

The list of thinkers from the Enlightenment and pre-Enlightenment period who professed a more than passing interest in Eastern philosophy is impressive and includes Montaigne, Malebranche, Bayle, Wolff, Leibniz, Voltaire, Montesquieu, Diderot, Helvetius, Quesnay, and Adam Smith.[8] They were fascinated by its philosophy, by the conduct of the state, and by its education system, and in all kinds of ways sought to hold it up as a mirror in which to examine the philosophical and institutional inadequacies of Europe, as a model with which to instigate moral and political reform, and as a tool with which to strip Christianity of its pretensions to uniqueness. In the sixteenth century Guillaume Postel had set up the Orient as a kind of utopia (an allegedly real one by contrast with the imaginary one of Thomas More) with which to reproach and to provoke reform in an erring and degenerate Christendom, and even as late as 1769, when sinomania was on the wane, Pierre Poivre could proclaim that

> China offers an enchanting picture of what the whole world might become, if the laws of that empire were to become the laws of all nations. Go to Peking! Gaze upon the mightiest of mortals [Confucius]; he is the true and perfect image of Heaven.
>
> (quoted in Dawson 1967: 55)

Frequent use was made of the Orient as a means of satirising European institutions by affecting to scrutinise them with the eyes of a foreigner, a literary device which helped to elude the attentions of the official censor. Most famous in this genre is Montesquieu's *Lettres persanes*, first published in 1721, in which two Persian gentlemen travel to Paris and take note of the absurdities of French social life and customs. Other notable examples are the Marquis d'Argens' *Lettres chinoises* of 1739, and Oliver Goldsmith's *The Citizen of the World*, published in 1762, in both of which pagan China is used as a means of satirising the manners of Christian Europe. And if Confucian China was the chief object of interest, Confucius himself attained almost cult status, 'the patron saint of the Enlightenment' as one historian ironically expressed it (Reichwein 1925: 77). As early as 1642 La Mothe le Voyer wrote a pamphlet entitled *La vertu de payens* in which he placed Confucius firmly alongside and equal to Western sages, and a hundred years later the Marquis d'Argens proclaimed that Confucius was 'the greatest man the world has yet produced', such views being typical of the period.[9]

There has been much dispute in recent times concerning the validity of the Enlightenment interpretations of Confucianism; the latter is certainly more complex conceptually, and historically more diffuse than the *philosophes* and their Jesuit teachers liked to believe, and there are strong elements of projection and wishful thinking in their accounts both of the Confucian philosophy and its social and political circumstances. Thus, they tended to see *neo*-Confucianism – the term itself was coined by the Jesuits in the seventeenth century – as a corruption of ancient Confucianism which had unfortunately become infused with superstitious beliefs, and there was little grasp of, or indeed interest in, the nature of Taoism and Buddhism and the role they played within the whole web of Chinese cultural and intellectual life.[10] It would be wrong to deny that the Enlightenment period saw a spectacular enhancement in the European understanding of the philosophical and political shape of China, that genuine sympathy was generated, and a sincere desire to learn was manifested. But it is evident, as for example in the case of the dispute over whether the Confucians were theists or not, that this understanding was filtered through and distorted by the concerns and disputes of contemporary Europe, and was to that extent a European construction. Thus, just as the Jesuits tended to see Confucianism in terms of their own project, so too the *philosophes* interpreted it in the light of Enlightenment ideas, and as reflecting their own political philosophy and utopian image of a transformed Europe. Whatever the accuracy of its European representations, however, China certainly became closely integrated into the consciousness of the European Enlightenment, touching on many aspects of the intellectual and cultural life of the time, and in the next section we will examine some of the more prominent thinkers of the period who contributed to this process.

THE *PHILOSOPHES* AND CHINA

We begin with two thinkers who predate the great wave of sinomania in France, but who anticipate its preoccupations in interesting ways. The first of these is the great French essayist Michel de Montaigne (1533–92), an eloquent advocate of a humanistic morality and critic of the religious intolerance of his day, who was quick to seize on scraps of information newly arrived from the East and to use them for his own polemical purposes. In several of his essays he drew on the example of China to encourage his readers to take a broader and more open-minded view of European affairs, urging them to reflect on 'how much wider and more various the world is than either the ancients or ourselves have discovered' (1958: 352); as the historian David Lach points out, he 'uses the East to support his beliefs about the uncertainty of knowledge, the infinite variety in the world, and the universality of moral precepts' (1977: 297). The interest of the French philosopher Malebranche (1638–1715) goes somewhat deeper, reflecting the wide dissemination of interest in China since Montaigne's time, and telling us a lot about the role that Chinese philosophy was beginning to play in the intellectual life of the period. Here we need to take note of his *Dialogue between a Christian Philosopher and a Chinese Philosopher on the Existence and Nature of God*, a tract whose very title is indicative of a new inter-cultural impetus within philosophy. In this work Confucianism is presented as a form of Spinozism – an association commonly canvassed in his day – and the dialogue is designed to demonstrate the orthodoxy of his own position. What is interesting here is not only that Malebranche takes it for granted that his readers will be familiar with Confucianism, assuming they will see its relevance to the debate in which he was engaged, but also that, as with many subsequent Enlightenment thinkers, Oriental philosophy is being deployed as a potent weapon with which to engage with purely European objectives, a strategy which we will encounter in many contexts right up to the present time.[11]

The interest of Pierre Bayle (1646–1706) in the Orient continued and developed that of Montaigne, for he was similarly concerned to exploit it as a polemical weapon, in particular in his assault on the climate of intolerance which followed the revocation of the Edict of Nantes in 1685. Bayle, a thinker whose subversive methods powerfully influenced the eighteenth-century Encyclopaedists, was a member of a group of radical philosophers called *les libertins* (freethinkers) whose hallmark was an anti-authoritarian scepticism and who seized upon China as a compelling instrument in the struggle against the establishment, using China's antiquity to upset traditional biblical chronology, and exploiting its apparent enlightened attitude of toleration to attack religious intolerance and persecution at home. As one historian puts it: 'Bayle represented the ultimate achievement of a long line of freethinkers who used the Chinese example in attempting to liberate themselves from preconceived modes of thought' (Guy 1963: 127). Unlike Malebranche, who was concerned to defend his particular version of Cartesianism, Bayle's philosophical efforts were directed towards the undermining of all metaphysical and religious claims to truth. In his famous *Historical and Critical Dictionary* of 1697 he set out to question the philosophical assumptions underlying every sort of systematic belief, not only of theologians but also of philosophers such as Spinoza and Leibniz, seeking to establish in general the principle of toleration. Moreover, contrary to the Jesuits he insisted that the Chinese were atheists, a view designed to demonstrate that Christian theism was not a necessary prerequisite for the establishment of a sound moral order in society.

The leading French sinophile of that period was undoubtedly Voltaire (1694–1778). In dramatic works such as *L'Orphelin de la Chine* (1755) and stories such as *Zadig* (1748) he followed the orientalist genre of his day in using a fictionalised East as a way of holding up a critical mirror to European customs. But it was in his *Essai sur lex moeurs* (1756) that he elaborated most explicitly his views on Confucian philosophy and exploited it in a frontal assault on the political and religious institutions of his day, arguing for the inherent superiority of Chinese moral philosophy, as well as of its political system, which he claimed was based not on a hereditary aristocracy, but on rational principles. In the *Essai* he claimed that in the Orient was to be found the most ancient civilisation, the most ancient form of religion, and the cradle of all the arts, and it is therefore to the East that 'the West owes everything'. To understand this somewhat ambitious claim we must necessarily set on one side the notion that Voltaire approached the East in the spirit of a disinterested scholar. His whole life was devoted to the task of overturning the established order of Christendom as embodied in Church and State, and just as in his *Lettres philosophiques* he used the England of Newton and Locke to attack French institutions, so he conscripted Confucian China in his battle against the tyranny, bigotry, and intolerance of the *ancien régime*. From his former teachers, the Jesuits, he learned that Confucius was an ideal philosopher-statesman, an archetypal rationalist who not only propounded a political philosophy that was free from religious dogma, but whose ideals were supposedly the foundation of the tranquil and harmonious political order that was believed to prevail in China.

China was also used by Voltaire as a weapon with which to mount an assault on the Catholic Church, '*l'infâme*' as he called it. Following the lead of the Jesuits, and contrary to Bayle who considered the Chinese to be a godless nation, Voltaire insisted that the Confucians were deists and that their belief in a supreme deity rested not on faith but on the natural light of reason. Worship of this deity, he believed, was largely devoid of superstitious practices such as image-worship and miracle-mongering, and was mostly limited to seasonal rituals carried out by the emperor, and to expressions of respect for the deceased. The success of Confucianism in providing a foundation for the moral and social order, one which appeared to be conspicuously more effective than its European counterpart, implied for Voltaire that the great theological edifice of Christianity, with its superstitious beliefs, its flamboyant rituals, and its corrupt institutions, was redundant. While he certainly had no liking for what he described as the 'poly-theistic rubbish' to be found in the East, especially in India, and – following the Jesuit lead again – was contemptuous of Buddhism and Taoism, he nevertheless 'believed he had found in the Middle Kingdom the flower of a tolerant religion, without dogma, and without priests, in a word, pure deism' (Guy 1963: 255).

Voltaire played an important part in the elaboration of yet another subversive tactic against Christianity, one which illuminates clearly the revolutionary potential of orientalist discourse. One of the great controversies which raged throughout the Enlightenment period concerned the origins of the human race and of civilisation, an issue that was related to the question of the age of the earth itself. According to the orthodox view, the genealogy of humankind was to be discovered in its basic outlines in the Bible: not only did humankind as such descend from Adam and Eve, but all the civilisations of the world could be traced back to Abraham and the Israelites. With the growth of scholarship and the expansion of European consciousness that accompanied the voyages of global exploration, this standard view was subjected to doubts and criticisms arising from a variety of quarters. In particular, the discovery of the great civilisations in the East, and the acknowledgement of the great antiquity of China and India, meant that the historical priority given to the Israel of the Bible began to look highly questionable. In a book entitled *On the True Antiquity of the World* published in 1660, Isaac Vossius challenged the traditional biblical chronology by claiming that Chinese civilisation stretched back to 2900 BCE, thereby pre-dating the Flood by about half a millennium, and Voltaire was quick to seize on this as being in clear contradiction to the orthodox views concerning the priority of the Judaeo-Christian tradition. The antiquity of Indian religions was also beginning to be a subject of interest among scholars at that time, and Voltaire later came to the conclusion that India was the world's oldest culture and that it was here, rather than in Israel, that the roots of monotheism were to be found.

Voltaire's interest in the vexed issue of biblical chronology could be seen as part of a much larger project on which he was engaged for many years, namely the construction of a universal history. The importance of this enterprise is acknowledged by the historian Colin Mackerras who notes that Voltaire was 'the first person of any nation to attempt a history of the world which would include not only his own culture but those of distant civilizations as well' (1989: 95). This work included two chapters on China, along with several on other non-European countries, and in these he set out explicitly to show that there were other major civilisations alongside that of Europe which were of at least equal extent and equivalent cultural achievement. This is an attitude which even in our own supposedly more enlightened times cannot be taken for granted, but in the eighteenth century it represented a deep and wounding affront to a tradition which had long maintained its sense of uniqueness and special status within the historical, and even the cosmological, order of things.[12]

The use that Voltaire made of his Jesuit-filtered image of China to attack and undermine the established order and orthodoxy of Church and State was repeated and refined by many of his contemporaries. Amongst these Diderot, editor of the *Encyclopédie*, and the philosopher Helvétius, were the most eminent. These thinkers were prominent representatives of the so-called 'Radical Enlightenment', and their particular brand of orientalism was, with regard to Christendom, essentially negative and destructive in its implications, since for them the old order had to be swept away completely before a new order could replace it. The other, perhaps less radically revolutionary, side of this process was best represented by the great German philosopher Leibniz (1646–1716). He was in frequent contact with the Jesuit missionaries, and from his early youth took a close interest in the ideas emerging from China, his personal library eventually containing as many as fifty books on China. By contrast with Voltaire whose writings on China are scattered and unsystematic, Leibniz produced two substantial works on this subject, one in 1697, *Novissima Sinica*, which was a compendium of reports and letters from the Jesuit missionaries, his own contribution being a Preface of some seventeen pages, and in 1713 a treatise on Chinese philosophy, *Discourse on the Natural Theology of China*, in which, like Voltaire after him, he claimed that the Chinese had formulated a natural religion based on reason rather than revelation.[13] More of an establishment figure than Voltaire, Leibniz's life-task was not so much the destruction of the status quo as a search for principles of harmony whereby the warring religious and political factions of Europe could be reconciled with each other, adopting China 'as an ally in the fight to break down moral and spiritual barriers separating man from man' (Guy 1963: 87). As David Mungello points out, this search, which began as a reaction to the continuing conflicts between Catholics and Protestants, took on a universal dimension, and following the example of some of the early Jesuits, Leibniz sought to build foundations for an ecumenical accord of truly global dimensions in which 'the revealed religion of the West would be an equal trade for the natural theology and ethics of China' (1977: 9). His interest in Chinese natural philosophy led him to an analysis of its characteristic organicist metaphysics and its concept of universal harmony based on the complementarity of opposites, and though there is some dispute about the extent of Leibniz's indebtedness to Chinese philosophy, there are some remarkably close parallels between his theory of monads, in which all aspects of the universe mirror all others and act together harmoniously, and the Chinese system of correlative thinking in which all parts of nature cohere and co-operate spontaneously without external direction.[14]

Leibniz's ecumenical interests are also evident in his search for a universal language. The quest for such a language, the language of Adam and Eve, was not unique to Leibniz, and many distinguished thinkers in that epoch, including Bacon, Boyle, Bayle, Hartlib, and Shaftesbury, had engaged in the quest for a 'lingua humana' which would encourage the advancement of learning, dispel scepticism, and transcend sectarian and national differences. Furthermore, since such a language would correspond to the tongue given to humankind by God it also held out the promise of penetrating the divine secrets of creation. China offered Leibniz two struts in support of this extraordinarily powerful idea. The first was the pictographic nature of the Chinese language itself which could arguably be seen as more ancient and closer to nature than the more abstract alphabetic languages of Europe, and which therefore suggested itself as a candidate for the original Adamic tongue. The possibility that the pre-Babel language was Chinese rather than Hebrew was, of course, one which was unlikely to appeal to Christian orthodoxy, and indeed, even prior to Leibniz, several thinkers had already speculated openly about the possibility that Chinese might represent the original Adamic language. These included Francis Bacon, and John Webb, whose case was fully worked out in a book entitled *An Historical Essay Endeavouring a Probability that the Language of the Empire of China is the Primitive Language* (1668). The second strut was the binary symbolism of the *I Ching*, an ancient text built around the elementary notation of a line which can be either broken or unbroken, on the basis of which a complex symbolic system was constructed for the purpose of giving practical and moral guidance. Leibniz was introduced to the *I Ching* by the Jesuit, Father Bouvet, who, like Leibniz, was interested in numerology, and immediately saw in it not simply a manual for divination, but a key to all symbolic systems, and indeed the foundation of a universal science. It is well known that Leibniz conceived the possibility of a binary number system, a system which is now the basis of most computer operations; what is not so commonly realised is that this was for him not a purely mathematical scheme, but part of a more ambitious project for the construction of a universal calculus, and that such a language could help to bring about reconciliation, not only between the warring religious factions of Europe, but also between the nations of Asia and Europe.[15]

In many ways Leibniz could be seen as the last great Renaissance figure, a successor to Marsilio Ficino and Pico della Mirandola, in his search for a universal philosophy, a *philosophia perennis* – the term was probably coined by Leibniz – that would combine and synthesise all others and lead towards a universal harmony amongst nations. Although he remained true to his Protestant origins, he thought that by distilling and conserving all that was true and valuable in the intellectual traditions of the nations of the world, he could demonstrate the fundamental compatibility of all philosophical systems, East as well as West, and thereby lay the foundations for philosophical accord. Thus in his *Discourse on the Natural Philosophy of China* he argued that Chinese concepts such as *li* (first principle) and *ch'i* (vital energy) could be compared closely with Western philosophical concepts, and that on this basis a common core of philosophical beliefs could be established. His interests here had important practical implications including the establishment of the Berlin Society of Sciences (later the Royal Prussian Academy of Sciences) in 1700, which he envisioned as a means for the 'Opening up of China and the interchange of civilizations between China and Europe' (quoted in Reichwein 1925: 81), and he had plans for the establishment of a similar academy in Moscow and the exploration of a land route to China via Russia.

The importance of Leibniz in the East–West dialogue is often overlooked, and one can peruse many modern commentaries on his work without getting even an inkling of the depth of his importance in this sphere. It is significant that his writings on this subject were not translated into English until 1977, and as N. P. Jacobson laments: '[Leibniz] remains what history books in philosophy have chosen to ignore, the chief transmitter of Asian ideas into seventeenth century Europe' (1969: 156). Nevertheless his enthusiasm for China affected a number of his contemporaries. Most notable of these was the philosopher Christian Wolff (1679–1754), a pupil of Leibniz who became the leading exponent of rationalist thinking in Germany, and was an important influence on Kant. Wolff studied Confucianism closely, holding its ethical teachings in especially high regard, and in a famous lecture delivered at the University of Halle in 1721 he proclaimed that Confucian moral teaching, though based on the natural light of reason rather than on revelation, was the equal of the moral teaching of Christianity. He argued that Confucianism represented a vindication of the idea of a natural morality, and as such was in close agreement with his own rationalist premises. As was intended, the lecture outraged his orthodox Protestant colleagues, who were able to engineer his dismissal from the university and his banishment from Prussia. He was later reinstated, however, and the episode led to his widespread fame amongst European savants for whom Wolff had become something of a martyr to the cause of Reason.[16]

The influence of Leibniz's orientalism is questionable. David Mungello points out that his ecumenical plans did not bear fruit until, perhaps, the founding of the United Nations in our own century (see Mungello 1977: 134), and his hermeneutical engagement with the *I Ching* was based on a misunderstanding of that text, an interest that was not renewed until the twentieth century. The case of the physiocrat François Quesnay (1694–1774) leads to a quite different judgement; though a less original thinker than Leibniz, the mark of his economic theory is evident on the whole of the modern world. The term 'physiocracy' means literally the 'rule of nature', and Quesnay's theory, published in 1758 in his *Tableau Économique*, was based on the belief that the nation's wealth came ultimately from the land and from agriculture, and that the full exploitation of this wealth depended on the freeing of producers from government restraint and interference so that the natural laws of the market place (as we would now call it) could operate freely. The market place is therefore subject to natural law like everything else in nature, and the freeing of its activities from unnatural and artificial restraint would inevitably lead not only to wealth but to the happiness and harmony of all.

Quesnay's revolutionary ideas amounted to a liberation from the economic orthodoxy of his day known as mercantilism – which could be described as the economic counterpart of political absolutism – and his influence on the free-market theories of Adam Smith was profound. What is often omitted in accounts of Quesnay's place in modern thought is his debt to China – unlike in his own day when he was widely known as 'the European Confucius'. The title of the treatise he wrote on China in 1767, *Le despotisme de la Chine*, might lead one to suppose that he was critical of China, and indeed some of the practices of that nation, such as slavery, were not entirely to his liking. But it must be remembered that for the *philosophes* 'despotism' was by no means a term of criticism, and that China was looked upon as a model of the kind of autocracy favoured by the Enlighteners, namely one that was not based on arbitrary whim but which was subject to the rule of law and in which the happiness of the people and the harmony of all aspects of society's operations were the despot's central concerns. Quesnay himself, like so many of his contemporaries, regarded China as an ideal society that provided a model for Europe to follow, and in discussing Chinese despotism he wrote that 'I have concluded from the reports about China that the Chinese constitution is founded upon wise and irrevocable laws which the Emperor enforces and which he carefully observes himself' (in Schurmann and Schell 1967: 113). Furthermore Quesnay also greatly admired the Chinese system of education whereby young men were prepared for public service through a rigorous programme of study, and gained advancement through competitive examinations. This aspect of China was, not surprisingly, attractive to the *philosophes* in general who saw in it a key to government through merit and learning rather than through privilege and heredity, and it later had an influence on the introduction of competitive entry into the civil services of France and Britain.[17]

But Quesnay's use of the example of China goes well beyond these general sentiments of approval. His most direct source of inspiration came from Pierre Poivre who had journeyed extensively in China between 1740 and 1756 and who painted a rosy picture of China as the happiest and best organised country in the world because it was founded on a mode of activity that was closest to nature's own way of operating, namely that of agriculture. This foundational principle was consciously supported by the state which sought to encourage agriculture and to free it as far as possible from the burdens of regulation and taxation. It was expressed philosophically in the idea that nature inclines towards a condition of harmony and balance, not through being forced and constrained but rather through following its own way – its *tao*. The function of the emperor, therefore, was not to direct and manipulate the economy but to ensure that the ways of nature were respected, a role which was largely a symbolic one. Thus, for example, every spring the emperor began the planting season by ploughing the first furrow, a practice briefly emulated in France by Louis XIV. Nature must be respected, then, not because it is divine or sacred in any way – such a view would have been abhorrent to the *philosophes* – but rather because as a self-regulating system it tends, through the workings of its own laws, to produce the best outcome for all. The wise ruler knows that, at a certain level of operating, the best policy is in a sense to do nothing, a policy summed up in the central philosophical concept of *wu-wei* which is translated into French as *laissez-faire*. The historian Basil Guy comments that 'Both lawmaker and law had to recognize the principles of . . . natural order, and in so doing conform to the Chinese ideal of *wu-wei*, which has ever inspired their theories of government' (1963: 350). It was this principle which also inspired Quesnay and which, through his disciple Adam Smith, entered into modern economic thinking.[18]

ENGLISH DEISTS AND GARDENS

The enthusiasms of the French *philosophes* were never fully shared by their British counterparts, though from early in the seventeenth century in Britain there is evidence of a growing respect for and interest in the philosophy and constitution of China in a way that echoed quietly many themes played fortissimo in France. Thus the essayist and diplomat Sir William Temple thought that 'It were endless to enumerate all the excellent orders of [China], which seem contrived by a reach of sense and wisdom, beyond what we meet in any other government of the world', and John Webb, whose work on the Adamic language was referred to above, agreed that 'if ever any monarch in the world was constituted according to political principle, and dictates of right reason, it may be boldly said that of the Chinois is' (quoted in Marshall and Williams 1982: 23). In the international world of Enlightenment scholarship the channel did not represent a barrier to ideas, and a number of French works were translated into English, for example the anonymous publication of 1691 entitled *The Morals of Confucius, a Chinese Philosopher*, and at about the same time the Latin translation of Chinese classics,

Confucius Sinarum Philosophus, became available in English. These, along with the accounts of travellers in the East, such as Sir William Chambers, helped to feed both the popular imagination and the minds of thinkers in Britain in that period.

The group of British thinkers most responsive to the allures of China were undoubtedly the *deists* who frequently drew on Confucian philosophy in support of their views, maintaining that the Chinese literati were essentially in agreement with their own point of view; indeed, according to David Hume the Chinese were 'the only regular body of Deists in the universe' (1898: 149). Following ideas first expounded by the poet/philosopher Lord Herbert of Cherbury (1582–1648), the deists believed in a natural religion which rejected the authority of church or revelation, but which rested on the 'light of reason' which is inborn in every human being. Herbert maintained that certain fundamental, rationally based, religious beliefs were universal possessions of humankind and were basic to all institutionalised religions, whereas sectarian and ethnic differences with regard to beliefs were merely modifications of universally attested truths. In pursuit of this idea, heretical enough in its day, the deists went even further and argued that the Old Testament was by no means the oldest religious text, or the unique word of God, but was only one among many sources of religious truth. Christianity itself was therefore only one of many religions which relied on the universal power of human reason. Later, Matthew Tindal (1657–1733), the most learned of the British deists, sought to give support to such views by again emphasising the fact that Confucian moral teachings, which were the equal of Christian teachings, were based on rational rather than revealed foundations. He approved of Leibniz's idea of China sending missionaries to Europe, and went so far as to declare that 'I am so far from thinking the maxims of Confucius and Jesus Christ differ, that I think the plain and simple maxims of the former will help illustrate the more obscure ones of the latter' (quoted in Appleton 1951: 50).[19]

The influence of China on Britain in this period is perhaps most evident in the cultural and artistic spheres, and it will be useful to look briefly at the latter, not only for their own sake but because of their close connections with the history of the ideas of the period. In the broader European context the impress of Chinese decorative motifs in the baroque and rococo period is well known, as too is its influence on the painting styles of artists like Watteau and Boucher. Furthermore, the enthusiasm for '*chinoiserie*', the fanciful European adaptation of Chinese styles in furniture, pottery, and textile design, rampant on both sides of the channel in the seventeenth and eighteenth centuries, is well documented. What is perhaps less well explored is the influence of China on the emergence of the Romantic sensibility in the middle years of the eighteenth century. In the first place the development of watercolour painting in the work of Alexander Cozens and his son John, which became a popular form of artistic expression in the Romantic period and afterwards, was strongly influenced by traditional Chinese painting techniques, methods which encouraged a more immediate and spontaneous relationship between the artist and the natural world. Second, and of even greater significance, was the evolution of the so-called Anglo-Chinese garden, a development which helped to shift attitudes away from the ideals of classical formality and regularity which had predominated in the Enlightenment period, towards a greater sense of naturalness and freedom. According to the art historian Michael Sullivan, the image of the Chinese garden, transmitted to Europe by Sir William Chambers *inter alia*, helped to provoke 'a reaction against the formal, geometrical gardens of Italy and France, and helped to bring to birth the natural gardens that were so much more in accordance with English taste' (in Ropp 1990: 286). Some critics believe that this transmission had a crucial influence on the formation of Romantic attitudes towards nature (see Lovejoy 1948), and in the opinion of the historian Adolf Reichwein, what was involved here was not merely a revolution in garden design as such but an epochal shift in attitudes towards nature from those associated with Augustan ideals of classical symmetry and proportion to the more liberated, imaginative, spontaneous view that blossomed in the Romantic period (see Reichwein 1925: 113ff).[20]

THE DECLINE OF SINOMANIA

Enthusiasm for China, though widespread, was by no means universal, and began to suffer a significant decline towards the end of the eighteenth century, by which time the cults of *chinoiserie* and sinophilism 'had run their natural course and completely lost their impetus' (Dawson 1967: 132). The revival of Hellenism, following the excavations of the remains of Pompeii in mid-century, contributed to the eclipse of sinomania, as did the expulsion of the Christian missionaries from China in 1770. Of even greater significance in distancing China from Europe was the growing suspicion that the image of that country propagated by the European sinophiles had been somewhat inflated, and that the picture of China's wisdom, its political and economic institutions, its moral philosophy and its religious practices, were 'somewhat more flattering to China than the realities would warrant' (Mackerras 1989: 41).[21]

A definite change of heart is detectable amongst the *philosophes* in the second half of the eighteenth century, with Diderot and Helvetius, both one-time devotees of the China cult, recanting their earlier enthusiasms. Diderot, who in the *Encyclopédie* had rated the Chinese people at least the equal of the European in culture and civilisation, came to regard the reports concerning the elevated moral and religious practices of the Chinese as biased and unscientific, and substituted the idea of the Noble Savage as the ideal for Europe to follow; while Helvétius in *De l'esprit* came to condemn the much-lauded Chinese despotism as unenlightened tyranny. In 1776 Friedrich Grimm pronounced China-worship to be excessive and in bad taste, insisting too that China was an unenlightened despotism, a view which was encouraged by Montesquieu who believed that the Chinese state was a tyranny based on fear and that political freedom was virtually unknown in the East. The most powerful anti-Chinese voice, however, was undoubtedly that of Rousseau. Like Diderot his desire for an ideal for Europe to copy tended more towards that of the Noble Savage, the Chinese appearing to him to enjoy an existence even more artificial and unnatural than that of his fellow Europeans. In his *Nouvelle Héloise* he characterised China as just another example of a decadent civilisation to be contrasted with the naturalness of the savage, and went on to declare that 'there is no sin to which they [the Chinese] are not prone, no crime which is not common among them' (quoted in Reichwein 1925: 94). And finally Condorcet, in his famous *Sketch of a Historical Picture of the Human Mind* (1795), which outlined a picture of the progress of the human race from barbarism to enlightenment, saw China with its lack of freedom as an impediment to political and moral progress. Where the culture of China had once seemed fresh and provocative, it now took on the character of torpor and apathy by contrast with the supposed vigour and progressiveness of Europe, and sinophilia gave way to a new orientalist enthusiasm – India.[22]

Chapter 4

Passage to India
The age of Romanticism

INDIA AND THE ROMANTICS

Whereas China was the chief object of interest for the philosophers of the Enlightenment, it was India that captured the minds and imagination of the Romantics. China indeed faded almost completely from serious Western philosophical interest and throughout the nineteenth century became instead largely an object of contempt and racist condescension in the West. From being a model of political and moral enlightenment, China become a corrupt and degraded civilisation in European eyes, and the great nineteenth-century political scientist Alexis de Tocqueville 'found it incomprehensible that the eighteenth-century Physiocrats should have had such an admiration for China' (Bernal 1987: 238). Amongst the complex reasons for this change of heart must be listed China's own increasingly hostile attitude towards Western incursions, as evidenced in its closure of Christian missions and the humiliation it dealt out to the Macartney and Amherst embassies, an attitude which ran in the face of rising nationalist sentiment in Europe. At a purely intellectual level, however, Chinese thought, as requisitioned by European thinkers, ceased to respond to the new sorts of questions and concerns that emerged in the period after the Enlightenment, and so the bridge-building that had been so promisingly begun in the seventeenth and eighteenth centuries ceased more or less abruptly.[1]

India had indeed been known to the Enlightenment *philosophes*, initially through the reports of Jesuit missionaries, and a large body of information about that civilisation became available in Europe from the seventeenth century onwards. By the latter half of the eighteenth century there were widespread discussions concerning India amongst the European intelligentsia, and Voltaire among others held up Hinduism as an example of a natural deistic religion with a pedigree much older than that of Judaeo-Christianity. But its political institutions failed to inspire respect, its mythology, rampant polytheism, and ritual extravagance were ridiculed by the *philosophes*, and practices such as *suttee* provoked attitudes of moral superiority among many writers in that period. As the historian Peter Marshall remarks: 'Even if some intellectual curiosity about Hinduism was aroused, the attitude of the great mass of Europeans who came into contact with it was always either ridicule or disgust' (1970: 20). Furthermore India's supposed moral 'quietism' and 'love of nothingness' were viewed as exemplifying a civilisation in decay, one which, by contrast with China, had suppressed the natural light of reason, and which had, according to Kant, 'become adulterated with many superstitious things' (quoted in Halbfass 1988: 61). Naturally the metaphysical speculations and 'mystical' inclinations of Indian thought were in conflict with Enlightenment taste, but it was precisely these aspects, appropriately refracted through European lenses, which appeared to mirror so lucidly the Romantic frame of mind and with which the Romantics engaged with enthusiasm.

The interest in and enthusiasm for Indian literature and ideas during the Romantic period was almost as pervasive as was the interest in China during the earlier epoch, and it was the extent of this interest that led Raymond Schwab to revive the idea of the 'Oriental Renaissance', first mooted in the early nineteenth century by Friedrich Schlegel. Schwab believed that the introduction of Indian thought into Europe from the late eighteenth century onwards and its integration into the cultural and philosophical concerns of the period amounted to a cultural revolution of the same order as that of the Renaissance of fifteenth-century Italy, and that

> the revival of an atmosphere in the nineteenth century brought about by the arrival of Sanskrit texts into Europe . . . produced an effect equal to that produced in the fifteenth century by the arrival of Greek manuscripts and Byzantine commentators after the fall of Constantinople.
>
> (Schwab 1984: 11)

The Italian Renaissance had been provoked by the influx of Greek manuscripts from the collapsing Byzantine empire, and in a parallel way the Oriental Renaissance was precipitated by the decline of the Mogul empire in the latter half of the eighteenth century and the consequent opening up of the Indian subcontinent to French and British commercial and political interests, which in turn led to the translation and study of Indian Sanskrit texts by European scholars.[2]

As in the Enlightenment period, the primary intellectual impetus for the new orientalism lay not so much in disinterested scholarship as in the growing sense of disillusionment with prevailing European modes of thought and belief, on the one side Judaeo-Christianity whose spiritual traditions were proving unsatisfactory, and on the other the materialism and anti-religious stance of the Enlightenment which appeared to abolish the possibility of spirit altogether. As one historian puts it: 'To the Romanticist, who had become painfully aware of himself in the icy breath of the rationalist, European–Christian atmosphere of sobering disengagement from his own roots, India appeared like the promised land' (Willson 1964: 113).

As with the *philosophes*, there was a perceived need for renewal, which in the case of the Romantics took the form of a search for childlike innocence, a vision of wholeness, a yearning for the recovery of what the poets and philosophers of the period felt the age had lost, namely a oneness with humankind and a oneness with nature, and for a reunification of religion, philosophy, and art which had been sundered in the modern Western world. Thus, where the earlier Oriental interest had sprung largely from ethical and political needs, the new version largely arose from what can only be described as a metaphysical thirst, and where China had been taken to heart as a political utopia, India came to be seen as the realm of Spirit. Mirroring the philosophical preoccupations of the time, Indian thought became selectively identified in the minds of European intellectuals with the monistic and idealist philosophy of the *Vedānta*, an attitude which inevitably gave rise to the myth of the exalted spirituality of India by contrast with the materialist West; as one commentator puts it: 'the notion of a subcontinent of idealists captured the Western imagination', thus giving rise to the long-lasting perception of India as a land of dreamers and mystics (Tuck 1990: 26). Political considerations were present also, however, even though they played a more muted role than in the Enlightenment period, and the fascination of German intellectuals for India can partly be explained by the fact that the growing spirit of national liberation inspired by the French Revolution caused many of them to look, paradoxically, to supposed archaic connections with India as a way of asserting their own distinct identity. The Enlightenment had often appeared in Germany as a largely French affair, and the Romantic movement, aided by an almost mystic affinity with the East, expressed Germany's search for a cultural and political identity beyond the French sphere of influence. The full implications of this in terms of racism and anti-semitism were only to emerge later in the nineteenth century, and we will return to these later.[3]

SOURCES OF THE NEW CULT

In the meantime let us look more closely at the origins of this new enthusiasm. Though the Jesuit missions had been the first to open up for European eyes the cultural treasure house of India, and accounts of the wonders of that sub-continent were being readily absorbed by educated Europeans from the early part of the eighteenth century, it was the commercial interests of Europe, especially those of the East India Company, that provided the main vehicle for the passage of ideas between India and Europe in the Romantic period. The decline of the Mogul empire in the eighteenth century and the penetration of French and British interests first into Bengal and then into the rest of India laid the groundwork, not only of the British Empire, but also of the Oriental Renaissance. Notable amongst the earliest pioneers in the world of Indian scholarship who were able to make use of this opening were two Englishmen, John Holwell and Alexander Dow, who carried over from the Enlightenment period leanings towards deism and a tolerant, universalistic outlook. Both served in India and produced widely read commentaries on India, its culture, and its religions. Holwell was for a while governor of Bengal, and in his writings gave a highly favourable account of the religious and philosophical ideas of India, and encouraged the belief that India was the source of all wisdom and had profoundly influenced the philosophical traditions of Ancient Greece. Their books were translated into German and French in the 1760s, and among their readers was Voltaire, whose views on the antiquity of Indian religion and civilisation were largely shaped by their writings.[4]

An equally important early pioneer was the Frenchman Anquetil Duperron (1723–1805). He produced the first translation of the Upanishads, the publication of which made a considerable contribution to the understanding by European thinkers of Indian thought. His translation, rendered from a Persian translation and known as the *Oupnek'hat*, exerted a powerful influence in Europe well into the nineteenth century, and became the favourite reading of Arthur Schopenhauer. Duperron visited India between 1754 and 1761, and while he remained a faithful Christian he developed at the same time 'an openness for extra-European and non-Christian achievements of thought, and a readiness for comprehensive comparisons which . . . transcended the limits of "orthodoxy"' (Halbfass 1988: 66). This openness was evident in his recommendation that the Indian classics should be treated and studied on a par with those of Greece and Rome, and that the teachings of the *Oupnek'hat* should be subjected to serious philosophical study, rather than read for merely antiquarian interest. He was indeed one of the first thinkers of his age to draw attention to parallels between Indian and Judaeo-Christian ideas, and to make comparisons with Western philosophical teachings. Of particular importance was the connection he made between Indian philosophy and Kant's transcendental idealism, asserting that

> Anyone who carefully examines the lines of Immanuel Kant's thought, its principles as well as its results, will recognize that it does not deviate far from the teachings of the Brahmins, which lead man back to himself and comprise and focus him within himself.
>
> (quoted in Halbfass 1988: 67)

Such comparisons were, for Duperron, of more than just academic interest. As a child of the Enlightenment he was driven by a deep-seated belief in the unity of humanity, and the correspondences he found between the two civilisations served as an 'incentive to general concord and love', and as a key to the moral regeneration of Europe. Powerful motives such as these were to become a characteristic feature of the whole Romantic attachment to India.

The most influential phase of Indic studies began with the arrival of British civil servants in Calcutta in the 1780s, many of them in the pay of the East India Company, and operating under the enlightened patronage of the governor, Warren Hastings. The central figure in this story was William Jones (1746–94), of whom Arthur Versluis writes: 'Jones's Herculean efforts . . . without exaggeration profoundly and almost single-handedly transformed the European view of Asia . . . to a vision of an exotic and highly civilized world in its own right' (1993: 18). Educated at Harrow and at Oxford, he was not only a distinguished lawyer and linguist, but also made a name as a poet and as a radical pamphleteer, and with his deep knowledge of Sanskrit was in effect the first true scholar of Hinduism. He was appointed judge in the Supreme Court in Calcutta in 1783, spending the rest of his days there, and founded the *Asiatick Society of Bengal* which became a focus of Hindu scholarship and which published the first journal of Oriental Studies, *Asiatick Researches*. In many ways Jones was more of an Enlightenment figure than a Romantic. He was a friend of Benjamin Franklin and Joseph Priestley, and his support for the cause of American independence led to a long delay in his appointment to the judiciary. But his influence on the Romantics, both English and German, was considerable. His writings on India and translations of Indian texts were widely disseminated in Europe, and in them were first elaborated many of the themes which were later to be developed in Germany by the Indophiles. The extent of Jones' influence on the continent is emphasised by Schwab when he writes that

> The publications of the Indic scholars at Calcutta ignited a kind of fervid intensity in certain young Germans. In philosophy they included Schelling, Fichte and Hegel – not to mention Schopenhauer and Schleiermacher. In poetry they included Goethe, Schiller, Novalis, Tieck, and Brentano. And among the great innovators of the new ideas that were to become Romanticism, a certain Herder passed the word to a certain Friedrich Schlegel.
>
> (Schwab 1984: 53)

The most important of the themes which carried through into Germany was the claim that European and Indian languages bore remarkable resemblances to each other, from which Jones conjectured that the European and Indian races may have sprung from a common source. The question of the origins of the European peoples had been the subject of intensive debate for some time, and, as P. J. Marshall notes, 'Jones was the heir to over a century of speculation about migrations from Asia', but with his knowledge of Sanskrit he 'was able to bring a new element of precision to these speculations' (1970: 16). In a paper 'On the Origin and Families of Nations' he argued that there was 'incontestable proof . . . that the first race of Persians and Indians, to whom we may add the Romans and Greeks, the Goths, and the old Egyptians or Ethiops, originally spoke the same language and professed the same popular faith', adding the suggestion that Iran was the common place of origin (quoted in Marshall 1970: 15). This idea was to have huge repercussions in later years, but as far as the Romantics were concerned it was useful ammunition in their fight to break out of what some of them saw as the narrowness of the Judaeo-Christian tradition and, as with the links made by the *philosophes* with Chinese religion, marked a further step towards a more universal conception of humanity. In addition to the work of Jones, mention must be made of two other British civil servants who made important contributions to the early development of the Oriental Renaissance: Charles Wilkins (1749–1836), who in 1785 produced the first translation into English from the Sanskrit of the great Hindu epic, the *Bhagavad*

Gītā, a work which was re-translated into many languages and 'which was to exercise enormous influence on the mind of Europe and America' (Sharpe 1985: 10); and Thomas Colebrooke (1765–1837) whose *Essays on the Religion and Philosophy of the Hindus* introduced the public to many hitherto unknown facets of Indian culture and was widely read in the nineteenth century.

The influence of these early explorations of the great Indian classics is evident in the English literature of that time, providing an important alternative source of imagery in the Romantics' attempt to undermine eighteenth-century classicism. William Jones, who was as famous in England for his poetry as for his Indian scholarship, was much admired by the Lake poets, and the work of Shelley, Southey, Byron, and De Quincy all show evidence of Oriental influence. Nigel Leask has observed of Shelley that his 'interest in India transcends the level of biographical anecdote', and quotes Edgar Quinet's remark: 'Shelley completely Indian' (1992: 71), a view supported by H. G. Rawlinson who finds *Vedānta* philosophy 'magnificently propounded' in that poet's *Adonais* (in Garratt 1937: 33). The writings of Coleridge, whose thinking was greatly indebted to the German idealist philosophers, contain a considerable number of references to Indian mythical figures and themes, though as John Drew notes in his study of India and the Romantic imagination, Coleridge, after a youthful phase of India-worship, was 'at considerable pains to disparage or dismantle an idealized view of India', and finally rejected Indian philosophy as a form of pantheism (1987: 186–8). Nevertheless, as Drew suggests, the very vehemence of Coleridge's rejection of Indian metaphysics is indicative of the extent to which he had at one time been intimately concerned with and in awe of it, and speculates that 'Coleridge never did free himself of the original debt of homage he paid to the Indian scriptures' (ibid.: 126).[5]

It was not in England, however, that the Oriental Renaissance came to maturity but in Germany. While the Romantic phenomenon in England centred mainly on poets and painters, in Germany it was given voice among playwrights and musicians as well. Even more significantly it also found powerful expression amongst the remarkable family of philosophers and thinkers who flourished at the end of the eighteenth and the beginning of the nineteenth centuries, a lineage running from Herder and Goethe through Hegel and Schelling to Friedrich Schlegel and Schopenhauer. All of them were coloured in one way or another by what Schwab has called 'an Indian tint' (1984: 206), and were infected by what Said describes more luridly as 'the virtual epidemic of Orientalia affecting every major poet, essayist, and philosopher of the period' (1985: 50). Kant, in some ways the fount and origin of this whole philosophical movement, is an exception in this regard, though he drew favourable attention to the absence of dogmatism and intolerance in Indian religions, and expressed admiration for Buddhist moral ideals.

There are interesting parallels between the German Indophilia of the Romantic period and the French Sinophilia of the Enlightenment, which provide evidence of the continuity of a number of common themes, while at the

same time pointing to radically different assumptions and values. As I emphasised above, in both cases the Orient was approached, not primarily in a spirit of
objective scholarship, even less through a desire to understand contemporary
India, but rather as an instrument for the subversion and reconstruction of
European civilisation, and though much was undoubtedly learned of Indian traditional culture, it was deployed primarily as a means of treating what were seen
as deep-seated ills at the heart of contemporary European culture. Inevitably,
therefore, the obsessional concern with Europe's own problems led, for the
German Romantics as much as for the French *philosophes*, to a measure of idealisation and of distortion, and the construction of an idyllic paradise where, as
one historian put it, 'nature is entwined with love; the emotion and the object are
inseparable, each includes the other. In India there was a pure golden innocence,
the innocence of childhood' (Willson 1964: 89). Just as the *philosophes* projected
onto Confucian China their concept of an ideal polity governed by wise and
philosophically educated rulers, so the Romantics projected onto India their idea
of a more fully realised human existence and a more holistic and spiritually driven culture. The Indian people themselves were seen as a child-like nation,
genial in their manners, and graceful in their deportment, living closer than the
Europeans to the natural order of things, given to quiet, sober, orderly living,
and abstaining from the violence connected with meat-eating and the consumption of alcohol. They, like the Chinese in the eyes of an earlier generation, were
seen as displaying a high level of moral conduct, by contrast with the greed and
rapacity of Europeans, standards which had to some extent been ruined by foreign incursions, first the Moguls and more latterly the French and British. This
sort of Rousseauesque primitivism extended deep into the perception of Indian
culture and philosophy. It was noted, for example, that many ancient Sanskrit
texts, even on such topics as astronomy, were written in verse, a fact which
helped to confirm a pet Romantic theory, namely that the original human
speech was poetic in form. This in turn was part of a general belief that India in
its classical literature possessed a kind of primitive wisdom, a fundamental truth,
which had become lost in the West – and in India too – and which needed to be
recovered. India was for many Romantics the source of all wisdom, and indeed
the fountainhead of civilisation as such. This idea, which, as we saw earlier,
Voltaire had eagerly adopted a generation earlier, was one which inevitably
called into question the priority of Israel and Greece in the formation of
European culture, and suggested to some that the linguistic and ethnic link
between Germany and India was stronger than the one with the ancient civilisations of the Mediterranean. Even Immanuel Kant, no romanticiser of the
Orient, repeated the common opinion that the arts of Europe, such as agriculture, numbers, and the game of chess, came from India.

The link with the ancient wisdom of India had important philosophical reso-
nances as well. This wisdom was seen at its most profound and highly developed
in the Upanishads where a monistic doctrine, associated with the idea of
brahman, replaced the pluralism of the earlier Vedas, and where the central con-

cept of *ātman* (soul or mind) was seen to parallel directly the role which mind or spirit (*Geist*) played in German idealist philosophy. The Germans were greatly attracted to the Upanishadic teaching (as they understood it) that the world as we know it through our ordinary senses is not the 'real' world, but only appearance, even an illusion (*māyā*), and that the goal of life was the realisation of the self – *ātman* – through its identification with the absolute – *brahman*. This view seemed to harmonise well with some central and characteristic features of German idealist philosophy, which could be summed up as the view that the phenomenal world exists essentially through, and is unified in, spirit or mind, and that the individual mind is but a moment in the unfolding of Absolute Mind. Thus, just as Confucianism had offered the *philosophes* a model for a rationalist, deistic philosophy, so the Hinduism of the Upanishads offered an exalted metaphysical system which resonated with their own idealist assumptions, and which provided a counterblast to the materialistic and mechanistic philosophy that had come to dominate the Enlightenment period.

These then are some of the general themes which flow through the German dialogue with ancient India. It is now time to examine them in more detail as they apply to some of the major thinkers of the period. We will concentrate attention on the key figures, bearing in mind that Indophilia left hardly any of the Romantic generation of poets, philosophers, and theologians untouched.

GERMAN THINKERS

Johann Gottfried Herder (1744–1803), who in many ways set the agenda for Romanticism, was the first of that generation to conscript the Orient in pursuit of the goals of Romanticism. The Romantic tone of his Indophilia is clearly evident in such comments as: 'O holy land [of India], I salute thee, thou source of all music, thou voice of the heart' (quoted in Edwardes 1971: 152), and 'Behold the East – cradle of the human race, of human emotion, of all religion' (quoted in Iyer 1965: 188). He was not the first to proclaim the venerable antiquity of India and to claim that the source of all civilisation, even of language itself, lay not in the Mediterranean or even the Middle East, but in India. But in so doing he helped to place the question of the origins and identity of European, or more particularly of German, cultural identity right at the heart of the Romantic movement. Though he was by no means uncritical of Indian culture – for example he disliked its practice of *suttee*, its caste system, and what he perceived as its attitude of resignation – he also helped to propagate the Rousseauesque picture of a decadent Europe contrasted with an ancient idyllic society, setting up India as an ideal against which Europeans might observe and measure their own moral failings.

Concern with the nature and identity of cultures was at the heart of Herder's thinking. Leaving aside the Confucian factor the classical world of Greece and Rome had hitherto been held up as the ideal to be followed in all humanistic endeavour from philosophy and the pursuit of virtue, to art, architecture, and poetry. This implied in turn the postulation of universal values which in practice were seen to have their most perfect embodiment in the ancient classical cultures of the Mediterranean. The German people had never found themselves sitting happily with this classical model, especially as in the eighteenth century it had come to be embodied most conspicuously in French culture. Herder's theory of history and of cultures spoke eloquently to this German problem. Contrary to the universalist and rationalist tendencies of the Enlightenment, he saw human history as comprising nations and traditions that were living wholes, organic entities with a life and soul of their own, whose cultural products and religious tendencies could only be assessed from within each living tradition. Metaphors of organic growth and development were typical of his thinking, and with the aid of these he sought to demonstrate close living ties between Europe and India. As Halbfass observes, writing about Herder: 'the development of mankind "from the Orient to Rome" is likened to the trunk of a tree, out of which branches and shoots grow. . . . The Orient was the infant state, and thus innocent, pure, and with unexhausted potential' (1988: 70).

Like William Jones, Herder, a Lutheran pastor, never doubted the intrinsic pre-eminence of Christianity over India and the Orient, but his sympathetic understanding of Hindu philosophy, and especially his empathy for the poetry of its ancient classics, provided the impetus for a whole generation of German thinkers. We have already seen that the idea that India represented the childhood of humanity, though it was later to be used for different ends by Hegel, helped greatly in the formulation of Romantic primitivism, which in turn became a powerful weapon in the critique of contemporary culture. His image of the Indian people as gentle, childlike vegetarians was an implicit criticism of the ineffectiveness of Christian morality, and he was vehemently opposed to the activities of Christian missionaries who sought to impose on Indians their alien formulae. This picture was linked with the question of Biblical priority. Again, as a Christian minister, Herder did not aim to attack the orthodox account, but his recognition of the great age of the civilisations of the East, and his belief that the European nations sprang from Asia, inevitably had the effect of placing question marks over the belief that the Book of Genesis contained the definitive account of the early history of the human race. His sympathies for Indian thought extended further. He rejected the doctrine of metempsychosis (transmigration of souls) as false, but at the same time he recognised in it the source of the ideal of sympathy for all creatures, and linked it to the notion of the fundamental unity of all living beings. He was also attracted by the Indian ideas of pantheism and of the world-soul (*ātman*), both of which came to be viewed by the German Romantics as providing support for their own views about the transcendent wholeness and the fundamentally spiritual essence of the natural world.

Equally influential on the course of the Romantic movement was Herder's friend, the great poet and dramatist Goethe (1749–1832) who, along with Herder, had inspired the proto-Romantic *Sturm und Drang* (Storm and Stress) movement of the 1770s. Goethe never became an outspoken supporter of the

Indophile movement, and indeed he came to distance himself from the Romantic movement in general, identifying himself more as a champion of Greek civilisation and Hellenic culture. Nevertheless, as a man of wide sympathies, he took a close interest in the ideas coming through from the East, China as well as India, and there is much evidence of Oriental influence in his writings. He was acquainted with the leading German orientalists of the day, such as Friedrich Majer and Silvestre de Sacy, an enthusiast for the Indian drama *Sakuntala*, and an admirer of the writings of 'the incomparable Jones'. His contributions to the orientalist genre included verse in the Chinese manner, the *Chinesische-Deutschen Jahres- und Tageszeiten* (1827), and a set of poems entitled *Westöstliche Diwan* (1819), which were to influence a whole generation of German poets including Heine and Rückert. In the Preface to the latter work he voiced his debt to Herder and wrote that he wished 'to penetrate to the first origin of the human race, when they still received celestial mandates from God in terrestrial languages' (quoted in Schwab 1984: 211). He was less enthusiastic about India's mythological profusions, but his own pantheistic leanings, like those of many contemporaries, found a resonance in the philosophy of the Upanishads.[6]

The appeal of the Upanishads to Goethe, Herder, and to the great philosophers of the Romantic period, lay in what was perceived as that scripture's monistic idealism, namely the belief that all things are, in the final analysis, one single whole, and that this oneness arises from the fundamentally spiritual nature of reality, the multiplicity of things being an illusion of our finite senses. The German idealist philosophical movement from Fichte and Schelling to Hegel and Schopenhauer comes remarkably close in many respects to this way of thinking. Of these, only Schopenhauer unreservedly acknowledged, even glorified in, this affinity, while at the same time denying that he had been influenced in his thinking by the East. Fichte was well versed in the new orientalist ideas, and his idealist philosophy bears many intriguing comparisons with Hindu thinking, but he could not be described as a leading member of the Indian cult. In the case of F. W. J. Schelling (1775–1854), however, a crucial figure in the development of German idealist and nature philosophy, Eastern ideas pervade and colour much of his thinking.

Throughout his life Schelling expressed great interest in and support for Indian and Oriental studies, and in his 1802 lectures he lavished praise on the 'sacred texts of the Indians', claiming that they were superior to the Bible. His philosophy underwent several transformations in the course of his long career, but the two elements of which we need to take note from the orientalist perspective are, first, his early 'nature philosophy', and second, his later work on mythology. In the 1790s Schelling had developed a philosophy in which nature is viewed in terms of dynamic growth and development, as a unified organic system in the process of self-formation through the reconciliation of opposing tendencies, with Spirit emerging from the womb of nature as its highest manifestation, its most complete state of self-fulfilment being identified with the

Absolute. His 'system of absolute identity' as he called it, which involved the resolution of differences in unity, his central notion of the Absolute as the ultimate perfection and unity of all things in nature, physical as well as mental, his belief in the illusory nature of the finite world, his pantheism, 'world-soul', and pervasive intuitionism, all were recognised in his day as arising from the same intellectual source as the philosophy of the Upanishads. Schelling himself underlined the affinity in his statement that Hindu philosophy is 'nothing but the most exalted idealism' (quoted in Halbfass 1988: 102), though at the same time he expressed regret at the lack of theoretical clarification in the Upanishads.

His relationship with Indian mythology was more fully developed, and over one hundred pages of his *Philosophy of Mythology* were devoted to India, in the course of which the religious histories of East and West were systematically drawn together. In the second half of his life Schelling moved away from the idealist monism of his earlier days and returned to a more orthodox Christian monotheistic position, and hence he was not, like many of his contemporaries, primarily concerned to use India as a weapon with which to belabour orthodoxy. Even so, in his studies of mythology he found in the Vedic poems a source of myth that was more ancient than the Bible, and which was clearly not a product of the Mediterranean world. In his earlier days he had expressed interest in the typically Romantic idea of 'a single God for all mankind', and in his later work on mythology he developed this into the thesis that there is but one mythology in the world shared by all traditions, and sought to create 'a fusion of the mythological traditions of all humanity' (quoted in Schwab 1984: 217). What the Vedas demonstrated to Schelling was that the human race shared a primitive unity, and his effort in this regard must be counted as one of the great constructive attempts to see the universal spiritual history of mankind as a single whole. It represented the ideal of a universal humanity that transcends all surface local and historical differences, an attempt which, as we shall see later, had important echoes in twentieth-century orientalism.

The desire to trace everything back to India was even more in evidence in the writings of Friedrich Schlegel (1772–1829) who in a letter to Tieck wrote that 'Everything, yes, everything has its origins in India' (quoted in Schwab 1984: 71). A novelist, historian, and a diplomat, he was of all the leading Romantics the most knowledgeable in Sanskrit. His *Essay on the Language and Wisdom of the Indians*, published in 1808, began by lauding the beauty and antiquity of this sacred language, and of its aptitude for expressing philosophical ideas, and went on to elaborate a linguistic and anthropological thesis, reminiscent of Jones and Duperron, according to which the origins of the peoples of Northern Europe could be traced back to India. He imagined that a dynamic new people had formed itself in Northern India, who, goaded 'by some impulse higher than the spur of necessity', had swarmed towards the West, even claiming that Ancient Egypt had been colonised by the Indians (quoted in Poliakov 1971: 191).

This whole approach marks out Schlegel as one of the sharpest critics of the supposedly lamentable state of contemporary European culture, with the Orient held up as a model of moral and religious purity, and of the lost wholeness of original human existence. There is in the writings of Schlegel 'a nostalgia for the idyllic existence of ancient Hindu culture, where a happy people lived in closest communion with nature, and there is also a longing for the harmony of the arts and sciences as perceived in that culture'. He complained that 'Man cannot sink any deeper; it is impossible. Man has indeed come very far in the art of arbitrary division or, what amounts to the same thing, in mechanism, and thus man himself has almost become a machine', advocating a return to the source of civilisation in the East 'from where every religion and mythology up to now has come' (quoted in Halbfass 1988: 74 and 75).

According to Schlegel, India was 'the real source of all tongues', even 'the primary source of all ideas' (quoted in Iyer 1965: 194 and 200), and, in sharp reaction against a classicism which had become indelibly associated with France, sought to trace the source of Germanic culture back to ancient India. The Romantic search for *Humanität*, an exalted state in which humanity could transcend its fragmented condition, was especially evident in the case of Schlegel, and his dialogue with India revived an ideal that Leibniz, in the more sober and measured tones of the Age of Reason, had earlier speculated upon, speaking of Asiatics and Europeans as forming a 'single great family', and as 'a single indivisible whole'. The idea that India was somehow the fount and origin of all civilisation was therefore no mere poetic conceit, and Schlegel spoke for his generation when he wrote that 'In India lay the real source of all tongues, of all thoughts and utterances of the human mind. Everything – yes, everything without exception – has its origin in India', and 'The primary source of all intellectual development – in a word the whole human culture – is unquestionably to be found in the traditions of the East' (quoted in Iyer 1965: 194 and 200). Rooted in this was the belief that a 'universal revelation' underlay the great religions of mankind; as Schwab puts it, the universal 'myths and mysteries were assumed to hold secrets common to the faithful of all nations', a single truth veiled beneath the clothing of local legends and faiths, 'a single God for all mankind' (1984: 216–17).

Something of this attitude, namely the demand of the Romantics for a global conception of the human spirit and of human history, penetrates the writings of the greatest philosopher of that period, G. W. F. Hegel (1770–1831). He was in many respects critical of the Romantic outlook as a whole, and certainly did not share the unbridled enthusiasm of the Romantics for the East. He detested the 'wild excesses of fantasy', the 'unrestrained frenzy' and the chaos of myths and icons which he found in Indian culture, and generally regarded the East as stagnant, frozen in its past, and incapable of resuscitation. Nevertheless he studied the cultures of the East in some depth, and had as comprehensive a view of them as was possible in his day, deriving much of his understanding of Indian philosophy from the researches of Colebrooke and of his friend the indologist Franz Bopp. Many references to the cultures and philosophies of India and China appear in his later work, and he devoted a lot of time in his lectures on the history of philosophy, on the philosophy of history, and on the history of religion, to expounding his views concerning the place of China and India within a universal history of the human spirit. He was not, indeed, the first to include Eastern thought within a history of philosophy; Johann Gotlieb Buhle included sections on Chinese and Indian philosophy in his history of philosophy published in Germany in 1796. But he was the first to subject it to systematic treatment and to attempt to see it within the development of humanity as a single totality, as part of the unfolding of the world-spirit. His study of the Orient represented in many ways a unique hermeneutical enterprise in the history of ideas, and though his interpretation was later taken as a justification for dismissing India entirely from the historiography of philosophy, it nevertheless exemplifies, as Halbfass notes, 'once and for all one basic possibility of dealing with a foreign tradition' (1988: 98). In the judgement of the Indian philosopher J. L. Mehta, 'Hegel has been the only Western philosopher of rank to devote serious attention to Indian philosophical and religious ideas', and underlines 'the intensity of purpose with which Hegel grappled with the difficulties of understanding Indian ideas in terms of Western philosophical conceptuality' (Mehta 1985: 197).

The confidence with which Hegel subsumes the cultures of Asia under the categories of his system is indeed breathtaking, and in many ways reflects the historical position of Europe in that period as the emerging world power. It has also led many critics to dismiss his ideas in this field as too abstract and speculative, and as lacking in any real hermeneutical sensitivity towards an alien culture; his European 'horizon' does not so much fuse with that of the East as transcend and obliterate it. This obstacle to a more favourable response to Hegel's theory is most evident in his belief in the irreversible direction of history, a direction which moves inexorably from East to West. Unlike the Romantics he did not glorify the past, and hence the antiquity of China and India did not rouse him to the heights of enthusiasm typical of his day. Quite the contrary, he viewed those civilisations as occupying an earlier stage in the development of the human spirit. Universal history is essentially 'the development of the consciousness of Freedom on the part of Spirit, and of the consequent realization of that Freedom' (Hegel 1956: 63), and within this framework it was clear to him that progress towards freedom was manifested in a historical movement of the spirit which culminated in the modern Christian civilisation of Europe, a view summed up in his famous statement that 'the Eastern nations knew only that *one* is free; the Greek and Roman world only that *some* are free; while *we* know that all men absolutely (man *as man*) are free' (ibid.: 19). This did not mean that the insights of the earlier period were destroyed, but rather that they were preserved and carried forward – *aufgehoben* – into the higher synthesis of later times. The East itself, therefore, is petrified, a stagnant culture bound to a past which it cannot itself overcome. Furthermore, it can only adequately be comprehended from our present, superior, European standpoint, a view which was to license European orientalists to take over and make sense of the East in European terms, a task which the Orient, according to this theory, is incapable of exercising for itself.

In spite of the fact that Hegel was consistently critical of his contemporaries such as Friedrich Schlegel whose fascination for India led them, in his view, to betray the present and to distort history, he clearly thought that understanding the Orient had its uses, and was of more than purely antiquarian interest. In the first place it provided material for the articulation of a comprehensive global history of human culture, enabling Hegel to construct an historical model of the development of the human spirit as such. Even though the values and ideas of the ancient civilisations of the East could no longer instruct us, they contributed to self-knowledge in the way that a reflective understanding of childhood (as in psychoanalysis, for example) can furnish an adult with an ampler understanding of their present condition. Second, knowledge of the East, as indeed of all foreign cultures, could also provide a corrective and an antidote to contemporary excesses and one-sided tendencies, such as those of Romanticism itself, and to the extreme individualism of European thought by contrast with which oriental thinking displays a 'solid unity'. As Halbfass points out, Hegel's interest in India 'is inseparable from his anti-Romantic attitude', and from his reservations about the 'excessive subjectivism and anthropocentrism' of modern Western thought (1988: 94–5).

FROM HINDUISM TO BUDDHISM

While Hegel saw the philosophy of India as belonging irrevocably to the past, Arthur Schopenhauer (1788–1860) saw it as a key moment in Europe's contemporary philosophical life, and his attitude towards it was one of almost unreserved admiration. In the history of thought he was in some ways a transitional figure. In the first place he can be seen as representing the quintessence of Romantic philosophy with his idealist outlook and his anti-rationalist stance, but at the same time his deep psychological studies of the human condition and his pessimism look forward to later developments such as psychoanalysis and existentialism. Second, he straddles the European interest in Hinduism and Buddhism, for while in his early years he was deeply involved in the philosophy of the Upanishads, he later came into contact with Buddhism and was one of the first Western thinkers to investigate its philosophical implications. His reputation in twentieth-century philosophy has, until recently at any rate, been decidedly mixed, but this should not lead us to overlook the fact that in the latter part of the previous century he was one of the most widely read and influential thinkers in Europe.

Schopenhauer denied that his philosophical system had been influenced in its basic structures by the East, a judgement confirmed by Bryan Magee who points to the fact that he had already completed his work *The Fourfold Root of the Principle of Sufficient Reason* prior to becoming acquainted with Indian philosophy, and insists that Kant is the major source of his thinking (see Magee 1987: 15 and 316). Nevertheless it must also be pointed out that Schopenhauer had been familiar with the ideas of the Upanishads for several years prior to the publication in 1818 of his major work, *The World as Will and Representation*. It was in fact in 1814 that he met the orientalist Friedrich Majer who awakened his interest in Indian philosophy and who introduced him to Duperron's translation of the Upanishads, a work which had an especially powerful effect on him, and of which he later wrote rapturously that it was 'the most profitable and elevating reading which . . . is possible in the world. It has been the solace of my life, and will be the solace of my death' (Schopenhauer 1974b, 2: 185). Influenced or not, Schopenhauer drew many close parallels between his own philosophy and that of Hinduism, and later of Buddhism, and urged that an understanding of the Upanishads would not only help towards an understanding of his own philosophy, but would bring about a fundamental change in European thought. Contrary to Hegel's belief that history has a determinate direction and must be understood in teleological terms, Schopenhauer saw history as a 'farce', a product of blind cosmic will, without direction or purpose, and this enabled him to view Oriental philosophy not as a juvenile antecedent to the mature adulthood of Western Christendom but as a universal wisdom which was perennially alive and relevant. Thus while recognising the historical differences between East and West, he insisted on the possibility that philosophical insights could be significant within diverse historical contexts, a view which permitted him to claim that his own teachings were essentially identical with those of both the Buddha and Eckhart. This did not mean, however, that he saw his own thinking as merely a repetition of the philosophy of the Upanishads, but rather that the essence of Indian thought found in his philosophy was its systematic completion and fulfilment, the uncovering of its true meaning. Especially important for Schopenhauer was the Hindu concept of *māyā* which for him indicated the illusoriness of the phenomenal world of multiplicity, and the Upanishadic teaching that all things are ultimately one appealed to him as the precise equivalent of his notion that the apparent separateness and individuality of things is a mind-made illusion. His ethical philosophy was also closely linked in his mind with certain central Oriental teachings, both with the Hindu doctrine of the identity of *ātman* and *brahman*, namely the belief that the individual soul is in reality an aspect of a much larger, more inclusive reality, and also with the Buddhist teaching of compassion for all sentient beings. By contrast with Kant, who rested his moral philosophy on the idea of the 'categorical imperative', Schopenhauer argued that the root of morality must be found in compassion, in fellow feeling for other sentient beings, and that this feeling in its turn rested on the intuition – it cannot be validated rationally – that 'all of us in our deepest nature are one with each other, are undifferentiable from each other' so that I am not merely similar to other human beings but 'at the very bottom they and I are literally one and the same thing' (Magee 1987: 199).

In tune with Romantic sentiments, Schopenhauer viewed India as 'the land of the most ancient and most pristine wisdom, the place from which Europeans could trace their descent and the tradition by which they had been influenced in so many decisive ways' (Halbfass 1988: 112). Furthermore he anticipated later speculations with his claim that Christianity had 'Indian blood in its veins'

(Schopenhauer 1974a: 187), and that the moral teachings of the New Testament had their historical source in Asia beyond Israel: 'Christianity taught only what the whole of Asia knew already long before and even better' (1969, 2: 627). More portentously he used this argument to drive a wedge between Judaism and Christianity, arguing that 'it is not Judaism . . . but Brahmanism and Buddhism that in spirit and ethical tendency are akin to Christianity', and went on to suggest that the 'sublime truths' enshrined in the great religions of East and West expressed an underlying, universal wisdom (ibid.: 623). Taken together, these points amounted for Schopenhauer to the belief that the influx of Indian ideas into Europe represented a new Renaissance which would bring about a fundamental transformation in European thought, a transformation of far greater impact than that of Europe on Asia. He was convinced that Christianity would never take root in India and that 'the ancient wisdom of the human race will not be supplanted by the events in Galilee. On the contrary, Indian wisdom flows back to Europe, and will produce fundamental changes in our knowledge and thought' (Schopenhauer 1969, 1: 357).

Schopenhauer's engagement with Indian philosophy displays a number of inadequacies, many of which he shares in common with other Romantic enthusiasts. As we noted earlier, the Hindu teachings they drew upon were clearly torn loose from their cultural matrix, reconstructed out of highly selective textual fragments, and approached through translations and philological methodologies which, by modern standards, were very inadequate. Furthermore it will be evident from our discussion so far that these teachings were conceptualised primarily from within the frame of Western philosophical interests, and indeed one critic goes so far as to claim that the Romantics 'created Hinduism in their own image' in order to confirm their beliefs, and that 'Hinduism emerged from their work as adhering to an undogmatic Protestantism' (Marshall 1970: 43). Schopenhauer's attempt to identify some of his own central notions with Hindu concepts, such as 'will' with *brahman*, is a case in point, and Schlegel's exaltation of India as the source of all wisdom is as much to do with Europe as India for, as Halbfass points out, 'the Romantic interest in India was inseparable from a radical critique of the European present' (1988: 83). But in spite of such evident shortcomings, it is difficult not to feel admiration for the attempts of Schopenhauer and the Romantics to integrate these remote and foreign ideas within the horizon of Western thinking. The deployment of Indian thought as a critique of a certain kind of quantifying, mechanistic way of thinking, and against the forms of rationalist and materialist philosophy which were becoming dominant modes of modern Western thought, is of more than passing historical interest. Schopenhauer's own understanding of Indian philosophy, however inadequate, is an outstanding representative of the orientalist aspiration to use Eastern thought in pursuit of a fundamental rethinking of the Western intellectual tradition. Moreover the impact of the Romantic orientalists on the development of comparative studies and on the formation of linguistic and philological studies was immense, and constituted an important foundation for the development of orientalist scholarship later in the century.

One of the most significant outcomes of these advances in scholarship was the 'discovery' of Buddhism. In the case of Schopenhauer, certain Buddhist concepts such as *nirvana* had entered into his early work, but with the rapid enlargement in the understanding of Buddhism in the first half of the nineteenth century Schopenhauer was able in his later writings to expand even further his hermeneutical links with Eastern thought. We will investigate these links, along with the impact of Buddhism on nineteenth-century European thought as a whole, in the next chapter.[7]

Chapter 5

Buddhist passions
The nineteenth century

ROMANTIC SEQUEL

The nineteenth century saw considerable growth in the study of Eastern religious and philosophical ideas, not only at the scholarly level but increasingly among the educated public as a whole. As far as the more academic end of the spectrum is concerned, it must be remembered that this was the great age of specialisation when many of the academic disciplines and divisions with which we are now familiar were carved out. Orientalism was no exception. The work of such pioneers as Anquetil Duperron, Jones, and Colebrooke marked merely the beginning of the great European campaign to conquer the languages, traditions, and literatures of the Orient, one which marched side by side with the rapid imperial expansion which took place in that epoch. The opening up of the East through colonisation and the imposition of spheres of influence not only facilitated the expansion of European commerce and political power, but also gave to European scholars the opportunity to investigate with ever increasing ease its intellectual and cultural traditions, leading to the founding during the first half of the century of a number of orientalist societies, journals, and university chairs in Europe and America. The impetus was sustained into the second half of the century, which saw the publication of seminal works such as Paul Deussen's *The System of Vedānta* (1883), Richard Garbe's *The Philosophy of Ancient India* (1897), and Friedrich Max Müller's *Six Systems of Indian Philosophy* (1899), and the beginnings of the huge task of translating and editing the classical religious texts of South and East Asia.

Interest amongst intellectuals was by no means confined to specialist orientalists. France's greatest historian of the nineteenth century, Jules Michelet, writing in 1864 concerning the *Rāmāyana*, urged that

> Whoever has done or willed too much, let him drink from this deep cup a long draught of life and youth. . . . Everything is narrow in the West – Greece is small and I stifle; Judaea is dry and I pant. Let me look a little towards lofty Asia, the profound East.

He went on to claim that Comte's positivism was 'but Buddhism adapted to modern civilization; it is a philosophical Buddhism in a slight disguise' (quoted in Radhakrishnan 1939: 249). In the same period the French philosopher and historian Edgar Quinet went even further, claiming that orientalists had discovered 'an antiquity more profound, more philosophical, and more poetical than that of Greece and Rome'. Better known today is the figure of Victor Hugo who, along with many French Romantics such as Lammenais, de Maistre, and Lamartine, had a profound respect for the ancient religions of India and whose work, such as his *Orientales* of 1829, was stimulated in many ways by fashionable images and ideas coming from the East. In Germany, even after the wave of Romantic enthusiasm had subsided, many philosophers continued to give a place in their thinking to Indian metaphysics. For example, Edward von Hartmann, whose highly influential book *Philosophy of the Unconscious* (1869) had been written under the spell of Schopenhauer, allotted places to Hinduism and Buddhism in his philosophy of religion alongside Judaeo-Christian theism, and anticipated a future synthesis between Christianity and the religions of India. In England, the scientist Thomas Huxley took a keen interest in the new ideas coming from the East, and in his Romanes Lectures of 1893 he pointed out that the agnostic character of Buddhism made it especially appealing to his contemporaries. In Russia too the orientalist enthusiasms flourished as intensively as in Western Europe, and made an impact on Leo Tolstoy (1828–1910) who, during his period of spiritual crisis, drew comfort from the teachings of the Buddha. The universal compassion and non-violence of the Buddhist creed found an especially important place in Tolstoy's thinking and writing, and Schwab comments that he 'doubtless remains the most striking example, among a great many, of those who sought a cure for the Western spirit in India' (1984: 451).[1]

Some influential voices, however, spoke in opposite tones, and the earlier enthusiasm for India and for Hinduism waned somewhat after the end of the Romantic period. This change of attitude could be ascribed to a number of factors, including the decline of Romantic metaphysical enthusiasms and the countervailing rise of positivist and materialist philosophies, along with the growing ascendency of the idea of progress. It undoubtedly reflects as well the steady growth of European political and commercial ascendency over the Orient: the waning of interest in Hindu philosophy and the rise of anti-Indian sentiment was, not surprisingly, most evident in Britain which became the dominant colonial power in South Asia in that period. The negative tone was set early on in the century by James Mill in his *History of British India* (1817), a work which offered a highly critical account of Indian religion and culture, proclaiming that 'there is a universal agreement respecting the meanness, the absurdity, the folly, of the endless ceremonies, in which the practical part of the Hindu religion consists' (1858, 1: 274–5). He never visited India and cannot be described as an Indologist, but as an employee of the East India Company Mill exercised a strong influence on the attitudes of the new class of colonial administrators, and his frequently republished *History*, with its utilitarian philosophical assumptions, helped to turn

British opinion away from the idealising tendencies of the early orientalists such as William Jones, and paved the way for the racist attitudes towards India which became pervasive in the second half of the century.[2] Mill's views were echoed by a number of writers in the period including the historian Thomas Macaulay whose remark that Indians were 'lesser breeds without the law' summed up the opinion of many. In 1885 he wrote of the 'monstrous superstitions' of India, and summarily condemned ancient Sanskrit texts as 'less valuable than what may be found in the most paltry abridgements used at preparatory schools in England' (in Young 1952: 722 and 728).

Another influential voice was that of John Stuart Mill. More enlightened than his father in his attitude towards India, he rejected in his essay 'On Liberty' any suggestion of racial differences between Asians and Europeans. Nevertheless he helped to confirm the widely held view that the East was historically backward and lacked the dynamism of the West (see Mill 1977: 272–3). This view had earlier been given intellectual respectability by the influential German historian Leopold von Ranke who referred to Eastern civilisations as 'nations of eternal standstill', and it later entered into the speculations of Karl Marx who, echoing Hegel's thinking about the Orient, represented the peoples of Asia as lacking in themselves the potential for further development, and as prone to despotism. This system of government was, he argued, the normal and distinctive political institution of the East, and was the consequence of what Marx called the 'Asiatic mode of production'. The characteristic features of this mode of production were, according to Marx, the absence of private ownership, the lack of class struggle, and the need to carry out large-scale public works such as irrigation canals, these factors giving rise in turn to a rigid centralised mode of government and forming a powerful bulwark against change and modernisation. This whole way of thinking is summed up in Tennyson's famous line 'Better fifty years of Europe than a cycle of Cathay'.[3]

Paradoxically European global ascendency in this period had the effect not only of encouraging condescending and racist attitudes towards India, attitudes which were evident at all social levels, but also of greatly increasing the popularity of and veneration for Eastern ideas. While the entry of Eastern ideas into European consciousness in earlier times had largely been confined to a small section of the public, the political developments in the nineteenth century, coupled with the rapid growth in literacy and in education in general, led to what could be described as a boom in orientomania. This is evident quite early on in the century in the pages of widely read journals such as the *Edinburgh Review* and the *North American Review* which provided extensive treatment of the very latest ideas coming from the Orient. Also figuring prominently in this boom was a series of writings from authors like Eugène Burnouf, Barthélemy Saint-Hilaire, Robert Spence Hardy, Friedrich Max Müller, Hermann Oldenberg, Edwin Arnold, and T. W. Rhys Davids, a growing body of work on Oriental topics designed not only for scholars but for a newly emerging class of readership which was eager to learn about the religion, culture, and history of the East. The *Oriental Series*, published in London at the end of the century, was a case in point, and the critic of *The Times* wrote of the series: 'A knowledge of the commonplace, at least, of Oriental literature, philosophy, and religion is as necessary to the general reader of the present day as an acquaintance with the Latin and Greek classics was a generation or so ago' (quoted from an advertisement in Edkins 1893). In America too 'there was a vibrant conversation about Buddhism . . . [which] became a serious option for the spiritually disenchanted' (Tweed 1992: 77), a trend evidenced in the popular *Harvard Oriental Series* of books. Many people derived their knowledge of Buddhism from writings connected with the newly regenerated activities of Protestant missionaries, and it is another of the many ironies in this whole story that works like Rev. Spence Hardy's *A Manual of Buddhism*, written to help missionaries understand Buddhism, served to propagate the very religion they were seeking to displace.

BUDDHISM: THE NEW 'DISCOVERY'

Buddhism as such represents a new chapter in the story of orientalism. It is true that in various shapes and forms Buddhism had been identified and written about since the seventeenth century, even though often confused with, or seen as just an heretical sect of, Hinduism. The Jesuit missionaries knew something of it in its Chinese and Japanese forms, but were largely ignorant of its teachings, and treated it for the most part, along with Taoism, as little more than a popular superstition. Pierre Bayle identified the teaching of Buddha as an extreme form of quietism and nihilism, likening it to the philosophy of Spinoza, and Hegel had written about Buddhism, believing it to be the most widely extended religion on the globe. Seven centuries earlier, Marco Polo himself made a flattering reference to Gautama Buddha, describing him as the equivalent of a Christian saint. However, prior to the nineteenth century, understanding of the distinctive identities and geographical extent of Buddhism was sparse, and interest in it was overshadowed by the involvement of the West in Confucianism and Hinduism.

The story of the irruption of Buddhism into nineteenth-century European culture must begin with Brian Hodgson, who, as an official of the East India Company in Nepal, came into possession of 400 hitherto unknown Buddhist manuscripts written in both Sanskrit and Tibetan, and in 1837 dispatched them to Calcutta, London, and Paris. One of the beneficiaries of this largesse was the French scholar Eugène Burnouf (1801–52) who oversaw their translation into French. His work in this field, including his book *Introduction à l'histoire du bouddhisme indien* (1844), was immensely influential in spite of its somewhat negative perception of Buddhism whose teachings it describes as 'naïve'. He was the first to establish a clear distinction between the northern and southern branches of Buddhism, and it was his emphasis on the latter as the more ancient and 'pure' version of the Buddha's teaching that led to the pre-eminence in the European mind in the nineteenth century of the southern Theravada tradition, the northern Mahayana schools remaining largely neglected until the following century.

The middle years of the century saw the multiplication of works expounding and debating Buddhist ideas, mostly written in terms accessible to an educated lay audience. Spence Hardy's *A Manual of Buddhism*, published in 1853, was widely read both in England and on the Continent, and equally popular, though considerably more critical in tone, was Jules Barthélemy Saint-Hilaire's *Le Bouddha et sa religion* (first published in 1858). He spoke of Buddhism's 'powerlessness for good', finding its supposed atheistical and nihilistic outlook 'deplorable'. Nevertheless he deemed the religion of Buddha to be 'not without a certain grandeur', and admitted that 'with the sole exception of Christ, there does not exist among the founders of religions a purer and more touching figure than that of the Buddha' (1895: 14). The second half of the nineteenth century saw a steady expansion of Buddhist scholarship, making available to the West – the New World now as well as the Old – a rich variety of texts from the Theravada tradition. The enterprise was on a large scale, reflecting the great extent of the scriptural inheritance from the southern schools, and was concentrated on texts written in the ancient Pali language, texts which at that time were considered to represent the earliest and most authentic record of the Buddha's teachings. In 1881 the Welsh orientalist T. W. Rhys Davids (1843–1922) founded with his wife Caroline Rhys Davids the Pali Text Society which set about the task of translating these scriptures, and by the time of his death ninety-four volumes, extending over 26,000 pages, had been published by the Society. Its work still continues to this day. In addition to his labours as a translator, Rhys Davids wrote a popular account of Buddhism, *Buddhism: Its History and Literature*, reprinted many times, in which he put forward his belief that Buddhism was a reasonable, even scientific religion, a view which, as we shall see, had important intellectual ramifications. He was convinced that the study of Buddhism would help to overcome European prejudice concerning the exclusively Greek origins of Western thought and culture, and sought to encourage Oriental studies by pointing out that it was 'a matter of historic fact that the great epochs of intellectual progress have been precisely those when two different and even antagonistic systems of thought have been fomenting in the same minds' (1896: 221).[4]

Another great enterprise of translation and publication was undertaken by Friedrich Max Müller (1823–1900), probably the greatest authority of his time in the field of both Indology and Buddhist scholarship. He studied Sanskrit at Leipzig University, embarked on Buddhist studies under Burnouf in Paris, and in 1854 was appointed Professor of Oriental Religions at Oxford University where he remained until his death. Fuelled by an eclectic, universalistic outlook, and by a commitment to the comparative study of religions, his influence on the expanding European awareness of Buddhism and Indian religions in the late nineteenth and early twentieth centuries was inestimable. His most important and lasting legacy is undoubtedly the *Sacred Books of the East* series which, begun under his editorship in 1874, helped to bring Eastern ideas to an ever-widening audience in the West. Many other individuals and enterprises could be mentioned in this context. For example there was the work of the German

Indologists Paul Deussen and Hermann Oldenberg, Neumann's popular translations of Buddhist texts into German, the production of the *Bibliotheque orientale* in
Paris in 1870, and the Sanskrit dictionary and translations of Mahayana
Buddhist texts produced by scholars in the St Petersburg Academy, all of which
helped to create a fertile new field of study.[5]

SCHOPENHAUER, WAGNER, NIETZSCHE

Amongst the enthusiastic readers of Burnouf and Spence Hardy was Arthur
Schopenhauer. References to Buddhism are sparse in his early writings, which as
we saw in the last chapter were bathed in the glow of Hindu teachings, but by
the time he came to produce the second edition of *The World as Will and
Representation* in 1844 Buddhist studies had begun to flourish in Europe and there
are extensive references to and discussions of Buddhist ideas in the substantial
Supplement that he appended to that edition. There he felt 'obliged to concede to
Buddhism pre-eminence over the rest' (1969, 2: 169), and made explicit use of it
as a radical critique of Judaeo-Christianity in a manner which was widely emulated later in the century. The Buddhist teaching of *nirvāna* was equivalent, he
argued, to his own view that in the final analysis all human strivings are empty
and worthless, and that the only sustainable, albeit finite, goal of life is liberation
from the blind forces of will. He saw in Buddhist philosophy a clear statement of
the vanity of all earthly happiness, complete contempt for it, and the turning
away to an existence of quite a different, indeed opposite, kind. He believed this
to represent the true spirit of Christianity as opposed to the 'optimistic' spirit of
Judaism and Islam (1969, 2: 444), but where Christianity sought redemption
through a divine saviour, Buddhism sought it in the denial of the will, a view precisely in agreement with his own. It was a view which, as we shall see, was also to
prove appealing to many others in that period for whom the Christian message
had lost its appeal.

Once again, however, we need to draw attention to important question
marks hanging over Schopenhauer's contribution to orientalism. His whole philosophy has often been characterised as 'pessimistic', even 'nihilistic', and can
be seen as the fullest expression of Romantic *Weltschmerz* (literally, 'world pain').
He viewed the world as driven ultimately by a blind, non-personal will, the
metaphysical basis of the world of which all phenomena are the external and
observable manifestations, and the destiny of individual human beings is
caught up in the aimless onward thrust of the world-process. The transitoriness
of life, the inevitability of annihilation, the impossibility of true and lasting
happiness, all these are the inescapable consequences, he believed, of the
relentless impulsions of the will, and for this reason his philosophy gives a central place to the sufferings and frustrations of life. This view of life, he believed,
was in complete agreement with the Buddhist outlook which taught that suffering is the central fact of human existence, and that release from suffering is not
a matter of salvation delivered from without, but rather a matter of achieving a

state of supreme detachment, which in Buddhist terms is identified with *nirvāna*. Now Schopenhauer himself did not take the view that *nirvāna* represented a state of complete annihilation: 'If *nirvāna* is defined as nothing', he wrote, 'this means only that *samsāra* contains no single element that could serve to define or to construct *nirvāna*' (1969, 2: 608).[6] Nevertheless, in view of the popular association of Schopenhauer with a distinctly pessimistic attitude, it was almost inevitable that the consequence of this was the parallel association of Buddhism itself with pessimism, an interpretation which had been promoted by Burnouf and which took some time to eradicate. N. P. Jacobson speaks of 'The long shadow of Arthur Schopenhauer [which] lives on from one generation to the next, depicting Buddhism as a pessimistic devaluing of persons and things' (1981: 3); and Guy Welbon laments that neither Schopenhauer nor India 'has benefited unequivocally from such popular association – Schopenhauer the pessimist' (1968: 156). A further consequence of this association has been the persistent ascription of the term 'irrationalism' to Eastern thought and religion, a concept which again has often been linked with Schopenhauer's philosophy in general, and hence by implication with the Eastern philosophies which he allied with his own.[7]

Among those influenced by Schopenhauer's oriental speculations were two giants of nineteenth-century culture, Wagner (1813–83) and Nietzsche (1844–1900). Buddhist ideas, transmitted not only by the works of Schopenhauer but also by his reading of Burnouf, penetrated deeply into Wagner's art and thinking, and for a period he actually described himself as a Buddhist, claiming Buddhism to be a world view 'compared with which every other dogma must appear small and narrow'. Like Schopenhauer he looked upon Buddhism as superior to the religion of his own tradition, writing to Franz Liszt: 'How sublime, how satisfying is this doctrine compared with Judaeo-Christian doctrine' (quoted in Welbon 1968: 176), and echoing Schopenhauer's conjecture that Christianity was 'nothing but a branch of that venerable Buddhism which, after Alexander's expedition, spread to the shores of the Mediterranean' (quoted in Goldman and Sprinchorn 1964: 277–8). Such, indeed, was his enthusiasm for Buddhism that he even began to sketch an opera based on the life of Gautama Buddha, to be called *Die Sieger* ('The Victor'), and though never completed, its material, along with some of its underlying spirit, later transmigrated into *Tristan* and *Parsifal*. There is some controversy concerning the extent of Buddhist influence on the theme of renunciation which is so characteristic of Wagner's works, but there can be no doubt that Indian thought became closely interwoven with his own, for, as Michael Edwardes puts it, he 'absorbed them into everything he wrote, creating perhaps the only real synthesis of India and Europe' (1971: 166).

In many ways Wagner, with his aim of reviving German culture in the face of what he saw as French cultural 'tyranny', represented a perpetuation and fulfilment of the attempt by some Romantics to root European civilisation, not in the classical world of the Mediterranean, but in the East. The fact that this search had become associated at this time with anti-semitism is one of the more shadowy sides of the nineteenth-century Oriental Renaissance. Wagner's anti-semitism is well known, but orientalism as a reaction against the Jewish influences on European civilisation makes its appearance with Schopenhauer, and the latter's popularity in the 1850s sanctioned 'a fundamental dispute between a spirituality born of India and carried on through a long Aryan tradition which was allegedly pure and wholesome, and a corrupting semitic exploitation of this spirituality' (Schwab 1984: 185). There is little evidence to suggest that Schopenhauer held any racist theories concerning the Jews, the thrust of his attack on Judaism being directed more towards Judaic monotheism with its attendant legalism and its 'pernicious optimism' rather than to the Jewish people as such. Nevertheless Schopenhauer's influence, along with that of Friedrich Schlegel, was an important factor in the formation of the racist discourse that was to flourish later in the century. Orientalism certainly played a part in the development of this discourse, along with its distinctive vocabulary, encouraging the idea, which gained ever-widening currency from the early years of the century, that the Jewish cultural inheritance could be marginalised in the construction of Europe's historical identity. The view that all European thought originated in Asia, along with belief in a common Indo-Germanic Aryan ancestry, was, in Raymond Schwab's words, 'a grave turn for the new Renaissance', for it provided the opportunity for later thinkers such as Gobineau, who was himself well versed in the latest orientalist scholarship, to give specious scientific backing to ideas of racial inequality, and to 'rewrite history for the benefit of the superior races' (Schwab 1984: 431 and 433).[8]

Nietzsche's relationship with Buddhism was more complex and ambivalent, but nonetheless more important than it is usually perceived to be. The sources of Nietzsche's interest in the East were not only Schopenhauer and Wagner, both of whom were of course major influences on his early development. His personal library and the record of his borrowings from the library of the University of Basel suggest that he read widely in this area, and he was personally acquainted with a number of leading Indologists of the day, including Paul Deussen who was a lifelong friend. Deussen himself was the translator of sixty Upanishads, but he was also a philosopher of distinction, a disciple of Schopenhauer, who wrote a history of philosophy which embraced both Eastern and Western traditions, and which sought to revive the idea of a *philosophia perennis*.

The degree of influence that Eastern thought had over Nietzsche's intellectual development remains a matter of contention. Lou Andreas Salome, who had a brief but close relationship with Nietzsche, claimed that his later thought, especially the idea of the Eternal Recurrence, was influenced by Indian philosophy, and others have seen a Buddhist presence in Nietzsche's speculations about the Will to Power and the *Übermensch*. On the other hand, Nietzsche's teachings have often been widely viewed as completely hostile to Buddhism, though this view has been somewhat modified in recent years and many would now allow that there are striking parallels between the writings of Nietzsche and Buddhist teachings, and that they are 'recognizably affiliated and attest to the proximity of their ethical philosophy' (Mistry 1981: 9). What is certain, however, is that references to the ideas of the East, especially those of Buddhism, often enter into the dialectical to-and-fro of his arguments, and furthermore that he exploited Eastern philosophies, as did earlier thinkers such as Leibniz and Voltaire, as an instrument with which to develop a critique of Western philosophy and Christian values, a foil, as one commentator has put it, 'to lay bare the bankruptcy of the Christian tradition' (Frazier 1975: 146). In *The Antichrist*, for example, Nietzsche used Buddhism to show up the 'decadence' and 'self-deception' of Christianity. Buddhism, being without the metaphysical encumbrances of Christianity, is able to take an 'objective' view of human existence, and is 'the only *really* positivistic religion history has to show us' (Nietzsche 1968a: 129), and hence Nietzsche's engagement with Asian philosophy can be seen as part of his general strategy of using the 'other' to gain a more critical perspective on Europe, 'to look *back* at his own situation from the perspective of the foreign' (Scheiffele in Parkes 1991: 44).

Two contrasting themes predominate in Nietzsche's comments on Buddhism. The first concerns his elaboration of the concept of nihilism. Here he associated Buddhism with the pessimism and life-denying qualities he saw in Christianity, and, following Schopenhauer's lead, interpreted the teachings of the Buddha as encouraging weakness, inertia, and the acceptance of pain and suffering, 'a passive nihilism, a sign of weakness', as he put it (Nietzsche 1968b: 18). He did indeed consider it to be a more 'aristocratic' form of pessimism than Christianity, lacking the latter's bitterness, guilt, and resentment, a religion of 'peace and cheerfulness' (1968a: 132). Nevertheless at the same time it represented for him a form of nay-saying philosophy – 'resignation . . . self-extinction' (1974: 36) – which he sought to combat with his concept of the *Übermensch*. The second theme is concerned with the psychology of suffering and placed Buddhism in a much more favourable light. While seeking to quell the fires of passion and hence to extirpate the source of suffering, Buddhism pursued this goal, not, as in the case of Christianity, by constructing an alternative 'illusory' world to compensate for the present vale of tears, but by offering an astute and uncompromising analysis of the nature of suffering and its origins within the human psyche. For Nietzsche, therefore, Buddhism represented a more psychologically honest account of suffering – 'a hundred times more realistic than Christianity' (1968a: 129), based on a strictly atheistic and pragmatic outlook, and avoiding the allure of metaphysical consolation. It was, he thought, the only genuinely positivistic religion, a 'system of hygiene' rather than of theological doctrine (1979: 46), perhaps even the religion of the future: 'a European Buddhism may prove indispensable', he speculated, and even suggested that he himself 'could be the Buddha of Europe'! (quoted in Halbfass 1988: 127 and 128).[9]

BUDDHISM AND THE VICTORIAN CRISIS OF FAITH

From a consideration of these three thinkers it becomes evident that the disclosure of Buddhism to European consciousness was not just a matter of a new and exotic discovery but also made a significant input into contemporary debates. The impact of Buddhism was indeed palpable, and far more pervasive than that of Confucianism and Hinduism on earlier generations. As one contemporary theologian put it: 'The interest that has been taken of late in Buddhism by a large number of intelligent people in various Christian countries is one of the most peculiar and suggestive religious phenomena of our day' (Kellogg 1885: 1). This interest was by no means merely academic for it touched the very heart of the contemporary religious controversies that, for various reasons, had blown up in the face of Christian orthodoxy at that time, and it was in this context of intense debate that Buddhism came to be used as a mirror 'in which [was] reflected an image not only of the Orient, but of the Victorian world also' (Almond 1988: 6). Moreover, in this hermeneutical engagement the 'mirror' itself was no neutral medium, for, as Almond points out, Buddhism was not merely a 'discovery' but, like Confucianism and Hinduism in earlier epochs, was in some respects a European construct, shaped by European agendas, 'materially owned by the West', and 'increasingly located in and therefore regulated by the West' (ibid.: 24 and 33).

This construcive phenomenon is evident in the ambivalent attitudes towards Buddhism, reflecting some of the pervasive ideological cleavages of the Victorian period. On the one hand the Buddha acquired the status of a hero, one of Carlyle's 'Great Men' who had changed the course of history, and whose ideas were morally and intellectually equal, or even superior, to the Christian philosophy. His teachings were favourably contrasted with those of Hinduism, and, by those for whom Catholicism was still seen as the work of Satan, he was frequently compared with Martin Luther as a religious reformer who did for India what the Reformers did for Christendom. Moreover, as a human being perceived to be of exemplary moral virtue, the Buddha was widely revered, even by those who rejected his teachings – his gentleness and compassion being most widely remarked upon. On the other hand his teachings were often dismissed as atheistical, even as degenerate, giving rise to corrupt and superstitious practices. 'It has been truly called the religion of despair' suited to 'the enervating agnosticism and sentimental pessimism of our generation', is how one Christian apologist put it (Scott 1890: 18). The example of Buddhism was often used to bolster the developing sense of European superiority and to argue that 'the Oriental mind was less intelligent, more fanciful, childish and simple' than the European (Almond 1988: 41). Nevertheless it must be remembered that the Victorian period was an 'age of doubt', a period in which the validity of traditional Christian belief was far more widely debated than in any preceding epoch, and it is hardly surprising therefore that Buddhism was often presented in ways which posed considerable problems for Christian clergy and theologians who were already having to contend with assaults from Higher Criticism, Positivism, and Darwinism. Indeed, the newly disseminated Buddhist teachings had a great appeal to many seeking a religious alternative to the Christian tradition, and became a veritable battle-ground between Christianity on the one hand and the forces of atheism and secularisation on the other. As Kraemer puts it: 'The initial impress of the confrontation with Buddhism was the feeling of having met with a great and unexpected rival of Christianity', a process which he sees as contributing 'to the slowly rising tide of relativism' that was beginning to become evident in that period (Kraemer 1960: 234–5). In 1884 Ernst Eitel in a book on Buddhism went so far as to claim that 'most atheistic philosophy of the nineteenth century was the immediate result of Buddhist endeavours in the West' (Almond 1988: 98). Furthermore, the 'crisis of faith' afflicted America as much as Europe. As the historian Thomas Tweed observes, there was at that time in the USA, 'a vibrant public conversation about Buddhism . . . [which] became a serious option for the spiritually disenchanted' (1992: 77), and while Buddhism failed to establish lasting institutions in that period, it constituted a significant voice in the growing dissent from traditional Western values, expressing 'significant opposition to the reigning political, economic, and social forms' (ibid.: xxii).

Amongst the specific issues debated, there was the old question of origins. This was sparked off by the evidently pre-Christian source of Buddhist teaching, which, along with the remarkable parallels between their ethical ideals and between the lives of their founders, was used by some critics hostile to Christian orthodoxy to suggest that Buddhism might be a source, independent of Judaism, of Christian belief and practice. This idea offered open house to all kinds of speculation. Some, such as Louis Jacolliot in his *Bible dans l'Inde* (1868), suggested that the Bible itself had its origins in India, that Jesus studied in India, and that the cult of Christ was an adaptation of the cult of Krishna. Others, such as Ernest de Bunsen in 1880, following an earlier conjecture by Burnouf, claimed that Jesus was a member of the Essene community which in turn had been established by Buddhist missionaries. And in his book *Vie inconnue de Jésu Christ* (1894) the Russian historian N. A. Notovitch claimed that Christ had lived for sixteen years with Brahmins and Buddhist monks before embarking on his mission in Palestine. It was widely argued that many of the parables told by the two religious leaders, and many of the stories and miracles attributed to them, were strikingly similar, and that in terms of doctrine and ritual there were also intriguing parallels. For example, both teachers attacked the legalism and ritualism of prevailing orthodoxies, both taught sublime ethics of universal love, both preached the primacy of the spiritual quest, and urged their disciples to seek the salvation of all humanity. The Rev. Archibald Scott, for example, referred to the 'Many agreements [that] are alleged to subsist between the contents of the New Testament and those of the sacred books which profess to record the life and express the teaching of Buddha' and to 'the resemblances between the central figures in both sets of scriptures' (Scott 1890: 20). Even the judicious orientalist Max Müller came to the conclusion late in the century that Christianity originated under Buddhist influence.[10]

Then there was the matter of the evident nobility of certain aspects of Buddhist teaching. As with Confucianism in the eighteenth century, there was excited admiration for the lofty nature of Buddhist ethics, with its emphasis on universal compassion, an ethic which was all the more disturbing because it lacked the benefit of Christian revelation and seemed to demonstrate the possibility of a morality without God or religion. There was naturally some difficulty in accepting this teaching as superior to that of Christ, but it was deemed to be a matter of urgent necessity to combat this foreign threat to the uniqueness and superiority of the Christian message, and it was a recognition of both the intellectual force and the growing popularity of Buddhism that many Christian apologists felt it necessary to 'refute' its philosophy. An authority no less eminent than the Professor of Sanskrit at Oxford, Sir M. Monier-Williams, devoted a large volume to this task, claiming that 'Buddhism – with no God higher than the perfect man – has no pretensions to be called a religion in the true sense of the word'. Like many critics of Buddhism, Monier-Williams concentrated his fire on its supposed nihilism, and asked rhetorically:

> Which Book shall we clasp to our hearts in our last hour – the book that tells us of the dead, the extinct, the death-giving Buddha, or the book that reveals to us the living, the eternal, the life-giving Christ?
>
> (1889: 563)

For another Christian apologist, Buddhism was simply 'the most unmitigated system of pessimism the world has perhaps ever seen' (Kellogg 1885: 373).

The interpretation of Buddhism as atheistic had been encouraged by a number of scholars, and was the focus of furious controversy – one which echoes an earlier dispute concerning the Confucians. Some declared it to be abhorrent, grounds for rejecting Buddhism out of hand. On the other hand, it was inevitable that this interpretation of Buddhism should be exploited by the advocates of agnosticism and secularism, who, like their eighteenth-century counterparts in relation to Confucianism, saw in Buddhist ideas a model of a purely rationalistic morality, and of a non-metaphysical religion. From the time of Burnouf's *Introduction*, Buddhism had been described as a 'faith without God', and while this feature was used by some to Buddhism's disadvantage, others, for whom the attractions of Christian theism had palled, yet who felt unable to abandon a religious outlook entirely, found this approach attractive.

This view of Buddhism, along with the belief that it rested its claims not on faith but on verifiable experience, had the further consequence of aligning it with the radical positivist creed that was making rapid headway amongst intellectuals in the latter part of the century. Within the hard-fought debates during the Victorian period concerning the relationship between science and religion, Buddhism was portrayed as inherently in tune with the scientific outlook, specifically with Comte's positivism, Darwinism, Spencer's evolutionism, Buchner's materialism, and Haeckel's monism. According to Edwin Arnold there prevailed a 'close intellectual bond between Buddhism and modern science' (Tweed 1992:

104), an attitude which became almost commonplace amongst intellectuals at the turn of the century. Thus, Buddha was seen by one influential thinker as 'the first prophet of the Religion of Science' (Carus 1897: 309), and, as we noted earlier, both Nietzsche and Huxley associated Buddhism with positivism. In response to such provocative associations, the Rev. Samuel Kellogg lamented that 'another element contributing to the sympathetic interest in Buddhism which is felt in the anti-Christian camp, should probably be named the wide acceptance of various theories of evolution', the Christian view of creation being seen 'to stand in the way of all true scientific progress' (1885: 6). The assumption that the Buddhists were atheists was by no means universally accepted, however, and was questioned both then and in more recent times, but it certainly played an important role in challenging the premiss of Christian uniqueness and superiority.[11]

In spite of the acerbity which was inevitably aroused in such debates, there were those on both sides of the argument who made some attempt to distance themselves from partisanship and to articulate the idea of a more open-ended dialogue between Christianity and Buddhism, reflecting the emerging cosmopolitanism at the turn of the century. The theologian Archibald Scott, for example, though committed to advancing the cause of Christianity, saw that the study of Buddhism could provide Christians with an objective external viewpoint from which to 'educate and reform' itself, and was prepared to allow that 'Even Christians may have something to learn from Buddhists' (1890: vi). He accepted that the intrusion of Buddhism and other Eastern religions into Christian consciousness in recent times had helped to engender the study of comparative religion, a scientific approach which, in his view, should not be resisted but welcomed as an encouragement to 'investigate the origin of our religion, and to search its scriptures in the fuller light which we now enjoy' (ibid.: 5).

Another example of this dialogical trend can be seen in the figure of Paul Carus (1852–1919), a polymath who was born in Germany where he studied Oriental religions, and who settled later in the United States. There his influence was widely felt through a number of popular books such as his *Gospel of Buddha* (still in print), and through his editorship of the journals *Open Court* and *The Monist*. Though not an atheist, Carus was less partisan in his approach than Scott, and was warmly sympathetic towards Buddhism which he found more tolerant and open-minded than Christianity. He informed his readers that 'I have not as yet met a Buddhist who would not look upon Christ with reverence as the Buddha of Western nations' (Carus 1897: 263), and he was sharply critical of the zealotry of missionaries which led them to distort and to vilify Buddhism. He lamented the exclusivism of Christianity, and rejected the prevalent view that Buddhism was a nihilistic doctrine: 'Far from being pessimistic in the Western sense of pessimism,' he wrote, 'the Buddhist possesses a cheerful disposition which in this world of tribulation lifts him above pain and suffering' (ibid.: 131). The importance of Buddhism lay for him, as for an increasing number of people in his day, in the similarities between its doctrines and Western scientific thought. He proclaimed Buddha to be 'the first positivist' and 'the first radical free-thinker', and in drawing Buddhism and Western thought close together he looked forward to the reconciliation of science (in particular Darwinism) and religion. In spite of his enthusiasm for Buddhism, however, he went out of his way to offer an even-handed account of the relationship between Buddhism and Christianity, and to encourage a comparative approach which emphasised the positive content of both religions, and which sought to rise above party squabbling towards a universal non-sectarian approach to religious truth. In his book *Buddhism and its Christian Critics* (1897) he expressed the belief that 'Mankind does not want Buddhism, nor Islam, nor Christianity; mankind wants the truth, and the truth is best brought out by an impartial comparison', and urged that 'every religious man should study other religions in order to understand his own' (1897: 9 and 5). The book ends with the statement that

> For the sake of purifying our conception of religion, there is no better method than a study of comparative religion; and in comparative religion there is nothing more fruitful than a tracing of the analogies that obtain between Buddhism and Christianity.

> (ibid.: 310)

The approach of both Scott and Carus is indeed a marker for the Buddhist–Christian dialogue which, as we shall see in later chapters, has become a significant feature of the encounter between East and West in the twentieth century.[12]

THE AMERICAN TRANSCENDALISTS

The spirit of dialogue and a reaching out for mutual respect and understanding was evident much earlier in the American transcendentalist movement. There is a virtual absence of interest in Oriental ideas in America in the eighteenth century, but during the early years of the nineteenth, interest, both scholarly and popular, began to increase, stirred especially by the writings of Sir William Jones, and in the middle years of the century there began to develop one of the most remarkable and most influential conjunctions of Eastern and Western ideas, associated first and foremost with the names of Emerson and Thoreau. The underlying philosophy of New England transcendentalism, of which these two men were the leading figures, represented a commitment to ancient and universal ideas concerning the essential unity and ultimately spiritual nature of the cosmos, combined with a belief in the ultimate goodness of man and the supremacy of intuitive over rational thought. Its deeply spiritual outlook was one which sought to go beyond creeds and organised religions in favour of a religious experience deemed to be universal. It represented in many ways a continuation and development of ideas of the European Romantic movement, especially those of Goethe, Wordsworth, Coleridge, and Carlyle, and like Romanticism was inspired by neo-platonic and mystical traditions. It can also be seen as a reaction against Lockean materialism, utilitarianism, and Calvinistic Christianity, and was associated with a broadly reformist and innovatory outlook, having a long-term impact in America on such areas as education, feminism, and ecology. But at its heart was a search for religious and spiritual values which were not tied to orthodox Christianity or indeed to any religious sect but which expressed a truth which transcended credal boundaries.

Like the European Romantics, the transcendentalists found inspiration in ideas emanating from the East; the chief object of attention was Hinduism, or more specifically *Advaita Vedānta*, but Buddhism and Confucianism also had a place within the frame of interest. *Vedānta* philosophy played an especially important role in the thinking of Ralph Waldo Emerson (1803–82), the founder of the transcendentalist movement. Because he wrote no single treatise on Indian philosophy it is easy to downplay this influence, but from about 1837 onwards he read widely in this area, and a perusal of his public writings and his private journals points to the pervasiveness of Indian ideas in his thinking. As F. I. Carpenter points out:

> His reading of Indian literature forms one of the most important chapters in the story of his literary development; for not only did he owe his poems 'Brahma' and 'Hamatreya' entirely to Hindu works, but large parts of his essays on 'Plato', 'Fate', 'Illusions' and 'Immortality' are based on Hindu thought.
>
> (1930: 104)

From an early age he had become well acquainted with the works of Jones and other orientalist writings, and later studied closely Charles Wilkins' translation of the *Bhagavad Gītā*. In his journal for 1 October 1848 he wrote of this work as 'the first of books; it was as if an empire spake to us, nothing small or unworthy, but large, serene, consistent, the voice of an old intelligence' (quoted in Schwab 1984: 201). Another important influence on him was the brilliant Indian reformer Rammohan Roy who had fashioned a universal theology from both Christianity and *Vedānta* sources. In spite of the fact that he had drawn away from orthodox Christianity and abandoned a career as a Unitarian minister, Emerson never exploited orientalism as a polemic against Christianity, though Indian thought in many ways became a substitute for and part of his rebellion against the evangelical Christianity he had left behind, and it would be true to say that his concern lay more with the perennial truths underlying all religions than with the falsity of any of them.

Central to Emerson's thinking was the idea of the 'Over-Soul', a neo-platonic World Soul or pantheistic Universal Mind that pervaded, enlivened, and spiritualised all of nature. Through this concept he sought to construct a unitive – we might now say holistic – philosophy whereby distinctions between the divine and the human and between spirit and matter could be transcended. He wrote that within the Over-Soul 'every man's particular being is contained and made one with all other . . . within man is the soul of the whole; the wise silence; the universal beauty, to which every part and particle is equally related; the eternal

ONE' (Emerson 1978: 150). There is no doubt that these ideas were formed prior to his immersion in Eastern thought, and can be traced back to the influence of neo-platonism on his thinking. Nevertheless he was eager to accept the support which the non-dualist *Advaita Vedānta* system gave, and was quick to perceive the close parallel between his idea of the World Soul and the Indian concept of *brahman*. The identity of *ātman* with *brahman*, the idea of the phenomenal world as *māyā*, and the doctrine of the transmigration of souls all locked smoothly into his own thinking, as indeed they had done a generation previously for the German Romantics. In his later writings it is difficult to separate out the Eastern and Western components, and nowhere is this more evident than in his poem *Brahma* which, according to Carpenter, 'Probably expresses the central idea of Hindu philosophy more clearly and concisely than any other writing in the English language' (1930: 111). Similar thoughts are expressed in his essay 'Plato' where he argues that the universal tendency in religious thought towards unity 'found its highest expression in the religious writings of the East, and chiefly in the Indian scriptures such as the Vedas.

Emerson was by no means uncritical of Eastern philosophy as he understood it, and found some of the attitudes and practices that emanated from it not to his taste. He was averse to what he saw as Hindu quietism and resignation, and for the same reasons was unsympathetic towards Buddhism. He disliked, too, the over-rational quality as well as the fatalism of the latter, and the concept of *nirvāna*, which he took to mean complete annihilation, repelled him. Less choosy, and altogether less intellectual, as well as much shorter lasting, was the approach to the East of his friend Henry David Thoreau (1817–62). His enthusiasm, inspired initially by Emerson, is evident in the following remarks in his journals:

> I cannot read a sentence in the book of the Hindoos without being elevated as upon the table-land of the Ghauts. It has such a rhythm as the winds of the desert, such a tide as the Ganges, and seems superior to criticism as the Himmaleh Mounts.
>
> (Thoreau 1961: 85)

Like Emerson he was clearly moved by the sacred writings of the East, remarking in *Walden*, with a rhetorical flourish which by this time had become almost statutory in this context, 'I bathe my intellect in the stupendous and cosmological philosophy of the *Bhagavat Geeta* . . . in comparison with which our modern world in its literature seems puny and trivial' (1961: 198). Thoreau's interest was drawn not so much to the metaphysics of the East, as to its images and symbols, and above all to its methods for attaining inner equilibrium and spiritual fulfilment. As Rick Fields suggests: 'He discovered in the Orientals something akin to his deepest spirit rather than another religion to replace . . . Christianity', and was 'perhaps the first American to explore the nontheistic mode of contemplation which is the distinguishing mark of Buddhism' (1986: 62–3). It might be going too far to suggest, as does Arthur Christy, that Thoreau embarked on his *Walden* experiment in the spirit of Indian asceticism (1932: 199), nevertheless he was evidently influenced by oriental concepts of self-discipline, detachment, and contemplation, and repeatedly expressed admiration for the emphasis of Hinduism upon meditation and non-attachment. In a letter written in 1849, he remarked: 'Depend upon it, rude and careless as I am, I would fain practice the yoga faithfully. . . . To some extent, and at rare intervals, even I am a yogi' (quoted in Christy 1932: 201).

This by no means exhausts the roll-call of transcendentalists who turned their minds to the Orient. Mention must also be made of James F. Clarke (1810–88) who, through his widely circulated book *Ten Great Religions* (1871), did far more than either Emerson or Thoreau to evoke a sympathetic response amongst the American public to Eastern religions. He spoke strongly on behalf of a comparative, scientific approach to the study of religions, and insisted that not only was there truth to be found in the non-Christian religions, but that the West had much to learn from the East, for example the Buddhist principle of toleration which he contrasted with the Catholic Inquisition. This universalist outlook found even fuller expression in the writings of Samuel Johnson (1822–82), a transcendentalist who, like Emerson, was an early apostate from the Unitarian ministry, preaching thereafter from a non-denominational church where he propounded what he called 'Universal Religion'. His knowledge of Eastern thought was unequalled in America at that time, and in 1873 he began the publication of a massive three-volume work entitled *Oriental Religions and Their Relation to Universal Religions*, in which he advocated the idea of the fundamental identity of all religions. Lying behind this agenda was a grand evolutionary design in which all the world's religions were viewed as part of a developmental process from primitive myth towards Universal Religion, a process which, in ways that echoed Hegel, was a manifestation of the unfolding of the divine spirit. There is a strong indication in Johnson's writings that Christianity, rather than Hinduism or Buddhism, will ultimately lay the foundations of this 'Universal Religion'. Nevertheless it is a Christianity that will be radically transformed by its historical encounter with the East, a revolutionary transformation 'compared with which the passage from Judaism to Christianity itself was trivial' (Johnson 1873: 31).[13]

FIN DE SIÈCLE

Our discussion of the work of Clarke and Johnson has hinted at the great widening of popular interest in Eastern thought, especially Buddhism, in the last decades of the nineteenth century, and in concluding this chapter I shall outline a number of factors which gave important impetus to this trend. In the first place this period saw a much more positive attitude towards Buddhism emerging, due partly to the reconsideration of the concept of *nirvāna* by Max Müller and Rhys Davids.[14] The transformation in the understanding of this central Buddhist concept was not a matter of purely scholarly interest, but helped to shift emphasis to the salvific potentialities of Buddhism rather than its philosophic peculiarities, and opened the way for a much wider acceptance of its relevance to the religious and spiritual needs of Westerners.

The man who first fully expressed this new attitude was indeed not an Oriental scholar but a journalist and poet, Edwin Arnold (1832–1904). His epic poem *The Light of Asia*, first published in 1879, came at the right time to exploit the changing scholarly approach to Buddhism, and at the same time, by offering an image of the Buddha and his teaching which was in tune with the growing spirit of optimism of the late Victorian era, helped to disseminate the Buddhist message to a wide and receptive audience.[15] It reflected, too, the growing pluralism and eclecticism of its day, and, while not confronting indigenous religions directly, supported the growing belief that truth speaks many languages and that spiritual wisdom is not exclusive to Christianity. The poem's success was phenomenal, both in Europe and America. It sold nearly a million copies, was translated into six languages, and for thirty years was a household classic, one of the best-sellers of its day. Moreover, it was transformed into an opera, into a Broadway play, two cantatas, and a movie! It drew many favourable reviews, for example from Oliver Wendell Holmes who considered it worthy to be classed with the New Testament, and from Richard Henry Stoddard who compared its verses with those of Rossetti and Swinburne (see Peiris 1970: 28). There were also fierce criticisms, especially from the ranks of the clergy who recognised in the poem a sinister threat. Thus, W. C. Wilkinson described Arnold as 'antichrist', Robert Moncrieff condemned the book as having 'produced darkness of the grossest kind' (quoted in Almond 1988: 2), and the American theologian Samuel Kellogg felt sufficiently angry to write a whole book by way of refutation, *The Light of Asia and the Light of the World*, in which he wrote of the need to combat 'the Buddhist menace' (1885: 373).

Arnold's objectives in writing the poem were 'inspired by an abiding desire to aid in the better mutual knowledge of East and West' (quoted in Peiris 1970: 7). Questions have been raised about his own beliefs, and about the extent to which Arnold was personally committed to Buddhism, but according to his biographer 'he never regarded his admiration of Buddhism as involving any disloyalty to Christianity; it would never have occurred to him that the truth could be diminished by being shared' (Wright 1957: 107). What is clear is that he was a conspicuous representative of a growing body of liberal opinion which held that the divine truth could be found in many religions, even if Christianity remained its most favoured vehicle. Far from being in any sense a religious fanatic or fundamentalist, therefore, Arnold was in fact part of the late Victorian liberal/intellectual *avant-garde* – he was friendly with Darwin, Huxley, Herbert Spencer, and John Stuart Mill – which constituted the radical and progressive wing of late Victorian cultural life. Arnold was well aware of the controversy over the many suggestive parallels between the lives and teachings of Buddha and Christ, and his poem undoubtedly contributed to the emerging climate of opinion which favoured a more even-handed and objective approach to the religions of the world. It is notable that this sea change was occurring at precisely the moment when Western, and most specifically British, imperial expansion was at its height, and at a time when Christian missionary endeavour was reaching a climax in terms of self-confident belief in its inevitable triumph. This makes the popularity of Arnold's poem all the more intriguing as part of an apparent contra-flow to the prevailing mood of Western triumphalism.

The emergence and rapid growth of the Theosophical Society is further evidence of the radical implications of orientalism in the late nineteenth century. It was founded in 1875 by Madame Blavatsky (1831–91), a woman of noble Russian descent, and Colonel Olcott (1832–1907), an American lawyer who had served in the Civil War. The term *theosophy* (meaning 'divine wisdom') can be traced back through the neo-platonist and gnostic traditions to the fourth-century philosopher Porphyry. It was adopted by Blavatsky and Olcott to reflect links with these traditions, and hence was a way of identifying their new movement with the notion of an ancient universal truth underlying all religious traditions. After earlier involvement in the currently fashionable pursuit of occultism, their interest shifted towards the East which helped to provide them with a philosophical framework for their spiritualist practices, and in 1878 they travelled together to India and to Ceylon, both of which countries became important focuses for the Society's activities. They were greeted in Ceylon as champions of Buddhism, and shortly after their arrival they publicly embraced Buddhism, perhaps the first Europeans to do so. As the Buddhologist Edward Conze put it: 'rather suddenly and unexpectedly [a] few members of the dominant race, white men and women from Russia, America and England, Theosophists, appeared among Hindus and Ceylonese to proclaim their admiration for the ancient wisdom of the East' (1975: 211).

The central message of theosophy, elaborated by Blavatsky in a number of works including *Isis Unveiled* (1877) and *The Secret Doctrine* (1888), was essentially a revival of the idea of the *philosophia perennis*, and can be summed up as the belief that all phenomena arise out of an eternal, unitary principle which is spiritual in essence and which is manifested most conspicuously in individual enlightened souls. Her writings became increasingly infused with Oriental ideas, and were in effect an amalgam of Hindu *Vedānta*, Buddhism, and Western esoteric philosophy, combined with contemporary evolutionary ideas. In attempting to define her beliefs in Asian terms, she made extensive use of such ideas as *māyā*, *karma*, reincarnation, and meditation, terms which the Theosophical Society was responsible for introducing into the European vernacular. However, while proclaiming a universalist philosophy, Blavatsky held institutionalised Christianity in some contempt, and reproached it for having betrayed the esoteric truths which, happily, had been preserved in the East. It was to the Orient, therefore, that the West must turn in order to recover the source of true wisdom.

Theosophy has indeed come to be seen as misrepresenting its claimed oriental sources and, even from its very early days, the Society has been criticised on the grounds that it offered a distorted interpretation of Eastern teachings. It was seen as promulgating an essentially Westernised version of Eastern wisdom, engineered solely as a vehicle for the purpose of propagating occultist ideas and practices, and encircled by a wall of mystification. Max Müller, for example, while acknowledging the wide influence of the Society, dismissed Blavatsky's writings as unscholarly, especially in their failure to distinguish adequately between *Vedānta* and Buddhism, and rejected the idea of an occultist/esoteric form of Buddhism (see Chaudhuri 1974: 327–8). Among its most severe twentieth-century critics, René Guénon has been outspoken in condemning the movement's falsification of Buddhism, and C. G. Jung has accused theosophy of merging East and West in a synthesis which ignores the individual features of each tradition. Accusations of racism have been levelled against Blavatsky herself, and the historian James Webb, while rejecting any suggestion that she was personally or actively anti-semitic, agrees that her writings permitted 'a passive acceptance of some elements of the [racist] myth' that was gaining currency at that time (1976: 227). Be that as it may, theosophical teachings, with their openness to a variety of paths to truth, and their emphasis on the underlying congruence of the great religious traditions, represented in many ways a radical challenge to orthodox religious attitudes, and, in their attempt to construct a philosophy which reconciled recent scientific discoveries with ancient wisdom traditions, appealed widely to educated Westerners and Indians alike. Furthermore, while it has become almost routine to dismiss the Theosophical Society as the disseminator of superstitious, and probably fraudulent, occultist practices, it is important to remember that in that period there was a strong intellectual dimension to occultism which was often taken seriously by members of the scientific community and by the educated classes generally.

The theosophical movement, through its various activities and numerous publications, certainly proved highly effective in popularising Asian religious and philosophical ideas in the West, and in encouraging the East–West dialogue. At its height around the turn of the century it could boast as many as 400 branches in India, Europe, and America, and by 1920 had a membership of over 45,000. Although its influence has declined considerably in the course of the twentieth century, partly due to internal disagreements and schisms, its impact has continued to be felt in many quarters. For example, its influence has been important in the foundation of Buddhist societies which received their initial inspiration from theosophy, even though moving away from this source towards a more 'purist' interpretation of Buddhism. The missionary work of Krishnamurti, who was originally brought to the West and set on his path by the Society, has had a powerful popular appeal, Jacob Needleman writing of him that 'no philosopher, teacher, or poet of our time has attracted the respect of more people over such a period' (1972: 150). And yet another interesting aspect of the movement, not always adequately acknowledged, lies in the fact that it had a considerable impact on the modern movement in literature and art; we will return to this connection in the next chapter.

Mention must also be made of the fact that the Theosophical Society has gained a considerable reputation on the Indian sub-continent, and that it not only contributed to the emergence of an orientalist counter-culture within the Western context, but also gave substantial assistance to the revival of Hindu and Buddhist self-awareness and self-respect in Asia itself. In modern Sri Lanka the name of Colonel Olcott is still associated with the revival of Buddhism in the late nineteenth century in circumstances where it was all but obliterated by the Christianising policies of the colonial government. The Society helped in the founding of the Hindu University of Benares in 1916, its chief aim being the preservation of the cultural heritage of India, and through its influence on the founding of the Mahabodhi Society by Dharmapala Anagarika in 1891 it played an important role in the recovery for Buddhism of its holy places. Of even wider historical significance was the role played by the theosophical movement in helping to redirect the young Mohandas Gandhi's thoughts towards his Hindu roots by encouraging him to recover the philosophical riches of the Hindu traditions. An important role in this was played by Annie Besant, an English Fabian socialist who succeeded Olcott as president of the Theosophical Society in 1907, and who made a significant contribution to the rise of the Indian independence movement, serving for a brief period as president of the Indian National Congress. When the Indian scholar Nirad Chaudhuri wrote that the 'contributions made by European Orientalists to Indian nationalism is now recognized by all', he had the Theosophical Society very much in mind (1974: 311).[16]

The eclecticism and internationalism of the Theosophical Society can be seen, then, as a challenge to Western intellectual and cultural hegemony at the end of the Victorian period. So too can the World's Parliament of Religions held in Chicago in 1893, formed to complement the World Columbian Exhibition held there the previous year. The symbolism of these two juxtaposed events is significant, for whereas the 1892 events consciously celebrated the West's political and commercial supremacy, the World's Parliament of Religions helped to give rise to attitudes and expectations of a profoundly unsettling kind from the West's point of view. The Parliament was indeed shaped in part, as one historian notes, by a powerful Christian missionary impetus and by a 'strong dose of Anglo-Saxon triumphalism' (Seager 1993: 7), and it is noteworthy that the Anglican Church refused to participate on the grounds that the format of the Parliament implied an unacceptable equality of faiths. Nevertheless, there was present right from the start a strong idealistic impulse which encouraged the world's faiths to embark on some sort of dialogue, and to work towards a more universalist and less sectarian outlook than that which prevailed in the Christian West. Amongst the 200 or so delegates from forty-five denominations there were representatives from Japan, China, Siam, India, and Ceylon, and the delegates of Hinduism and Theravada Buddhism – Swami Vivekananda and Anagarika Dharmapala – proved through their eloquence and sincerity especially successful in awakening their audiences to the spiritual and philosophical sophistication of Asian religions. The warm response to these figures and to the Asian presence as a whole, stirred by the highly charged emotion of the occasion, was somewhat evanescent in the short term, but in the longer term the Parliament had a major impact on American public opinion, and produced waves which persisted long after the event, its message constituting a marker for significant orientalist developments that were to unfold in the century which followed.

A universalist spirit of reconciliation was never far from the surface of the Parliament. The inspiration for the event came from one Charles Carroll Boney, a Chicago lawyer and a member of the Swedenborgian Church, who helped to inject into the proceedings the ideal of international understanding and toleration, and who in his opening address spoke of the rising of 'the sun of a new era of religious peace and progress . . . dispelling the dark clouds of sectarian strife' (quoted in Seager 1993: 21). The idea of some form of religious convergence, perhaps even the development of a world religion, was, as we have seen, already beginning to take shape in the minds of some at the end of the century, and reflections such as these, with their Leibnizian echoes, could perhaps be viewed as the culmination of orientalist explorations which began 300 years earlier. They could also be regarded as anticipating important developments in the East–West dialogue over the following century, ones which, as we shall see in the next section, had repercussions over a wide range of intellectual endeavour.[17]

Part III

Orientalism in the twentieth century

Chapter 6

East–West encounter in the twentieth century

In his great unfinished novel, *The Man Without Qualities*, Robert Musil summed up the agitated spirit that became apparent at the turn of the century as a 'kindling fever' which broke out suddenly in Europe, a veritable cultural epidemic in which 'nobody knew exactly what was on the way; nobody was able to say whether it was to be a new art, a new man, a new morality, or perhaps a reshuffling of society' (1953–65, 1:15). The developments within orientalism which were recounted at the end of the last section clearly anticipate this mood of questioning, change, and renewal. Our task in this chapter will be to outline the way in which the themes that have become evident over the past centuries in the West's encounters with the East reach a new pitch of intensity in the twentieth century, and to locate these themes within the whole polyphony of the cultural life of the period. The remaining chapters in this section will then examine in closer detail how these transformations have been manifested in four distinct fields of intellectual endeavour.

THE CENTURY'S 'KINDLING FEVER'

A number of factors help to explain Musil's 'kindling fever'. In broad terms, the end of the nineteenth and the beginning of the twentieth centuries witnessed a growing sense of disenchantment amongst educated Europeans with the rationalist ideals of the Enlightenment and the Victorian faith in progress, accompanied by a fascination with ideas of degeneration and decadence, and a willingness to explore strange new seas of thought. The very speed of progress, the rapid transformation from traditional to modern social and economic formations, the growth of science-inspired materialist philosophies, and the ever-slackening hold of ancient religious beliefs and rituals, all of these combined to breed a mood of discontent with the comforts and promises of Western civilisation, and to encourage a search for more satisfying and meaningful alternatives.

As Musil perceived, this was a period of great cultural ferment which generated an extraordinary vortex of intellectual strife gyrating round a set of ideas and debates including movements such as positivism and psychoanalysis, issues such as social Darwinism and eugenics, artistic and literary theories associated with symbolism and expressionism, and a variety of cults ranging from Tolstoyism and Wagnerism to neo-paganism, and occultism. A powerful and influential voice at the turn of the century was that of Friedrich Nietzsche which undoubtedly helped to articulate the growing disillusionment with established Western ideals, not only with Christianity but with the whole Enlightenment preoccupation with progress and scientific rationalism, and to motivate the urge to explore new values and world views. In this broad context it is possible to see orientalism as one of many interacting responses to the unsettling cultural forces that mark the beginning of this turbulent century. Many of the age's deepest intellectual and cultural concerns, including racism, nationalism, post-Newtonian science, psychoanalysis, environmentalism, and feminism can all be traced back to this seminal period, and have all in one way or another formed challenging associations with orientalism. As we shall see, these relationships have often been productive and have encouraged the creative involvement of Eastern thought in fields such as philosophy, theology, and psychology. On the other hand such associations, in particular those with occultism and the mystical undercurrents of fascism, have also proved less than enlightening and have often contributed to the sometimes negative perception of orientalism in this century.

These unsettling cultural forces have acquired the potency of a veritable hurricane in the course of the century. In Chapter 2 of this book I argued that the whole of the modern world was characterised by cultural, social, and intellectual transformations which produced a deep sense of uncertainty and anxiety, expressed in terms such as 'anomie', 'alienation', and 'the homeless mind', a major consequence of which has been the calling into question of traditional beliefs and values, and the relativising of all world views. These factors have acquired both wider and more acute significance in the twentieth century where the plurality of belief systems, and hence the risks and conflicts associated with choice, has emerged as an issue of fundamental importance in cultural and intellectual debates. We have been obliged in this century to confront, not only a disturbing – yet at the same time stimulating and inspiring – transformation and pluralisation of cultures and institutions, but also an unprecedented fragmentation and dissolution of traditional ways of thinking about the world, of values, and of matters of ultimate concern. Above all the century has experienced a collapse of spiritual authority and a crisis of religious faith which, while representing the maturation of factors that have been germinating in the West since the Enlightenment period, has had unprecedented cultural consequences in recent times. The secularising implications of what Nietzsche so graphically described as 'the death of God' have indeed in many respects had an emancipatory and liberating effect, but at the same time the drastic weakening of the supporting framework of the Christian tradition has left a deep sense of loss and bewilderment.

It is this disturbing confrontation with and disengagement from the West's own traditions that has allowed, even encouraged, the increasing exploration – some might say exploitation – of oriental philosophies. The West's own indigenous world views have been seen as simply not working any more, a situation which has led to an extraordinary quest, in the East and elsewhere, for more serviceable alternatives. And whereas in earlier centuries the encounter with the Orient was confined to a relatively few intellectuals, from the turn of the twentieth century we can witness its effects increasingly amplified over a much wider range of cultural and intellectual endeavours, from popular religious quests to scholarly research.

This proliferating involvement with the East must also be viewed against the background of the imperialistic expansion of the European powers. The colonial interests of France and Britain had been well established in Asia in the nineteenth century, but the full cultural impact of these developments on the European mind becomes most evident in the twentieth, both in the context of the rapid growth and consolidation of these interests in the first half of the century, and their collapse and disintegration in the second half. It is partly a matter of the growth of communications consequential upon the work of imperial expansion, which not only encouraged an increasing involvement of European peoples with the beliefs and practices of far-away cultures, but also facilitated the explorations of scholars and intellectuals. At a deeper level it helped to shape a variety of influential attitudes towards the East. On the one side it helped to engender a sense of the otherness of the East, its cultural difference from the West, a difference which inspired contrasting attitudes of contempt and of veneration, confirming for some the inherent superiority of Western civilisation, and for others the need to draw from the ancient traditions of the East qualities which the West conspicuously lacked. On the other hand the colonial factor has helped to produce a feeling of anxiety tinged with guilt towards the East, and has encouraged a variety of intellectual responses ranging from grand speculations about a universal philosophy or a global religion to more modest proposals for the encouragement of hermeneutical dialogue. In either case the traditional philosophies of the East have increasingly been drawn into interaction with Western intellectual traditions, and have helped to rouse and amplify a range of contentious issues in a variety of fields.

NEW WAVES FROM THE ORIENT

The social and political transformations of the twentieth century, then, constitute an important context in which to understand the extraordinarily luxuriant growth of the orientalist enterprise in that period. In many ways, though, we can see continuities with the previous era and ways in which the interests and attitudes of earlier centuries have carried through into more recent times. The interest in Buddhism which first flowered in the mid-nineteenth century has come to full growth in our own day, and Theravada Buddhism, which so appealed to the rationalist and humanist tendencies of the nineteenth century on both sides of the Atlantic, has continued to offer both a spiritual path and an intellectual stimulus to many who firmly rejected the transcendental aspects of the Christian teachings. Important in this regard was the founding of Buddhist societies in

Germany and England in 1903 and 1906 respectively, both organisations helping in the propagation – albeit in quiet and unassuming ways – of Buddhist ideas
and practices.[1] Chinese thought and culture, long neglected, even despised, after
its eclipse in the Romantic period, regained some of its popular appeal through
the series of translations of Chinese poetry undertaken   by Arthur Waley
(1889–1966) which had a profound effect on modern poets such as Yeats and
Pound, and has become once again an object of interest to Western scholars and
philosophers. Hinduism, especially in its *Vedānta* form, has acquired renewed
favour and has attained a popularity in our century which far exceeds that which
it elicited in the Romantic period. This revival was largely initiated by the missionary work of Swami Vivekananda (1862–1902) who had a powerful impact in
his day, and his influence has been carried through into the twentieth century by
the Vedānta Society which he had founded in 1894 after the World's Parliament
of Religions.

    However, in addition to these continuities, the range of Eastern ideas and
philosophies with which the West has sought to engage has been greatly widened
in the present century. Most conspicuous is the emergence into Western consciousness of the northern schools of Mahayana Buddhism, which in the nineteenth century were usually dismissed as degenerate and corrupt versions of
'original Buddhism'; here the work of scholars such as Louis de la Vallée Poussin
and Étienne Lamotte was crucial. Of the Mahayana schools, Zen Buddhism has
had the most powerful impact on the West. Zen first appeared in the West at the
time of the World's Parliament of Religions, and even prior to that the American
scholars Ernest Fenollosa and Lafcardo Hearn had visited Japan and drawn
comparisons between that culture and the West. But it was in the inter-war period that the writings of D. T. Suzuki helped to awaken the Western mind to the
strange but enticing world of Zen, and, following the defeat of Japan in 1945
and the lowering of cultural barriers between that country and the West,
Suzuki's writings reached a wide audience and elicited warm acclaim throughout
America and Europe. During the post-war period, and especially during the era
of cultural efflorescence associated with the beat and hippie movements, there
emerged in the West a desire for cultural liberation and spiritual fulfilment which
was felt by many to be left unsatisfied by established traditions and creeds, and it
is not surprising that Zen, with its aesthetic purism, its non-dogmatic spirituality,
and its promise of instant enlightenment, has been assiduously cultivated in the
West.[2] More surprising, perhaps, is the fast-growing appeal of Tibetan
Buddhism which has come to prominence in the West as a result of the Chinese
assimilation of Tibet and the exile of the Dalai Lama and many of his fellow
monks. More colourful and exotic than their Japanese counterparts, the esoteric
teachings and practices of the Tibetan schools of Buddhism have found fertile
soil in the West, and their psychological insights have surprised Western scholars
by their remarkable level of spiritual and intellectual sophistication. Though
scorned in the earlier period as a corrupt deviation from the Buddha's original
teaching, in recent years Tibetan Buddhism has begun to be taken seriously by

Western intellectuals, and as Peter Bishop points out, 'has been active in the emergence of the new physics, meditational psychotherapy, transpersonal psychology, as well as depth psychology'.[3]

Chinese Taoism represents perhaps the last major wave of Eastern philosophy to break over the Western mind. Though known in the West since the Jesuits first went to China, Taoism was routinely dismissed in the Enlightenment period as a popular superstition containing little that could edify the mind of the modern Western world. Following the early translations of James Legge and V. M. Alekseev, and the interest of people like C. G. Jung and Alan Watts, however, it has in recent decades begun to emerge from the shadows and to play a not insignificant role in the formation of radically new conceptions of mind and of nature. In the words of Martin Palmer, 'The term Tao has been used to describe and to justify a vast array of alternative positions and ideas from the famous Tao of Physics to the Tao of Computer Technology' (not to mention the Tao of Pooh), and he goes on to claim that Taoism in its 'challenging and uncomfortable' way 'has a great deal to say to our culture of individualism, of power, of dualistic thinking and of materialism' (1991: 127–8).[4]

Mention must also be made of the interest that Tantric yoga has attracted in recent years as a path of psychological healing, a school which has little interest in metaphysical speculation, but which offers a way of personal transformation embracing the physical as well as the spiritual dimensions. The use of sexual intercourse as a means towards spiritual enlightenment has, of course, been one of the reasons for its popularity, but in addition to this Tantra's emphasis on the integration of body and spirit has proved appealing for a culture whose indigenous religions have not always been seen to give adequate place to the physical and emotional dimensions of human existence.[5]

New also is the *manner* in which ideas have been transmitted from East to West. In earlier times orientalism was a largely textual matter, its images and opinions constructed out of Eastern texts which were selected, brought to the West, translated and interpreted by generations of scholars, philosophers, and intellectuals of all kinds, and hence often remote from their original contexts and from direct experience of the living practice of Eastern religions and from their contemporary exponents. There were of course Westerners – for example Ricci, Duperron, Jones, Arnold – who made the journey Eastwards and gained a first-hand knowledge of Asian cultures, but it was not until the twentieth century that a significant number of Westerners, both scholars and religious seekers, went East precisely in order to acquire direct knowledge, or even enlightenment itself, often adopting Oriental names (Swami Govinda, Ajahn Sumedho, Sangharakshita, for example) and returning as teachers to bring the practices of Eastern wisdom as well as new texts and information Westwards. Of equal significance is the number of distinguished Eastern thinkers, including Vivekananda, Suzuki, Tagore, Aurobindo, Radhakrishnan, and Trungpa, who, well educated in Western intellectual traditions, became actively involved in the orientalist enterprise, propagating Eastern ideas in both academic and more popular contexts, often subtly transforming their own teachings in the process. Related to this is the exponential growth of immigration of Eastern peoples to the West, a factor which has meant not only the multiplication of centres of oriental cultural life within the West, but a cultural interaction at first-hand level which has provoked a mixture of interest, controversy, and conflict. The importance of these factors from our present point of view lies in the fact that orientalism in the twentieth century has increasingly become a matter of complex interaction between cultures, involving a variety of interweaving agendas and ideological interests, rather than simply a matter of remote projection by one culture upon another, and in the greater awareness of the voice of 'orientals' in Western discourse concerning the East. Furthermore, both these factors, combined with the increasing sophistication of scholarly methodologies, have had the consequence of breaking up some of the earlier orientalist oversimplifications – for example 'Hinduism', 'Buddhism', 'the East' – and encouraging greater attention to the complexities of historical context, to the historicity of our own apprehensions, and to the disclosure of ideological deformations.

CULTURAL CONTEXTS

Let us now examine in more detail some of the cultural forces that have helped to energise these new waves. At the turn of the century there were a number of movements beginning to respond to the historical factors just outlined in ways which set the trend for the proliferation of orientalism in the following decades. We have already taken note of some of these: the rapid expansion of the Theosophical Society, the popularising efforts of Arnold and Carus, the impact of the World's Parliament of Religions, the missionary work of Vivekananda, and the establishment of Buddhist societies in Europe in the first decade of this century: all of these contributed to the encouragement of the wider engagement with Eastern teachings. These institutional factors have been accompanied by a communications explosion through the medium of the printed word. From the closing years of the nineteenth century the dissemination of translations of Eastern texts in the West has steadily increased, and as the century has progressed classics such as the *I Ching* and *The Tibetan Book of the Dead* have become best-sellers, sometimes attaining almost cult status. Writings about Eastern philosophies and religions, in popular as well as academic format, have proliferated, the buoyancy of the market for such books being demonstrated by the existence of a growing number of specialist publishers in this field. Furthermore, in recent decades groups and organisations devoted to the study and practice of Eastern ways, from yoga and t'ai-chi ch'uan to Transcendental Meditation and the cult of Hari Krishna, have multiplied and flourished.

One of the earliest cultural manifestations of orientalism was associated with *avant-garde* literary developments early in this century. An adequate examination of the place of orientalism in modern Western literature in general, and in particular its relation to Western imperialism, would require a separate study,[6] but the influence of oriental ideas on the formation of the so-called *modern* movement early in this century – in the visual arts as well as in literature – requires some discussion here, particularly in view of its association with the 'kindling fever' of change and uncertainty of pre-World War I Europe, and the way in which it anticipates motifs that were to develop throughout the century. Oriental images and themes abound in popular modern literature, of course, but where for the most part the East has been little more than a peg on which to hang Western fantasies, for certain of the founders of the modern movement the East was far more than just a source of exotic tropes or romantic plots. In the words of Zhaoming Qian 'Orientalism [was] a constitutive element of the Modernism of the 1910s and 1920s' (1995: 5), for it helped to give expression and substance to a sense of deep cultural crisis and to loss of faith in the West's idea of progress through scientific rationalism, and to a need for new modes of representation. Responding to the cultural crisis at the turn of the century, modernism meant, in essence, the demand for a new and purified consciousness, one that could replace the discredited tastes and conventions of the Victorian period with a new spiritually-cleansed and progressive attitude. The theme of some kind of spiritual crisis and the need for cultural renewal, inspired in part by Eastern ideas, first becomes evident in the group of writers associated with the Irish Literary Renaissance of that period, in writers such as W. B. Yeats, George Russell (better known by his pen-name Æ), and George Moore. Russell's enthusiasm for the East is evident enough in his remark that with regard to the work of Goethe, Wordsworth, Emerson, and Thoreau 'we can find all they have said and much more in the grand sacred books of the East . . . [which] contain such godlike fulness of wisdom on all things' (quoted in Radhakrishnan 1939: 250), and in his novel *The Brook Kerith* George Moore represents Christ as couching his teachings in explicitly Vedantist terms.

The orientalist theme is most consistently present, however, in the work of Yeats (1865–1939), described by T. S. Eliot as 'the greatest poet of our time', and whose famous line 'Things fall apart; the centre cannot hold' sums up the prevailing sense of cultural crisis in the period preceding World War I. Like Emerson before him, his interest in Eastern philosophies has sometimes been underplayed by commentators, and has been overshadowed by his involvement with the neo-platonic tradition, nevertheless it is clear that he had a considerable knowledge of Eastern religions, and that this knowledge made a significant impact on his writings. Yeats could be described as a visionary who was repelled by the age of science, by Lockean empiricism, and by the current materialist philosophies, and was drawn by contrast to the poetic mysticism of Swedenborg and Blake as well as to the neo-platonism that lies behind these figures. In 1887 he joined the Theosophical Society in London shortly after its foundation, and through it he became acquainted with the *Advaita Vedānta* teaching concerning the self, namely that each individual is only a manifestation of a higher Self which is identical with *brahman*. He felt ill at ease with the dominant dualistic outlook of Western thought, particularly as manifested in the perception of God as a distant, authoritative Other, but in the Upanishads, which he assisted in translating into English, he found an ancient way of expressing his deepest conviction concerning the wider reality within which the human spirit ultimately dwells. He discovered in Eastern philosophy not only 'an alliance between body and soul [which] our theology rejects', but also 'the mind's direct apprehension of the truth, above all antinomies' (Yeats 1961: 451 and 437). Later, at the instigation of his friend Ezra Pound, he became an enthusiastic admirer of Japanese *No* plays, and through the writings of Suzuki became acquainted with Zen Buddhism which he viewed as the culmination of Eastern wisdom through its ability to cut through all intellectual abstractions.[7]

Yeats was, of course, a crucial figure in initiating the modern movement in literature which, in parallel with the visual arts and music, challenged many of the cultural assumptions of the Victorian period, and it is interesting to note that several other important contributors to this movement were also closely involved with Eastern traditions. A common factor here was the influence of the Theosophical Society which inspired many thinkers and writers at that time to look to the East as a source of cultural renewal. One such was Ezra Pound (1885–1972). We have just noted his interest in Japanese *No* plays, but his oriental concerns extended well beyond this. His best known poetical work, the *Cantos*, displays strong oriental influences, and at various times he was engaged in the translation of Chinese poetical and philosophical writings into English. Following the lead of the American orientalist Fenollosa, he became convinced that the pictographic, and hence non-abstract, nature of the Chinese script was ideal for poetry, and his work on this led Eliot to pronounce that 'Pound invented Chinese poetry for our time'. [8] The oriental influence on T. S. Eliot (1888–1965) himself is well attested. At the instigation of Irving Babbitt he studied Sanskrit and oriental religions as an undergraduate at Harvard, and Hindu scriptures, especially the *Bhagavad Gītā*, later became an important factor in the writing of the *Four Quartets* with their themes of time and eternity and their attempt to grasp in poetical terms the mystical experience of the timeless moment. He was also familiar with Buddhist teachings which find echoes throughout *The Waste Land*, and at the time of its composition, according to Stephen Spender, he was seriously considering becoming a Buddhist.[9]

Some of the characteristic features of the beginnings of the modern movement in literature are evident also in the revolution in the visual arts taking place in the early decades of the century. The deployment of orientalist themes to transform Western visual sensibility was nothing new, of course. We have already noted the influence of Chinese representations of the natural world on the burgeoning Romantic movement in the mid-eighteenth century. We noted too the challenge to artistic traditions brought about by the introduction of Japanese prints in the nineteenth century which influenced not only the decorative arts (for example the work of Christopher Dresser) but also movements such as Impressionism and *Art Nouveau*, an impact described by the historian John MacKenzie as 'a break with tradition, a vehicle for radicalism' which stimulated renewal of 'the flagging or reactionary tastes of Europe' (1995: 130 and 133). The influence of the East on the birth of the modern movement in painting was of parallel scope and significance, though it is one which has been consistently played down by critics and historians. The key figures in these profound changes in the visual arts are Kandinsky and Mondrian, both of whom became associated with the theosophical movement in their formative years and came under the influence of the writings of Madame Blavatsky in their search for a more spiritual approach to painting. Abstract art may indeed seem a long way from orientalism, but both of these painters discovered in the East inspiration for a mode of expression which broke completely with the aims they associated with traditional Western representational art. For them abstractionism was not merely a revolutionary new style of painting but originated in nothing less than a vision of a new epoch of enhanced spirituality, a way of penetrating through to a level of reality beyond the material and the sensual surface of things.[10]

Themes of cultural/spiritual crisis and renewal along with a turning towards the East are present in a number of other important literary figures of the twentieth century, of whom two deserve mention. The first is Aldous Huxley. He too, like the modernist poets, had undergone a 'crisis of faith', precipitated by despair over what he experienced as the spiritual barrenness of modern civilisation in the West, and sought in the mysticism of the *Vedānta* a way of recovering a sense of meaning in life. Eastern themes appear prominently in works such as *Island*, a utopian novel which, through an alliance between Buddhism and ecological ideals, offers a radical alternative to Western scientism and militarism. The second is Hermann Hesse, in whose writings we also find a sense of anxiety and disillusionment over the state of civilisation – expressed most eloquently in *The Glass Bead Game* – and a search for a lost sense of spiritual purpose that leads Eastwards. As the son of a missionary he spent part of his youth in India, travelling there again in later years, and throughout his life he sought to attain a synthesis of Christian and oriental-mystical religiosity. One of his best-known works, the novel *Siddhartha*, was based on the early life of Gautama Buddha, a work which he himself described as a confession of faith, and in which we find a moving expression of the Buddha's personality and teachings.[11]

The works of both Huxley and Hesse, like Edwin Arnold's *The Light of Asia* in an earlier period, had a powerful impact on the imagination of a readership which, from the 1950s onwards, shared their desire to reach out to new artistic and spiritual horizons. This period witnessed a rapid growth of interest in Eastern ideas amongst both intellectuals and the educated public in general, and orientalism as a conspicuous socio-cultural phenomenon can conveniently be dated from the emergence of the so-called 'beat' movement in this period. This movement, which centred on bohemian artist communities in the USA, and which was inspired by the nineteenth-century American transcendentalists and by the existentialist movement in France, played a crucial role in propagating an interest in the Eastern way to personal authenticity and heightened states of consciousness. Zen Buddhism proved especially attractive, with its emphasis on spontaneity and its offer of instant enlightenment, and the writings of Gary Snyder, Jack Kerouac, Alan Ginsberg, and Alan Watts, as well as of Aldous Huxley and Hermann Hesse, helped to introduce a whole generation of young people to Eastern philosophy and spirituality. Gary Snyder first encountered Zen Buddhism in 1951 through the writings of D. T. Suzuki, and, after ten years of study under a Zen master in Japan, he attempted to work out an alternative ethic which drew on both Buddhist and Native American ideals, as well as American natural rights ideology. The writings of Alan Watts, such as his famous essay 'Beat Zen, Square Zen, and Zen', had a wide impact through their endeavour to translate Zen and Taoist ideas into Western terms. His attempts to link Zen with science and with psychology have often been dismissed by scholars as amateurish, but there is no doubt that his eloquent and provocative style helped to make Zen accessible to the average reader. His *Psychotherapy East and West*, with its emphasis on the transformational and liberating potential of Eastern practices, provoked widespread interest when it was first published in 1961, and the historian Theodore Roszak assures us that Watts 'has made the most determined effort to translate the insights of Zen and Taoism into the language of Western science and psychology' (1970: 132). No less inspiring were the writings of Jack Kerouac. His novel *The Dharma Bums* contains an enticing vision of

> a great rucksack revolution, thousands or even millions of young Americans . . . all of 'em Zen lunatics who go about writing poems that happen to appear in their heads for no reason . . . wild gangs of holy men getting together to drink and talk and pray.
>
> (Kerouac 1959: 78)

It has frequently been pointed out that the beats for the most part misunderstood and distorted Zen. Charles Prebish, for example, accuses them of ignoring 'the very basis of Zen monastic life and its incumbent discipline', and of transposing the 'ecstatic' quality of Zen experience into inappropriate erotic and alcoholic terms. Nevertheless, as Prebish himself concedes, the beats 'with their zany antics' came close to 'providing a real American beginning for Buddhism', even if authentic Zen eluded them (1979: 24).

The hippie phenomenon of the 1960s was in many ways a continuation and apotheosis of the beat movement, and a fulfilment of Kerouac's vision. At the social level it represented a counter-culture which reacted against the standardisation and the competitive materialism of conventional culture, at the philosophical level a radical critique of scientific rationalism, and at the religious level a search for new routes to spiritual enlightenment through the use of mind-expanding techniques and drugs. Eastern philosophies and practices were eagerly studied in pursuit of these goals by many in this period, providing a powerful tool for the re-evaluation of, and ready-made alternatives to, Western values and lifestyles, offering a way not merely of escape but of political liberation. It was in this period, too, that works such as the *I Ching*, the *Tao Te Ching*, the *Bhagavad Gītā*, and *The Tibetan Book of the Dead* made their appearance in Western bookshops, and that gurus such as the Maharishi and Bhagwan Rajneesh, and movements such as the International Society for Krishna Consciousness, gathered troupes of young disciples around them, eager to embrace the wisdom of the East. As living social phenomena the beat and the hippie movements are now part of history, or survive on the margins as vestigial remnants, but in all sorts of ways their legacy lives on, not least in the continuing popularity of Asian philosophies. Though the utopian rhetoric has cooled, and the revolutionary fervour given way to a-political pragmatism, the quest for personal authenticity and for a new form of spiritual growth has continued to preoccupy later generations, and indeed in many respects the Eastward search for alternatives to home-grown philosophies has if anything gained in depth and seriousness. As one psychologist puts it: 'The faddish wave of interest in Eastern religions . . . has broken, leaving behind it a lasting, more serious swell of understanding and enquiry' (Claxton 1986: 7).[12]

The New Age movement represents at least one manifestation of this 'more serious swell'. This movement is a rather loose-knit collection of beliefs and practices, at once less politically committed but more philosophically focused than the earlier post-war movements, which centres on the idea of the emergence of a new *Weltanschauung*, and seeks to substitute a more holistic paradigm for old mechanistic and dualistic ways of thinking. In broad terms, it is concerned with the recovery of the sacred within nature and within human life, and in pursuit of this is prepared to draw on and to adapt a variety of ancient creeds and practices. Here too the example of Eastern philosophies has proved highly stimulating, and though the idea of a 'new age' has a specifically Judaeo-Christian ancestry, oriental traditions have offered New Agers a whole menu of concepts and techniques to draw on in such fields as personal growth, health, psychotherapy, and ecology. As with the beats and the hippies, the New Age thinkers are convinced of the spiritual bankruptcy of the West, and have been prepared to draw syncretistically on Eastern as well as Christian symbols and concepts to provide a new overarching philosophical framework, though some would argue that the utopian strain within New Age thinking fits uncomfortably with Eastern religions such as Hinduism, Buddhism, and Taoism which have no significant eschatological tendencies.[13]

SCHOLARLY AND INTELLECTUAL DIMENSIONS

Beyond the cultural and literary movements examined in the previous section, it is important to recognise as well the role played in the dissemination of Eastern ideas and values by the huge growth in this century of oriental scholarship. As we noted earlier, orientalism as an academic study began much earlier with the pioneering work of such men as William Jones, Anquetil Duperron, and Wilhelm Schlegel, and came to maturity in the nineteenth century in the work of men such as Burnouf, Max Müller, Deussen, and Rhys Davids. Notable too was the arduous work of translating the huge corpus of Eastern religious texts, undertaken most conspicuously in the work of the Pali Text Society, in Max

Müller's *Sacred Books of the East* series, and in James Legge's translations of the major Confucian and Taoist texts. With the exponential growth in our century of academic institutions, along with the accompanying emphasis on specialisation and on the application of methods and approaches imported from the natural and social sciences, oriental scholarship has flourished in all kinds of ways and produced an abundance of riches which has not only served the needs of scholars but has helped to encourage and inform a much wider following. Research centres like The School of Oriental and African Studies in London, The Institute of Sinology in Leiden, the East–West Center in Hawaii, and the Leningrad Oriental Institute (closed by Stalin) have provided a focus for orientalist research and for the teaching of oriental studies at a high level. And this century, like the last, has also produced a long line of distinguished orientalist scholars, such as Thomas Cleary, Edward Conze, Helmuth von Glasenapp, A. C. Graham, Marcel Granet, Hermann Oldenberg, Giuseppe Tucci, and Heinrich Zimmer, whose work has directly or indirectly contributed to the wider intellectual ferment that has been provoked by the East–West passage of ideas.

Looking beyond the domains of oriental scholarship as such, it is important to recognise that Western intellectual culture has in many aspects, including as we shall see a number of academic disciplines, become increasingly intertwined with ideas originating in the East. The roll-call in this century of thinkers and creative writers who have taken a close interest in Eastern philosophies is a distinguished one and includes such names as Roland Barthes, David Bohm, Paul Claudel, Erich Fromm, Charles Hartshorne, Martin Heidegger, Aldous Huxley, C. G Jung, R. D. Laing, Robert Ornstein, Albert Schweitzer, Erwin Schrödinger, Rudolf Steiner, Paul Tillich, Arnold Toynbee, H. G. Wells, and W. B. Yeats. None of these is in any sense an orientalist, yet they all have found inspiration by linking their own ideas and projects with the ancient traditions of India and China. It would be an exaggeration to claim that figures such as these have transformed Western thought and culture with the aid of Eastern ideas, but at the same time their work is indicative of the way in which ideas from one culture can interact with and fertilise those of quite a different culture by means of a creative dialogue. For some of them, indeed, the encroachment of Eastern philosophies on the West represents a phenomenon of considerable historical and cultural importance. According to Jung, for example, the East is 'throwing our spiritual world into confusion' and pushing us to 'the threshold of a new spiritual epoch' (1961: 249–50). The philosopher N. P. Jacobson speaks of the West's encounter with Buddhism as 'a part of the most significant event of our time, an event without precedent in the historical development of man', believing that 'the Buddhist orientation has played a central role in humanity's continuing discovery of its organic wholeness' (1983: 17–18). The Catholic theologian Thomas Berry echoes this with the claim that this encounter 'has become one of the most potent forces in the intellectual, spiritual, and aesthetic life of the contemporary world' (1974: 239), and the Protestant theologian Hendrik Kraemer speaks of the mutual influence and interpenetration of the Eastern and Western religious traditions as 'one of the cardinal events of our time' (1960: 12). This latter assessment is spelled out even   more forcibly by the historian Arnold Toynbee who went so far as to claim that the East–West cultural and intellectual encounter would usher in a new historical epoch. In his book *Civilization on Trial* he asked: 'What will be singled out as the salient event of our time by future historians, centuries hence, looking back on the first half of the twentieth century?' Not, he replied, the 'sensational or tragic or catastrophic political and economic events', but rather the impact of West on East and of East on West leading to the ending of age-old 'parochial' distinctions between the civilisations of East and West and the emergence of a world community, a revolution that will be seen to be the product not of economic forces but of religious convergence (Toynbee 1948: 213).

COMMON IDEALS AND MOTIVATIONS

It is time to round off this preliminary discussion of twentieth-century orientalism by attempting to identify common orientalist themes, some of which have already emerged clearly, while others will become more apparent in the chapters which follow. The diversity of movements and writers discussed in this section of the book, and the complex and heterogeneous nature of the East–West encounter in the twentieth century, make this task difficult, but a number of related motifs stand out.

The first of these is one that we have observed over the whole of the modern period, namely the deployment of the East as a means of intellectual and cultural criticism. We will come to see in the following chapters how, over a wide range of disciplines, and in the hands of an equally wide range of thinkers, the East has continued to play the role of Socratic gadfly on the Western body, stinging and cajoling it into critical reflection by holding up to view radical alternative conceptions. In this reflexive spirit Joseph Needham writes that 'It is necessary to see Europe from the outside, to see European history, and European failure no less than European achievement, through the eyes of that larger part of humanity, the peoples of Asia (and indeed also of Africa)' (1956: 279). Similarly, Alan Watts has emphasised the importance of approaching Western psychotherapy through oriental eyes by pointing out that 'cultural patterns come to light and hidden metaphysical assumptions become clear only to the degree that we can step outside the cultural or metaphysical systems in which we are involved by comparing them with others' (Watts 1973: 23). Buddhism has proved especially well suited for the role of cultural gadfly, for, as N. P. Jacobson insists, it is a philosophy which, by dint of its astringent analysis of all conceptual frameworks and presuppositions, 'is one of humanity's most persevering efforts to keep from enveloping itself in those linguistic and symbolic systems that reduce awareness and understanding to the limits of the tribe, social class, age, race, ethnic background or nation' (Jacobson 1983: 18). By its very nature it possesses a self-corrective methodology which can release us from the 'hypnotic grip of mental habits, or parochial patterns and social convention', and which 'constitutes one of the major resources, therefore, in the struggle of the contemporary world to free itself from the culture-bound astigmatisms of the past' (ibid.: 52). This freeing from 'culture-bound astigmatisms' has proved on the whole salutary and productive, contributing an enriching ingredient to Western cultural life, though as we shall see later it has not proved uniformly liberating and enlightening, and its role in the intellectual life of the West has in some respects come to appear ambivalent and questionable.

The second of these themes, exemplified in the remarks of Toynbee quoted above, is more constructive than the first, and involves the search for common ground in a fragmented world, the quest for some kind of intellectual and spiritual convergence between disparate and often warring nations and doctrines, for a 'unified humanity' as Joseph Kitagawa puts it (1990: 15). It is a theme which clearly has special significance in the context of the inter-cultural conflict of the twentieth century. The East–West encounter of ideas in recent times has indeed often focused on the ideal of global reconciliation, and many thinkers have earnestly explored the idea that bringing East and West together at an ideological level might provide a key to a new world order of peace and reconciliation. Such thinkers point out that in one sense the world is indeed coming closer together under the pressure of economic, social, and technological factors, but that the human race is still at peril if this is not accompanied by a deeper unity that brings together the hearts and minds of diverse peoples. This is a theme which received particular encouragement in the West from a number of Indian thinkers, and is indicative of the way in which orientalism transcends its Western origins, and in which the tangled web of interactions between East and West often precludes any simple judgements concerning the source and direction of influences. Radhakrishnan is a conspicuous example here. He has been a leading exponent of the ideal of intellectual and spiritual convergence, expressing the hope that, with the intermingling of peoples, races and religions, 'neighbourhood will now be transformed into brotherhood', and that by means of 'a cross-fertilization of ideas and insights, behind which lie centuries of racial and cultural tradition and earnest endeavour, a great unification [will] take place in the deeper fabric of men's thoughts', urging the creation of 'a world society with a universal religion of which the historical faiths are but branches' (Radhakrishnan 1939: 51 and 347–50).[14]

High-minded – some would say excessively inflated – aspirations such as these can be found in a great number of orientalists. For example, W. Y. Evans-Wentz hoped that his translation of *The Tibetan Book of the Dead* would 'serve as one more spiritual strand in an unbreakable bond of good will and universal peace, binding East and West together in mutual respect and understanding, and in love such as overleaps every barrier of creed and caste and race' (1960: xxi). In similarly expansive vein, Romain Rolland saw East–West understanding as a key to global reconciliation and to the 'unity of the human spirit' (1930: 521); and Joseph Needham began his *Science and Civilisation in China* by looking forward to 'the dawn of a new universalism which . . . will unite the working peoples of all races in a community both catholic and co-operative' (1954: 9). For many such thinkers it was not enough that there should be mutual understanding and a tolerant cross-cultural fertilisation. What was required if real global understanding and peace are to be achieved is nothing less than the creation of a world religion. The American philosopher W. E. Hocking, for example, believed that the emergence of a world civilisation inevitably draws together East and West and makes it a matter of urgent necessity that the traditions of both should come together to assist in the creation of a new world religion (see Hocking 1956). For others this aspiration has taken more secular forms. One such was the popular philosopher Count Hermann Keyserling (1880–1946). After an extensive world tour beginning in 1911 he published his most famous book, *The Travel Diary of a Philosopher* (1919), in which he attempted to propagate an internationalist outlook and an attitude of toleration and understanding. He persistently urged the need for some kind of synthesis between Eastern and Western thought, and in pursuit of this in 1920 he founded at Darmstadt the School of Wisdom, whose aim was to foster mutual understanding and respect between East and West, and which hosted an annual colloquium attended by a number of distinguished sinologists and scholars from various fields. The school was characterised by its internationalism and by its commitment to free and open dialogue, attributes which are worth underlining in view of the ever-growing racism and fanaticism characteristic of that period of Germany's history.[15]

Connected with this is the theme of cultural sickness, one which, as we noted earlier, has been amplified and embellished by a number of modern Western thinkers. The theme of moral and cultural decline is indeed one of the dominant themes of the East–West encounter throughout the whole modern period. We observed it in the case of the Romantics and then in the religious and cultural debates of the nineteenth century, and it reaches a veritable crescendo in the twentieth. On a purely cultural level, minus any obvious religious overtones, this theme is often expressed in terms of the supposed unbalanced, unharmonious, even neurotic, character of modern Western life, addicted to instant satisfactions and the frenetic pursuit of economic goals, in a word, a cultural neurosis. At one level this kind of dissatisfaction has taken the form of a profound reaction against the modern world with its ideals of rationality, progress, and liberal democracy, and in Germany we can witness a disturbing affinity between orientalism and some of the anti-modernist trends associated with the rise of fascism and racism. At another, less politically charged, level modern Western civilisation is viewed in the words of one writer as 'hyper-active, over-rational, out of touch with nature' and therefore 'in need of restoring the balance between activity and repose'. She is by no means alone in suggesting that the Eastern way 'is a practical way for the alleviation and cure of the tensions and pressures of life today and for taming the "monkey mind" with its restless and purposeless leaping about' (Cooper 1990: 129). Much earlier in the century, G. Lowes Dickinson, following a trip to the East, wrote *An Essay on the Civilisation of India, Asia and Japan* in which he sought to break down some of the deeply entrenched prejudices about the East, and argued that the East had developed qualities which the West had lost and now badly needed to recover. He took the view, which has since achieved almost the status of commonplace wisdom amongst certain orientalists, that Asians live closer to nature and in harmony with its rhythms, they have developed higher forms of religion, literature and art, and have a spiritual outlook which contrasts sharply with the materialistic attitudes in the West (see Dickinson 1914: 85). The theme of cultural sickness is often linked closely with what is perceived as the perilous spiritual plight of modern Western civilisation. A good example of this is to be found in the writings of a somewhat eccentric Englishman, Paul Brunton, who after travelling extensively in India wrote a series of books in which he sought to offer the wisdom of ancient India as a message of hope to a world torn by war, and suffering from loss of spiritual purpose. His first major book, *A Search in Secret India*, published in 1934, sold a quarter of a million copies in several languages, and played an important role in conveying Indian spiritual practices and their philosophical background to the West. In later writings he reflected on the spiritual failure of Western civilisation, arguing that the only possible hope for the future lay in the direction of some kind of harmonisation between Western science and Eastern mysticism.[16]

Running through all these themes is the motif of *dialogue*, a notion which has attained almost cult status in this context. As we shall see later this motif has become especially important among certain leading Christian theologians who have come round to the belief that 'we must move from the Age of Monologue to the Age of Dialogue', and who advocate this as a means towards a greater measure of mutual understanding and toleration (Swidler *et al.* 1990: vii and 3). And from a philosophical point of view there are those who speak of the need for a dialogical spirit which depends 'not on one system of thought replacing the other, but on an integrated growth which maintains and expands both tendencies' (Allinson 1989: 23). Nevertheless the notion of dialogue, benign-sounding though it is, has not escaped censure, and some view it as simply a more subtle form of colonialism which, in its one-sidedness and its Eurocentric impetus, is hardly preferable to outright missionary zeal. In more general terms, the commonly evoked theme of an East–West dialogue turns out, in the hands of such critics, to be simply a more acceptable way of expressing the well-established practice of appropriating Eastern traditions within a Western discourse.[17]

Parallel complaints have been made concerning all the themes just enumerated: how legitimate, for example, is the claim that East and West represent complementary opposites, and what Western interests lie behind the quest for a world religion or a global philosophy? Worries such as these can be seen as manifesting a much wider critical development, a new set of orientalist motifs and a whole series of debates in which can be seen a greatly enhanced awareness of the methodological assumptions and ideological prejudices underlying the whole orientalist enterprise. Where earlier in the century thinkers from many fields and backgrounds have sought with the aid of oriental ideas to confront some of the major issues of the age such as international conflict and spiritual decay, lately the discourse of orientalism itself came under scrutiny, and many of the concepts and strategies outlined in this chapter – from the ideal of a universal wisdom to the very possibility of dialogue between cultures – have themselves been subjected to close analysis. In philosophical and related fields orientalist studies have shown a growing inclination to step back and examine their own methods and presuppositions, and to raise questions about the epistemological problems implicated in transcultural studies, leading to debates concerning the nature of these disciplines themselves as well as to questions about language, translation, and interpretation. In domains such as cultural and area studies discussion has more and more centred on orientalism as a form of *praxis*, specifically one related to colonial and postcolonial experience, where attention has been focused on the ideological assumptions underlying Western representations of colonised peoples. Here the issues of power, Eurocentrism, and the construction of orientalist discourse, which we broached earlier on, come to the fore once again. Increasingly it is recognised that the historical fact of colonisation has not only provided a context in which orientalism has been able to thrive, but that the relationship is deeply symbiotic, and that, arguably, categories in which the East has been understood cannot be uncoupled from the more overt instruments of colonial oppression. At one level this is a matter of the objectivity and ethics of scholarship, but at another it provokes troublesome questions about the role of power and interest in the pursuit of inter-cultural understanding. These reflexive tendencies and strategies, as well as the other themes elaborated here, will become apparent in what follows, and in the remaining chapters of this section of the book we look more closely at some of the major disciplinary areas in which orientalist discourse has evolved over the past century.

Chapter 7

Philosophical encounters

WESTERN PHILOSOPHY AND ORIENTAL TRADITIONS

Academic philosophy in the twentieth century has sometimes been slow to respond to the allures of the East, and in investigating its history one is sometimes reminded of Chuang-tzu's image of the 'cramped scholar' whose world horizon is unduly narrow and blinkered. As a recent book on the subject of 'world philosophy' puts it, philosophy has 'become overly narrow, insulated from other disciplines, and in many quarters oblivious to its own culture as well as to others' (Solomon and Higgins 1993: xi). In some Western philosophical traditions Eastern thought is simply ignored or marginalised. Marxism and positivism, with their scientistic and anti-metaphysical inclinations, have inevitably bracketed Eastern systems of thought with the metaphysical and religious systems of the European past, and from these perspectives oriental philosophies are seen as reflecting the benighted attitudes of pre-scientific ages. In the case of Marxism they represent the ideological superstructures of pre-bourgeois societies which, though they may survive in certain cultural enclaves, represent mentalities which belong essentially to the past;[1] and for positivists they represent little more than a repository of pre-scientific mystification, to be dismissed as 'meaningless' along with the products of Western metaphysics. Linguistic philosophy has adopted a less exclusivist view than positivism concerning the proper objects of philosophical interest, but while questions of inter-cultural understanding have for some time entered into philosophical debates, in which context some serious attention has begun to be paid to Eastern traditions of thought, philosophers of this school have tended to carry out their discussions within a purely European idiom.[2] A greater level of interest is evident in continental philosophy, where, according to Graham Parkes, 'the realization has dawned recently that the European Continental tradition . . . has developed philosophical terminologies that are far more in harmony with many strains of Asian thought than are those of Anglo-American philosophy' (1987: 6), but while the names of Jaspers and Heidegger are witnesses to a broader outlook in this respect, there is still a tendency here as well to concentrate on purely Western traditions of thought and to leave the East to colleagues in specialist departments of oriental studies. Edmund

Husserl went so far as to claim that 'the Europeanization of all foreign parts of mankind' is the 'destiny of the earth', and that Western philosophy is a unique spiritual expression which can encompass, but cannot be encompassed by, the thinking of China and India (see Husserl 1970: 273–5).

A good yardstick for measuring the breadth of Western philosophical attitudes is to be found in histories of philosophy and histories of ideas. Histories of philosophy written in the nineteenth century tended to focus exclusively on European philosophy, following Hegel's treatment of the Orient as a land of 'sunrise' which represents the early history of the world spirit but is not part of its philosophical fulfilment, a consummation which begins only with Thales. Paul Deussen's *Universal History of Philosophy*, begun in 1894, was a notable exception in this regard with its attempt to break out of what the author saw as the one-sidedness of Western philosophies,[3] but many histories in that period either ignored non-European philosophy or else, following Hegel, treated it as a precursor to philosophical developments which were to find their culmination in Europe. Thus for example the German philosopher W. Windelband in an influential history of philosophy first published in 1892, *Lehrbuch der Geschichte der Philosophie*, referred to Eastern thought as the 'pre-history of philosophy' and explicitly excluded it from his textbook. And Eduard Zeller in his important work on Greek philosophy helped to set the seal on a purely Eurocentric approach to the history of philosophy by viewing it as peculiarly and exclusively Hellenic in nature and origin. Telling examples from more recent years include the widely read histories of W. K. C. Guthrie and Anthony Flew, both of which consider Eastern thought to be 'utterly different' from Western philosophy and hence to be excluded from their studies. It should be added that this historical exclusivism is not confined to philosophy, for as the historian Raymond Dawson complains: 'It is easy to detect in the writings of many European historians the constant assumption that history is co-extensive with the European historical tradition' (1967: 80).[4]

Nevertheless, in spite of this negative overall picture, there is evidence in Western philosophy in the twentieth century of a growing awareness of alternative traditions and a desire to bring about some kind of 'fusion of horizons' (to use Gadamer's phrase) between East and West, and, as we shall see, a number of distinguished philosophers have begun to take a serious interest in Eastern ideas and to locate their Western philosophising within a wider perspective. As early as the 1920s the Russian philosopher Th. Stcherbatsky, leader of a group of orientalist scholars in Russia between 1920 and 1935, was seeking to build bridges between Buddhism and Western philosophy. In a pioneering work he set out to show the limitations of Western logic by engaging in an extensive comparative study of the traditions of Buddhist logic, and in the process he attempted the first fully worked out analysis of Buddhism as a philosophical system (see Stcherbatsky 1958 and 1968). He was the first Western philosopher to take seriously the thinking of the Indian philosopher Nāgārjuna whom he construed in neo-Kantian terms.[5] A German philosopher who had more than a passing interest in the East was the existentialist Karl Jaspers. In his study of *The Great Philosophers* he attempted to locate the ideas of Buddha and Confucius within a global framework of philosophy, arguing that they arose from the same 'common root' as, and shared certain 'eternal questions' with, the great Western thinkers, and that their 'historicity and consequent uniqueness can be perceived only within the all-embracing historicity of humanity' (1962: 13). This global outlook was a dominant factor in his thinking, and in his book *The Origin and Goal of History* Jaspers argues that the 'axial age' of the first millennium BCE witnessed the simultaneous emergence across many different civilisations, East and West, of cultural 'transcendence' – a form of critical and reflective thinking which for the first time in human history engaged with reality as a whole.

In more recent years it is possible to discern an increasing recognition by philosophers of the need to take account of this oriental 'other', if only as a means for clarifying and reconceptualising indigenous philosophical concerns. Thus the French existentialist Merleau-Ponty writes that 'Western philosophy can learn [from India and China] to rediscover the relationship to being, and to estimate the possibilities we have shut ourselves off from in becoming "Westerners", and perhaps reopen them' (1964: 139). A similar goal of self-reappraisal by using the external standpoint of Eastern philosophy is suggested by a leading exponent of an entirely different philosophical tradition who writes that 'The treatment for philosophical parochialism, as for parochialism of other sorts, is to come to know alternatives. . . . There may even be ways of catapulting oneself, at least temporarily, into different philosophical perspectives, e.g. from Eastern thought' (Nozick 1981: 19). Another American philosopher from an earlier generation, E. A. Burtt, who had an unusually wide knowledge of Indian thought, asked: 'What can Western Philosophy Learn from India?', and replied that it 'can give us a new provocative perspective in which to pursue our philosophical thinking. It can give us a more inclusive orientation in our understanding of what sort of thing philosophy is' (Burtt 1955: 197 and 210). A more recent example of this kind of approach is offered by the Israeli philosopher Ben-Ami Scharfstein. In a collection of writings on comparative philosophy he accuses Western philosophers of 'cultural myopia', claiming that 'philosophy is not confined to the West', and going on to express the hope that he and his fellow contributors 'are taking a genuine step out of our provincialism and towards the world in which the different philosophical traditions exist as equals and together express the single humanity of them all' (Scharfstein *et al.* 1978: 1 and 5). The cultural and geographical situation of Israel, straddling East and West, gives an added force to these comments, and it is interesting to note that a similar move away from Eurocentric provincialism is evident in Australasia, where in 1988 the Asian and Comparative Philosophy Society of Australasia was founded as a result of a strong growth of interest in Asian thought amongst hitherto largely Oxford-centred philosophical communities in Australia and New Zealand.[6]

The most important twentieth-century philosopher to engage with the Orient, however, is Martin Heidegger, of whom the theologian John Cobb wrote: '[he] may well be the most Buddhist thinker the West has produced' (1980: 19). Heidegger's lifelong interest in Asian thought is not readily apparent in his published writings where references to it are sparse, and it is only recently that the full extent of this interest has become manifest. On the face of it such an interest should not be surprising for, as Graham Parkes notes, there is a 'pre-established harmony' between Heidegger's thinking and Eastern philosophies, and a reading of *Being and Time,* as well as his later work, makes it 'comprehensible why he should have found Taoism and Zen so congenial' (Parkes 1987: 9 and 107). Heidegger's radical questioning of the entire Graeco-Christian metaphysical, logocentric tradition, culminating, he claimed, in modern scientistic and technological modes of thinking, with their calculative and objectifying tendencies, invites comparison with Eastern, and especially Chinese and Japanese, modes of thinking. It is not surprising, therefore, that Heidegger, like so many other critics of the Western tradition, found an affinity with the more meditative and intuitive thinking of Taoism and Zen.

There is evidence that as early as 1930 he was acquainted with the Taoist philosopher Chuang-tzu and saw the relevance of the latter to his own philosophy. When later he encountered Suzuki's writings on Zen he exclaimed that 'if I have understood Suzuki correctly, this is what I have been trying to say in all my writings' (quoted in Schrag 1970: 295). His search for an appropriate language in which to 'think Being' led him progressively away from the conceptualising methods born out of European linguistic modes towards non-representational modes of utterance such as those found in Asian philosophical texts, and his lifelong attempt to free us from the prison-house of Western philosophical categories and to open up the 'clearing' of Being led him to turn towards meditative thinkers such as Lao-tzu and Chuang-tzu. It is significant, therefore, that in 1946 he embarked in company with a Chinese scholar on a translation of the *Tao Te Ching,* a project which was never completed but which enabled him, according to his student Otto Pöggeler, 'to confront the beginnings of Western thinking with the beginnings of one of the great east Asian traditions [which] transformed Heidegger's language in a critical situation and gave his thinking a new orientation' (in Parkes 1987: 52). His attitude towards the East–West dialogue remained ambivalent, however, for, unlike his one-time friend Jaspers who advocated the spirit of a trans-historical unity of East and West, he continued to insist on the European roots of his thinking. In his view philosophy is essentially a Western phenomenon and he was doubtful about the possibility of engaging in a dialogue with Eastern thought as long as the European mode of thinking retained its role of planetary domination. In a discussion with a Japanese philosopher he remarked that the language of the dialogue between East and West 'shifted everything into European', and that the current domination by Western ways of thinking led to 'the complete Europeanization of the Earth and of Man' (Heidegger 1971: 4 and 15). In spite of this he affirmed late in life that 'Again and again it has seemed urgent to me that a dialogue take place with the thinkers of what is to us the Eastern world' (in Parkes 1987: 7).[7]

ORIENTALISM IN AMERICA

It is in America, however, that the influence of Eastern thought on Western philosophy is greatest,[8] and a tradition of East-directed scholarship and interest has flourished there in the schools of philosophy since the late nineteenth century when Harvard University first included Indian thought in its philosophy curriculum. The strong influence of the home-grown transcendentalist movement on the American cultural climate in that period may help to explain this, in addition to which it was natural that, in its endeavour to emancipate itself from its European past, American philosophy should turn its attention to non-European traditions. Dale Riepe, in his account of the influence of Indian philosophy on America, has argued that from the nineteenth century an intellectual pluralism prevailed in America which encouraged a comparative approach to philosophy, and thereby helped to transcend purely European traditions of thought (see Riepe 1970: ix). This more outward-looking trend is apparent in histories of philosophy produced in America, most conspicuously in Will Durant's best-selling work *The Story of Philosophy* first published in 1926, in J. C. Plott's *Global History of Philosophy*, and in works like Paul Edwards' *Encyclopedia of Philosophy* and the *Dictionary of the History of Ideas* all of which devote more than just token space to Eastern philosophies and ideas. Furthermore, a number of histories of specifically Oriental philosophy have been produced in America this century, including F. Grant's *Oriental Philosophy*, published in 1936, and L. A. Beck's *The Story of Oriental Philosophy*, published eight years earlier. Beck notes that 'The value of the thought of Asia is daily more realized by Western thinkers' (1928: v), and goes on to argue that the values of East and West do not clash but are complementary, and that understanding between nations 'is the most vital need of the present day', one whereby 'men may yet reach that Brotherhood for which all Teachers of the East and West have willingly consecrated their lives' (ibid.: v and xi). Such sentiments are, as we have already seen, not untypical of this genre of writing in the twentieth century.

The story begins even further back. Josiah Royce (1855–1916) was the earliest American philosopher of any significance to take Indian philosophy seriously, and became an important stimulant for later American philosophers' interest in Asian thought. He discovered in *Vedānta* useful support for his version of monistic idealism, using Indian metaphysics as a weapon with which to attack prevailing realist and dualist views, though after reading Schopenhauer his interest switched to the moral teachings of Buddhism. William James (1842–1910), a colleague of Royce at Harvard, though not especially sympathetic to Indian thought, was well read in it and made frequent references to it in his lectures and writings; as Riepe comments: 'it may be said of James that he was both attracted and repelled by Indian thought' (1970: 81). His emphasis on pluralism put him at odds with Indian metaphysical monism, and his pragmatist outlook did not dispose him well towards Buddhism's supposed quietism, but in his famous Gifford Lectures *The Varieties of Religious Experience* his knowledge of Eastern mystical traditions enabled him to place Western mystical traditions within a global context. Indicative of James' open-minded attitude is the following story concerning the visit of the Ceylonese Buddhist, Anagarika Dharmapala, to one of his lectures at Harvard in 1903:

'Take my chair', Professor James said when he recognised Dharmapala seated in the hall, 'you are better equipped to lecture on psychology than I', and after Dharmapala's talk outlining the major Buddhist doctrines, James turned to his class and announced, 'This is the psychology everybody will be studying twenty-five years from now'.

(see Fields 1986: 135)

James Haughton Woods (1864–1935), a student of Royce who also studied comparative religion in Europe under Deussen and Max Müller, visited India twice, lectured on Indian philosophy, and in 1914 produced the first full-length scholarly work in America on Indian philosophy: *The Yoga System of Patanjali*. Another Harvard philosopher who lectured on Indian philosophy was W. E. Hocking (1873–1966). As a young man, Hocking attended the World's Parliament of Religions in Chicago and heard the famous address by Vivekenanda, and though not uncritical of *Vedānta* and Buddhism, he used Eastern philosophical and religious ideas as corroborations of his own insights. He was a powerful advocate of the broadening out of Western philosophy through comparative studies, and in his keynote address to the first East–West Philosophers' Conference held in Hawaii in 1939 he argued that such studies would demonstrate 'just how much akin the minds of men are under all circumstances', and that the 'influx of new knowledge about Oriental philosophy ought to be a powerful means of reaching for ourselves a better grasp of universal principles' (in Moore 1946: 2 and 4).

The American philosopher from this period who took the closest interest in Eastern philosophies, 'the most genuinely receptive to the totality of Indian philosophy' (Riepe 1970: 107), was George Santayana (1863–1952). He taught philosophy at Harvard where he came into contact with Royce and James and where his interest in Indian philosophy and in Buddhism was aroused. The importance of Indian *Vedānta* philosophy for him lay in the opportunity it gave him to establish a point of reference outside Western philosophy with which to clarify his own metaphysical views, and Buddhism was especially evident in his writings on morality where he sought to construct an alternative ethic to the materialism and rationalism of his age, a 'post-rational morality' as he called it, which pointed to the inadequacies of egoism and emphasised instead the values of inner equilibrium and sympathy for others. Buddhism as a redemptive system was, he believed, superior to Christianity in so far as it quiets the emotions and the will rather than rousing them, and generates a condition of peace and inner liberation.[9] Mention should also be made of Irving Babbitt (1865–1933) who, though not strictly a philosopher, had a considerable influence on the intellectual climate of America in his day. He is especially remembered for his fight against the influence of Rousseau and Romanticism, but what is often forgotten is that he studied Sanskrit at Harvard and later devoted much time to study of Buddhism, producing a translation from the Pali of the Buddhist text, *The Dhammapada*. He drew heavily on the teachings of India in the articulation of his 'Neohumanistic' doctrine, an ethical outlook which aimed, like the philosophy of Santayana, to combat the industrial and utilitarian values of his day.

The distinctiveness of American philosophy vis-à-vis Eastern traditions is especially visible in the emergence to prominence there of *process thought*, a school in which Eastern ideas, especially those of Buddhism, have come to play an important role. Process philosophy represents a direct challenge to a central tradition of Western philosophy that goes back to Aristotle. This latter tradition rests on the belief that the fundamental constituents of the material world are enduring substances, that is to say distinct entities which persist through time and to which all complex phenomena are ultimately reducible. By contrast with this, process philosophy maintains that the basic constituents of reality are events or processes. Reality is viewed as being like an ever-flowing river, dynamic and mobile, and that the changes we perceive taking place are not merely the reshuffling of unchanging particles but are in some way radically creative. Inspired by Heraclitus and by the French philosopher Henri Bergson, it is a way of thinking which has flourished chiefly in America and has been associated with names such as Peirce, James, and Dewey, but mostly with those of A. N. Whitehead and Charles Hartshorne. Whitehead did not study Eastern thought in depth, nor was he significantly influenced by it, but he did come to see the kinship between his own metaphysical thinking and certain forms of Eastern philosophy, especially Buddhism with its regard for organic unity and its preoccupation with change rather than substance.[10] Charles Hartshorne, who became the chief proponent of process philosophy, had extensive knowledge of Buddhism and was much more concerned than Whitehead to integrate it with his own speculations. He discovered in Buddhism a way of thinking about the physical and the mental world which anticipated in many ways the approach of process philosophy, and advocated the study of Buddhism as a corrective to endemic errors in Western philosophy deriving from its long-held views about substance. He wrote that 'enduring substances in a living world constitute an elemental confusion contrary to both logic and life, a fact taken into account by countless Buddhists for two thousand years', and that 'at long last we should join the Buddhists in recognizing that an enduring individual is a society or sequence of occasions [a Whiteheadian term] rather than a soul-substance' (Hartshorne 1970: 87–8). Many of these ideas have been refined and developed by N. P. Jacobson, a more recent exponent of process philosophy who claims that Buddhism 'anticipated by over two thousand years the efforts of a whole series of philosophers of the West – Bergson, Dewey, Darwin, Fechner, James, Hartshorne, Whitehead, and Peirce – to construe the world of events in their novel, emerging forms of togetherness' (Jacobson 1981: 48).[11]

UNIVERSALISM

In discussing the development of philosophical contacts with the East in this century it will be useful to think of a sequence of three stages. These stages could be called the *universalist*, the *comparative*, and the *hermeneutical* respectively, and while they do not represent distinct phases but overlap to a considerable extent both chronologically and conceptually, they are convenient labels for simplifying and making sense of the complex developments within this philosophical genre in recent times.

'Universalism' could be defined as the search for a single world philosophy, one which brings together and synthesises the diverse philosophical traditions of East and West. It has a pedigree that goes back at least as far as Leibniz, and is often linked with the search for what Leibniz himself called the *philosophia perennis*. It aims to find some basic assumptions which these traditions hold in common, and thereon to build a global system of thought which will not only bring philosophers together in agreement but might also contribute to some kind of cultural and political reconciliation among the nations. There are, inevitably, different versions of this, ranging from the quest for a single global philosophical system to the elaboration of a methodology which would enable divergent philosophies to communicate in a fruitful way, but all share the belief that Western philosophy has hitherto been confined too narrowly within its European–American boundaries, and that there is an urgent need to break out of this enclave. The urgency of this need is seen to arise, not only from within philosophy itself, which for the benefit of its own health needs to be set within a much wider context, but also from the demands of a new world order in which old cultural boundaries are shifting and a new interpenetration of peoples and ideas is taking place at all levels. For some the ideal of a world community is more than a philosophical imperative, therefore, it is a historical necessity, an inevitable consequence of political, economic and cultural convergence, for, according to one philosopher, 'mankind is entering a new phase of evolution, a phase of a higher dimension of consciousness [where the] distinction between Eastern and Western, American and Chinese philosophy will soon become a thing of the past' (Saher 1969: 261).

Historically and geographically the universalist tendency within philosophy has a very precise locus in the remarkable East–West Center in the University of Hawaii, and its key moment was the first East–West Philosophers' Conference held in Honolulu in 1939. Charles Moore was the driving force behind this enterprise, and while it has broadened out and proliferated in various ways over the years, the initial impetus came from his passionately held belief in the need for philosophers from East and West to engage in dialogue and thereby to bring about a synthesis of East and West, even to forge a global philosophy. In his *Preface* to the proceedings of the first conference he spoke boldly of 'a new Renaissance', and stated unequivocally that the underlying purpose of the conference was 'to determine the possibility of a world philosophy through the synthesis of the ideas and ideals of East and West', a purpose which was driven by what he saw as the West's need for a 'wider perspective', one 'for which the East may provide inspiration' (Moore 1946: vii). Here as elsewhere Moore's motives were not purely academic but were clearly driven by a deep personal commitment to what he called 'a truly cosmopolitan and international world order, in which the diverse basic conceptions and resultant valuations of the two cultures are combined into a single world civilisation' (ibid.: 234).

Something of Moore's early vision is captured by F. S. C. Northrop, the most distinguished and influential North American philosopher in the mid-century period to articulate a theoretical framework for comparing Eastern and Western thought. In his eyes, world understanding, tragically in short supply at the time of the first Hawaii conference, required a unified philosophy which would embrace all existing philosophies. In his book *The Meeting of East and West* he elaborated the view that there are fundamental differences between Eastern and Western ways of thinking which nevertheless are mutually complementary and can be reconciled with each other through philosophical analysis. With greater philosophical acuity than Moore, he understood the methodological pitfalls which beset attempts to draw East and West together, at least to the extent that he recognised the necessity to construct a philosophical framework within which East–West comparative studies could begin to operate. In pursuit of this goal he distinguished between concepts of 'intuition' and concepts of 'postulation', applying these to Eastern and Western thinking respectively, and arguing that each represented a complementary aspect of a total philosophical outlook. Such a totalising approach based on a polarising of essential differences would find little favour today, and his analysis of global differences between Eastern and Western mentalities represent by any standard hugely distorting simplifications, but his ideas were widely discussed and contributed an important impetus to the East–West dialogue. Underlying his thinking was the conviction that enhancement of world understanding requires a unified philosophy, and he concluded his contribution to the 1939 conference with this ringing act of faith:

> It appears that by independent developments in the East and the West a new and more comprehensive philosophy is being made articulate. . . . This new philosophy, by enlarging the outlook and values of each part of the world to include those of the other, may well serve as a trustworthy criterion of the good for a truly cosmopolitan and international world order, in which the diverse basic conceptions and resultant valuations of two great cultures are combined into a single world civilisation.
>
> (in Moore 1946: 234)[12]

A second East–West Philosophers' Conference was held in Hawaii in 1949 with the title 'An Attempt at World Philosophical Synthesis', and in his report Moore stated once again that 'The general problem of the Conference was to study the possibility of a world philosophy through the synthesis of the ideas and ideals of the East and the West', though this was qualified by excluding the idea of 'a rigidly homogeneous single philosophy' in favour of what he describes as an 'orchestrated unity' in which 'different emphases and perspectives would be harmonized as supplementing points of view' (Moore 1949: 4–7). In spite of its title the mood of the second conference appears to have shifted away from the idea of a universal philosophical synthesis towards the encouragement of open-ended dialogue, and there was evidence of a growing recognition of the methodological problems that beset any such universalising project.

The theme of universalism, and the ideal of some kind of synthesis between East and West, continued to find voice in the Hawaii conferences and in the journal, *Philosophy East and West*, which grew out of them. The ideal remains alive, albeit in more methodologically nuanced form, in the thinking of philosophers such as David Dilworth who calls for 'a new and essentially comparative hermeneutical expertise to be able to understand and appreciate the major texts of world philosophy' (Dilworth 1989: 6). His aim is to elaborate a 'universal categorial structure' that would be common to the philosophical texts of diverse cultures and which could deliver 'a single intertextual picture' that would enable us to combine the world's major philosophical texts into 'a single purview' (ibid.: 6–7). Nevertheless, there has been a gradual shift of emphasis during the years following the war, away from the vision of a global philosophy towards the more limited aims of comparative philosophy, a shift which in recent years has been marked by a growing distaste for 'grand narratives' and a critique of the 'foundationalist' aims that have become associated with the universalist assumptions of European Enlightenment philosophy. And regardless of purely philosophical considerations, universalism appears increasingly in an ideologically reflexive age to carry a Eurocentric stigma and to represent the continuing authority of Western thought, even where this authority is no longer backed by imperial power. Even Moore himself had shifted ground by the time of the 1964 East–West Philosophers' Conference where he defined its aims as to 'examine – and attempt to overcome – common pertinent misunderstandings and antagonisms which exist between East and West', and in his concluding remarks spoke in modest terms of the need for 'improved mutual understanding' and for a philosophical outlook that moved beyond narrow provincialisms and nationalisms (Moore 1968: 6 and 548).[13]

COMPARATIVE PHILOSOPHY

Though the idea of making comparisons between Eastern and Western thought has been a powerful driving force behind orientalist studies since the seventeenth century, it was not until the 1920s that the discipline of comparative philosophy came to be explicitly formulated by the French philosopher Paul Masson-Oursel (1882–1956).[14] In his book *Comparative Philosophy*, which became an influential text in France between the wars, he followed closely the aims of Comte's positivism, claiming that the comparative method would become the indispensable prerequisite for the development of a truly scientific philosophy. This meant in the first place treating the philosophical traditions of the world's civilisations as on a par with each other, for, as he put it, 'No one philosophy has the right to put itself forward as co-extensive with the human mind', and hence 'philosophy cannot achieve positivity so long as its investigations are restricted to the thought of our own civilisation' (Masson-Oursel 1926: 35 and 33). It also meant recognising that the philosophies of different civilisations expressed different mentalities which could not be understood purely in terms of European categories, a view which he derived from his teacher Lucien Lévy-Bruhl, and which led him to believe that comparisons are more worthwhile the greater the differences amongst the traditions in question. By drawing analogies, and by comparing and contrasting the philosophical insights and techniques characteristic of the great traditions of Europe, China, and India, he hoped to show that comparative philosophy must ultimately lead to an understanding of 'the unity of the human mind under a multiplicity of aspects', an enterprise which, Masson-Oursel claimed, is 'capable of unlimited progress' (ibid.: 200 and 203).

However, as in the case of C. A. Moore's quest for a universal philosophy, such ambitious tasks for comparative philosophy have over the years become on the whole progressively moderated and diffused. Just as philosophy in general has increasingly backed away from its claims to global hegemony, and adopted a more critical and complementary role, so too in its relationship with Eastern thought it has scaled down some of its earlier grand designs and been content with adopting a more modest posture, dealing with individual concepts or thinkers, and working towards tightly defined goals. This has meant an emphasis on such activities as comparing individual philosophers with each other – Confucius with Aristotle, Mencius with Aquinas, Sankara with Spinoza, Kant, and Bradley, Nāgārjuna with Nietzsche, Heidegger, and Derrida, Dōgen with Heidegger – and drawing comparisons between Eastern and Western systems of thought – Advaita Vedānta with transcendental idealism, Spinozism with Mahāyāna Buddhism, Platonism, and existentialism. Studies in this genre have also tended to be concentrated more and more on specific concepts and ideas such as the self, causality, and scepticism, and on issues connected with epistemology, philosophy of mind, and ethics. There is still, though, a tendency amongst practitioners to envision these limited goals as having a much broader historical and social significance. Many involved in this activity take the view that comparative philosophy can enable Western philosophers to rethink their assumptions by placing them in a wider context. Steven Collins, for example, in his study of the Buddhist no-self doctrine suggests that by examining philosophical issues concerning selfhood within a cross-cultural perspective it becomes possible 'to widen a little our cultural horizons in which both our common sense and our philosophy set their ideas of the person and of selfhood' (1982: 3). Others go much further. Ben-Ami Scharfstein argues, as we saw above, that through comparative studies philosophy breaks out of its provincialism and gives expression to the ideal of a 'single humanity' (1978: 5); and in somewhat apocalyptic terms Troy Wilson Organ insists that, while the original motivation for comparative philosophy was intellectual curiosity, 'our motivation now is survival', and that 'we need to look beyond the West for therapy' (1975: 7).[15]

In order to illustrate the comparative approach it would be useful to look briefly at some examples. First Chris Gudmunsen's comparison between Buddhism and Wittgenstein. An analytical philosopher by training and profession, he was led through his personal interest in Buddhism to believe that the juxtaposition of the two had interesting philosophical possibilities, ones which could prove illuminating for both sides of the equation in spite of the historical differences between the two. He began by rejecting the possibility of any historical influence of Buddhism on Wittgenstein, a theory which has at times been canvassed because of the latter's admiration for Schopenhauer, but at the same time he also rejected Edward Conze's uncompromising view that parallels between Eastern and Western thought are 'spurious', arguing – in harmony with Masson-Oursel – that it is the very difference of context and background which 'makes the whole thing so interesting' (Gudmunsen 1977: viii). The specific focus of his interest was the *Mādhyamaka* philosophy, the 'Middle Way' of Nāgārjuna, which he believed anticipated by about 1,800 years 'much of what the later Wittgenstein had to say' (1977: 113). Thus, according to Gudmunsen, the *Mādhyamaka* philosophy is concerned essentially with language, and, like Wittgenstein's later thinking, seeks to emancipate us from the grammatical fictions in which we are trapped. For both, the meanings conveyed in language do not lead us to the essence of things, but rather are conventions, socially constructed language games, which we create and which mislead us into imagining, for example, that the mind or self is a real, persisting entity. The aim of both, therefore, is not to convey truths about the world, but to free us from pathological fixations and to provide a kind of therapy for the diseases of language. What is particularly interesting about Gudmunsen's whole approach is that, in addition to showing the way in which a Buddhist hermeneutic can place a leading modern Western philosopher in a refreshing new perspective, it also casts light on the way in which Buddhism itself is constructed and reconstructed as it passes through the reducing valve of changing Western philosophical preoccupations, for it is his contention that Wittgenstein's linguistic turn provides the basis for a new interpretation of Buddhism, one which should replace the Kantian and idealist approaches which have dominated Western thinking about Indian philosophy as a whole since the Romantic period.[16]

Gudmunsen's approach has been echoed in recent years in a number of other comparative studies, particularly with regard to Nietzsche who is yet another important Western thinker who has been drawn into comparisons with Buddhism. As in the previous case it is Nāgārjuna who is the favoured partner, indeed he is a thinker who, with increasing frequency in recent years, has been drawn into comparative studies and into the net of deconstructive discourse of which Nietzsche himself is seen as a precursor. What has proved especially compelling about this second/third-century Indian thinker is the way in which he was seen as focusing on the ambiguities and mystifications inherent in language and used these in order to substantiate a broad critical perspective, a project which bears more than a passing resemblance to Nietzsche's critique of traditional Western ways of thinking. Thus, for example, Glen T. Martin argues that

> Nāgārjuna's dialectical analysis of the common categories by which people understand existence carries radical implications, somewhat comparable to those of Nietzsche's philosophy, in which a deconstructive process ultimately leads to the realization that both everyday existence and the categories by which we comprehend it are self-contradictory and incoherent.
>
> (in Parkes 1991: 91)

Martin is quick to point out that the writings of Nāgārjuna come from an entirely different historical background, and carry with them, on the face of it, very different purposes; where Nietzsche's aim was to reflect on and provoke the transformation of European culture in an age of incipient nihilism, Nāgārjuna's aim was release from the bondage of suffering caused by distortions in our understanding. Nevertheless the latter's method is equally concerned with what Martin describes as 'the dialectical deconstruction of the central categories by which language seduces us into accepting its "thought constructions" as realities' (ibid.: 99–100), and both thinkers converge in their deep practical concern for humanity, for, as Martin points out, Nāgārjuna and Nietzsche are both involved with the question of liberation from bondage. Moreover, for both thinkers, the critical thrust of their approach is not a form of anti-religious scepticism, but rather 'opens up unheard of creative possibilities latent within the human situation' (ibid.: 109), a reflection to which we will return in the final chapter. Similar considerations can be observed lying behind the more unlikely comparisons between Nietzsche and Taoism. At first glance Taoism might seem too mystical and esoteric to be placed in any useful relationship with Nietzsche, yet the Taoist emphasis on the conventional, and hence misleading, nature of language and on the need to return to a closer kinship with nature have interesting echoes in Nietzsche's own thinking, and, as the Chinese philosopher Chen Guying notes, there is about both Nietzsche and the Taoist Chuang-tzu a profound eccentricity and rigorous individualism which leads both to become severe critics of the respective historical traditions and values that they have inherited (see Parkes 1991: 115–29). The concept of individualism is also central to a comparison drawn by Roger Ames. 'There is no difficulty', he writes, 'in identifying a resonance between Nietzsche's will to power . . . and the classical Chinese notion of "virtuality" (de)' (ibid.: 146). The common ground here is the notion of self-transformation, with both the 'will-to-power' and 'de' pointing towards a superior ideal of self-cultivation and self-overcoming.

Comparative studies such as these arise out of a variety of motivations, and find a place in a diversity of philosophical agendas, but what is noticeable in many such cases is that Eastern thought is treated, not just as an interesting new discovery, like the revelation of a hitherto little-known Western thinker, but rather as a way of reflecting on the Western tradition itself. As Graham Parkes points out with regard to Nietzsche, such studies bear precisely on the issue concerning the 'end' of the Western metaphysical tradition, an issue with which Wittgenstein and Heidegger as well as Nietzsche are associated, and that the question of Nietzsche's attempt to extricate himself from the Western metaphysical tradition 'is lent greater force if his thought can be shown to be congruent with ways of thinking . . . stemming from totally alien traditions' (1991: 15).

HERMENEUTICAL APPROACHES

The hermeneutical approach, which I have nominated as the third phase in the East–West philosophical dialogue, emerges out of and in many respects is closely tied to the comparative approach. Like the latter it seeks to relate Eastern and Western ideas and movements, but it goes beyond the earlier goals of comparative studies by seeking more explicitly to engage the East in philosophical argument, and by developing a more reflexive and self-critical stance, thereby drawing such studies into contemporary debates about language and the limits of philosophical discourse. Thus, while on the one hand it demands awareness of cultural and historical differences, at the same time it encourages the embracing of Eastern thought within the orbit of current philosophical debate, seeking as far as possible to treat it as part of what Richard Rorty has called 'the conversation of mankind', rather than as some alien 'other' that needs an especially athletic intellectual leap in order to encounter it. Something of the tone of this hermeneutical approach is captured in the following remark by Eliot Deutsch:

> we are ready to pursue new goals in comparative philosophy and to bring comparative philosophy into the mainstream of *creative* thought – East and West. . . . Students ought to be able to study Asian thought simply for the purpose of enriching their philosophical background and enabling them to deal better with the philosophical problems that interest them.
>
> (Deutsch 1968: Preface, np)

Comparative studies have inevitably given rise to intriguing and awkward questions about the nature and validity of the comparative process itself, and in recent years this kind of hermeneutical reflexiveness has become such a hallmark of East–West studies that we are warranted in assigning it to a new and distinct phase. Where postulating parallels and drawing analogies between distinct traditions was typical of the comparative method, the hermeneutical approach goes beyond such comparisons by treating them in a self-critical way as integral to the proper task of philosophy, and by reflecting at the same time on the historical relativity of such a process. This sometimes involves mediating Western philosophical concepts through Eastern ideas rather than, as has traditionally been the case, the other way round.[17] It also involves the recognition of diversity, otherness, difference, without thereby separating out East and West into substantive and incommensurable enclaves. Thus Troy Wilson Organ, after dismissing the universalist approach as 'an intellectual smörgasbord' and as 'pathological eclecticism' (1987b: 7), claims that what is needed

> is not a world of one philosophy, but a world that appreciates diversity, a world in which philosophers in each culture have knowledge of and appreciation of other philosophies, a world in which there is a willingness to respect, to understand, and in some instances to assimilate ways of thinking and acting of other peoples.
>
> (Organ 1987b: 27)

Coming at the matter from the Eastern side, Zhang Longxi in his book *The Tao and the Logos* suggests that the justification for intercultural dialogue 'lies in the universality of the hermeneutic phenomenon', going on to argue that

> In bringing together historically unrelated texts and ideas, I attempt to find a common ground on which Chinese and Western literatures can be understood as commensurable, even though their cultural and historical contexts are different. The ultimate goal of such thematic comparisons is to transcend the limitations of a narrowly defined perspective and to expand our horizon by assimilating as much as possible what appears to be alien and belonging to the Other.
>
> (Zhang 1992: xiii–iv)

The task of this new hermeneutical approach to comparative philosophising, as Gerald Larson sees it, is 'to get away from talking *to* one another . . . in favour of talking *with* one another' (in Larson and Deutsch 1988: 18). At one level this has meant the increasing involvement of Asian scholars in this enterprise, and a growing number of occasions, face-to-face and literary, in which philosophers from East and West have worked in co-operation with each other. At another level it has involved the proliferation of philosophical studies in which Western philosophers engage directly with Eastern thinkers and movements, not in order to compare them but simply as part of the philosophical enterprise. In this latter spirit, the British philosopher Ray Billington examines certain fundamental existential questions in which issues are illuminated at various junctures by reference to Eastern philosophies, but avoids any attempt to elaborate systematic comparisons. Like other thinkers we have considered in this chapter he believes that 'Western philosophy is incomplete without its Eastern counterpart', and argues that the achievement of 'a comprehensive ontological perspective' requires drawing Eastern ideas such as those of Buddhism and Taoism into a close relationship with the more familiar language of existentialism (Billington 1990: xv and 210).[18]

Billington's approach implicitly calls into question the distinction between Eastern and Western philosophy, and in doing so confronts certain typical underlying attitudes in the traditions of the latter. Indeed an increasing number of writings in this area portray East–West comparative studies as challenging the familiar foundational claims of philosophy, and as part of a sea-change in which the rather narrow agendas of analytical philosophy are giving way to a more catholic attitude which embraces, *inter alia*, continental philosophy, feminism, and postmodernist criticism. This attitude is evident in an important recent work of David Hall and Roger Ames, *Thinking Through Confucius*, in which they attempt to formulate the idea of 'a single hermeneutical community serving as the context of viable philosophical dialogue' (1987: 5). Their aim is nothing less than the reconceptualisation of the nature of thinking: 'It is our belief that by thinking through Confucius we shall be able to make a contribution to the discussion currently defining the center of philosophical thinking' (ibid.: 9), and they make it clear that, while they are seeking to offer a 'truer' account of Confucius, thereby dispensing with some typical Western distortions, their chief aim is 'to promote the relevance of [Confucius'] vision as a potential participant in present philosophical conversations' (ibid.: 6). They give emphasis to differences at least as much as to similarities in their study, and indeed it is these very differences which, in their view, make a hermeneutical engagement possible.[19]

On more specific questions, discussions of issues concerning self, mind, consciousness, mind–body dualism, and the emotions, offer good examples of this hermeneutical approach, and increasingly Western philosophical debates concerning these issues draw on Eastern traditions without necessarily engaging in systematic comparisons, and without assuming any essential differences – or indeed identities – between the various traditions. A good example here is the question of the ontological status of the self or subject, an issue which has, of course, been of central philosophical concern in the West since Descartes. A number of thinkers have drawn on the Buddhist no-self doctrine in an attempt to illuminate this issue, and indeed, as we noted in Chapter 3 of this book, Jacobson has attempted to demonstrate that David Hume's theory of personal identity – namely that there is no substantial self, but only a 'bundle' of fleeting ideas and impressions – was not only remarkably similar to the Buddhist notion of consciousness (*citta*), but that there was strong circumstantial evidence for supposing that he was actually influenced by Buddhist thought in this as well as in other aspects of his philosophy. Whatever the merits of Jacobson's historical argument, the importance of the Buddhist concept of the self has become increasingly recognised in recent Western philosophical debates, and has frequently been drawn into attempts both to criticise traditional Western notions of the human subject and also to articulate new approaches. In a parallel way discussions of the issue of mind–body dualism have begun to draw on both Buddhist thought and the *Advaita Vedānta* philosophy of Sankara. For example, Paul Griffiths argues that the Buddhist concept of 'the attainment of [mental] cessation' has important implications for traditional Western concerns about the relationship between mind and body, and offers this as an example of philosophy as 'a trans-cultural human activity', which in turn has implications for questions of rationality and cultural relativism (1986: xvii). And David Loy, while eschewing any simplistic East–West polarity, proposes that the non-duality theory of Sankara represents an important 'challenge . . . to the dualist categories that have largely determined the development of Western civilisation since Aristotle' (1988: 13). Similar hermeneutical engagements involving both Eastern and Western thought have arisen in connection with traditional Western philosophical assumptions concerning the emotions, involving such issues as the relationship between reason and emotion, and the social construction of the emotions (see Marks and Ames 1995).[20]

There still remain important questions, of course, about the extent to which this new hermeneutical enterprise continues to be conducted on Western grounds, and hence the degree to which Eastern thought systems are being refracted through the lenses of Western philosophical categories. The first point to be made is that such methodological questioning has itself become a characteristic feature of this new phase, and the hermeneutical self-reflexiveness of much of recent East–West comparative work, over questions such as inter-cultural interpretation, and ideological distortion, has been explicitly factored into debates which are central to contemporary philosophy. A good example of this is the Sixth East–West Philosophers' Conference which was held in Honolulu in 1989 on the topic of 'Culture and Modernity'. Long gone are the days in which the conference searched earnestly for a grand synthesis, and instead there was, according to the convener Eliot Deutsch, a celebration of difference and of otherness, and a keen awareness of the dangers of cultural imperialism. Amongst the main issues addressed in the conference was that of cross-cultural communication, and the related questions of rationality, relativism, and incommensurability. These issues have come to occupy the centre ground of contemporary philosophical debates, and, as demonstrated in Honolulu, it is clear that the question of the East–West communication of ideas is directly relevant thereto. It was shown to be equally relevant with regard to the issue of modernity debated at the conference, for here too the serious philosophical – as opposed to historical – attention paid to Eastern thought also serves to challenge one of the foundational claims of Western philosophy, namely that the European Enlightenment concepts of rationality and progress have universal validity, a challenge which, as we have emphasised, has been implicit in orientalism from its very beginnings. Although many of the papers remained obdurately rooted in the Western philosophical tradition, the conference demonstrated that East–West studies are no longer perceived as a specialist and somewhat esoteric corner at the edge of philosophical space but a task that relates intimately to it at all levels.

There was little appetite evident, either at this conference or in most other contemporary work in this area, for a renewal of the search for a global or perennial philosophy. Yet in one sense the great syncretistic ideals of Leibniz and of his Renaissance forebears are with us once again, only transformed by history and refined by philosophical debate. While the search for a grand synthesis of East and West, a cosmopolitan world-philosophy, is surely *passé*, many of the cultural and conceptual boundaries which once seemed so forbidding have come to be seen as pathways rather than barriers to communication, and the recognition of difference and plurality is seen as an essential prerequisite for the formation of a global philosophical community. This ideal may still seem a long way off, but orientalism has made serious contributions to issues concerning the scope and limits of European philosophy, and has thereby helped to make it possible for the Western philosophical tradition to move beyond its traditional boundaries.[21]

Chapter 8

Religious dialogue

THE CHALLENGE OF ORIENTALISM

If the East has preyed only on the margins of twentieth-century Western philosophy, its influence has penetrated much more deeply into the field of religion and theology. The role which Buddhism played in the Victorian crisis of faith has been re-enacted and enhanced in many respects in our own epoch, producing an impact on the West which, according to the theologian Geoffrey Parrinder, is 'one of the most significant events of modern times', amounting to nothing less than another 'Reformation' (1964: 12 and 22). The kind of intellectual issues and social forces which beset the theologians and churchgoers of the Victorian period have, of course, continued to expand and proliferate in the twentieth century, and the East has increasingly been drawn into the fray, a power at once threatening and redeeming, both an unwelcome stimulant to an already agonising debate, and an inspiration for renewal and a model for future developments. According to the Jesuit William Johnston 'we are now entering a new religious era, an era in which the most important event will be the meeting between Christianity and the great religions of the East' (1981: 70). In this chapter we will investigate this epochal 'meeting', and examine the role of Eastern thought in the religious debates of recent times, sketching in outline the historical development of a remarkable dialogue that has begun to take place between hitherto alien and often embattled religious traditions.

To begin with we need to recognise the broad cultural scope of this phenomenon, and see the extent to which the religious consciousness of the West has been penetrated by the East well beyond boundaries of intellectual and theological debate. A brief comparison with the previous era will serve to underline this. As we noted earlier, the publication of Arnold's *The Light of Asia* and the foundation of the Theosophical Society, amongst other factors, helped to generate an interest in Eastern religions that went well beyond the confines of oriental scholarship and theological argument, but few people in the nineteenth century sought openly to adopt or to profess an Oriental creed. In the twentieth century, by contrast, Eastern religions have exerted an increasingly powerful influence over an ever-growing number of people in the West, and many have sought therein either a supplement or an alternative to the Christian and Jewish beliefs whose attractions for them have waned. For many it seems that the West has undergone a spiritual crisis, a deeper and more pervasive one than the crisis of faith associated with the Victorian era, one in which the loss of Christian belief has often led, not to atheism or agnosticism but to a spiritual vacuum into which the religions of the East, along with other spiritual movements, have been eagerly drawn. Old certainties have decayed, and new substitutes associated with science and with material welfare have proved unsatisfying, and in these circumstances it is not altogether surprising that many have sought in the oriental path a way to the renewal and the deepening of the spiritual life. C. G. Jung saw this as part of a wider contemporary malaise which is manifested in a growing concern with the psychic, as opposed to the material, aspects of life, pointing to 'the fascination which psychic life exerts upon modern man' (1961: 51). It was not just a passing fad, therefore, but expressed a deep need which 'arises undoubtedly from psychic energy which can no longer be invested in obsolete forms of religion' (ibid.: 239).

Whatever we may think of Jung's diagnosis, the fact remains that in the inter-war period when he formulated these opinions Eastern religions had begun to have an impact on the personal lives of many individuals in Europe and America. The theologian Harvey Cox speaks of 'a wave of interest among Americans in Oriental spirituality whose scope and intensity is unprecedented in the history of American religion', a wave which 'seems both broader and deeper than the ones that preceded it' (1977: 9). The sense of spiritual crisis and the search for alternatives to Christianity reached something of a crescendo in the 1960s and 1970s, a period which saw a remarkable outburst of popular interest in Eastern religions. In his account of this phenomenon, Jacob Needleman speaks of a 'spiritual explosion', and writes that 'men are moving away from the forms and trappings of Judaism and Christianity, not because they have stopped searching for transcendental answers to the fundamental questions of human life, but because that search has now intensified beyond measure' (1972: xi). Movements deriving from Hinduism, such as the International Society for Krishna Consciousness, drew many youngsters into its ranks, Indian gurus such as the Maharishi and Bagwan Rajneesh attracted large numbers of devoted followers, Transcendental Meditation became widely practised, and the books of writers such as D. T. Suzuki and Alan Watts provided many with the spiritual sustenance that they craved. In subsequent years the intensity of this orientalist phenomenon has waned somewhat with the decline of the popular counter-culture movement, but its scope and range have continued to widen with the establishment of many new meditation and retreat centres, and with ever-increasing numbers of books on Eastern spirituality coming onto an apparently insatiable market.

The Christian churches themselves have been faced, not only with the rise of secularism and the challenges of scientific rationalism and Marxism, but also, as a result of the unprecedented migration of peoples in recent times and the interaction of cultures through the global media, with the growing presence in their midst of alternative, and to many highly attractive, modes of religious belief and expression, a situation described by the Protestant theologian Paul Tillich as the 'dramatic encounter of world religions' (1963: 12). The demands made by competition from religious alternatives from the East have been complemented and reinforced by the decline of Western colonial power and by the growth world-wide of national and cultural awareness which has forced Christianity in its Western embodiment to acknowledge the existence of a plurality of faiths, a fact which has enormous theological consequences. Such plurality, and the disruptive cultural consequences which it implies, would be a severe challenge for any culture or religion, but it is especially acute for Christianity with the long-felt sense of its own uniqueness, allied with the West's belief in its own cultural superiority. As Parrinder puts it: 'The challenge is acute for the Semitic or Western religions, Christianity, Judaism and Islam. They have been accustomed to think of themselves as supreme, in religion and culture, possessing the highest truths and the oldest and best philosophy' (1962: 21). And according to the theologian David Tracy, 'we are in fact approaching the day when it will not be possible to attempt a Christian systematic theology except in serious conversation with the other great ways' (1990: xi).[1]

COMPARATIVE STUDIES AND THE UNIVERSALIST OUTLOOK

The response to this challenge on the part of Christianity has been varied, some looking upon the rising tide of interest in the East as a dangerous threat, others greeting it as an opportunity for self-appraisal and renewal. Some theologians, such as the Protestant Karl Barth, have sought in the face of the threat of rising pluralism and theological liberalism to reinforce traditional doctrines and to reiterate the time-honoured beliefs concerning the exclusive nature of Christian revelation and the unique historical mission of Jesus Christ, a position recently reiterated by Pope John-Paul II. Others have sought to enter into dialogue and in varying degrees to arrive at some kind of accommodation with Eastern religions, at one extreme allowing an exchange of ideas for the sake of good neighbourliness, at the other opening up the possibility of some form of doctrinal syncretism. Harvey Cox, for example, sees Buddhism as an especially dangerous challenge to Christian faith, and while recognising the need for debate and mutual understanding, sees the new wave of oriental enthusiasm as a serious threat to Christianity. Paul Tillich, unlike his fellow religionist Karl Barth, has tended towards a more accommodating position, arguing that the recent encounter with the East is in many respects not new and represents part of a long tradition of doctrinal re-evaluation through dialogue with other faiths, that it is part of 'the rhythm of criticism, counter-criticism, and self-criticism throughout the history of Christianity' (1963: 89). The philosopher of religion Ninian Smart is also a strong advocate of dialogue. He speaks of the emergence of a global culture, a 'planetary world [which] harbours unparalleled opportunities of mutual fecundation and challenge', in which traditional religious loyalties must inevitably give way, not to a global blending of identities but to what he calls 'interactive pluralism'. He is one of the growing number of Christian thinkers who have ceased to regard the oriental invasion as a sinister threat but rather as the opportunity to revitalise the Christian tradition, for 'we have to live in the tensions which are created by pluralism and change [and] use those tensions creatively' (1981: 285 and 294).

One of the earliest manifestations of this pluralistic outlook, and of the problems it raises, is to be found in the growth of *comparative religion*. Its history, from the point of view of Eastern religions, could be traced back to the Romantic period, but a more realistic starting point can be located in the work of Friedrich Max Müller. His Royal Institution lectures of 1870, later published under the title *Introduction to the Science of Religion*, and his popular Hibbert Lectures entitled *On the Origin and Growth of Religion as Illustrated by the Religions of India* (the latter delivered in Westminster Abbey to an audience of 1,000!), was amongst the first systematic attempts to set out a rationale and methodology for the study of comparative religion. Like so many intellectuals at that time, he was under the influence of the climate of positivism and evolutionism, and he saw this new discipline as a 'science of religion', based on 'an impartial and truly scientific comparison of . . . the most important religions of mankind' (1893: 26), one which arose naturally out of the then well-established field of comparative philology. He regarded the subject, therefore, as neutral from a doctrinal standpoint for, as he put it, 'science wants no partisans' (ibid.: 28), but at the same time he was sensitive to the fact that his advocacy of this new discipline would antagonise many Christians who were not only unwilling to apply the methods of science to their faith, but who saw in it a subtle threat to the unique status of their religion. They had every reason to be apprehensive. Max Müller himself remained a professed Christian, but in the course of his lectures he enunciated views about the universality of the religious instinct and of revelation which implicitly called into question certain fundamental principles of Christian theology, claiming for example that 'there is a faculty of faith in man independent of all historical religions', and that 'the word of God [is] revealed in the heart of man' (ibid.: 13 and 51).

The field of comparative religion continued to grow and proliferate in the late nineteenth and early twentieth centuries. In Germany the work of such scholars as Paul Deussen and Rudolph Otto helped to generate wide scholarly interest in this field, and a distinguished tradition of comparative studies in India was initiated in 1899 with the publication of *Comparative Studies in Vaishnavism and Christianity* by Brajendranath Seal. In 1904 the great Welsh orientalist T. W. Rhys Davids was appointed Professor of Comparative Religion at Manchester University, and subsequently the discipline has been integrated into academic institutions and university curricula throughout the world. Amongst the more orthodox Christians the goal was often seen more or less explicitly as the ultimate triumph of Christianity, whereas the more liberal-minded Christians involved in such studies looked forward to a convergence, even a synthesis, of the world's religions. Early in the century the American theologian A. J. Edmunds, in his comparative study of Buddhism and Christianity, expressed the hope that work such as his 'will finally have the effect of making them respect each other, and hasten the day when mankind will be one' (1908: 9).[2]

Many of the central themes and problems that wind their way through research and writings in this area are to be found in embryo in Max Müller's pathmaking work. One of the most prominent of these themes is, once again, that of *universalism*. We examined this idea in the last chapter where we saw that it meant the search for a truly global outlook that might be formed through some kind of synthesis between Eastern and Western intellectual traditions, based on the belief that 'at the deepest level of human wisdom there is a unity of vision embracing all mankind' (Ward 1957: 77). A parallel search in the realm of religious belief obviously bears close resemblances to this philosophical goal, and not surprisingly overlaps historically and conceptually with it to some degree. Both clearly represent a yearning to unite humankind at a time when on the one hand there continues to be tension and conflict between peoples, yet on the other hand the peoples of the earth are in many respects coming closer together. What gives the search especial urgency in theological circles is the fact that, while the Christian religion is concerned with ultimate truths, there is at the same time an evident diversity of religious views, even within Christianity itself. This 'scandal of plurality', as W. E. Hocking called it, might be agreeable to philosophy where ultimate truth is itself a philosophical question, but in the case of religion such diversity presents an acute dilemma: if there are so many divergent claims to ultimate truth, then perhaps none is right. This is an issue that has beset Christianity ever since the Reformation fragmented the unity of the mediaeval church, but the invasion of Eastern religions in more recent times has given the problem added depth and urgency.

There has been a number of Western intellectuals who, outside the realms of professional theology, have elaborated the universalist theme. One of the most famous of these was Aldous Huxley (1894–1963) who, as we noted above, became disillusioned with Christianity and repelled by the materialism of Western civilisation, and turned to the study of Buddhism and *Vedānta* philosophy, and to the study of the world's mystical traditions. He had a long and close involvement with oriental religions, and from an early age read widely in the world's religious scriptures, as well as, later, in writings of orientalists such as Conze, Suzuki, and Heinrich Zimmer. After settling in the United States in 1937 he became closely associated with the Vedānta Center in California where, with Christopher Isherwood and Gerald Heard, he edited the magazine *Vedānta and the West*.[3] Much of Huxley's writing can be seen as evidence of his belief that in the religious thought of India lay the solutions to many of the modern ills of the West – its tendency towards aggression, its excessive rationalism, its moral confusion – and his wide reading in mysticism led him to the belief that beneath the surface variety of the world's religious traditions there lay a core of truth, and that this core was most closely identifiable in the *Vedānta* philosophy of India. In his famous work, *The Perennial Philosophy*, which was first published in 1946, and which carries more than just an echo of Leibniz, he collected together the sayings of many mystics and philosophers over the ages and from a variety of traditions, illustrating the belief in the ultimate unity of the human with the divine reality, and thereby seeking to demonstrate the fundamental agreement and essential unity of all the world's major religions.

The quest for some universal, perennial wisdom that transcends the particularities of creeds and sects is often associated with so-called 'esoteric' traditions, a term which usually serves to designate types of secret spiritual knowledge and practice which lie beyond or beneath institutional religious orthodoxies. The sources of such 'hidden' traditions are usually perceived to lead back to the ancient world, often to the East, and in the late nineteenth and early twentieth centuries esotericism proved to be a powerful magnet attracting many who sought an alternative to prevailing orthodoxies, especially Christianity and scientific rationalism, taking the form both of a renewed interest in the occult and in the mystical traditions of the East. Two distinguished, though now somewhat neglected, twentieth-century thinkers who have been closely associated with the study of esoteric teachings, are René Guénon (1886–1951) and Fritjof Schuon (1907–), both of whom acquired extensive knowledge of Eastern religions, and expounded a global religious outlook which drew heavily on the traditional teachings of Hinduism and Buddhism. Guénon was a trenchant critic of various contemporary views and fashions with regard to the East. He rejected the 'intellectual myopia' of academic orientalism which views the East as an extinct curiosity, seeing it on the contrary as an essential component of the West's cultural and intellectual history, and second, as a vital perennial spiritual force. He rejected too the positivistic interpretations of scholars such as Max Müller, and was scathing about the 'Westernised Vedānta' of Huxley *et al.* that had become popular in the West, and the 'distortions' and 'idle imaginings' of the Theosophists (Guénon 1945: 317). He urged instead a return to the pure original teachings of the *Vedānta*, teachings which could only be acquired through 'an assimilation of the essential modes of Eastern thought', through a rediscovery of these ancient doctrines which, though once the common property of mankind, are now represented most conspicuously by Hinduism (see Guénon 1945: 334–7). Schuon, a follower of Guénon, was equally 'fundamentalist' in his outlook, and in his book *The Transcendent Unity of Religions* he argued that all religions are, at the level of their esoteric teachings, identical, a level where, in all faiths, a direct participation in the divine reality is attainable. Like Guénon, his overriding aim was to combat what he saw as the debilitating secularism and materialism of the modern world, and to recover the perennial spirituality that the West had lost, but which was preserved, so he believed, in the mystical traditions of India. Another, but more widely influential, figure associated with esotericism is Rudolf Steiner, once a member of the Theosophical Society but who in 1912 broke away to set up his own movement, the Anthroposophical Society. He was a man with wide philosophical sympathies who sought to draw close links between Buddhist and Christian spirituality, insisting that:

> As to the study of Eastern wisdom, one can only be of the opinion that this study is of the highest value, for the Western peoples have lost a sense for the esoteric while Eastern peoples have retained it. . . . Only in this esotericism can blossom the harmony of science and religion.[4]

MYSTICISM AND UNIVERSALISM

Both universalism and esotericism have in their turn often been associated with *mysticism*, which has proved an attractive idea to those Western thinkers who have sought a universal bond underlying the surface differences between Eastern and Western religions. The philosopher W. T. Stace, for example, has argued that mysticism represents the central core of *all* religions, and hence is that which most closely binds Christianity to the religions of the East. William James, in his famous analysis of religious experience, concluded that 'In Hinduism, in Neoplatonism, in Sufism, in Christian mysticism, in Whitmanism, we find the same recurring note, so that there is about mystical utterances an eternal unanimity' (1902: 410).

Several important thinkers have subsequently elaborated this thesis in one form or another. The first and most celebrated is the German Protestant theologian and historian of comparative religion, Rudolf Otto (1869–1937), who took a close lifelong interest in Hinduism and Buddhism, studied Sanskrit, and paid two extended visits to the Indian sub-continent. His work on the Indian religious traditions has been overshadowed by the popularity of his *Idea of the Holy*, a work in which he argued that the sense of the numinous was the universal basis of religious belief, but he also wrote extensively on comparative religion and discussed Hindu spirituality in depth. The thesis of a universal stratum of mystical experience that transcends cultural boundaries is most fully elaborated by Otto in *Mysticism East and West* (1926). In this work he offered a detailed comparison between two mystics, the Hindu Sankara and the Christian Eckhart, and, while accepting that 'there are within mysticism many varieties of expression', he attempted to demonstrate that 'in mysticism there are indeed strong primal impulses working in the human soul which as such are completely unaffected by differences of climate, of geographical position or of race'. His broad conclusion was that a 'deep-rooted kinship . . . unquestionably exists between the souls of the Oriental and the Occidental' (1957: xvi–xvii).[5]

Two further important, though in many ways contrastive, thinkers who found in mysticism a significant point of comparison between Eastern and Western spirituality are Martin Buber (1878–1965) and Pierre Teilhard de Chardin (1881–1955). Buber, a friend of the Indian poet and mystic Rabindranath Tagore, was an early advocate of the idea of dialogue between Eastern and Western religions, particularly with regard to the comparative study of mysticism, and like so many of his contemporaries his interest in the East was in large part a response to the perceived spiritual crisis of the age. The extent to which Eastern thought helped to shape some of Buber's most characteristic ideas is not always appreciated. Thus, in his famous contrast between 'I–thou' and 'I–it' relationships he drew on the Taoist idea of *wu-wei* to elucidate the relationship in which the other is 'let be', and according to one commentator 'the dialogue with Taoism remained of central importance to him throughout his life' (Friedman 1976: 415). In addition to this he was also concerned with linking both Zen's interest in immediately lived experience and Indian spiritual traditions with Jewish Hasidic mysticism. Teilhard de Chardin's interest in Eastern mysticism is even less well known, in spite of the fact that he spent many years in China. According to the theologian Ursula King who has sought to correct this misunderstanding, Teilhard, though critical of aspects of Eastern religion, 'looked for seeds of renewal and inspiration' in the East, and admitted that 'my own individual faith was inevitably peculiarly sensitive to Eastern influence' (in King 1980: 13 and 14). In spite of his belief that European Christendom represented 'the principal axis of anthropogenesis' (Teilhard de Chardin 1958: 211), he advocated 'spiritual collaboration' between Christianity and China, stressing the need for Christians to 'rethink' their own religion in the light of experience of world religions, and expressing the hope that in China he would discover 'a reservoir of thought and mysticism that would bring fresh youth to our West' (quoted in King 1980: 123). From the early 1930s he increasingly engaged in comparative studies of Eastern and Western mysticism, and, on his return to France in 1946, devoted himself to the examination of Eastern mystical traditions. One of the fruits of this research was an essay entitled 'The Spiritual Contributions of the Far East'. There he made quite clear his debt to oriental religious traditions, and while rejecting what he saw as the monistic pantheism of the East in favour of Christian theism, he nevertheless anticipated a future synthesis which would take forward and go beyond both 'the road of the East' and 'the road of the West'. King draws special attention to the universalising influence of the East on Teilhard who, without the experience of the East 'would not have developed . . . the same perspectives of unity, universality, and courageous searching for a spirit of one earth which ultimately transcends both East and West' (ibid.: 88).[6]

Questions have been raised from various perspectives about this sort of approach. The term mysticism itself is of course notoriously elusive, and the idea of employing it as a means of cross-cultural comparison has been questioned by philosophers such as S. T. Katz who rejects the contention that mystics from different traditions are in some deep sense having the 'same' experience, since in his view 'mystical experience is over-determined by it socio-religious milieu' (1978: 46). Moreover, from an ideological perspective it has sometimes been argued that the use of the term 'mysticism' in this crucial role underscores the West's hegemonic role in relation to the East in so far as it tends to canonise the belief that there is something inherently mystical about Eastern thought by

contrast with the typically rational essence of Western thinking, thereby privileging the latter over the former. For a variety of reasons, some echoing the foregoing, the whole universalist approach has declined in popularity in recent decades.
On the one side it has been rigorously contested by those religionists who see it
as a threat to the integrity of the Christian faith. For example, R. C. Zaehner,
while recognising the need for mutual understanding and dialogue between religions, has emphasised the differences between Eastern and Western mysticism,
and has vehemently rejected any notion of creating a synthetic world religion,
proclaiming that for him 'the centre of coherence can only be Christ' (1970: 16).
On the other side, there are those who reject this form of universalism, not out
of credal commitment, but out of the conviction that universal understanding
and harmony can be pursued as much through difference as through identity.
Thus, for example, F. J. Hoffman claims that 'differences between religions are at
least as important as similarities', and that diversity is not a weakness but 'a sign
of great human vitality rather than as something to be homogenized' (1987: 3).
From a more philosophical standpoint there are those who argue that universalism in general fails to take account of historical differences and of the relativising factor of cultural and historical context, and that religious experience in
particular is always culture-relative. In an even broader perspective, univer-
salisms of all sorts have come to be viewed as part of the 'totalising' discourse of
Western cultural imperialism and hence as tending to suppress cultural differences, and though the universalising tendencies within the East–West religious
dialogue have drawn profitable attention to the multiplicity of forms of religious
belief, they have sometimes been seen to be seeking to transcend these in the
(unspoken) name of only one of the faiths concerned. We will return to these
issues in the final section of the book.

THE INTER-FAITH DIALOGUE

The decline of ambitious universalistic designs has not, however, marked the
decline of East–West comparative religious studies, but rather has led to a new
phase which can be summed up in the word *dialogue*, a concept which, as was
noted in Chapter 6, has attained something of a cult status in recent times.
Where once arrogance, dogma, and missionary preaching prevailed, the mood
has changed and the Christian churches have increasingly in recent years
become committed to the value of dialogue, first between the different Christian
sects, and then with the religions of the East.

As we shall see, the term 'dialogue' can mean any one of a number of different things, but first it would be useful to investigate the historical origins of this
new phase. The idea of a face-to-face exchange of views between religionists
from the two ends of the earth can be traced back to the World's Parliament of
Religions in 1893 when representatives of most of the world's major religions
gathered together in one place for the first time, and which according to its
organiser succeeded in 'striking the noble chord of universal human brother-

hood' (Barrows 1893: viii). The mood of the Parliament was reflected in a number of subsequent writings, including the book entitled *Buddhist and Christian
Gospels* by the theologian A. J. Edmunds, who, as we noted earlier, sought to
establish a climate of mutual understanding in which 'mankind will be one'
(1908: 9). This conciliatory approach was somewhat premature, however, and
for a while after the initial euphoria of the Parliament it seemed that Christians
were most often interested in dialogical exchange solely for the furtherance of
missionary aims. During the early decades of this century much interest was
shown in the neo-Hegelian view that Eastern religions were not precisely false
but were rather to be seen as preparations for the coming of Christ, and hence
all investigations of Eastern religions tended to be seen in that light. The Scottish
Protestant missionary John Farquar, for example, published a book in 1913 in
which, while urging Christians to make an attempt to understand Eastern religions, he argued that Hinduism finds its fulfilment in Christ in a way exactly
analogous to Christ's fulfilment of the law and prophets of Judaism: Christ is
'the crown of the faith of Hinduism' (1930: 458).[7]

   The inter-war years saw a rapid growth in inter-faith dialogue, both
East–West and intra-Christian, with conferences and congresses proliferating in
both Europe and America. In 1921 Rudolf Otto founded the Inter-Religious
League (*Religiöser Menschheitsbund*) which aimed at the facilitation of inter-religious
understanding, and in the same period the International Congress of the World
Fellowship of Faiths and the World Congress of Faiths were founded with similar
aims. The latter was brought into being through the inspiration of the explorer
and mystic Sir Francis Younghusband, and is still active today in promoting
inter-religious dialogue. The idealistic spirit of these initiatives was captured at
that time by the American philosopher of religion J. B. Pratt, who explicitly set
on one side the question of the truth or falsity of the respective claims of
Christianity and Buddhism, arguing instead that 'Both possess much truth, and
neither one is wholly beyond illusion' (1928: 746), and predicting that they would
come close together in dialogue without coalescing. A similar spirit is evident in a
pamphlet entitled 'A Vision of Christian and Buddhist Fellowship in Search of
Light and Reality' by the Protestant missionary Dwight Goddard in which he
advocated a dialogue on points of doctrine and worship, and argued that the
contemporary world desperately needed a mingling of Christian social awareness with Buddhist personal piety.[8]

   This new openness to dialogue and recognition of plurality is nowhere better
reflected than in the series of meetings known as the *Eranos* seminars that were
held every summer at a villa overlooking Lake Maggiore from 1933 to 1969.
These meetings were international gatherings, the primary purpose of which
was the task of finding common ground between Eastern and Western religious
thought, though they broadened out later to include discussions over the whole
range of subjects relating to the history and psychology of religious experience,
and gave an important stimulus to the study of comparative religion. C. G. Jung
was a key figure in setting the agenda and tone, but it was not an explicitly

Jungian gathering and the seminars were attended by a wide range of scholars including the physicist Erwin Schrödinger, the anthropologist Paul Radin, the theologians Martin Buber and Paul Tillich, the orientalists Caroline Rhys Davids and D. T. Suzuki, and the historian of comparative religion Mircea Eliade. The latter was an especially significant figure in the pursuit of dialogue between East and West. Born in Romania in 1907, he spent four years as a young man studying philosophy and yoga in India, and wrote his PhD on the subject of yoga philosophy, and his later work ranges far and wide over the world's religions and mythologies. In his writings can be seen an underlying criticism of modern Western culture, similar to that found in the writings of the French anthropologist Claude Lévi-Strauss, and a deep concern to overcome what he saw as the narrowness of the European outlook. In this vein, he warned that

> Western culture will be in danger of a decline into a sterilising provincialism if it despises or neglects the dialogue with the other cultures. Hermeneutics is Western man's response – the only intelligent response possible – to the solicitations of contemporary history, to the fact that the West is forced . . . to this encounter and confrontation with the cultural values of 'the others'.
>
> (Eliade 1960: 10)[9]

This need to confront the cultural values of 'the others' has evidently become a matter of some urgency in the second half of this century. Something of the mood of this new outlook, and the epochal significance it evokes, is captured in Tillich's remark: 'Not conversion, but dialogue. It would be a tremendous step forward if Christianity were to accept this' (1963: 95), and in Leroy Rouner's claim that inter-religious dialogue 'is as formative for Protestant theology today as the struggle with Darwinism was in an earlier generation' (in Küng and Moltmann 1986: 114). As we have noted, the growing consciousness of religious plurality since the middle of the century, and the realisation that the world no longer recognised without question Christianity's unique divine mandate, represented a serious challenge to the Church's authority. This had important theological implications, raising questions such as whether there is salvation outside the Christian Church, whether the Christian revelation of divine truth is unique and exclusive, and whether Christian doctrine is subject to development. It has also provoked practical questions such as the propriety of using Buddhist meditational techniques in prayer, or Hindu scriptures in the liturgy, and the place of Eastern religions in Western educational curricula and in communal school worship. The need for dialogue has, in some minds, been made more urgent by the growing recognition that the political and the theological considerations are not wholly distinct, and that Christians have through their doctrinal exclusivism and missionary fervour been, as Rouner puts it, 'responsible for colonizing and even subjugating people of the Third World' (in Küng and Moltmann 1986: 109).

The growth of consciousness of oriental faiths amongst Christians is of course part of a wider movement in the post-war period towards a more ecumenical outlook. As far as the Protestant churches are concerned this has taken most evident shape in the World Council of Churches which was founded in 1948. It was dedicated to the renewal and the reunification of the specifically Christian churches, but at its Fourth General Assembly in 1968 it committed itself to a widening of its remit to include dialogue with non-Christian religions. In 1970 the first multilateral meeting on religious pluralism was held in Beirut under the auspices of the WCC, and a year later a new sub-unit, Dialogue with Men of Living Faiths and Ideologies, was set up, leading to an ongoing debate concerning the relationship between Christianity and other religions, and the practice of dialogue at various levels within the churches. Almost simultaneously, the Roman Catholic Church was undergoing a similar transformation in its attitude towards non-Christian religions. Ever since the Council of Florence (1438–45) the Church of Rome had maintained the principle that 'outside the Church there is no salvation', but at the Second Vatican Council (1962–5) the emphasis shifted dramatically to the principle that 'God desires the salvation of all mankind'. The Council proclaimed that, while the Church has a unique role in mediating mankind's salvation, God works for salvation in and through all religious traditions, though in the case of non-Christian faiths in an implicit and anonymous way. It even went so far as to proclaim that God has revealed himself in many ways, and that other religions often reflect a ray of that truth which enlightens all human beings, a teaching which authorised and encouraged Catholics to engage in dialogue with non-Christians.

EXCLUSIVISM, INCLUSIVISM, PLURALISM

We need to examine more closly now the outcome of these earlier initiatives. The spectrum of attitudes towards dialogue is customarily divided into three categories or 'paradigms'.[10] The first is that of *exclusivism* which is characterised by the traditionalist belief that Christ, or Christianity, offers the only valid path to salvation, and that other religions are therefore false and idolatrous. The second paradigm is *inclusivism* which, in Gavin D'Costa's words, 'affirms the salvific presence of God in non-Christian religions while still maintaining that Christ is the definitive and authoritative revelation of God' (1986: 80). Finally, *pluralism* denotes an attitude of neutrality to the relative claims of religions, maintaining that Christianity has no higher or more exclusive claim to truth than non-Christian faiths. These three categories are not themselves mutually exclusive, of course, but overlap in various ways, and within them, too, a range of differing and competing views can be discerned. Looked at overall, the debate is in active and continuous process, and we can do little more, therefore, than give a still snapshot of a controversy which is in ever-quickening motion.

Standing behind the exclusivist position is the dominating figure of Karl Barth (1886–1969). His attack on the liberal tradition of Protestant theology which developed in the nineteenth century led to what became known as 'Neo-Orthodoxy', and involved a reaffirmation of the uniqueness of the Christian revelation. Barth contrasted 'religion', which is a human product to be found in many different forms, non-Christian as well as Christian, with 'revelation' which he thought was to be found exclusively in the person of Jesus Christ, and which was not shared with any other religious traditions. The consequence of this view is not so much to condemn other religions as to marginalise them, and hence to render dialogue pointless for theological purposes. An eminent Protestant who adopted Barth's overall theological viewpoint, but who nevertheless felt it necessary to develop an understanding of Oriental thought and culture, was the Dutchman Hendrik Kraemer (1888–1965). He was in fact trained as an orientalist, having spent twelve years as a missionary in Indonesia before becoming Professor of the History and Phenomenology of Religions in Leiden. While affirming the uniqueness and sufficiency of Christ's Incarnation, and vehemently rejecting all forms of relativism, he saw the practical necessity for promoting a religious understanding of the East, seeing the meeting of East and West as 'one of the cardinal events of our time', and something of great significance for the future: 'The real play has not yet begun', he prophesied, 'it is in the process of being staged' (1960: 12 and 14). Not surprisingly he rejected universalism, but he thought it essential that understanding between East and West, between Christians and non-Christians, should be enhanced, and that dialogue could lead not only to mutual understanding and toleration, but also to greater self-understanding and self-clarification on the part of Christian theology. Kraemer's approach to dialogue, therefore, was circumscribed and based on a conservative theological foundation, but it did at least point to the need for an active engagement between East and West, one which he thought could be of benefit to Christians in helping to remove some of the worst vestiges of colonial intolerance and arrogance, and which in some respects represents the first steps towards the articulation of a philosophy of inter-religious dialogue.

The move towards a more *inclusivist* position is evident in the writings of the Catholic oriental scholar R. C. Zaehner. In his early work he stood firm against the view that there is a fundamental doctrinal unity underlying all the great religions (here he was particularly concerned to refute Schuon), and clung to the conviction that 'Jesus Christ fulfils, not only the law and the prophets of Israel, but also the prophets of Iran and the sages of India' (1958: 184). Nevertheless, following the Second Vatican Council, he took a more liberal line, arguing that the various faiths can usefully begin to listen and to learn from each other, and that 'Indian religions have something to teach us [which] can help us to deepen our own religion and open up insights that were only dimly perceived before', going so far as to admit that 'There is much in Eastern religions that is still valid' (1970: 19 and 20). However, the inclusivist view proper goes somewhat further than this, maintaining that, while the central claims of Christian faith remain unchallenged, the divine truth may also be found in other religions. The Catholic theologian William Johnston, for example, asks whether non-Christian religions may 'possess aspects of the truth that we have not seen', and whether 'they will even cast light on the mystery of God and Christ', concluding that 'if we wish to grow in truth we must listen to other people' (1981: 5). A leading member of this category is Karl Rahner (1904–84), perhaps the most influential Catholic theologian of this century, and indeed from a Roman Catholic standpoint the chief architect of the inclusivist paradigm. His position, clearly more radical than that of Kraemer or Zaehner, is that God works salvifically everywhere, while nevertheless maintaining the special role of the Christian dispensation in God's design, arguing that though non-Christian religions find their fulfilment in Christ, they mediate the word and saving grace of Christ to non-believers of good will. Unlike Kraemer, he was in no sense an orientalist, but his 'liberal' theological position had a powerful impact on the deliberations of the Second Vatican Council, and on the surge of interest in dialogue with non-Christian religions that followed in its wake.

Another theologian of world standing who has taken up more explicitly the challenge of Eastern religions, and who has adopted a more radical stance than the previous thinkers on the question of East–West dialogue, is Paul Tillich (1886–1965). After visiting Japan in 1960 he became deeply interested in the idea of *satori* (enlightenment), and saw in the training provided by Zen Buddhism methods that could be incorporated into Christian spirituality. Already, with his idea of God as 'ultimate concern', rather than as a quasi-human person, he had forged a link with oriental religions, and he recognised in Buddha as well as in Christ an anti-religious figure who represented not a founder, but a challenger to religious institutions. He came to the conclusion that revelation is not confined to Christianity but is a universal human phenomenon, each religion embodying an answer, however fragmentary, to the problem of human existence. He accordingly rejected the missionary role of the Church in favour of dialogue through which the historical biases and distortions of the Christian religion could be opened to self-criticism.[11]

The inclusivist position provokes a number of awkward theological issues, issues arising out of the recognition of the existence of a plurality of religions, and the refusal simply to condemn non-Christian religions as false and beyond the pale, and leading to questions about the uniqueness of the Christian message. In addition, it raises deep philosophical questions concerning the very nature of knowledge and truth, for, as the theologian Leonard Swidler puts it in his discussion of inter-religious dialogue, 'our understanding of truth and reality has been undergoing a paradigm shift', one which leads from an absolutist to a hermeneutical standpoint where all statements about reality are seen to be 'historical, praxial or intentional, perspectival, language-limited or partial, interpretive, and dialogic' (in Swidler *et al.* 1990: 59). Some of these awkward issues are outflanked by the position known as *pluralism*, according to which 'no single religion can be considered somehow normative or superior to all others. All religions are in their own way complex historically and culturally conditioned human responses to the one divine reality' (Netland 1991: 26). In recent years this kind of view has attracted a growing number of supporters amongst the leading theologians of both Catholic and Protestant persuasions, including John Cobb, Don Cupitt, John Hick, Paul Knitter, Hans Küng, Raimundo Panikkar, Wolfhart

Pannenberg, Geoffrey Parrinder, Ninian Smart, Wilfred Cantwell Smith, and David Tracy. These and many like them have protested against the lingering arrogance, as they see it, of the inclusivist position, and the one-sidedness of dialogical exchanges so far entered into, and hold with Tracy that religious pluralism is no longer a contentious outsider but 'is now our true home' (Tracy 1990: 39). They have also tended to view the growth of pluralism at the present time as representing a radical transformation in Christian theology, Paul Knitter speaking of a 'paradigm shift' in Christian attitudes towards the unique status of Christianity, and John Hick of a 'Copernican revolution' in which Christian teachings are displaced from their hitherto perceived central position in relation to other religions. Clearly in the arena of such a lively debate we should not expect unanimity amongst thinkers such as these, for the issue of pluralism strikes at the very heart of traditional orthodoxy, and provokes some of the most agonising and divisive questions that contemporary theology has to face.

John Hick is a good example of a pluralist thinker who has engaged in dialogue with Eastern religions in order to re-examine his own theological presuppositions. He adopted an explicitly pluralistic position in 1973 with the publication of *God and the Universe of Faiths*, where he came to the conclusion that there is no privileged position from which the various claims of the world's religions can be judged since all human experience is radically interpretative, arguing that all religions are true in so far as they provide authentic channels for salvation. For him, as for many contemporary thinkers, pluralism is therefore no longer seen as a scandal to be overcome, for the scandal lies in the Church's traditional teaching that there is no salvation outside the Church; rather, pluralism is a condition to be celebrated, for it is through differences that one's own perspective is broadened and enriched, and that the vestiges of Western Christian imperialism can be cast off.[12] In a similar vein, the philosopher of religion Ninian Smart, who has written extensively on Eastern religions and their relationship with Christianity, insists that Buddhism should be a mandatory study for all students of religion, for it challenges the assumptions of and provokes a critical self-awareness amongst those of the Christian faith. It challenges, *inter alia*: theism as a necessary basis for religion, the necessity of worship and the sense of the numinous, the patriarchalism of Judaeo-Christian teaching, the idea of a Lawgiver as necessary for morality, and the idea of an enduring soul-substance as a necessary condition for personal salvation (see Smart 1992: 3). The radical Catholic theologian, Hans Küng, has also been active in recent years in the field of inter-religious dialogue and, like Smart, strongly advocates 'Christian self-criticism in the light of other religions' (1987: xvii). Though not going all the way with Hick's egalitarianism, he nevertheless has come to the conclusion that 'The Christian possesses no monopoly of truth', and that while openness to other religions does not lead to the abandonment of Christian commitment or to a purely relativist position, it does imply 'a constant readiness to learn, so that the old faith is not destroyed but enriched' (in Küng and Moltmann 1986: 121 and 125). Another important contemporary theologian who can also be considered a pluralist is John B. Cobb who has gone further than most in examining the theoretical basis of dialogue, and who, like Smart and Küng, is convinced of the transformative benefits of the East–West dialogue. His advocacy of process theology has led him to believe that, in the words of Paul Ingram, 'Christianity needs to continually submit itself to creative transformation through dialogue with non-Christian ways' (Ingram and Streng 1986: 85). For Cobb, the recognition that 'the Christian claim does not contradict the core affirmations of other traditions' opens up the possibility that 'we will all be purified and enriched' (in Swidler *et al.* 1990: 13 and 18).[13]

It is hardly surprising that such considerations have led Küng, Cobb, and others into a philosophical maze over the question of *relativism*. Both adamantly reject any relativistic implications that may seem to flow from their pluralist viewpoint. Thus, Küng rejects what he calls the 'cheap tolerance of "anything goes"' and 'untenable indifferentism' (1987: xviii). The concession that Christianity does not have a monopoly of truth does not imply for him the corollary that all religions are *equally* true, with its implication that strictly speaking none is. Cobb rejects, too, what he calls 'the corrosive acid of relativism' (in Swidler *et al.* 1990: 4). He recognises the potential threat to the peace of mind of the faithful implicit in the open-ended dialogue he advocates, but at the same time he holds that each religion can affirm the special truth of its own position, while at the same time acknowledging the truth in that of others, thereby preserving the notion of truth while avoiding unproductive confrontation of alternative doctrines. On the question of comparisons between the Christian concept of God and the Zen concept of emptiness, for example, Cobb takes the view that 'in the full complexity of reality, so far exceeding all that we can know or think, "emptying" identifies one truly important aspect, and "God" another', and he asks: 'Would acknowledging that possibility contradict fundamentally what it is most important to either Zen Buddhists or Christians to assert? I think not. But to come to that conclusion does require that one rethink the insights on both sides' (in ibid.: 6). Whether such attempts to preserve some notion of objective truth, while acknowledging religious and cultural diversity, prove successful is a matter of dispute, but it is clear that East–West dialogue has provoked a debate with deep philosophical and theological implications which are destined to preoccupy thinkers, whether Christians, Buddhists, or otherwise, for a long time to come, and that many long-established positions are likely to be radically altered in the process.[14]

The issue of relativism, with its disturbing postmodernist connotations, brings the East–West religious debate sharply into contemporary focus. What, then, is the current situation? As in the case of the philosophical debates we examined in the previous chapter, there is some evidence that dialogue is leading beyond dialogue into truly hermeneutical terrain where there is no longer a self-conscious counterpointing of East and West, of Christian and Buddhist, but rather an engagement with fundamental issues which integrate themes from Eastern and Western sources without the artificial polarisations that characterised the earlier stages of this process. An indication of this development is to be found in works such as Francis Clooney's *Theology after Vedānta*. Here the author seeks to open up paths to a new kind of theology by avoiding any attempt to enter into a generalised dialogue between *Vedānta* and Christianity, but rather by engaging in a 'selective reading of certain Advaita texts and a reconsideration of certain Catholic theological texts [from Thomas Aquinas] thereafter' (Clooney 1993: 3). Such an approach, he argues, resists making any generalisations about religion, or using the study of texts to reach wider conclusions or 'sensational new teachings', but concentrates instead on the immediate benefits to be gained from the reading of theological texts, from whatever tradition they come. This new hermeneutical approach can be seen in other recent writings such as the symposium *The Christ and the Bodhisattva*. Here too the ambitious aims of earlier dialogical endeavours have been scaled down, and the agonisings over philosophical issues of truth and relativism replaced by the desire to exchange ideas from the respective traditions within a modest compass and with more limited aims and expectations. A strong historical consciousness is evident in works such as these, and a recognition of ineradicable differences. As the Introduction to the latter book expresses it:

> To claim that all religions in the final analysis teach the same truth is to run the risk of ignoring the complexity and richness of the doctrines of the religions and of disregarding the significance of their historical and cultural context.
>
> (Lopez and Rockefeller 1987: 32–3)

There is also a recognition in some quarters that dialogue itself is a questionable category, that it carries the taint of its imperialistic ancestry, and needs to be subjected to ideological scrutiny. After all, its motivation and its impetus seem to be largely Western, and thus theologians such as Joseph Kitagawa are led to ask whether the idea of dialogue is merely used 'as a gimmick to camouflage the bankruptcy of the historical missionary approach of the Western Churches' (1990: 11).

This does not mean that dialogue is at an end. For many it has hardly begun, and work of a more traditional comparative kind is still being done; the Confucian–Christian dialogue, for example, has been initiated only relatively recently.[15] At the grass-roots level, too, there are many Christians for whom dealing in the religious concepts and practices of Buddhism and Hinduism remains profoundly alien and threatening. But the movement towards and beyond dialogue which I have narrated in this chapter may, in spite of the recent rise of fundamentalisms, be pointing towards a new era in the relationship between the world's religious faiths, one in which, as the historian of religions Wilfred Cantwell Smith suggests, 'young people of today . . . are beginning to see and feel themselves as heirs to the whole religious history of humankind' (1981: 18).

DIALOGUE IN SPIRITUAL PRACTICE

So far the emphasis has been on the purely theological and philosophical aspects of the inter-faith dialogue, but in concluding this chapter we need also to take note of some of its outcomes in terms of spiritual practice. Here the growing interest in Eastern meditation methods amongst Christians calls for special attention. According to William Johnston, this phenomenon amounts to 'a revolution in Christian spirituality', whereby 'Christians who dialogue with Buddhists are discovering that levels of consciousness previously dormant are opening up to the presence of God', a movement which, he prophesies, 'will dominate Christian experience in the future' (1981: 23). Another Catholic theologian, Heinrich Dumoulin, who has worked for many years in Japan and has taken a close interest in Zen, regards Far Eastern meditation as a necessary counterbalance to Western man's obsessive 'rushing from achievement to achievement', whereby he has 'lost the harmony of his self and the inner balance of stillness and motion', and indeed as 'the prerequisite of all higher spiritual life'. Though staying close to biblical roots, he continues, 'the faithful Christian may gain a better and deeper understanding of Far Eastern spirituality, while the contact with Far Eastern meditation can help him toward a fuller realization of biblical truth' (1974: 13, 12, and 16). More intrepidly, attempts have been made from time to time to adapt some of the Eastern scriptures for Christian use, and to integrate selections and chants from the Vedantic literature into Christian liturgical practice. One of the earliest pioneers in this field of East–West spiritual confluence was the French Benedictine monk, Dom Henri le Saux (1910–73) who in 1950 founded a Hindu–Christian ashram in Tamil Nadu, South India. There he lived the life of a Hindu *sannyāsin*, and wrote extensively on Hindu contemplative traditions, and on the lessons which Christian contemplatives could learn from the Indian orientation towards the inner life. His ashram was a practical expression of these ideals where he sought to integrate Hindu spiritual practices with Benedictine monasticism. The leadership of le Saux's ashram was taken over after his death by an English Benedictine, Dom Bede Griffiths (1906–93), who not only sought to integrate Hindu yoga practices into his own monastic tradition, but also, following the inspiration of the early Jesuit missionaries in China, attempted to interpret Christianity in Upanishadic terms. In his book *The Marriage of East and West* he speaks of the need to engage in dialogue with the Hindu traditions, a process which 'is not a compromise with error, but a process of enrichment by which each religion opens itself to the truth to be found in the other religion' (1982: 25). Another Benedictine who should be mentioned in this context is Dom Aelred Graham who, in his provocatively entitled book *Zen Catholicism*, urged that the directness and simplicity of Zen practices have great merit as against what he saw as the often rigidly artificial and self-conscious programmes of Christian spiritual practice.

Perhaps the most famous proponent of an inclusivist-inspired integration between Christian and Eastern monastic and spiritual practices is the American

Trappist monk, Thomas Merton (1915–68). His writings have been widely read and admired, and, prior to his fateful journey to the East, he had already become familiar with Eastern religions and had written a number of books and articles in which he sought to illuminate his own spiritual journey and the tradition of Christian contemplation and mysticism by means of the teachings and practices of oriental sages. He believed that Zen in particular 'offers us a phenomenology and metaphysic of insight and consciousness which has extraordinary value for the West' (1961: 254), and while emphasising the wide divergences in tradition and outlook between East and West, he nevertheless undertook a close study of Buddhism, and found in Buddhist methods of meditation, with their emphasis on mindfulness, on the attainment of mental clarity, and on the dispelling of illusions, ways which could complement and enhance the traditional Christian contemplative practices, ideas which have been taken up and developed more recently.[16] In pursuit of his ecumenical path, Merton left his monastery in 1968 to undertake a journey to South-East Asia in order to build bridges between Christian and Asian monasticism, meeting the Dali Lama and other religious leaders, and travelling, in his own words, 'as a pilgrim who is anxious to obtain not just information, nor just facts about other monastic traditions, but to drink from ancient sources of monastic vision and experience' (quoted in Burton *et al.* 1974: xxiii). In a lecture given in Calcutta he spoke of the need to engage in dialogue as part of the process of renewal of Christian monasticism, insisting that

> we have now reached a stage of (long-overdue) religious maturity at which it may be possible for someone to remain perfectly faithful to a Christian and Western monastic commitment, and yet to learn in depth from, say, a Buddhist or Hindu discipline and experience.
>
> (ibid.: 313)[17]

Chapter 9

Psychological interpretations

NEW PSYCHOLOGICAL PERSPECTIVES

In 1951 the Buddhist writer Christmas Humphreys wrote: 'in the world of mind, including that Cinderella of mental science, psychology, the West has more to learn from Buddhism than as yet it knows' (1951: 223). In fact, as Humphreys was well aware, the learning process had already begun, for in the inter-war years a number of thinkers had started to speculate about the possibility of opening out Western psychology to Oriental influences, and indeed even in the nineteenth century the potential of Buddhism for psychological insight had been recognised. In the period since these words were written the process of accommodation between ancient Eastern ideas and the newly emerging psychological disciplines has grown and proliferated in a number of ways. Earlier suspicions and prejudices about the irrelevance of the 'mystical Orient' to rigorous psychological concerns are now giving way to genuine respect for the insights of ancient Asian cultures such as that of Tibetan Buddhism, and a willingness to engage in some sort of dialogue. According to the psychologist Guy Claxton: 'things have changed rapidly over the last few years. . . . Concern with the impact of the spiritual traditions [of the East] on psychology and psychotherapy is now legitimate and psychological meditators can come out of the closet' (1986: 8), a view confirmed by another psychologist John Pickering who believes that 'Buddhism is indirectly contributing to a shift in the balance between reduction and holism' within psychology (1995: 31). It would be an exaggeration to say that psychological discourse has been profoundly altered by this new East–West hermeneutical process, and, in European universities especially, Eastern psychology has received little attention. Nevertheless, its insights have had a significant impact in a number of different areas.

Amongst the best known points of impact is undoubtedly that of psychotherapy, for although orthodox Freudian psychoanalysis has not been concerned with any cross-cultural perspective, a number of individuals and schools which have moved away from the founding father have attempted to build bridges between their own disciplines and practices on the one hand and the ideas and techniques of the ancient East on the other. This is commonly thought to represent the limit of Eastern influence on Western psychology, but, as I shall attempt to show in this chapter, the East has begun to have an impact as well on academic psychology, and as psychology has sought to break out from the confines of the behaviourist methodology it has not only discovered interesting psychological material in the oriental traditions, but has in some respects drawn them into the whole process of its self-reorientation and recontextualisation. Some psychologists have indeed already begun to speak of new developments within their discipline that will draw on the two complementary traditions of East and West. Pickering, for example, holds that within the contemporary reappraisal of psychology, and the belated recognition of the importance of the study of consciousness, Buddhism will play an important role 'in the development of a more pluralistic psychological science' (1995: 23), and the psychologist John Crook insists that 'we need to go beyond the duality of East and West . . . to create a genuine East–West psychology' (in Crook and Fontana 1990: 22). Thus we see once again that what is involved here is the perceived need for renewal and reconstruction, a need that arises out of the belief that, in this particular instance, Western psychology is in some way limited or even fundamentally flawed. At the very least, according to some, the encounter between East and West leads to the demand for self-criticism, for, as the psychotherapist S. Ajaya (Allan Weinstock) points out, 'By juxtaposing the systems of East and West, the hidden assumptions in each emerge, along with their implications for developing therapeutic processes' (1983: 10). A similar point is made by Claxton who argues that 'Buddhist teachings provide a mirror that reflects the insights of . . . psychologists back onto our selves, and that urges us to apply those insights reflexively' (1986: 313).

For some time a vigorous debate has been in progress about the fundamental assumptions and methodology of psychology, and while it is true that in recent decades there has been a development away from behaviourism as the dominant model towards one which takes account of the cognitive processes of the mind, for some in the field this falls short of a basis for an adequate understanding of the human person.[1] Even more inadequate, according to such critics, are the models of the mind drawn from neuroscience and from artificial intelligence, both of which have exerted a powerful influence on recent psychological thinking, and which equally fail to address adequately questions concerning consciousness and self-awareness. As John Welwood puts it:

> Western psychology has so far failed to provide us with a satisfactory understanding of the full range of human experience. . . . It appears that we have largely overlooked the central fact of human psychology – our everyday mind, our very real, immediate awareness of being.
>
> (Welwood 1979: xi)

According to this view, therefore, Western psychology has so far failed to furnish us with a picture of the whole human personality, a picture which can only begin to be completed by taking into account and integrating the conscious, subjective side of the personality, the inner life of awareness and self-awareness, and by linking these factors within a conceptual scheme which goes beyond mind–body dualism to a holistic view of the human person. It is in this area that ideas from Eastern systems, with their long-established commitment to introspective studies, and their emphasis on the inseparability of mental and physical functions, have been thought to have most to offer and where they have been seen as a most powerful challenge to prevailing Western orthodoxies. Speaking in a symposium on the relationship between modern neuroscience and ancient Buddhist psychology, the Tibetan scholar Robert Thurman suggested that while the West has been adept at understanding the 'hardware' of the mind, it has much to learn from the sacred traditions of India and Tibet which have long investigated the mind's 'software'. He goes on to argue that the failure of the Indian civilisations to develop 'outer sciences', often represented as a failure of intellect, is far less a failure, and far less portentous in practical and political terms, than the West's failure to develop 'inner sciences' (see Goleman and Thurman 1991: 57–9).

It might be thought that this supposed shortcoming in terms of the 'software' or of 'inner science' is not shared with those therapeutic traditions which descend from Freud, for here surely there is a commitment to the investigation of the world of consciousness and self-awareness. But in this field too we hear an increasingly loud voice of protest against what is seen as an all-too-narrow Western approach which, as in the case of academic psychology, demands to be revitalised by the spiritual energies of the East. Thus the strictly Freudian approach has been accused of being too reductive and too biologically slanted, leaving out or explaining away large areas of human mental life, especially those connected with religious experience and expanded states of consciousness. It has also been accused of emphasising too strongly the role of the ego, thereby reinforcing a largely Western notion of the individual as an independent competitor in an essentially hostile social environment. In both these respects Eastern models of the human subject have seemed to be more promising, and to offer a fuller account of the human person. Buddhism in particular is increasingly being looked on, not just as a religion, but as a system for understanding and promoting personal growth, and as such it is seen as offering a much more positive idea of the nature of mental health, and a much richer repertoire of methods for attaining a sense of mental balance, well-being, and personal fulfilment. The American psychologist Daniel Goleman, for example, contends that 'the model of mental health one finds in Eastern psychologies – and Tibetan Buddhism is the example *par excellence* – really overreaches and extends, in a very powerful way, our own notion of mental health' (in Goleman and Thurman 1991: 91).

The model of human personality which is emerging from these speculations can be summed up as one which takes a holistic and contextualised view of mental life: holistic in the sense that it is able to integrate consciousness, brain, and behaviour without lapsing back into the reductionisms of either materialism or dualism; and contextualised in that it is able to understand selfhood as situated within and interactive with a broad social and material frame. It is also a model which promises to draw closer together the rigour and objectivism of scientific understanding and the demands of a renewed subjectivity or spirituality. Oriental insights, especially those of Buddhism, appear increasingly to have an important part to play in these developments.

How far back, historically, can these developments be traced? Attention is inevitably trained most sharply on Buddhism, though it is worth recalling that the development of the idea of the unconscious in the nineteenth century in post-Romantic thinkers such as C. G. Carus and Eduard von Hartmann owes something to the influence of Hindu Vedantism. Hints of the psychological significance of Buddhism appear in Nietzsche's writings, as we noted earlier, and Thomas Tweed points out that in the late nineteenth century Buddhism seemed to many to be 'compatible with the latest findings in the emerging "science" of psychology' (1992: 104). But it was the orientalist Caroline Rhys Davids (1858–1942) who, in her book *Buddhist Psychology*, was the first to develop this theme *in extenso*. Drawing on half a century of debate amongst Buddhist scholars in which concepts such as *anātta* (no-self) and *nirvāna* had increasingly been detached from any metaphysical or religious assumptions, she subjected Buddhist ideas to an analysis which focused on human experience rather than religious belief, arguing that 'Buddhist thought is very largely an inquiry into mind and its activities', and that the self-examination carried out by means of Buddhist meditation practices had much to teach the West (1914: 9). D. T. Suzuki, too, played an important role in bringing out the psychological, rather than the religious, significance of Buddhism. It is not always appreciated that, while obviously drawing heavily on his native Japanese traditions, his thinking owes a lot to that of William James, not so much because of the latter's interest in Eastern thought, but because of James's pragmatic approach to religion, his emphasis on experience rather than metaphysical theory, and most especially because of his phenomenological analyses of mysticism. Suzuki taught that the very quintessence of Zen lay in the experience of *satori* (enlightenment), laying emphasis in his early works on the *kōan* (paradoxical question-and-answer method used in Zen training) which he presented chiefly from a psychological angle.

PSYCHOTHERAPY AND MENTAL HEALTH

The inter-war period saw the first attempts to draw explicit links between Eastern traditions of thought and the new field of psychotherapy. As early as 1918, when psychotherapy was still in its infancy, the orientalist Friedrich Heiler suggested that Zen meditation should be seen, not just as an adjunct to a religious cult, but as a mental health technique whereby 'the temporary suspension of thought and feeling serves as a nerve-strengthening, psychotherapeutic means' (quoted in Dumoulin 1963: 276). A few years later Oskar Schmitz drew detailed parallels between psychoanalysis and yoga, and shortly after that the Berlin neurologist and psychiatrist J. H. Schultz formulated a technique called 'Autogenic Training', which was based in part on the Eastern meditation practices that were beginning to become known in Europe at that time. Initially it was intended not as a method of therapy but rather as a technique of relaxation, but subsequently it came to be seen to have specific clinical applications, particularly in the alleviation of psychosomatic disorders. Schultz encouraged his patients to develop 'meditative exercises' in which they visualised bodily states and processes in order to promote serenity and self-healing, methods which could be considered the first attempt to adapt Eastern psychosomatic techniques to a Western therapeutic context. The method has been thoroughly researched over the years and is still widely practised both as a technique of mind control and in the treatment of a number of chronic medical conditions.[2]

Similar visualisation techniques were being developed at that time by the Italian psychiatrist Roberto Assagioli (1888–1974). His system, known as 'Psychosynthesis', was acknowledged by him to have many sources of inspiration including William James, Pierre Janet, Freud, and Jung, but in addition to these, he was deeply influenced by the Jewish, neo-platonic, and Christian mystical traditions, and had early on developed an interest in Eastern mystical traditions via the Theosophical Society. Furthermore, in the 1920s he came into contact with Keyserling and his School of Wisdom at Darmstadt which, as we noted in Chapter 6, promoted the idea that the West had become narrowly materialistic and one-sided, and needed to tap into the spiritual resources of the East. He was well versed, then, in the world's mystical traditions as well as in the ancient writings of the East, and as a consequence he became especially interested in the investigation of what he called 'superconsciousness' and in the formation of the 'higher self', an aspect of the human personality which he thought contemporary theories ignored, but which had been recognised and cultivated in the mystic traditions of both East and West. The main technique used for the exploration and cultivation of such higher states of consciousness was visualisation, and meditation in general, he believed, offers a technique which 'helps the patient to an expanded consciousness and impersonal experience and knowledge', and which 'will continue to develop into a systematic technique which can aid men towards their goal of developing their highest psychic potentialities' (Assagioli 1975: 314–15).[3]

The most celebrated East–West explorer in the field of psychotherapy was undoubtedly C. G. Jung (1875–1961), though his debt to Eastern ideas in the formulation of his own has often been obscured by his followers for fear that it would tarnish his scientific credentials.[4] He too developed a strong interest in oriental ideas and practices in the early decades of the century and sought to integrate oriental insights into his own thinking. His interests in this field span almost the whole range of the most important Eastern religious systems, including Taoism, Mahāyāna Buddhism in its various forms including Zen, and Indian Yoga, and date back to his teenage reading of Schopenhauer who was a considerable influence on the shaping of Jung's outlook. He began his investigations into Eastern religions in earnest in 1909 when, still a close colleague of Freud, he sought to expand his psychological insights by studying myth and religious symbolism on a comparative and world-wide basis, an inquiry which led to the postulation of his theory of the collective unconscious, which in turn led to his estrangement from Freud. By the time he came to write his two early major works, *Psychology of the Unconscious* (1912) and *Psychological Types* (1921), he had acquired a basic understanding of Hindu, Buddhist, and Taoist ideas and mythology which he closely interwove with Christian symbols and symbols from Western cultural sources. His interest in the Orient became more precisely focused in the 1920s through contact with Herman Keyserling's School of Wisdom, and then by contact with several distinguished orientalists including Heinrich Zimmer and Richard Wilhelm. It was the latter's translation of the Taoist alchemical text, *The Secret of the Golden Flower*, which rekindled Jung's enthusiasm for Eastern thought and provided the opportunity to embark on an investigation of the relationship between Eastern thought and Western psychology. Though he never developed his thinking in this field in a systematic way, the psychological commentary he wrote for this text at the translator's instigation was the first of a number of short pieces, including introductions to translations of *The Tibetan Book of the Dead*, the *I Ching*, and to Suzuki's *Introduction to Zen Buddhism*, as well as studies of yoga and meditation, in which he expanded and refined his ideas. His three-month visit to India and Ceylon (now Sri Lanka) in 1938 was the culminating point in his oriental researches, and even though the main focus of his intellectual interest subsequently turned elsewhere, he retained his interest in Buddhism right to the end of his life.

In his commentary on *The Secret of the Golden Flower* Jung set out explicitly to construct 'a bridge of psychological understanding between East and West' (1978: 57), and to set up a hermeneutical dialogue with the text whereby he sought to mediate its 'strange' ideas through his own developing psychological theories. By using this technique he claimed to discover in this ancient text an unexpected 'agreement between the psychic states and symbolisms of East and West', which not only helped to provide confirmation for his theory of the collective unconscious, but also indicated that the goal of becoming a conscious and fully realised person 'unites the most diverse cultures in a common task' (ibid.). The idea of self, the psyche, as something irreducible, and whose full development is the goal of psychic life, was at the heart of Jung's thinking, and in his reading of this and other Eastern texts, he claimed to find confirmation of this. In his commentary on *The Tibetan Book of the Great Liberation*, for example, he underlined the emphasis in that work on the fundamental reality of mind or consciousness, and its teaching that all things, including material reality, are in the final analysis mind-made, insisting that the text 'bases itself upon psychic reality, that is upon the psyche as the main and unique condition of existence' (Jung 1978: 109).

Jung was careful to distinguish between what he took to be the psychological significance of such ideas and their articulation in terms of metaphysical or religious beliefs, insisting that 'I quite deliberately bring everything that purports to be metaphysical into the daylight of psychological understanding . . . [and]

strip things of their metaphysical wrappings in order to make them objects of psychology' (1978: 51). What Jung claimed to be seeking from the East, therefore, was not a new metaphysical system to replace Christianity or science, but a way of finding fresh evidence and support for his own view about the centrality of the psyche, and for his belief that the psyche is a kind of inner cosmos, corresponding to the outer world, one which can be systematically explored. In the West, he believed, we have adopted an extraverted attitude which has on the one hand enabled us to acquire unprecedented knowledge of and power over the physical world, but on the other hand has led us to neglect or to underestimate the importance of the inner life. Here the ancient philosophies of the East, with their strongly introverted orientation, have much to teach us. Furthermore, he argued, the spiritual crisis that the West is plainly going through at the present time, manifested both by the loss of a sense of individual meaning and by the periodical outbreak of violent social and political storms, is a consequence of this unbalanced psychological condition in the West, one which needs to be counterbalanced by re-emphasising the introverted and spiritual values to be found in the East.[5]

It might be supposed that, given his belief in the need for the West to compensate for its extraverted tendencies, Jung would be eager to adopt the methods of yoga and to integrate them into his therapeutic practice. He was, however, very circumspect on this matter, even to the extent of disappointing some of his admirers by his unnecessarily extreme caution. Some critics, as we shall see later, have gone further and argued that his polarity between an extraverted West and an introverted East, along with his emphasis on essential differentiations between European and Asian cultures, helped to provide a conceptual framework for racist ideas in the 1930s. Be that as it may, he was wary of the artificiality and the possibly dangerous consequences for Westerners who, with their ingrained acquisitiveness and impatience, would simply grasp at the superficial aspects of yoga techniques, seeking to 'put on, like a new suit of clothes, ready-made symbols from a foreign soil, [and to] cover up [their] nakedness with the gorgeous trappings of the East' (Jung 1959: 14). Moreover, Eastern techniques of spiritual transformation had grown over many millennia out of an ancient culture, very different from the West whose spiritual development 'has been along entirely different lines from that of the East and has therefore produced conditions which are the most unfavourable soil one can think of for the application of yoga' (1978: 85).

In spite, therefore, of the high esteem in which he held Eastern thought, a spiritual achievement which in his view was 'one of the greatest things the human mind has ever created' (1978: 85), he did not advocate the emulation of its practices by Westerners, and indeed saw the urge to take over Eastern ideas and practices as typical of the Western desire to appropriate, to control, and to manipulate. 'Study yoga', he urged, 'you will learn an infinite amount from it – but do not try to apply it' (1978: 82). What can be gained from it, in his view, is the inspiration to develop our own, Western, form of yoga: 'we must build on

our own ground with our own methods' (ibid.: 111). The techniques of psychoanalysis represented one such method, and while he avoided making direct borrowings from   yoga, and claimed never to have used Eastern meditation
techniques as such in his practice, he found in such techniques, and the ideas
underpinning them, models which emboldened him to develop his own. Thus,
his method of active imagination, a visualisation technique whereby a patient
follows through a sequence of fantasies in a consciously deliberate way, was, he
thought, a modern Western version of certain ancient Tantric yoga techniques.
Similarly, his use of the mandala symbol[6] and of expressive drawing and painting in general, though developed in the course of his own self-analysis, found
support and confirmation from similar symbols and methods that had long been
used in the East. Indeed the whole individuation process, which was at the core
of Jung's analytical method, was seen by him as equivalent to the methods of
yoga in so far as both, in his view, sought to integrate the unconscious with the
conscious.

Jung was, indeed, aware of significant differences between his own approach
to the human psyche and the traditional spiritual philosophies of the East; the
Advaita Vedānta teaching of non-duality was unacceptable to him, and he maintained that the Buddhist belief in the possibility of complete redemption from
suffering was an illusion. Nevertheless his writings in this area represent an
important and influential attempt to engage in a hermeneutical dialogue with
the ideas of the East, and provide an extended example of the way in which
Eastern ideas are interpreted and exploited for Western polemical purposes.[7] For
this reason I have spent some time with Jung, but it is important to record that a
number of others in this field, some of comparable repute, have made expeditions Eastwards and have explored Eastern concepts and practices as a way of
illuminating their own.

The most important of these to be noted is Erich Fromm (1900–60). Like
Jung he was at pains to link his analytical work and ideas with broad moral and
social questions, and his emphasis on freedom, responsibility, and the quest for
meaning, rather than on the unconscious, set him apart from Freudian orthodoxy. In the 1950s he became acquainted with Suzuki, and through him developed a close interest in Zen. In 1957 he participated with Suzuki and others in a
conference on Zen and psychoanalysis which led him, as he put it, 'to a considerable enlargement and revision of my ideas', specifically with regard to 'the problems of what constitutes the unconscious, of the transformation of the
unconscious into consciousness, and of the goal of psychoanalytic therapy' (in
Fromm *et al.* 1960: viii). He makes it clear that his study of Zen Buddhism 'has
been of vital significance to me and, as I believe, is significant for all students of
psychoanalysis' (ibid.: 78). In spite of Fromm's disagreements with Jung, there
are many interesting parallels between their approaches, for like Jung he
acknowledged the differences between Zen and psychoanalysis, while at the same
time recognising that the one could cast illumination on the other, especially in
so far as their goals were virtually identical, insisting that 'the knowledge of Zen,

and a concern with it, can have a most fertile and clarifying influence on the theory and technique of psychoanalysis', and that 'Zen thought will deepen and widen the horizon of the psychoanalyst' (ibid.: 140).

The premise from which Fromm began, however, was not psychoanalysis as such but rather 'the spiritual crisis which Western man is undergoing in this crucial historical epoch' (Fromm *et al.* 1960: 77) – a further point of contact with Jung. He characterises this crisis as ' "malaise", "ennui", "mal de siècle", the deadening of life, the automatization of man, his alienation from himself, from his fellow man and from nature', noting that such a 'crisis' has been identified by many thinkers from Kierkegaard and Marx to Tillich and David Riesman (ibid.: 78–9). Psychoanalysis represented for Fromm a characteristic expression of this crisis, and an attempt to find a solution. Moreover, it was not to be construed as a purely medical procedure whose aims are tied to conventional concepts of 'illness' and 'cure', but rather had the wider aim of achieving self-knowledge and self-transformation. It is at this point that the affinity with Zen Buddhism becomes evident, and where it is possible for psychotherapy to draw on the latter's traditional ideas and practices. At the heart of the therapeutic process, he argued, is the growth of self-awareness, the expansion of consciousness, and of self-realisation, and it is precisely this goal which is also at the heart of Zen Buddhism, for Zen is 'the art of seeing into the nature of one's being; it is a way from bondage to freedom' (ibid.: 115). It is not, as has often been wrongly supposed, a form of world-denying narcissism, nor a means towards a trance-like state in which reality is dissolved, but rather a wakening up to and a direct confrontation with one's present condition. *Satori* (enlightenment) is not an abnormal state of mind, nor, as Jung was inclined to suggest, an oriental art which is remote from Western experience, but rather 'the immediate, unreflected grasp of reality . . . the realization of the relation of myself to the Universe' (ibid.: 134–5). Moreover, the Zen path of enlightenment, in so far as it resembles the psychotherapeutic process, can help us better to understand the latter by virtue of its emphasis on *experiential*, rather than *intellectual*, knowledge, for it 'transcends the kind of knowledge and awareness in which the subject-intellect observes itself as an object, and thus it transcends the Western, rationalistic concept of knowing' (ibid.: 111). Another way of putting this is that Zen, like psychotherapy, confronts directly the existential condition, for it both raises the question 'What am I?' and encourages emancipation from any kind of external authority; 'it means to wake up, to shed fictions, and lies, to see reality as it is' (ibid.: 129).

The connection between Zen and existentialism is made quite explicit by Fromm, and has been echoed by several other thinkers. The French psychiatrist Hubert Benoit, for example, who had a considerable impact on early Western students of Zen, maintains that Buddhism, with its emphasis on the human condition and on the sources of mental suffering, has much in common with existentialism. For him Zen enlightenment represents simply 'the becoming conscious of existing', and 'seeing into one's own nature', a method which is characterised by suddenness, spontaneity and the non-intellectual process of 'emptying-out'

(Benoit 1955: 25). The existential theme is even more evident in the work of the Swiss psychoanalyst Medard Boss who pioneered an approach to psychotherapy called *Daseinanalysis*, a method based on the philosophy of Martin Heidegger. In the 1950s he made two extended visits to India where he met a number of sages who impressed him as 'living examples of the possibility of human growth and maturity and of the attainment of an imperturbable inner peace', and came to the conclusion that 'we should call them psychotherapists rather than philosophers' (Boss 1965: 187 and 184). He had long been highly critical of the Western materialist outlook in general, and in particular of what he saw, from his existentialist standpoint, as the absence in Western psychology of any real understanding of the person as a conscious subject: 'Western psychology tells us absolutely nothing about the subjectivity of the subject, the personality of the person and the consciousness of the mind . . . [it] can see man only as a thing, or as a conglomeration of objects' (1965: 10). Like Jung he discouraged the straightforward adoption of yoga techniques, and warned of the possible dire psychological consequences for Westerners who 'attempt to sink into meditation in the Indian fashion' (ibid.: 186), but at the same time he thought that the analyst had much to gain personally from Zen, especially in terms of the ability to develop a receptive and meditative state of mind, the ability to listen to 'the root-melody of all being' instead of 'a straining of the intellect' (ibid.: 190). Two other distinguished analysts who have been involved in cross-cultural interchange are Karen Horney, who attended, along with Erich Fromm, Suzuki's lectures at Columbia, and who visited Japan to observe the life of a Zen monastery; and R. D. Laing, who spent some time with Buddhist teachers in Sri Lanka, Thailand, and Japan; but to my knowledge neither expedition bore any other than personal fruit.[8]

Many of the themes which we have been dealing with in the last few pages, such as the need to complement Western with Eastern approaches to the study of the human person, and the contribution that the traditional techniques of the East can make to the practice of psychotherapy, are evident in humanistic psychology. One of the salient characteristics of this school is its aim of approaching psychology in a radically novel way, and while it can certainly be seen as a development out of more orthodox traditions, at the same time it represents a powerful and sustained critique of those orthodoxies. This critique touches on many of the issues that we have just been dealing with, and it is not surprising, therefore, to discover that humanistic psychologists have actively and explicitly drawn on Eastern models in their attempt to articulate a distinctive viewpoint, with the stress for example on receptivity, non-interference, spontaneity, and the immediate experience of the here-and-now. It also needs to be recalled that the emergence of humanistic psychology coincided with and reflected some of the concerns of the counter-culture movement of the 1960s when, as we have seen, Eastern thought became a focus of widespread interest. The major proponents of this movement, such as Abraham Maslow, Rollo May, and Carl Rogers, did not, by contrast with some of the earlier therapists we have been dealing with, study Eastern thought closely, but the whole flavour of their enterprise, with its emphasis on self-actualisation and on the exploration and refinement of consciousness, has an Eastern tang to it, and as John Rowan, an historian of the movement, notes: 'Humanistic psychology today contains many things which came originally from the East' (1976: 14).[9]

One of the many points of confluence between humanistic psychology and the East is the desire to transcend mind–body dualistic thinking. Rollo May, for example, who has drawn attention to the similarities between existential analysis and such Eastern philosophies as Taoism and Zen, argues that the importance of Eastern thought for psychotherapy lies in the fact that 'Eastern thought never suffered the radical split between subject and object that has characterized Western thought' (1958: 19), a point underlined by Maslow's talk of 'dichotomy-transcendence'. Another point of confluence concerns the use made of therapeutic strategies inspired in part by Eastern meditation practices. This is most evident in the Gestalt school with its focus on the here-and-now and on experience unmediated by intellectual rationalisation. The Buddhist meditation practices of 'bare attention' and 'mindfulness' have provided powerful models, and the Gestalt theorist Claudio Naranjo, a prominent advocate of the integration of Eastern spiritual practices and psychotherapy, has emphasised the important influence of Buddhist meditation on the present orientation in contemporary psychotherapy, and concludes that Eastern spiritual disciplines – Zen in particular – have contributed greatly to the shaping of Gestalt therapy.[10] Yet another confluence is the cultivation of 'higher states of consciousness', an endeavour closely associated with an off-shoot of humanistic psychology known as 'transpersonal psychology'. The inspiration for the latter can be traced to the interest of James, Jung, and Assagioli in mystical experience as integral to 'normal' psychic development, and to Maslow's concern with 'peak experiences' and with the importance in the psychic life of such states as heightened awareness, ecstasy, creativity, and unitive consciousness. As with humanistic psychology in general, this movement has drawn heavily on oriental traditions, with their sophisticated elaboration of different levels of consciousness reaching from ordinary everyday states to experiences of 'pure consciousness' in which the sense of oneself as a distinct individual is attenuated. As Warwick Fox notes, 'thinkers with interest in transpersonal states of being have generally felt it necessary to look to Eastern thought as a source of conceptual language, theoretical models, and practical guidance' (1990: 299). The leading thinker in this field is Ken Wilbur who is a vigorous critic of prevailing psychological paradigms, and who has made use of ideas drawn from the East to help in the development of a comprehensive evolutionary model of consciousness. In *Transformations of Consciousness*, he and his associates have attempted to combine Eastern ideas with mainstream psychology in order to elaborate a '"full-spectrum" model of human growth and development . . . [one which] takes into serious account the "higher" or "subtler" lines and stages embodied in the world's great contemplative and meditative disciplines' (in Wilber *et al.* 1986: 5).

The idea of the expansion of consciousness points to the whole field of mental health and of personal growth which, in an age beset with problems of anxiety, alienation, and emptiness, has become increasingly prominent. The importance in this context of the spiritual traditions of the East lies in the growing determination that these latter should be thought of, not solely or even primarily, as religions, but rather 'as systems for understanding and promoting deep personal change', leading to transformations in attitudes towards questions of 'life and death, responsibility, relationship and identity' (Claxton 1986: 9). Mental health, as a positive quality contrasted with the mere absence of illness, and which can be actively promoted, is something which has not always been emphasised in modern Western medical traditions, and recent interest in this approach owes something to Eastern models with their techniques for the cultivation of calm, tranquillity, and mind–body equilibrium. In the area of personal growth, too, we are witnessing the seeding of Eastern ideas in a number of fields which, though linked to psychotherapy, go well beyond it. These include: self-awareness and self-management training, mind and memory control, visualisation techniques, biofeedback, and even behaviour therapy, all of which have applications ranging across many fields including psychotherapy, health care, personal growth strategies, and management and professional training. The British psychologist Malcolm Walley sums up the East–West link in the following way:

> The mind-training tradition developed within Tibetan Buddhism provides workers in Western psychotherapy and other helping professions with a valuable resource. Through an appreciation of [this tradition] psychologists may be encouraged to examine their own assumptions as to the potential which exists for modifying individual construct systems in the direction of greater psychological well-being.
>
> (in Crook and Fontana 1990: 143)[11]

MEDITATION AND CONSCIOUSNESS STUDIES

Consideration of mind-training and mental health inevitably lead to questions concerning the role of *meditation* in recent psychological discussions. Over recent years Eastern meditation practices have attracted increasing interest in Western societies, both at the professional and the popular levels, and we have seen first of all within the field of psychotherapy and then in the wider domains of personal and professional development how traditional Eastern spiritual techniques have been adapted to Western-originated purposes. The very breadth of their appeal is underlined by the British psychologist Michael West who emphasises the link between meditation and 'the wider concerns with fitness, health, and emotional well-being . . . a natural form of therapy and relaxation which enhances mental health and self-actualization', going on to emphasise the extent to which meditation is now practised by ordinary people in everyday non-clinical settings (1987: vii).

There has undoubtedly been much misunderstanding of meditation in the West. It has frequently been perceived as embodying all that is mysterious and alien about the Orient, and as far as psychology is concerned the tendency has been to lump it with mystical experience and hence to regard it as a form of self-induced hallucination and as an escape from the demands of the world. In recent years, however, a sea-change in attitudes has taken place, summed up in the words of the American philosopher Paul Sagal: 'There is nothing magical about meditation. It is not a vehicle of the exercise of secret powers . . . [it] is ultimately the practice of everyday life' (in Crook and Fontana 1990: 150). Naranjo, who has carried out much experimental work in this field, argues that, whereas Western mysticism points upwards and beyond the body and the physical world, oriental meditation techniques give importance to psycho-physiological factors and to the experience of everyday sounds, images, movements, and bodily functions (Naranjo and Ornstein 1971: 66), and the psychologist John Welwood underlines its pragmatic, everyday aspect in the following passage:

> Meditation proves a very direct, practical way to discover the larger awareness and aliveness in us and to learn to trust its natural direction toward well-being. Meditation also trains attention . . . as essential for therapeutic change. It helps us cultivate a friendly attitude toward all the phenomena of the mind – so that the inner struggle and conflict of trying to get rid of neurotic patterns can be replaced by what in Buddhism is called *maitri* – unconditional friendliness toward oneself. At the same time, it allows a person to tap into a larger awareness in which ordinary emotional entanglements are seen in a different perspective.
>
> (Welwood 1983: xii–xiii)

In view of such a moderation in attitude, and the recognition of wider practical application in modern secular contexts, it is not surprising that meditation has become the object of scientific inquiry. A considerable weight of psychological endeavour has been applied to this subject over the past quarter of a century, producing dozens of books and monographs, and well over 1,000 published research articles. In addition to its therapeutic implications, the main focus has been in the areas of physiological and personality changes, though, as we shall see shortly, these in turn are connected with wider questions about the nature of consciousness. As far as physiological changes are concerned, a number of investigations, carried out in the East as well as the West, have shown that significant physiological alterations take place during meditation in such areas as respiration, heart rate, blood pressure, skin resistance, and cerebral activity. Two interesting consequences of these investigations need to be mentioned. With regard to the first of these, some psychologists have argued, on the basis of investigations using EEG techniques, that in addition to waking, sleeping, and dreaming, there is a fourth major state of consciousness which is produced in meditation states and which is characterised by a pattern of lowered arousal indicated by alpha-wave activity. The second consequence relates to the possibility of directly controlling the autonomic nervous system, an area of investigation which 'is a clear example of the convergence of Eastern and Western sciences, of knowledge gleaned from ancient meditative systems and data gathered with the most sophisticated biomedical technology of the twentieth century' (Pelletier 1985: 142). Amongst the important clinical implications of this are new approaches to the treatment of hypertensive conditions.

As for personality changes, a number of investigations have been undertaken to determine the long-term effects of meditation practice on behaviour and personality, and have indicated a lowering of the levels of anxiety, depression, and neurosis, and the raising of the levels of self worth and authenticity. It should be emphasised that the results of all these experimental endeavours are by no means univocally positive, and research into the physiological and personality effects of meditation have not always fulfilled their early promise. Nevertheless the interest of experimental psychologists is by no means exhausted, and work in this area continues to give evidence of the fruitfulness of the meeting of psychological methodologies from two quite distinct cultural backgrounds. As Michael West puts it: 'Reference to Eastern philosophies provides sophisticated conceptual frameworks to guide hypothesis development', going on to suggest that 'one of the consequences of [the] meeting of methodologies of East and West is that we are forced to turn back and examine psychological methodology more carefully' (1987: 266). This examination, he argues, will inevitably help to turn psychologists' attention to aspects of human behaviour which have often been neglected. One of these aspects is subjective awareness or consciousness, and it is now time to examine the influence of meditation studies, and Eastern philosophies in general, on an area which is once again engaging the attention of psychologists.[12]

Within Western psychology the re-activation of research into consciousness, after a long gap since William James in America and the Würzburg school in Germany at the turn of the century, coincides with development of cognitive psychology in the 1960s and 1970s, and is linked with the growing influence of phenomenology within the human sciences. In the view of Robert Ornstein, one of the leading proponents of the consciousness movement, this renewed interest in what from a lay person's point of view might seem absolutely central to any study of the human person, represents a reaction against the 'parochialism' and 'unduly narrowed' approach of behaviourism, and points towards a more fully rounded study of the human person (Ornstein 1977: 5 and 7). Ornstein's own contribution to this movement centres on elaboration of the demarcation between the functions of the left and right cerebral hemispheres. The pioneering work in this area of Roger Sperry and Michael Gazzaniga in the 1960s led Ornstein to speculate that there are two major, complementary modes of consciousness, the one analytic, concerned with verbal and rational functions, the other synthetic or holistic, concerned with imaginative, intuitive and emotive functions – 'left-brain' and 'right-brain' respectively. In modern Western cultures, according to Ornstein, there has been a tendency to give privileged status to left-brain activities, and correspondingly to devalue a-rational, non-verbal modes of consciousness. The bi-hemispherical theory suggests that the Western concentration on verbal and intellectual training needs to be complemented by the more intuitive methods associated with Eastern meditation and yogic practices, practices which lead to 'a shift from the normal analytic world containing separate, discrete objects and persons to a second mode, an experience of "unity" and holistic perception' (ibid.: 187). Current psychology, Ornstein believes, is undergoing the first stirrings of a synthesis of these two modes and is pointing towards the beginning of a more complete science of human consciousness, a synthesis which in his view has much to learn from the 'esoteric' psychologies of the East.

Ornstein's theories about the wider implications of bi-hemispherical research have not been widely accepted, not least because of their tendency to reify cultural differences. Nevertheless, his project for a more complete science of consciousness, including the investigation of Eastern philosophies and practices, has been echoed in a number of psychological quarters in recent decades. This has been especially evident in investigations into altered states of consciousness (ASCs), i.e. into mental states typically induced by marijuana and by psychedelic drugs such as mescalin and LSD, near-death experiences, and out-of-body experiences, as well as those states of consciousness induced by meditation practices. Asian philosophers have often in this context been seen as describing and recommending techniques for attaining altered states of consciousness. Some have gone further and argued that ASCs not only indicate a richer concept of human consciousness than had hitherto been allowed in mainstream Western traditions, but that they also have epistemological implications by suggesting that there might be valid ways of knowing which are not standardly recognised in Western philosophy, and that Asian philosophies may be inherently broader and more encompassing than Western ones. As Amoury de Riencourt points out, whereas in the West ASCs are seen as 'an alien and inexplicable intrusion . . . never really absorbed or integrated', the East by contrast has long accepted them as an everyday experience (1981: 158). A similar challenge to what is perceived as the limitations of the Western approach to consciousness, compared with traditional Eastern approaches, is found in the work of Charles T. Tart, one of the leading psychologists in this field. In drawing a close link between spiritual experiences and ASCs he believes that an understanding of Eastern psychologies can assist us in our investigations into altered states, and while he does not advocate the wholesale adoption of Eastern approaches by the West, he nevertheless sees them as inspirations and guides for our own approach. 'I have no doubt', he writes, echoing the similar reservations of Jung and others,

> that many sacred scriptures contain a great deal of valuable information and wisdom, and I am certain that many spiritual teachers have a great deal to teach us that is of immense value, but even the greatest sorts of spiritual teachings must be adapted to the culture of the people they are presented to if they are really to connect with their whole psyches.

(Tart 1975: 58)[13]

While the idea of bringing about some kind of convergence between Eastern and Western psychologies continues to stimulate work in both the practical and theoretical fields of psychology, the whole question of comparing Eastern spirituality with Western psychology has provoked considerable discussion, leading some to claim that spiritual development has little to do with mental health, and that psychological growth has little in common with spiritual growth (see Welwood 1983: 33–42). Even the idea that meditation may be conducive to mental health has been questioned on account of perceived differences between Eastern and Western traditions concerning the role and value of the ego, for, while Western psychotherapy often seeks to expand the boundaries and powers of the ego, the Eastern spiritual path often leads to its dissolution. Furthermore the West's search for theoretical knowledge, for example concerning the nature of consciousness, is sometimes seen to sit awkwardly with the East's pursuit of self-knowledge as a spiritual goal, for science of its very nature cannot offer guidance on questions of meaning and value.

Such issues as these are unlikely to stem the flood of interest in Eastern paths to self-knowledge and self-development, but they do indicate the emergence in recent years of a more critical and reflexive approach to the whole enterprise. Simplistic phrases such as 'Buddhism is a form of psychotherapy' are going the same way as trivialising clichés about 'the mysterious Orient', and there are signs of a growing willingness to recognise and to respect differences arising from divergence of cultural background and outlook between East and West. As psychology itself becomes more aware of the epistemological problems that weave their way through its own discourse, so too those who seek to contribute to the construction of an East–West bridge are equally becoming aware of the need to recognise the contentious nature of their undertaking. Furthermore, the confrontation between the languages of Western psychology and Eastern spirituality may also be contributing to the erosion of categories and the widening of sensibilities, which in turn may lead to the transformation of the discipline of psychology itself. The difficulties we are confronted with when deploying essentially contested terms such as 'spiritual', 'religion', and 'psychotherapy' in this context force us into a reassessment of these terms, and hence of the languages in which they are embedded.

Chapter 10

Scientific and ecological speculations

THE EAST AND MODERN SCIENCE

The link between science and Eastern philosophies is, on the face of it, an unlikely one. The latter have often been perceived in the West as displaying an endemic mystical bent and a pervasive irrationalist tendency, and their role within Western orientalist discourse has sometimes appeared to be to act precisely as a counterweight to Western scientism and positivism. Nevertheless, as we saw in an earlier chapter, in the nineteenth century Western science and Eastern mysticism formed an improbable coalition, with many thinkers looking upon Buddhism as an ally in the struggle of science against indigenous metaphysical traditions. Even earlier in the Enlightenment period, Confucianism, though it had little intrinsic association with natural science, was nevertheless perceived on the basis of its rationalistic ethics to be in sympathy with the emerging scientific spirit of that age. This perception of a broad affinity between certain aspects of Eastern thought and the modern scientific outlook has continued into the twentieth century. The French writer Amoury de Riencourt has argued that contemporary science 'in its search for a philosophic framework, seems to be deliberately turning away from its cultural roots, finding a more compatible atmosphere in the totally alien metaphysics of the Orient' (1981: 18). And in terms which hark back to the previous century, the scientist Mansell Davies has written of the 'confluence between the basic position of Buddhism and modern science', and of Buddhist teachings as being 'offered entirely in a spirit of reason' (1990: 61 and 13).[1]

In one respect this alliance has been formed around a perception of Buddhism as offering a radical critique of tradition – any tradition – a role that has often been assigned to science itself within the modern period. The American philosopher N. P. Jacobson, for example, points to the power of both Buddhism and modern science 'to shift the conduct of life away from established beliefs, however reliable and legitimate, over to the self-corrective mode of behaviour', both being 'alert to what Wittgenstein called "the bewitchment of the intellect by language" ' (1983: 133), and argues that Buddhism, with its consistent refusal to beatify any conceptual, theoretical, or linguistic structures, has the capacity to act as a powerful countervailing influence to this tendency, and must to this extent become a complement to science. The future, he claims, 'may well depend upon the mutual understanding and support now possible between the two self-corrective legacies together as the Yang and the Yin of the self-corrective community of tomorrow' (ibid.: 149). This echoes similar sentiments expressed some thirty years earlier by Christmas Humphreys when he opined that

> the Buddhist attitude to all phenomena and to all teaching about it has ever been that of the modern scientist. Let all things be examined dispassionately, objectively, assuming nothing, testing all, for such was the Buddha's own injunction to his followers.
>
> (1951: 223)

It was precisely this perceived radicalism of the Buddhist method that helped to broker an intriguing, albeit brief, alliance between Buddhism and Soviet Marxism. As we noted in Chapter 7, Buddhistic studies had flourished in Russia since the end of the nineteenth century, and in the early years of the revolution attempts were made to work out some sort of accommodation between Buddhism and Bolshevism on the basis of the belief that Buddhism was essentially atheistic and scientific in outlook. The marriage came to a tragic end in the 1930s when Stalin launched his reign of terror indiscriminately against all religious creeds.[2]

Another important point of contact concerns the age-old conflict between science and religion. Christian theology has often had a difficult relationship with modern science, arising in part out of the former's inclination towards a literal interpretation of scripture and to truth in general, and it is not surprising, therefore, that Westerners have turned to the East as a way of reconciling a religious outlook with that of modern science. As we saw earlier, in the nineteenth century many thinkers seized on Buddhism as a religion which was compatible with science, for it made no metaphysical claims, based its 'truths' on the pure dictates of experience, and moreover could not conceivably have a quarrel with evolutionary theory. This kind of rapprochement has persisted into the twentieth century, and has often focused on the idea of *experience*, a term which, 'with its suggestive ambiguity and its broad range of connotations', William Halbfass suggests, 'seems to indicate a possible reconciliation or merger of science and religion, providing religion with a new measure of certainty and science with a new dimension of meaning' (1988: 399). For the Marxist Buddhologist Trevor Ling the issue is even more straightforward since Buddhism can hardly be called a religion at all but is rather 'a form of rationalism' with an 'empirical and analytical outlook' in which 'all propositions must be tested' (1973: 115–17).

An attempt to demonstrate a close affinity between science and Eastern religions was made early in this century by Sir John Woodroffe (alias Arthur Avalon), the author of a widely read book on Tantric yoga, *The Serpent Power*, in which he argued that there was an underlying affinity between *Tantra*, with its experiential methods, and modern science. He insisted that Indian religious teachings were based on 'experiments', and wrote that Tantric and Vedantic thought 'is in conformity with the most advanced scientific and philosophical thought of the West' (1966: 4). Among other early proponents of this idea were certain well-known neo-Vedantists living in California in the 1930s and 1940s whom we met earlier, a group including Aldous Huxley, Christopher Isherwood, and Gerald Heard. In their magazine *Vedānta and the West* they advocated what Huxley called, with self-conscious reference to the scientific method, 'The minimum working hypothesis' according to which the idea of *brahman*, the ground of being, was claimed to rest, 'not on blind authority, but upon empirical work which any inquirer may repeat . . . and confirm for himself'. Hence there was 'no conflict between true Religion and true Science'. The Vedantist world view was not only superior to the Judaeo-Christian tradition because 'it does not contradict the findings of science', but was actually supported by recent developments in science which suggested that 'the physical world is a construction of the human mind . . . a basic unity which our animal senses break up into a manifold' (Isherwood 1945: 33, 38, and 53–4).

This last suggestion points towards what is certainly the most conspicuous example of the science/Orient alliance in recent times, namely the marriage between the new physics and Eastern philosophies. Many influential thinkers have found in the natural philosophies of China and India important precedents for the swing within the physical sciences in this century from an atomistic/mechanistic mode of thinking to an organicist/holistic one, and although Fritjof Capra's *The Tao of Physics* constitutes the most extended and best-known statement of this 'union of opposites', conjectures along these lines had been in evidence for some time prior to its publication in 1975. In 1953, for example, J. P. McKinney argued that in the development of quantum physics 'Western thought has been brought round to a standpoint which has been the traditional assumption of Eastern thought' (1953: 263). This insight can be traced back even earlier to the work of C. G. Jung and his collaboration in the 1930s with Wolfgang Pauli, one of the leading figures in the development of quantum theory. At that time Jung was working on the ideas of the *I Ching*, and he came to the conclusion that the background assumptions of this ancient Chinese text bore an interesting likeness to those of the new physics, and some years later, alongside a parallel work by Pauli, he published an essay entitled *Synchronicity* where these ideas are elaborated, and in which he pointed out that 'the latest conclusions of science are coming nearer and nearer to a unitary idea of being' (Jung 1985: 133).

Pauli's involvement in these speculations is thrown into even sharper relief by the fact that several of the other key physicists involved in the development of quantum theory, whose concern with some of the wider epistemological and metaphysical implications of the new ideas drew them Eastwards, were also thinking along similar lines in that period. Niels Bohr, the leading figure in this group, was one of the first to see the close similarities between the revolutionary new model of nature that was being forged and the ancient philosophies of the

East, and his interpretation of quantum theory had the consequence of allowing the re-introduction of consciousness into the scientific understanding of nature. Following a visit to China he became especially interested in Taoist philosophy, and it is interesting to note that on being knighted by the Danish government he chose for his coat of arms the Chinese Taoist yin/yang figure of interlocking circles which he felt symbolised his most important idea, namely the principle of complementarity. The oriental interest of Werner Heisenberg, author of the indeterminacy principle, lay more in the direction of India, which he visited in the 1930s. There he was a guest of the philosopher and poet Rabindranath Tagore, and he later acknowledged that his discussions with Tagore on Indian philosophy had been an important stimulant to his thinking on physics.[3] The precise extent of the influence of Indian thought on the development of the quantum theory itself is a matter of dispute, and it must be borne in mind that many quantum physicists either disagree with or are indifferent to these philosophical speculations, but at any rate it is clear from the following passage in his book *Physics and Philosophy* that Heisenberg thought that the parallelism between the two could at least be helpful in attuning Western minds to the revolutionary ideas underlying the new physics:

> [The] openness of modern physics may help to some extent to reconcile the older traditions with the new trends of thought. For instance the great scientific contribution in theoretical physics that has come from Japan since the last war may be an indication of a certain relationship between philosophical ideas in the tradition of the Far East and the philosophical substance of quantum theory. It may be easier to adapt oneself to the quantum theoretical concept of reality when one has not gone through the naïve materialistic way of thinking that still prevailed in Europe in the first decades of this century.
>
> (Heisenberg 1959: 173)

The involvement of Erwin Schrödinger in Eastern metaphysics is even more significant. During the period immediately following World War I, when he was already qualified as a physicist, he immersed himself in philosophy, beginning with Schopenhauer and turning from there to a study of Indian *Vedānta* philosophy. His reading at that time, which took place immediately prior to the intense period of speculation in the field of wave mechanics, was by no means superficial, taking in the writings of Indologists such as Max Müller, Deussen, and Rhys Davids, as well as the Vedas and Upanishads. The precise influence of this reading on his scientific investigations is again difficult to assess, but it is certain that from that time onwards Indian philosophy became a central part of his thinking about life in general, and it is difficult to imagine that this did not influence his work in physics to some degree. In 1925 he began to write a book on his world view, completed some years later and published under the title of *Meine Weltansicht*, in which he expressed profound concern for the decline of Western civilisation, in particular its loss of a secure metaphysical grounding, and though he rejected Judaeo-Christian teaching, he still felt the need for some kind of religious framework, and believed that this framework could be provided by the Vedantist philosophy with its vision of the ultimate unity of the world – self, nature, and God. According to his biographer, *Vedānta* became a 'foundation for his life and work',[4] for it offered a unified picture of the world which was entirely consistent with the emerging view of physics in which the old mechanist/atomist model was being replaced by one of inseparable probability waves.

Another scientist – this time a biochemist – who has anticipated Capra's line of thinking is Joseph Needham, whose contributions to orientalist debates we have already noted. Needham himself has been one of the major agents in transmitting the ideas behind Chinese naturalism in general and Taoist philosophy in particular to the Western mind and in showing their relevance to modern thought. Taoist ideas have been relative latecomers as far as Western awareness of Eastern philosophies is concerned, and according to Joseph Needham they have, until recently,

> been much misunderstood if not ignored by Western translators and writers. Taoist religion has been neglected, Taoist magic written off wholesale as nothing more than superstition, and Taoist philosophy interpreted as purely religious mysticism and poetry. The scientific side of Taoism has been largely overlooked.
>
> (Needham 1978, 1: 86)

According to Needham, the central ideas stressed by Taoist natural philosophers were: that nature is one and that its activity is all-pervasive, that it is eternal and uncreated, and that its operations are entirely spontaneous and self-originating (see Needham 1956: 46ff, and 1978, 1: 89ff). This suggests a model of the universe which is organic rather than mechanical and which sees natural phenomena as if they are parts of a living organism rather than as parts of cause-and-effect chains or a mechanical process. In such an organicist model

> Things behaved in particular ways not necessarily because of the prior actions of other things, but primarily because their position in the ever-changing cyclical universe was such that they were endowed with intrinsic natures which made such behaviour natural for them.
>
> (Needham 1978, 1: 164)

It is not surprising therefore that Needham was concerned to emphasise the connections between Chinese natural philosophy and post-classical physics, arguing that 'the philosophy of organism, essential for the construction of modern science in its present and coming form, stemmed from [the correlative philosophy of China]', and that 'the Chinese shot an arrow close to the spot where Bohr and Rutherford were later to stand without ever attaining to the position of Newton' (1956: 339 and 467). Indeed one of his overriding aims was to exploit the history of Chinese science as a critique of the Galilean-Newtonian model and to use the neo-Confucian ideas of nature to assist in the elaboration of an organicist synthesis that goes beyond Western mechanistic thinking (see ibid.: 291).[5]

It is in the writings of Capra, however, that the intimations of these scientists are most fully articulated. In his popular book, *The Tao of Physics*, the argument is summed up as follows:

> In modern physics, the universe is thus experienced as a dynamic, inseparable whole which always includes the observer in an essential way. In this experience, the traditional concepts of time and space, of isolated objects, and of cause and effect, lose their meaning. Such an experience, however, is very similar to that of the Eastern mystics.
>
> (Capra 1976: 70)

He then proceeds to draw extensive parallels between the new physics and ancient oriental philosophies, and concludes that 'the principal theories and models of modern physics lead to a view of the world which is . . . in perfect harmony with the views of Eastern mysticism' (1976: 320). Two key notions for Capra are the basic oneness of the universe and the integrated role of consciousness. At the sub-atomic level he argues that modern physics offers us an 'organic' model of nature in which the world is envisaged as an inseparable whole, where all things are fluid and ever-changing, and where there is no room for any fixed, absolutely separate, fundamental entities such as those envisaged in the Newtonian dispensation. Moreover, developments in this area of science point to the possibility of re-introducing consciousness into an integrated account of nature, a notion excluded from the old Newtonian paradigm, for quantum phenomena 'can only be understood as links in a chain of processes, the end of which lies in the consciousness of the human observer' (ibid.: 318). In both these respects ideas from the Hindu, the Buddhist, and the Taoist traditions can be drawn on to flesh out a new world view. Thus, while, the various Eastern schools differ in many details, 'they all emphasize the basic unity of the universe' and in all of them the 'cosmos is seen as one inseparable reality – for ever in motion, alive, organic; spiritual and material at the same time' (ibid.: 23). And as in the new physics, 'this universal interwovenness always includes the human observer and his or her consciousness' (ibid.: 44). A point of contact which Capra particularly emphasises is that of the complementarity of opposites. In spite of the undivided unity affirmed by Eastern philosophies, they also recognise that there are differences and contrasts within the all-embracing unity, and that while at one level such opposites – good/bad, male/female, life/death – appear to be separate and polarised, at another they can be seen as complementary sides of the same reality. A similar consideration prevails in modern sub-atomic physics 'where matter is both destructible and indestructible; where matter is both continuous and discontinuous, and force and matter are but different aspects of the same phenomenon' (ibid.: 152).

Clearly, Capra does not imagine on the basis of such comparisons that Eastern metaphysics can contribute in some way to quantum physics as such. His purpose is a different one, namely to elaborate a new philosophical framework within which the new physics can be understood and out of which further philosophical consequences can be elicited. One of the most important of these is, once again, the reconciliation of science on the one hand and religious and spiritual goals on the other. In the West, he points out, these two paths have diverged and the consequence has been a cultural bifurcation whereby scientific and spiritual endeavours have lost the means of inter-communication and so failed to furnish an integrated world view. What Capra seeks to show is that

> Eastern thought and, more generally, mystical thought provide a consistent and relevant philosophical background to the theories of contemporary science; a conception of the world in which man's scientific discoveries can be in perfect harmony with its spiritual aims and religious beliefs.
>
> (Capra 1976: 24)

He has frequently been criticised for measuring against one another the incommensurable, and for disregarding the obvious differences between Eastern mysticism and modern science – differences in methodology, in practical applications, and in the whole cultural contexts from which they arise. Such criticisms may not be without their point, and we will return to them in the next chapter, but they miss the central target of Capra's argument which is the underlying assumptions of the Western view of the world. He is concerned not to give support to the new physics qua scientific theory, but to show that deep-rooted philosophical beliefs in such ideas as substance, in the absolute distinction between mind and body, and in rigid determinism are fundamentally at odds with new thinking in science, and he is in effect making use of these Oriental ideas as part of a strategy to subvert long-established Western beliefs and to articulate new ones – the forging, as he puts it, of a new paradigm. This strategy is not entirely novel. An interesting precedent can be observed in the scientific revolution of the seventeenth century, for there too, in order to subvert the authority of Aristotle, the precedents of other competing philosophies from the ancient Greek world, such as atomism and scepticism, were invoked.[6]

The idea of a revolutionary philosophical synthesis which combines new Western scientific insights with Eastern cosmologies has not been warmly welcomed within science itself, or indeed amongst philosophers, but it has nevertheless become the subject of wide speculation and interest, and has been discussed by a number of prominent thinkers. For example, the Russian-born physicist Ilya Prigogine, in attempting to deal with the radical changes that are taking place in physics, and to elaborate a new approach to the self-organising properties of matter, speculates that 'we will eventually be able to combine the Western tradition, with its emphasis on experimentation and quantitative formulations, with a tradition such as the Chinese one, with its view of a spontaneous, self-organizing world' (Prigogine and Stengers 1984: 22). Another prominent physicist, David Bohm, has also sought to build bridges between East and West, and has drawn Eastern ideas into the elaboration of his own distinctive interpretation of quantum theory. Contrary to the atomistic view of reality which has served physics well for several centuries, Bohm argues that it is necessary, in the light of the new physics, to map out a non-fragmentary view of reality which accounts for the essentially 'undivided wholeness of the universe' (1981: xi), a view which contrasts sharply with the classical idea of the analysability of the world into separate, independently existing parts. In pursuit of this aim he has constructed a theory of the 'implicate order' whereby phenomena are seen as containing within themselves, potentially as it were, the sum of all phenomena, a unitary order out of which the 'explicate order' of empirical reality is unfolded. Such a view makes possible, Bohm maintains, not only an understanding of the new properties of matter implied by quantum theory, but also the nature of consciousness, and hence makes possible the re-uniting of the human world of mind and the world of physical phenomena. Like Capra and Prigogine he sees this new unitary conception as having long been intimated and worked out in philosophical form in the philosophies of the East where 'such views still survive, in the sense that philosophy and religion emphasize wholeness and imply the futility of analysis of the world into parts' (ibid.: 19). Bohm goes on to ask:

> Why, then, do we not drop our fragmentary Western approach and adopt these Eastern notions which include not only a self-world view that denies division and fragmentation but also techniques of meditation that lead the whole process of mental operation non-verbally to the sort of quiet state of orderly and smooth flow needed to end fragmentation both in the actual process of thought and in its content?
>
> (Bohm 1981: 19–20)

In spite of his personal commitment to the Eastern 'way', this does not mean for Bohm the wholesale adoption of Eastern modes of thought and action, but rather the search for a 'new synthesis', as he calls it, one which has regard 'to the great wisdom from the whole of the past, both in the East and in the West' (ibid.: 24).[7]

ECOLOGY AND WHOLENESS

A central theme in the writings of Capra, Prigogine, and Bohm is that of *wholeness*. They all emphasise what they see as an important shift away from the atomism and mechanism that characterised the metaphysical basis of science, indeed of the Western world view as a whole, over the past three centuries or more, to a more holistic approach which emphasises the inextricable interconnectedness of things. This, as we have seen, is the main reason for their interest in Eastern philosophies where the underlying wholeness of things is a virtually universal assumption. It is also a factor which links them with two other fields closely related to science.

The first of these is medicine, with which we will deal briefly. In recent years there has been considerable interest in the West in the medical practices of China and India, and lying behind these practices certain holistic assumptions have been identified concerning health and the human person which, it is claimed, contrast favourably with the more mechanistic and dualistic assumptions lying behind Western medical practice. Where once modern Western medicine was used to demonstrate the inadequacy of non-Western varieties, the situation is now to some extent being reversed. Chinese and Indian medical systems are increasingly being seen as superior in certain respects to Western medicine in that they treat the whole person as a psychosomatic unity, and conceive illness in relation to the total human and natural environment rather than in terms of isolable dysfunctions. Traditional Chinese medicine and the ancient Ayurvedic medical system of India have both in recent years attracted attention in the West, not only because of their perceived healing powers, but also because they offer a completely different way of looking at health in terms of the harmony and balance of the whole person, physical, psychic, and social. For some these developments constitute a powerful challenge to the global hegemony of Western medicine, or at any rate to the view that Western scientific medical theory and practice are culture-free. For others they are seen to offer a stimulant towards a situation in which Western and Asian medical systems can develop in a mutually complementary rather than a competitive direction. This co-operative approach is emphasised by the historian of Chinese medicine Manfred Porkert who argues that 'the goal is not to exchange our original set of preconceptions for another [but] to establish a new kind of medicine that can freely accept the observations and accumulated knowledge of both cultures' (1982: 278).[8]

The second of these fields is ecological thinking which has emerged into prominence over the past few decades, and which we will examine in more detail.[9] Here, too, wholeness is a central theme, implying the fundamental interconnectedness of an ecosystem, humankind's symbiotic relationship with natural ecosystems, and the interdependence of mind and nature. Where, under the traditional way of thinking in the West, there has supposedly been a tendency to treat the world as a collection of distinct entities and areas of concern, and to see human beings as radically distinct from the rest of nature, ecological thinking is seen to formulate a different model which starts from more integrative assumptions. It is not surprising, therefore, that thinkers in this area have begun not only to draw comparisons between the holistic outlooks of ecology and Eastern philosophies with a view to uncovering hidden Western assumptions about nature, but also to use Eastern ways of thinking about nature as an alternative set of categories for rethinking environmental attitudes. The development of ecological thinking since the 1960s has indeed in many ways gone hand in hand with the growing popularity of Eastern religions. Both have given voice to a fundamental disillusionment with certain of the underlying assumptions and values both of science, with its atomistic-mechanistic model of nature, and of Christianity with its radical division between the spiritual and the natural worlds, and increasingly 'in the search for new integrative and moral paradigms by means of which to establish a more harmonious and mutually fulfilling and beneficial relationship of man to nature. . . . Eastern traditions of thought [have been found to] provide important conceptual resources' (Callicott and Ames 1989: 11–12). Some have sought a way forward from within a transformed

Christian tradition based on the inspiration of St Francis of Assisi, or on the idea of stewardship. For others, however, the traditional belief systems of the West are seen to be the problem rather than the solution, and they have therefore turned to the East for help in renewing basic assumptions about the natural world.[10]

This help has been drawn from a variety of sources in Asia, ranging from Hinduism with its traditions of non-violence and reverence for life, to Taoism with its sense of the symbiotic union between the human and the natural worlds. Here are some representative examples: the political scientist Hwa Yol Jung has argued that the principles of Zen Buddhism could be used to substitute attitudes of respect for nature in place of the utilitarian and exploitative attitudes that prevailed in the West, and that in the search for 'a Copernican revolution of the mind to avert impending ecological disaster . . . Zen could be the fountain-head of that revolution' (quoted in Callicott and Ames 1989: 7). Lawrence E. Johnson in his book on environmental ethics stresses that there are 'valuable lessons to be learned from Taoism' with its emphasis on the interconnectedness of natural phenomena, on harmony and balance, and on the principle of *wu-wei* – doing by not doing (1991: 269–71). And according to the Islamic philosopher Seyyed Hossein Nasr, we can find in Taoism 'a devotion to nature and comprehension of its metaphysical significance that is of the greatest importance', and in accordance with this philosophy we can learn to 'live in peace and harmony with nature or the Earth' (1990: 83 and 85). In a more practical vein, evidence for this desire to 'live in peace and harmony with nature' is to be found in the growing popularity in the West of *feng-shui*, the Chinese art of living in accord with the energy currents of the earth.

Eastern ideas have been used to challenge Western ideas and values on a broad front, with the former being seen as providing the foundation for an alternative paradigm based on sound ecological principles. A classic example of this approach was offered by E. F. Schumacher (1911–77) in his book *Small is Beautiful*. In a chapter entitled 'Buddhist Economics' he set out to expose the philosophical underpinnings of the Western economic system and to examine what the economy would be like if it were based, alternatively, on Buddhist principles. He argued that economists tend to suffer from 'a kind of metaphysical blindness' which leads them to imagine that 'theirs is a science of absolute and invariable truths' that is value-free and deals with laws as immutable as the law of gravity (1974: 44). One of these 'truths' is that consumption is the sole end and purpose of all economic activity, and that labour is simply an essential, if intrinsically unpleasant, means to that end. The 'standard of living' is measured in terms of consumption, and hence the aim of the economic system is to maximise consumption, and to encourage an optimal level of production without regard to the wider human and environmental consequences. By contrast with this he drew from Buddhism the view that the purpose of economic activity is the enhancement of human well-being, a factor which cannot be measured in purely quantitative terms, and that labour is an essentially human activity, not merely a means to a further end. Moreover, he argued, the Buddha enjoins a reverent and non-violent attitude to all of nature which means that the world's natural resources should not be exploited without consideration of their renewability and the overall balance of nature. What a Buddhist approach offers, in short, is a radical alternative to prevailing economic theories and practices, one which points to a 'Middle Way between materialist heedlessness and traditionalist immobility' (ibid.: 51).[11]

Since this pioneering work was published, a rising crescendo of debate has amplified and elaborated Schumacher's challenge to the fundamental principles of the Western socio-economic system from an ecological standpoint, and Buddhist ideas have continued to play a part in this debate. Two British thinkers who have been closely involved with this debate in recent years are Ken Jones and Stephen Batchelor, both of whom voice strong views about the need for a renewed spirituality at the heart of ecological thinking. In several closely argued books Jones has sought to draw close links between Buddhism and Green politics in such areas as non-violent change, decentralisation of power, non-exploitative work, and the treatment of animals, and argues that Buddhism can offer an 'engaged spirituality readily accessible to secular-minded people, rationalists and humanists' (Jones 1993: 170). He places special emphasis on the belief that, in the final analysis, no solution to environmental problems is viable which does not recognise the need for an inner transformation to take us beyond our current ego-centred ideologies, a task for which Buddhism is well suited. This means that 'we shall need to nudge the evolution of consciousness beyond its present high egoic level in order to build, as from new, the radically different green mutuality on which the steady-state economy will depend' (ibid.: 77). According to Batchelor, Buddhist teachings offer a fundamental challenge to the 'social structures which sustain and promote values which blind us to the ecologically destructive results of our actions', and to the belief that 'by accumulating enough agreeable pieces of reality – cars, household appliances, clothes, hi-fi systems, fine art or whatever – we will accumulate a sense of well-being' (in Batchelor and Brown 1992: 32–3). What Buddhism encourages us to do is to look for causes rather than treat the symptoms, and these causes are to be found, not in the operation of external processes but rather within ourselves, in our attitudes, beliefs, and values. There we discover in the West a starkly individualistic attitude, a romanticised sense of the self which seeks its satisfaction in competition with other selves, whereas by contrast, he argues, Buddhism sees personal fulfilment in interdependence, both with the world of nature and with other human beings.[12]

Similar ideas were elaborated by Capra in his attempt to demonstrate that a 'new paradigm' is in the process of evolving, 'a new vision of reality; a fundamental change in our thoughts, perceptions, and values' (1982: Preface, np), one which will provide the foundation for a new way 'to experience the wholeness of nature and the art of living with it in harmony' (ibid.: 325). In addition to the new physics, an important source of inspiration for this new holistic paradigm,

Capra believes, is to be found in the emergence of a new way of thinking in terms of *systems*. Systems theory, he explains, 'looks at the world in terms of interrelatedness and interdependence' and provides a conceptual framework for thinking about phenomena, in all kinds of different fields, so that 'properties cannot be reduced to those of its parts' (ibid.: 26). This new attitude is supported once again by reference to Eastern modes of thought. The new systems approach, Capra thinks, is in many respects a modern transformation of ancient Eastern ideas, and a new paradigm must necessarily be the result of a new kind of synthesis which, following the lead of Chinese Taoist philosophy, must seek a dynamic balance between the apparently opposing tendencies of reason and feeling, the masculine and the feminine, action and contemplation. The philosopher Joanna Macy has also drawn together ideas from systems theory, ecology, and Buddhism in her radical critique of Western ways and values, and has sought to address some of the contemporary world's most pressing problems by asking us to reconceptualise our world and its creatures as nothing less than an extension of ourselves. Rejecting as philosophically mistaken and ecologically unsound the idea of a separate 'skin-encapsulated ego', 'so separate and fragile that we must delineate and defend its boundaries', she argues for 'the creation of the eco-self' as part of 'the resurgence of nondualistic spiritualities'. The role of Buddhism in this creation lies in the way in which, like systems theory, it 'undermines categorical distinctions between self and other' and demonstrates 'the pathogenic character of any reifications of the self' (1991: 187–9).

Many of the ideas mentioned in this section have reached a philosophical apotheosis in the idea of *deep ecology*. This notion, which was first sketched out in 1972 by the Norwegian philosopher Arne Naess (1912–), involves an attempt to move beyond environmentalism, which is seen as applying superficial, piecemeal remedies within the confines of an orthodox scientific-rationalist world view. Deep ecology, according to Naess, seeks to undertake a more fundamental questioning of our relationship with the natural world, and calls for a new ecological paradigm to replace the mechanistic model that has dominated Western thought and practice for the past 300 years. Lying at the heart of this new paradigm is an attempt to establish the principle of the equality of value of all components of the interlinked web of nature, and to found a new psychology of the self based on a symbiotic relationship between person and planet. These ideas have a number of sources, including the traditions of native peoples, the *philosophia perennis*, eco-feminism, and the new physics, but amongst the most important are the philosophies of the East. Naess himself has frequently acknowledged his debt to Gandhi, and sees deep ecology drawing its basic principles from Buddhist and Taoist ideas, as well as from Christianity, Spinoza, Whitehead, and Heidegger. Other deep ecologists have emphasised the importance of the Eastern connection by stressing that these traditions 'express organic unity . . . and express acceptance of biocentric equality in some traditions', and that they 'relate to the process of becoming more mature, of awakening from illusion and delusion' (Devall and Sessions 1985: 100).[13]

At the heart of deep ecologists' thinking is a fundamental shift from our traditional Western anthropocentric attitude towards nature to a biocentric one. This revolutionary change demands nothing less than the extension of ethical boundaries from the purely human to other animals, and to the whole of the natural world, a change which is seen as being facilitated by ideas from traditional Asian cultures. In many Eastern traditions all beings, animate and inanimate, are thought to be permeated by some kind of spiritual quality; Hindus, for example, 'see life everywhere, notably in human beings, but in trees, birds, animals, and insects – a oneness of life in all creation' (Prime 1992: 96). This means that while moral obligation, on the purely natural plane, is normally seen in the West to extend only to the bounds of the human community, in the East it embraces all living things, and even the whole of nature. As the philosopher Roderick Nash puts it: 'The natural rights philosophy of John Locke and Thomas Jefferson secularized this concept [i.e. the sacredness of the individual human being]. In the East, on the other hand, intrinsic value extended to the limits of the universe' (1989: 113). To anyone brought up in the Judaeo-Christian tradition it seems perfectly natural to suppose that the domain of morality is confined to human-to-God and human-to-human relationships, and while the Church has not encouraged or condoned cruelty to animals, it has tended to condemn it on the grounds that it might encourage cruelty to other human beings rather than as something that is wrong *per se*.[14] The moral attitudes arising from the Buddhist Eightfold Path or from the Jain doctrine of *ahimsā* (non-violence) have encouraged in the West a radical re-thinking on this score. The East is by no means the only source of this change of heart, and in the nineteenth century the Buddhist and Jain attitude towards the relationship between humans and animals was looked upon with horror, but in more recent days it has certainly been an important factor in helping to alter attitudes towards the natural world in general and animals in particular. Among the influential contributors to this change of heart are Albert Schweitzer who, partly as a consequence of his study of Asian religions, formulated the ideal of 'reverence for all life', urging that animals had as much moral claim to our kindness as humans, and that the circle of moral concern should comprise 'the unity of mankind with all created things' (1936: 261).[15] More recently such notions have begun to enter into serious philosophical debate, and Stephen Clark confessed at the outset of his important study on the moral status of animals that he was 'strongly influenced by Mahāyāna Buddhism' (1977: 5).

As with the debates and dialogues that have been outlined in the preceding chapters, the East–West ecological debate has undergone a palpable transformation in its brief history.[16] In retrospect, its earlier manifestation in the era of the beats and hippies, inspired by the writings of Gary Snyder and Alan Watts *inter alia*, now seems somewhat naïve and over-inflated, often conveying the conviction that Eastern traditions could provide a ready-made solution to Western ills, a royal road to harmony between humanity and nature. Related to this was a tendency to conflate all forms of Asian thought into a generic 'Eastern wisdom', and to treat both East and West as monolithic and mutually exclusive traditions. Such attitudes are evident in a number of academic writings in that period, as well as in more popular works. In 1967, for example, Nash wrote: 'In the Far East the man–nature relationship was marked by respect, bordering on love, absent in the West' (1967: 192), and shortly thereafter the theologian J. Huston Smith spoke of Asia's 'unquestioned confidence in nature' and its dignified affirmation of it, in marked contrast with the West's 'oppositioned . . . reserved and critical' attitude (1972: 66). In more recent years Asian traditions of thought have been brought to bear in more circumspect and critical ways on environmental and ecological questions. Some of the earlier utopian enthusiasms for a 'new paradigm' which would sweep away and replace failed Western ways of thinking have given way to a more hermeneutical mode of discourse in which East–West intellectual interactions are viewed in a more dialectical and historically-tuned light. Thus, for example, there is an increasing awareness that Eastern attitudes to nature have in the past often been suffused in the West with an idealised glow which has tended to obscure the less-than-ideal ecological practices of Asian societies in the past, and those theoretical aspects of Eastern religions which might be at variance with ecological principles. There is a recognition, too, of the need to take account of the historical and cultural distance between ancient Eastern philosophies and the contemporary environmental problematic, and not to imagine that the West can simply cut itself loose from its cognitive roots and adopt alien intellectual traditions wholesale. At the same time it is also recognised that comparative environmental thinking can play an important facilitative role in enabling us to 'see the world through an alternative frame of mind', thereby 'revealing certain premises and assumptions concerning the nature of nature and who we human beings are in relation to it', and enabling us to take an outsider's point of view 'from which the West can more clearly discern the deeper strata of its inherited intellectual biases and assumptions' (Callicott and Ames 1989: 16 and 288).

This recent, more critical and discriminative stance is one with which we have by now become familiar in the course of the last few chapters. This is the stance which will be adopted in the final section of this book where some of the controversial issues implicit in the foregoing two sections will be brought more fully into the open.

Part IV

Conclusions

Chapter 11

Reflections and reorientations

It is now time to enter into a critical evaluation of the historical pageant presented in the previous two sections. In this chapter, therefore, we will draw out and
examine more closely some of the contentious issues that have woven their way
in and out of our narrative, and confront some of the criticisms that have commonly been made against orientalism in one form or another. It is one thing to
have chronicled the West's intellectual encounters with Eastern thought, but the
historian of ideas needs also to ask philosophical questions about the very possibility of crossing linguistic and cultural boundaries, and about the adequacy of
inter-cultural communication, and must reflect on the nature of the hermeneutical process which, so we have claimed, is at the heart of these encounters. And
we need also to confront awkward questions concerning the ethical and political
implications of the East–West encounter: has orientalism served to support a
racist ideology? Does it help to propagate an a-moral irrationalism? Is it a
masked form of colonial domination? We will deal with these and related issues
in the present chapter. Questions about the present state and potential of orientalism will occupy us in the final chapter.

INTERPRETING ACROSS BOUNDARIES

It might appear to be a reckless act of philosophical scepticism to doubt whether
communication has actually taken place between East and West. In spite of all
the distortions, exaggerations, and projections on the part of Western thinkers
which we have encountered, it is surely beyond dispute that some kind of cognitive exchange has taken place, something that, however tentatively and loosely,
could be called a 'dialogue'. At the very least, much has been learned, narrow
provincialisms have been transcended, tired old Western assumptions and prejudices challenged, stimulants to creative new thinking provoked. Nevertheless the
matter cannot rest there. Deep problems arise out of our historical narrative,
problems which recapitulate in a different key issues that are high on the agenda
of contemporary philosophy and critical studies, problems concerning for example cultural relativism, translation, incommensurability, historical understanding,
and the nature of rationality itself. These issues are clearly too large to be dealt

with adequately here, but some attempt must be made to draw out the implications that they may have for our study of orientalism.

It will be useful to frame our discussion within a rather simplistic polarisation of views. On the one hand there is the view that differences between cultures are so wide, and that texts, ideas, and values are so deeply embedded in individual cultures, that nothing is to be gained at all in attempting to communicate across cultural divides; orientalism on this sceptical or relativistic view is possible only as an exercise in narcissism. On this premiss our attempts to interpret concepts such as *tao* or *karma* will necessarily be frustrated since the meaning of such terms is generated within the linguistic and philosophical framework of cultures which are wholly different from our own. The hermeneutical exercise is therefore doomed from the start. At the opposite extreme there are those who might wish to sweep aside philosophical problems in their eagerness to harvest the fruits of dialogue, and who see no particular problem in the Western attempt to assimilate ideas from Eastern cultures. At various points in the orientalist literature we come across remarks to the effect that understanding the texts and philosophies of the East is simply a matter of open-mindedness and good will, that orientalism is no more and no less problematic than understanding the ideas of one's own culture. Thus according to Erich Fromm, 'Zen is no more difficult for the European than Heraclitus, Meister Eckhart, or Heidegger' (1986: 70), and Romain Rolland took the view that there is neither East nor West since 'All the aspects of mind that I found or felt [in the East] were in their origins the same as mine' (quoted in Smith 1930: xvii).[1] This polarisation of views is neatly summed up in the remark of Wilhelm Dilthey that 'Interpretation would be impossible if the expressions of life were totally foreign. It would be unnecessary if there was nothing foreign in them' (quoted in Zhang 1992: 22).

Let us begin then with the question of relativism, which in the present context I shall take to imply that, in view of the culture-bound nature of all knowledge, inter-cultural understanding is impossible. Taken at its extreme, this form of relativism is self-defeating, and moreover seems to imply that one can be on both sides of a supposedly impassable divide.[2] More pertinent in the present context is the fact that by implication if communicating across cultural boundaries is impossible, then so is *any* attempt at communication. The arguments which apply to communication between Europe and China apply with equal force, not only between modern and mediaeval Europe, but also between any two individuals attempting to communicate with one another. As the philosopher Robert Allinson points out, the 'task of crossing boundaries, rather than being something unusual, is something we are doing all the time' (1989: 2). Gadamer, likewise, has insisted that interpreting is not an occasional human performance, a heroic exploit of making sense of the incomprehensible, but something that is absolutely essential to our very being-in-the-world. Moreover, as Ben-Ami Scharfstein insists, 'the whole discussion for and against the possibility of comparative philosophy pales in the face of the history of thought. For the truth is that actual contacts have been made and influences exerted by cultures that might have been supposed to be incompatible' (1978: 35).

Nevertheless it might still be argued that communicating with the cultures of the East represents a special case, and that the East–West 'dialogue' presents problems which do not arise when communicating with one's boss, neighbour, or partner. A view such as this can be gleaned from Gadamer's own writings, according to which all understanding is grounded in *tradition*, and the fusion of horizons which is at the core of historical understanding can only arise through the mediation of a shared tradition. On this view the attempted fusion of past and present 'is not to be thought of so much as an action of one's subjectivity, but as the placing of oneself within a process of tradition' (1975: 258). However, as has frequently been pointed out, Gadamer's notion of 'tradition', and his sense of 'belonging' to a tradition, are questionable. Jürgen Habermas, for example, has accused Gadamer of adopting an overly simple and uncritical notion of tradition which fosters dogmatism and authoritarianism, and Halbfass urges us to go beyond Gadamer by recognising the historical 'openness and self-transcendence' of all traditions, most especially the Western/European (1987: 165). What is not always evident in Gadamer's writings, in spite of his admission that we 'can never have a truly closed horizon' (1975: 271), is the degree to which peoples and their ideas have throughout history perpetually interpenetrated and interacted; nor the fact that ways of thinking alien to indigenous traditions do not belong exclusively to 'other' cultures but are also frequently present in our very midst, that our own culture can be experienced 'as strange and as characterized by profound otherness' (Turner 1994: 103). After all, the European tradition itself is a hermeneutical community within which a great variety of radically diverse horizons have come into mutual engagement, to some extent fusing, to some extent retaining their separate identities. It has already accommodated and synthesised within itself all kinds of cultural extremes, with sources ranging from Jerusalem to Athens, from mysticism to logic, from metaphysical idealism to positivistic science, from the Celtic runes to Euclidean geometry. As Allinson puts it: 'Cultural boundaries have never been pristine' (1989: 5).[3]

A more direct critique of Gadamer's use of the idea of tradition arises out of the historical account of East–West interactions that was offered in the two central sections of this book. What I hope to have achieved there is a direct refutation of any notion that East and West have constituted distinct and unrelated traditions, and an affirmation that, from Alexander's and Ashoka's expansive aspirations to contemporary Buddhist–Christian dialogue, some kind of 'fusion of horizons', however spasmodic and fragmented, has indeed taken place.[4] The hermeneutical engagement between peoples must therefore be seen as a universal phenomenon that cannot be artificially confined to mutually closed-off traditions, but must be conceived as if having boundaries which stretch as far as the limits of human experience and language itself. According to this way of looking at things, therefore, there is no compelling reason why Gadamer's hermeneutical concepts and perspectives should not be applied to a wider, trans-cultural context, for, as Halbfass points out, even though we may belong to an identifiable European tradition, this tradition itself 'has been a "fusion" of different cultural horizons – Greek, Roman, Hebrew, etc.', and that therefore the 'phenomena of understanding and misunderstanding, which occur within a particular tradition, need not be fundamentally different from those which we encounter when we try to approach other traditions' (1988: 165).

Problems concerning the idea of tradition have frequently been posed in terms of *language*. It has sometimes been argued that different languages embody different forms of understanding, a thesis which would, in confirmation of our earlier worries, tend to undermine the kind of attempts at inter-cultural understanding we are concerned with here. The classic statement of this view was made by the anthropologist Benjamin Lee Whorf (1956) who argued that language determines perception and thought, a view anticipated by the French sinologist Marcel Granet (1934) for whom the fundamental differences between Chinese and European languages imply fundamental differences in ways of thinking. Similar views have been seen to arise out of the philosophical speculations of such influential thinkers as Wittgenstein and Thomas Kuhn. Stated in its extreme form this view – characterised by Karl Popper as 'the myth of the framework' – implies the impossibility, not only of translating from one language to another, but even of making any sense of another language-user's world view. This, once again, is clearly self-negating, for the hypothesis can be set up in the first place only on the assumption that we are in a position to compare the way different languages construct the world. Nevertheless, in a modified form the hypothesis helps to remind us that deep philosophical differences, involving fundamental divergences in how people conceptualise nature, human actions, and values, may be encountered as we move from one linguistic/cultural tradition to another. The strangeness that so often has been evident to Europeans in their encounter with Eastern ideas may therefore be neither a sign of total difference, nor yet a stage on the way towards total comprehension, but rather a manifestation of the difficult hermeneutical process in which the cultural horizons of two cultures move towards some kind of dialogical accommodation. These considerations may serve to remind us that the 'fusion of horizons', so lightly spoken of, does in fact involve a difficult and often frustrating set of transactions, the outcome of which is not a terminus but merely a stage along a path which offers no final resting place.[5] It may also serve to remind us that such explorations have now entered into the mainstream of philosophical discourse, and the question of East–West understanding is increasingly being drawn into current epistemological debates.[6]

The kind of linguistic relativism suggested by these speculations has obvious implications for our understanding of *translation*. The problem can be brought into focus by reference to the thesis of the indeterminacy of translation associated with the American logician W. V. O. Quine. He has argued that at the heart of any attempt to translate from one language to another there lies a radical and inescapable indeterminacy, for we have no standpoint outside of language from which to judge its adequacy. This clearly provokes urgent questions when considering East–West communication for this has largely relied over the past four centuries on the translation of oriental texts into European languages. Once again, stated in its starkest form this thesis is almost certainly self-refuting, but leaving philosophical puzzles aside it does serve to remind us again of the need to apply the hermeneutical dictum of critical self-reflexiveness when engaged in translating across wide cultural and linguistic divides. Even in the early days of the Jesuit China mission there took place agonised debates about the appropriate translation of the term 'God', and nearer to our own times concepts such as 'mind', 'spirit', '*tao*', and '*karma*' have caused notable difficulties. In this context the Buddhist scholar Herbert Guenther, in a discussion of Western interpretation of Tantric Buddhism, has warned that language in general 'is a treacherous instrument', and 'the question, whether the authors of the original texts actually meant the same as we do by those words about whose meaning we ourselves are not quite clear, should always be present . . . when translating texts' (Guenther 1989: 37–8). A sobering example of such problems is to be found in the new edition of *The Tibetan Book of the Great Liberation* where the translator, John Reynolds, comments wryly that the earlier rendering by Evans-Wentz was flawed to such an extent that Jung, who wrote his 'Psychological Commentary' for this edition, 'had no way to know what the Tibetan text was actually talking about' (1989: 108).

In view of such difficulties it is hardly surprising that there have been wide divergences between translations of classic oriental texts, a conspicuous example of this being the *Tao Te Ching* which has been subject to numerous translations and consequently to a bewildering variety of interpretations. Part of the problem here is that translations are not ideologically neutral but are shaped by the background and outlook of the translator. In the nineteenth century, for example, translations of Hindu and Buddhist works were often made by people who came from a neo-Kantian/idealist or a theological/Christian background and whose work was, often unconsciously, shaped accordingly. A good example of the former would be Max Müller who rendered Kant's *Critique of Pure Reason* into English before setting to work on Sanskrit texts. In the early twentieth century the work of translating Eastern texts has sometimes, as in the case of Evans-Wentz, been affected by the theosophical beliefs of the translator, and in the case of translations by James Legge and Richard Wilhelm of the *I Ching*, by their Christian missionary backgrounds. Another problem is that many of the texts involved are, if not deliberately elusive, often calling into question and deliberately undermining the conventional functions of language and are couched in linguistic forms – we might call them poetic – which often mock our standard methods of translation and interpretation.[7]

In case considerations such as these tempt us back into a more extreme sceptical position, we need to remind ourselves once again that the work of the translator is but a more formalised version of the universal hermeneutical structure of human communication. As we emphasised earlier, people cross conceptual, cultural, and linguistic boundaries, not only when rendering a foreign text into the vernacular, but also whenever they read a book, listen to a lecture, or engage in the most trivial conversation, for every act of communication involves a measure of decipherment and interpretation. The translator's work, even where there is a painful awareness of cultural and historical distance from the original, possesses, as Gadamer has noted, 'something of the effort to understand another person in conversation', every translator being involved in what is 'an extreme case of hermeneutical difficulty, i.e. of alienness and its conquest' (1975: 348–9). The underlying philosophical problems are roughly the same across the spectrum of communication, and hence the force of Quine's translation argument could apply equally within, as much as between, cultures and traditions.[8]

PROJECTING ACROSS BOUNDARIES

Even if we succeed in rescuing orientalist discourse from the jaws of relativism, we still need to square up to the common objection that Western interpreters have in practice been deficient in their attempts to cross cultural boundaries, and have consistently failed to recognise the need to place Eastern modes of thought in their indigenous contexts and to understand them in their own terms. In a word they have, according to this sort of accusation, appropriated Eastern ideas by simply *projecting* onto them the West's own categories, assumptions, and preoccupations, and in general terms the West has become 'a sort of omnivorous monster, one which swallows up all other cultures' (Rorty 1992: 588). Concerns of this kind were first clearly articulated by Edward Said in the late 1970s, and were articulated at the same time by Harvey Cox who argued that the East has become nothing more than 'a myth that resides in the head of Westerners . . . a convenient screen on which the West projects reverse images of its own deficiencies' (1977: 149). In recent years it has become fashionable to speak of the 'Orient' as a Western creation or construct, as constituting a Western discourse rather than an independently existing reality. Language itself, according to this view, becomes an unconscious instrument for the projection of Western assumptions and values, and serious questions arise, for example, out of the use of classificatory terms such as 'Orient', 'religion', and 'Hinduism' which are often used without reflecting adequately on the fact that such terms arise from a peculiarly occidental mode of thinking. By the same token, the efforts to transpose Buddhist teachings into the conceptual frameworks of Western psychotherapy, of Taoism into those of modern ecology, and of *Mādhyamaka* into the terms of linguistic philosophy suggest the widening rather than the bridging of the East–West divide. At a more subtle level there are the largely unspoken strategies of selectivity which, on the model of Western Christian and humanistic traditions, have led to a privileging of a canonical set of 'classical' Asian texts and the marginalisation of 'superstitious' and 'corrupt' practices such as polytheism and the veneration of 'idols', and of popular mythologies and cosmologies.[9] In brief, whole ways of thinking from non-European sources have been more or less consciously reconstituted in the mill of Western modes of representation such that, as one critic vividly expresses it, 'Asian thought must be shown to be positivistic in a time when positivism is in vogue, or existential for those who value existentialism, or scientific today if there is to be anything of worth in it' (Jones 1986: 172).

This sort of objection would amount to claiming that orientalism has failed to measure up to the high hermeneutical ideals specified by Gadamer who insists somewhat optimistically that 'a person trying to understand a text is prepared for it to tell him something', the important thing being 'to be aware of one's own bias, so that the text may present itself in all its newness and thus be able to assert its own truth against one's own fore-meanings' (1975: 238). Is there any evidence that orientalists have been prepared to let texts from Asian philosophical and religious traditions speak to them? As we saw again and again in the earlier part of this book, Western scholars, philosophers, theologians, and psychologists have not only torn oriental texts loose from their religious and cultural contexts, but have then proceeded to relocate them within Western frames of discourse, thereby inevitably simplifying and distorting them.[10] Eric Sharpe's comment that 'the Western tradition of [Bhagavad] Gītā hermeneutics has been its almost total lack of interest in the Hindu world's own estimate of its own Gītā' (1985: xiii); and Gai Eaton's accusation that 'Huxley [in *The Perennial Philosophy*] filched from various doctrines, without regard for their context, those elements which seem to support his attitude to life' (1949: 182) sum up what to many appears to be a pervasive defect of orientalism.

This syndrome is in evidence even where the conscious motives of the participants may appear to be of the highest kind. C. A. Moore's project of 'reconciling' Eastern and Western thought or the religions of East and West, within a wider and more global synthesis, was driven by nothing less than the desire to save the world from political and spiritual disaster. But it could be argued that in pursuing this worthy goal he and his co-universalists failed to reflect on the characteristically European authorship of the project, in particular its source in Enlightenment thinking. Some would go further and agree with Leroy Rouner that the universalistic tendency 'came easily to those whose mindset was fashioned by the politics of Western colonialism', and that such thinking, far from being genuinely universal, represents the tribal views of 'the dominant white Western male' (in Marks and Ames 1995: 91). Even in the case of 'comparative religion' and 'comparative philosophy', which on the face of it might appear to be more neutral and more open-ended than the project of Moore and his colleagues in Hawaii, there is in evidence a desire to control and manipulate foreign ideas in the service of home-spun purposes. Raimundo Panikkar, for example, worries that 'Comparative studies are still fashionable today because they belong to the thrust towards universalization characteristic of Western culture' (in Larson and Deutsch 1988: 116). Similar objections have been mounted against those who, with the very best of intentions, have reformulated Asian teachings within non-Asian evangelistic modes, such as Paul Carus's *The Gospel of Buddha* (first published in 1894), and David Goddard's *A Buddhist Bible* (first published in 1936).[11]

Even orientalist scholarship of the more 'scientific' kind does not escape this sort of criticism. The development of more systematic methodologies in the nineteenth and twentieth centuries has certainly helped to discredit some of the more blatant distortions and fantasies, and provided improved tools for translation and interpretation. But in spite of this, scholars have inevitably projected their own interests and prejudices, as well as those of the cultures from which they have sprung, onto the objects of their investigation. The sinologist Bernard Faure maintains that in spite of critiques of orientalism and attempts by scholars to free themselves from the attitudes and prejudices of earlier times, 'It would be an error to believe that much has changed: in all cases, whether the Oriental or primitive Other is caricatured or idealized, the ethnocentric and Orientalist premises of Western discourse are similar' (1993: 6). In like fashion, looking back at the disputes in nineteenth-century Europe concerning the idea of *nirvāna*, Guy Welbon points out that interpretations by scholars have been shaped to a significant degree by their ideological prejudices, and are to be seen as ultimately based 'not exclusively on philosophical and historico-critical considerations [but] in every instance reflect the individual scholar's personal commitment' (1968: viii). Thus for example Hermann Oldenberg, a leading Indologist of that period, was motivated in much of his research by a neo-Kantian suspicion of metaphysics, and the French orientalist Barthélemy Saint-Hilaire's judgement 'was buttressed by his deep and informed commitment' to certain philosophical and religious principles (ibid.: 208 and 76). On a more political plane there is the case of the 'scientific' support given by German Indologists to the Nazi cause, a portentous affair to which we will return later in this chapter.[12]

Is there any way of circumventing this, or is orientalism inescapably enmeshed in the language and the cultural attitudes and prejudices of its origins, and hence incapable of communicating with Eastern modes of thinking in anything other than distortive and manipulative ways? In responding to such questions as these it is important to bear in mind that any communication whatsoever carries with it an element of projection whereby one communicator will read his or her own preconceptions into the other. It has become conventional wisdom that scholars work within specific ideological, philosophical, and political environments, and the vision of a distortion-free understanding, at whatever level, has been challenged in recent years by recognition of the theory-laden, perspectival, and pre-judgemental factors that inevitably enter into human knowledge. Moreover, taken in its most literal sense, the view that all attempts to represent other cultures are constructed, and hence determine the nature of the object, would seem to preclude completely the possibility of ever understanding another culture. Take the following statement by T. W. Organ: 'To force Chinese humanism, Japanese Buddhism, and Indian metaphysics into a synthesis determined by Western philosophical assumptions would constitute a serious loss of variegated approaches to human life and thought' (1989: 118). The point is well taken, but at the same time it may not have escaped the reader's notice that terms like 'humanism' and 'metaphysics' used by Organ in this passage have a timbre which resonates more to Western than to Eastern intellectual traditions. This is not to imply that their use was necessarily an error, but rather to underline the point that Westerners simply cannot avoid using a vocabulary derived from their own culture, and that the point therefore is not to avoid such use – which is impossible anyway – but to do so with critical self-awareness. Thus David Mungello argues that some kind of 'sinological torque', whereby the preoccupations of the scholar are imposed on the object of study, is inevitable, but the point is not to try to eliminate it but to subject it to constant critical reflection (see Mungello 1978). A similar point is made by Edward Said who, while pointing out that 'to some German Romantics . . . Indian religion was essentially an Oriental version of Germano-Christian pantheism', admits that 'all cultures impose corrections on raw reality, changing it from free-floating objects into units of knowledge', which means that inevitably oriental concepts are transformed into patterns of thought like those of the receiving culture (1985: 67). But it would be a mistake to draw from this the conclusion that knowledge of the East is nothing but the imposition of 'correction' or meaning on an otherwise noumenal or essentially elusive reality, and is nothing but an arbitrary fabrication. All knowing is a two-way dialectical relationship in which our conjectures are both imposed on and corrected by the objects of our interest, and all accounts of the past, whether of one's own or another's culture, are as much discovered as constructed, as much found as imagined.

Gadamer's views are relevant here. According to him the projective tendency in human understanding is an essential component of the hermeneutical process: 'A person who is trying to understand a text is always performing an act of projecting' (1975: 236). All interpretation involves, however implicitly, a process whereby the text being examined, the sentence being heard, the work of art being scrutinised is assimilated into the conceptual horizon of the interpreter, and is shaped by current concerns and imperatives, an inter-textual process in which foreign writings are reflected and reconstructed from within domestic textual horizons. As the sinologist A. C. Graham puts it: 'We, like the Chinese, fully engage with the thought [of an other] only when we relate it to our own problems' (1989: ix), a view which echoes Gadamer's notion of 'application' (see Gadamer, op. cit.: 274 ff). Moreover there is a mutuality in the hermeneutical process which, though necessarily beginning with one's own cultural categories, may very likely lead to their transformation in the course of the encounter: 'interpretation begins with fore-conceptions that are replaced by more suitable ones' (ibid.: 236). This is not an occasional or accidental part of interpretation, but of its very nature, for it is logically impossible for the interpreter hermeneutically to engage with such a textual object without this presupposition, or to imagine that the meaning of the text can be 'present' to the interpreter without any mediating interference. Furthermore, there is no 'essence' of meaning lying elsewhere, hermetically sealed within the encasement of foreign languages and cultures. Meaning according to Gadamer is always the product of an interactive process taking place between two or more poles which are sometimes close, sometimes far apart, and it is precisely the tension between these poles which makes understanding possible. 'To interpret means precisely to use one's own preconceptions so that the meaning of the text can really be made to speak for us', a process which Gadamer sees as modelled on the conversational structure of question and answer rather than on that of intuitive insight or of passive recipience (ibid.: 358).[13]

A useful example of this dynamic interpretative process is to be found once again in attitudes towards Buddhism. In the nineteenth century two major interpretative perspectives became dominant, the one seeing Buddhism in deeply pessimistic terms, the other in terms of scientific rationalism. In the twentieth century both of these perspectives have been called into question and superseded by interpretations which are both more optimistic and positive in tone, and which emphasise the spiritual rather than the rational qualities of Buddhism. Throughout the same period, as we observed earlier, there has also been a shift from a predominantly Kantian-inspired interpretative tradition with regard to Indian philosophy, towards a linguistically-inspired one, a shift which is clearly related to the radical change in Western philosophical fashion that took place in this century.[14] But at the same time it would be difficult to argue that, by comparison with the nineteenth century, we have now reached a 'correct' interpretation; Thomas Merton's complaint about 'the irresistible temptation to think of Zen in Neo-Platonic terms [or as] a system of pantheistic monism' (1961: 14) is readily understandable, but this should hardly imply that we must try to understand Zen without the aid of any Western concepts whatsoever – including the ones that he mentions. Indeed one of the developments that has taken place over this period is the growth of methodological awareness, a greater degree of hermeneutical sensitivity which has not only encouraged us to reflect on the questions and assumptions that are implicit in our hermeneutical efforts, but has also led us to reflect on the fact that our own present interpretations have no claim to finality or definitive validity. Furthermore it might be inferred from this example that the inadequate renderings of Buddhism in the past are not mere mistakes which would better have been avoided, but necessary and salutary turnings of the hermeneutical wheel.

RACISM

Can we, though, continue to speak of 'dialogue' between East and West in these hermeneutical terms without facing up to the full social and political implications of this particular realm of discourse? Some critics see Gadamer's brand of hermeneutics as involving a complacent theory of history, and J. Caputo accuses him of articulating a theory of tradition which 'is innocent of Nietzsche's suspicious eye', and which does not face up to 'its capacity to oppress' (1987: 112). Indeed the very Eurocentredness of the orientalist agenda which we have documented in the middle sections of this book obliges us to look at orientalism through 'Nietzsche's suspicious eye' and to open up the possibility that these apparently benign activities may have helped to form and propagate cultural infirmities. Amongst the most obvious and virulent of these are racist attitudes, anti-semitism, and related fascistic ideas and movements. Racist attitudes have certainly been a pervasive feature of the West's historical engagement with the Orient. It may be an exaggeration to say that 'every European, in what he could say about the Orient, was . . . a racist, an imperialist, and almost totally ethnocentric' (Said 1985: 204), but in the mid- to late nineteenth century there was a growing racist culture in Europe directed, *inter alia*, towards China and India, and a rising tide of anti-semitism whose catastrophic consequences in the following century have plunged the whole question of Europe and its 'other' into acute agitation.[15] But how does this baneful episode in Europe's history relate to orientalism? Surely the whole demeanour of orientalism – as this term has been used throughout this book – has been predominantly one of goodwill towards the cultures and civilisations of the East, and has been precisely at odds with jingoistic, imperialistic, and racist postures. Can we not, then, without more ado set aside such questions as irrelevant to our present purposes?

On the face of it this riposte seems justified, for orientalists from the Enlightenment period onwards have in many respects encouraged attitudes of inter-cultural understanding and toleration, and by canonising the ancient scriptures and religions of the East have often run counter to the overbearing, oppressive demeanour of the colonising powers. However, even leaving on one side the demeaning attitudes that have persisted in popular orientalist writings, there is a significant other side to the story. In the first place some critics have pointed to the fact that this very idealisation of ancient texts, far from creating a bond of equality with Eastern peoples, has had the consequence of disparaging the denizens of contemporary oriental cultures, and of marking out a justification for their political and commercial exploitation by showing them to be inferior to modern Europeans.[16] Moreover, whether or not the creation of such attitudes could plausibly be described as actively or explicitly racist, it is beyond dispute that orientalism has in practice sometimes formed associations with racism, and that the way in which orientalism has implicated the East in specifically Western controversies has sometimes led to its being exploited for racially discriminatory purposes. The most significant point of contact occurred in the nineteenth century when racism, which was emerging in that period as an identifiable intellectual discourse, can be seen as having formed close ties with certain manifestations of orientalism. They both shared common roots in the Romantic movement, and the seeds of anti-semitism can be identified in the writings of Romantic orientalists such as Herder, Schlegel, and Schopenhauer. As we saw in an earlier chapter, Friedrich Schlegel, capitalising on ideas first intimated by Sir William Jones, made a significant contribution to the formulation of the concept of the Aryan race with his categorical disjunction between the Indo-European family of languages and others, and his matching of this distinction with a racial one. Schopenhauer, whose affinity with Indian philosophies was at least as close as Schlegel's, has been more specifically indicted with developing proto-racist and anti-semitic attitudes. But, as we argued earlier, neither of these thinkers could strictly be accused of racism or anti-semitism: Schlegel made no overt attempt to denigrate the Jewish race by comparison with the Indo-European, and with Schopenhauer it was not the Jewish people who were the object of his animosity but rather the theological doctrines of Judaism which he contrasted unfavourably with the teachings of Buddhism.[17] However, while the association of orientalism – from the Enlightenment period onwards – with a radical critique of the Jewish religious tradition and its relation to Western civilisation does not imply any *logical* connection between orientalism and anti-semitism, it may well be seen as opening up, in some historical circumstances at any rate, a facilitating pathway between the two.

This caesura between logical and practical implication is evident in the case of the orientalist Max Müller who was the first to formulate a fully worked-out theory concerning the Aryan family of languages in lectures given in Oxford in 1859–61. In these lectures he was careful to deny any racial implications, insisting that 'Aryan, in scientific language, is inapplicable to race; and if we speak of Aryan race at all, we should know that it means no more than Aryan speech' (quoted in Chaudhuri 1974: 314). Yet it cannot be denied that his ideas, along with the polarisation of the Jewish with the Indo-Germanic factors in European inheritance, helped to mark out a conceptual framework which proved crucial in the subsequent construction of an explicitly racist and anti-semitic discourse. According to the Indologist Sheldon Pollock, the identification of the Germanic with the Indo-Aryan peoples played an important part in Germany's 'Romantic search for self-definition', and led to the dichotomy between the 'Indo-Germanic' and the 'Semitic' races and to the affirmation of Aryan superiority. This was a process which Pollock refers to as the 'internal colonization of Europe' in which he sees orientalism as being vectored 'inward to Europe itself rather than outwards towards Europe's colonies, to constructing the conception of a historical German essence and to defining Germany's place in Europe's destiny', and he quotes the proto-fascist Houston Stuart Chamberlain as proclaiming that 'Indology must help us to fix our sights more clearly on the goals of our culture. A great humanistic task has fallen to our lot to accomplish; and thereto is Aryan India summoned' (in Breckenridge and van der Veer 1993: 83 and 86).

The perception of a symbiotic relationship between nineteenth-century orientalism and racism is reinforced by the fact that a number of proponents of racist doctrines such as Renan and Le Bon, as well as several other figures involved in the formulation of racist attitudes, such as Bopp, Boetticher-Lagarde, and of course Wagner, were all associated with orientalism. The French diplomat and historian J. A. de Gobineau (1816–82), in whose writings racist and anti-semitic doctrines were fully articulated, was well versed in oriental languages and made considerable use of orientalist references in the construction of his racist views. In his writings he followed Voltaire and Schopenhauer in emphasising Europe's cultural debt to the East, and building on and beyond Herder and Schlegel he elaborated the idea of a superior Aryan race from which both Indian and Germanic peoples stem. He lauded the white Aryans of India, seeing the caste system as a preserver of racial purity and the guarantor of India's survival of British rule, but at the same time he pronounced the 'dark races', including those of ancient pre-Aryan India, to be inferior to the European, and while asserting the pre-eminence of the white Aryan race who had invaded the Indian sub-continent, over its indigenous inhabitants, he viewed the Indian peoples as in reality a bastardised, and hence inferior, mixture of Aryan and native populations. Furthermore, he expressed contemptuous views, typical of his day, concerning the Chinese people who 'have little physical vigour and tend towards apathy . . . to mediocrity . . . [and] have an easy enough understanding of what is not too elevated or too profound' (quoted in Bernal 1987: 240)

However, it must be remembered that belief in racial inequality as a 'scientific' fact was widely held by intellectuals of the period, and moreover that nineteenth-century racism and anti-semitism was a highly complex, hybrid affair, a 'scavenger ideology', as the historian George Mosse puts it, which 'annexed diverse ideas', even ones like early socialism and traditional Christianity which appeared on the face of it to be incompatible with it (1981: vii). Most important of these 'diverse ideas' was *völkisch* thought, a potent amalgam of theories deriving from Herder and the Romantics which emphasised the common ethnic and cultural identity of the Germanic peoples and the related ideas of 'blood and soil'. Anti-semitic views were also linked to the crisis of Christian faith and the attendant belief that the Jews were a non-spiritual people who were seen as having all too easily capitulated to the growing materialistic outlook of the period. And they were also connected with the reaction against industrialisation and modernisation, both of which again were associated with the emancipation and secularisation of Jewish people in Western Europe. Bearing in mind that orientalism also represented for many people a reaction against both Christianity and certain hegemonic rationalist trends, it is hardly surprising that it shared some common ground with racism. It is evident that in the late nineteenth and early twentieth centuries orientalism sometimes became ensnared by and gave succour to the emerging racist discourse. However, the extraordinary web of ideological convergences which characterised European thought at that time, involving *inter alia* race, eugenics, nationalism, naturalism, evolutionism, and occultism, and responding to the 'kindling fever' that had taken hold of Europe, became entangled together in what must seem in retrospect to be a series of unlikely and contingent associations. It would be a mistake, then, to ascribe some 'essentially' racist taint to orientalism on the basis of a study of nineteenth- and early twentieth-century Europe. Apart from the awkward interwovenness of so many disparate intellectual and cultural strands, we need to keep in mind as well the fact that the intercalation of the languages, histories, and religions of India and Europe, sketched out by a series of orientalists from Jones and Schlegel to Quinet and Max Müller, represented a powerful force for the expansion and enrichment of traditional Western outlooks, laying foundations for an enhancement of inter-cultural understanding, and helping to moderate endemic xenophobic attitudes. Nevertheless, at the same time we must not overlook the other side of the picture, nor ignore the fact that Gobineau and his friends turned to the East in order to formulate their racist doctrines, and used orientalist theories in order to conceptualise redemptive options with which to combat the disorders and degeneracies which, in their minds, characterised the current condition of European culture.[18]

FASCISM

Analogous considerations emerge when we look at similar conjunctions in the early years of the twentieth century where we find that orientalism formed ominous links, not only with racist attitudes, but also with fascism. We referred in an earlier chapter to the close interest of W. B. Yeats, Ezra Pound, and T. S. Eliot in oriental ideas. What we did not bring to attention there was the fact that all three evinced anti-semitic tendencies, and that Pound displayed outspoken sympathy for fascist régimes. Once again, though, we need to bear in mind that such attitudes were not at all uncommon amongst intellectuals in that period, and also that many other orientalist-inclined thinkers showed no such tendencies; this is not to 'excuse' such attitudes but to indicate the extent to which orientalism and racism were both elements that have to be understood within the broader mix of loosely related belief systems and social agitations of the time. Nevertheless, we are still left with the nagging suspicion that the connection here is not entirely coincidental or adventitious. Taking our cue from the earlier Romantic period, we might conjecture that the connection lay not so much in any direct or logical connection between orientalist and fascist outlooks, but rather in the fact that in both cases a robust assault had been mounted on certain established Western ideas and traditions. It is worth recalling that Yeats, Pound, and Eliot were all central figures in the articulation of the modern movement in literature, a movement which set out self-consciously in a radically new direction, and mounted a concerted campaign whereby long-prevailing artistic and literary traditions were to be questioned. The precise objects of orientalist and modernist criticism are not identical, yet they do overlap at certain points. For example, as I pointed out earlier, the Theosophical Society, which was an influence on all three of these writers, considered itself and was considered by others to be radical in its outlook, attacking as it did the whole Judaeo-Christian foundation of Western culture. Its interest, and that of the early modernist poets, in the spiritual and the occult may appear at variance with all that we have come to associate with the 'modern' outlook, but we can begin to make sense of this paradox if we view this as part of an attempt, by no means confined at this time to theosophists and modernist poets, to bring about a renewal and transformation of Western cultural life. For many at the turn of the century the old world was moribund and a new beginning was needed, and orientalism and fascism were two amongst the many exemplifications of this transformative *angst*.

Can we apply the same argument to Heidegger and Jung, both of whom had significant orientalist leanings, and who have both been accused of anti-semitism and of pro-Nazi complicity? Heidegger was a member of the Nazi party, and for a brief time became Rector of Freiburg University where he carried out the party's anti-semitic policies. Jung, as a Swiss national, was not a party member, but some of his writings and activities in the 1930s have led to him being seen as a sympathiser. His idea of the collective unconscious was viewed by the Nazis themselves as supportive of their philosophy, and his theories concerning the psychological differences between races, though hedged about with denials of racist intent, could appear to give support to anti-semitism. Once again we need to ask whether there could be any intrinsic connections here, or only chance intellectual encounters, whether some central or key tenet of their thinking binds them inescapably to these pathologies. An adequate answer could only be given by a close study of both cases, which are in any event different from each other in many crucial respects. Nevertheless, a characteristic feature of both thinkers was a need to offer a fundamental critique of modern Western civilisation and to point ways towards more authentic modes of existence. For Heidegger it was the need to rediscover the meaning of Being; Jung's aims could better be understood in terms of the need for spiritual renewal as a means towards psychic health. For both, oriental thought offered, in various respects, a way back to a more direct engagement with human being and with the world of nature, and an experiential mode which offered the possibility of an alternative, or perhaps a complement, to Western scientific and technological rationalism. It is likely that for both men Nazi ideals initially appeared to offer a political framework for such hopes, and a dynamic driving force which they may have thought would bring about a much-needed spiritual revolution in Europe. But it is clear that both became disillusioned with this prospect as it was shaped by the hands of the Nazis, and that Jung – though not Heidegger – subsequently became profoundly hostile to all that Nazism stood for. There seems once again to be some kind of coincidence of overall objectives, but hardly a fusion of intellectual horizons. Jung's emphasis on highly personalised goals of individuation, his internationalist outlook, and his profound distaste for social collectivities have little in common with the mass hysteria and the nationalistic fervour of Hitler's Germany, and his employment of oriental thought to illuminate his concept of the 'self' is equally poles apart from the ideals expressed by Nazi apologists.[19]

What of the relationship between the Nazis themselves and orientalism? Once again the link appears, on the face of it, unlikely, but recent scholarship reveals a disturbing situation in which distinct congruences are evident at certain levels between orientalism and Nazi ideology. Sheldon Pollock, for example, has argued that Indologists played a significant role in the formulation of Germany's discourse of racial dominance in the years 1933–45 (see Breckenridge and van der Veer 1993: 86–96). He shows that in their quest for German self-identity and National Socialist self-legitimation in an Aryan past the Nazi apologists sought confirmation, not only from nineteenth-century scholarship, but also from contemporary sources, and drew into seemingly willing collaboration the services of a considerable number of German orientalists. In short, the 'science' of orientalist scholarship was drafted in to legitimate the order of the National Socialist state. Thus, the leading Vedic specialist and Nazi supporter, Walter Wüst, held up the ancient Hindu sacred texts as being not only free of any semitic taint, but also in fundamental agreement with the outlook of Hitler's *Mein Kampf*, 'a text that thus evinces a spiritual continuum stretching from the second millennium BC to the present' (quoted in ibid.: 90). He even went so far as to characterise the Führer's outlook as consonant with the Buddhist 'Middle Way', and to correlate the Buddha's confrontation with human suffering with Hitler's experience of the suffering of working people in his early Vienna period! Added to this is the fact that some of the Nazi leaders were familiar with Hindu teachings, Himmler, it is said, being particularly fond of the *Bhagavad Gītā*. Such worrying connections demand serious attention, but once again should not lead us to the conclusion that there is something inherently evil at the heart of orientalism; it is a truism that all powerful ideas carry potential for both good and evil, and it is worth noting that the work of two orientalists with Nazi sympathies, J. W. Hauer and E. Herrigel, on the *chakra* system and Zen respectively, appears now to carry no ideological stigma, and indeed has proved intellectually and spiritually stimulating to the present generation.[20]

Collusion between orientalism and fascism is also evident in the case of the Italian Giuseppe Tucci. One of the most distinguished Buddhologists of the twentieth century, his work ranges from India and Tibet to China and Japan, and has been particularly influential in opening up the field of Tibetan studies. During the Mussolini regime, however, he became entangled in fascist politics, and in a series of semi-popular articles he placed his scholarship at the service of the ideological campaigns of the Italian state. He was particularly concerned to strengthen ties between Italy and Japan, and to that end he set out to demonstrate that the central characteristics of Italian fascism were also to be found in the traditional practices of Zen with its warrior creed and its sense of authentic and immediate contact with an elemental nature which precedes the rationalisations of science and technology. In general terms, the spiritual riches and psychological integrity encountered in the East were contrasted by Tucci with the artificial, rootless, and fragmented life of modern Europe, and throughout his writings in the 1930s and early 1940s he elaborated the utopian theme of nostalgia for a more authentic mode of existence and a deep antagonism to the modernising tendencies of industrialism, urbanisation, and liberal democracy. They were in effect a means for coming to terms with modernity that echoed the fundamental agenda of fascist ideology. As Gustavo Benavides puts it: 'Tucci's Orientalism [was] a peculiar creature in which a deep dissatisfaction with modernity led him to imagine the Orient in which he could always find . . . the wholeness no longer available in the West' (in Lopez 1995: 182).

The lesson to be learned is, I believe, not concerned with any essential identity between orientalism and fascism but rather with the necessity for vigilance and critical reflexiveness; as the French philosopher Julien Benda argued in the face of racist obscurantism, the treason of the intellectuals lies in the betrayal of the pursuit of truth and justice for political considerations. Furthermore, as Pollock points out, there are wider implications here concerning humanistic scholarship in general, for 'German Indology was hardly different from the rest of German scholarship in the period', and he expresses the hope that the development of a more 'self-consciously responsible scholarship' will escape complicity in 'new forms of coercive power' (in Breckenridge and van der Veer 1993: 112). It is important to understand how it was that some orientalists came into close relationship with fascism in certain historical circumstances, and to face up to and come to terms with this, not in order to condemn orientalism as such, but rather in order to ensure that such dire mistakes should not be repeated. This warning is especially relevant for an age in which the metamorphosis of noble creeds into fundamentalist instruments for the pursuit of material gain or *Realpolitik* has again cast an ominous shadow, and we need constantly to remind ourselves that Eastern religious ideas, like those of the Abrahamic traditions, possess fissionable capability and embody potential for evil as well as good.[21]

IRRATIONALISM

Discussion of the Nazi connection suggests the need to probe further, and to raise the question whether the association between fascist outlooks and orientalism can be traced to a much deeper level. On the face of it the ideas of thinkers like Jung and Heidegger appear to have little affinity with fascism, but it may still be the case that if we dig further we will find a much more disturbing layer of significance. This layer could be summed up in the word *irrationalism*, and linked with the anti-modernist and anti-humanist leanings that have often been connected with orientalism. Both fascism and orientalism have at various times and in various ways been associated not only with the discouragement of critical rationality, but more widely with a psycho-epistemic syndrome which despairs of the products of the Enlightenment – reason, science, technology, individual liberty – and longs to rediscover the deep primal source of human nature in something primitive, something associated with a more direct, non-rational, ecstatic experience, and which puts us in touch with some true, but now lost, wellspring of our being. Does this irrationalist model fit the case of orientalism? Does the whole orientalist enterprise, associated as it frequently is with occult and New Age concerns, represent a dangerous retreat into irrationalism and fanaticism driven by personal illumination and mystical vision, and into what C. S. Peirce called 'the monstrous mysticism of the East'?

This kind of criticism of orientalism has frequently been voiced in recent times, especially in the aftermath of the 1960s counter-culture. The association of oriental ideas and practices with the drug culture and the hippie lifestyle has often been emphasised, and, as we saw in an earlier chapter, C. G. Jung and Medard Boss were both careful to point out the psychological dangers for Westerners in appropriating oriental methods without adequate safeguards. One of the most trenchant critiques came from the pen of the Indologist R.C. Zaehner. A Roman

Catholic who, as we saw in an earlier chapter, sought to maintain a certain distance between Christian and oriental spiritual traditions, Zaehner drew attention to what he saw as the dangerously a-moral implications flowing from Eastern thought. He built a case round the notorious figure of Charles Manson, instigator of the 'Sharon Tate murders', who, though not himself a devotee of any oriental doctrine, was to some extent influenced by Zen and Hindu ideas, and who came to represent in many minds all that the counter-culture movement had stood for, in particular its potentiality for evil. According to Zaehner, Manson, following a transformative religious experience arising from his acquaintance with Eastern religions, went into a 'liberated' state where all reason and morality were abandoned, a condition 'beyond good and evil' where he could murder serenely, without remorse. Although Zaehner is careful to avoid any implication that Eastern creeds would condone Manson's actions, he was nevertheless convinced that irrationalist tendencies in oriental religions, such as Zen *satori* and the *Vedānta* 'All is One' doctrine, could help to trigger behaviour in Westerners which was flagrantly evil. Another critique, similarly attacking the supposed irrationalist tendencies of orientalism and emphasising their supposed dangers for Westerners, has come from the even more eloquent pen of Arthur Koestler in his book *The Lotus and the Robot*. The monism and idealist metaphysics which he identified with Indian philosophy represented, in his opinion, so many 'logical monstrosities'. With its 'indifference to contradiction', Indian philosophy could only act as a 'solvent to Western conceptual thought' (1960: 49–50), and hence 'India, with all its saintly longings for samadhi, has no spiritual cure to offer for the needs of Western civilisation' (ibid.: 162). Zen is dismissed in similar terms, being surrounded by 'pseudo-mystical verbiage' which is 'at worst a web of solemn absurdities' (ibid.: 245 and 233), and its moral indifferentism shows Zen to be a positive menace, as witnessed by the failure of leading Zen masters to condemn Japanese and German war crimes. He claimed that students of Zen are taught to put reason and morality on one side and to act instead like robots, and that Zen's celebrated spontaneity amounted to little more than the conditioning of thoughtless, automatic behaviour.[22]

Some critics see these censures as having wider and more sinister implications. Dusty Sklar, for example, argues that the counter-culture of the 1960s, and the Manson cult in particular, are manifestations of a romantic irrationalism similar to that which gave rise to the Nazi movement early on in the century. She suggests that there is a strong link between the social and political disillusionments of both these periods, and that they both gave rise to orientalist and occultist movements that contained the potential for great evil. She points out that a couple of generations before the hippies, German youth had been equally caught up in a yearning for spiritual renewal, a yearning which expressed itself in a variety of preoccupations including theosophy, oriental religions, and the occult. She goes on to claim that 'the whole of Germany [at the turn of the century] was swept up in this esoteric wave', and represented 'a new romanticism [which was] above all irrational' (Sklar 1977: 105–6).[23]

Arguments such as this cannot simply be set aside as indicating little more than passing aberrations. It is clear that in certain historical circumstances oriental religious ideas have been found to open up alluring mystical pathways to a more fulfilling way of being that lies beyond the irksome constraints or the social fragmentations of the modern world. The quest for some kind of instant release from the toils of capitalism, the work ethic, and scientific rationalism – 'pop nirvana', as Koestler called it – was certainly a conspicuous feature of the 1960s, and the occult revival of recent years manifests similar characteristics and motivations to those of the turn of the century when, inspired *inter alia* by the Theosophical Society, many people sought alternative religious inspiration in esoteric traditions from both East and West. But we must be careful that these factors do not lead us to a one-sided perception of orientalism, and persuade us to return to old stereotypes in which the East is dismissed as the source of irredeemable obscurantism. If we glance back at orientalist pursuits over the past few centuries it becomes apparent that something that could be described as 'irrationalism', though evident at certain times and in certain circumstances, is not a central or dominant theme. It will be recalled that for the *philosophes* China represented not the irrational but on the contrary the very embodiment of reason. The teachings of the Upanishads, though to some extent appealing to the Romantics for certain mystical qualities, were viewed, not simply as a form of esoteric wisdom, but as marking out the fundamentals of a logically coherent system of thought which became fully articulated in the work of the philosophers. Moreover the interactions which we discussed earlier between Buddhism and evolutionism in the nineteenth century, and the intellectual traffic between Eastern philosophies and the new physics, though undoubtedly problematical in certain respects, cannot easily be identified with any cults of unreason. There is no doubt that enthusiasms for Zen, yoga, and Taoism have at times been associated with anti-intellectualist tendencies, with powerful reactions against Western scientific rationalism, and with the desire to find a truth that comes from an inner and often emotionally compulsive source of illumination. But in most of the cases we discussed in Part III of this volume in relation to philosophy, theology, psychology, science, and ecology, the direction of interest was more towards the achievement of *balance* between Western and Eastern outlooks, on the need to integrate the intuitive with the rational, the inner with the outer, the esoteric with the exoteric, and to show, for example, that 'both the scientific approach in physics and the Eastern mystical approach are complementary rather than opposite and antagonistic' (Riencourt 1981: 129).

Furthermore the concept of the 'irrational' is uncomfortably question-begging, and accusations of irrationalism can themselves be ideologically motivated, and can be turned round on the accuser. The postulation of a contrast between the rational West and the irrational East is one of the typical ways in which the West has frequently been seen as establishing its cultural and intellectual hegemony over the orient, enabling us, from a secure base in Western rationalism, to proscribe oriental thought as irredeemably mystical and esoteric, and to warn against dangerous lapses into Eastern mysticism and irrationalism. It is a view which has been given intellectual encouragement by a series of Western thinkers from Hegel onward, including Max Weber, who saw the modernising processes of Western capitalism as manifesting a form of rationality, and hence of world-mastery, for which there was no analogue in the Orient. Even if we ignore the political aspect of this, it is almost certainly flawed in purely philosophical terms. If we follow a well-worn path of philosophical debate that has taken place over the past few decades, it is difficult to see how it is possible to establish the inherently rational nature of Western thinking from within Western thinking itself. Whether it be from a Wittgensteinian, a hermeneutical, or a post-structuralist standpoint, the stereotype of Western rationalism versus Eastern irrationalism is readily dissolved. All thinking takes place from within an historical horizon, and from this it follows that no particular conceptual or linguistic scheme can arrogate to itself exclusive right to the label 'rational' and claim for it universal applicability. From this point of view it is plausible to argue that Eastern ways of thinking have a rationality that may differ in certain respects from those characteristic of the West, but which is not the less 'rational' for that. Moreover, even by broadly Western standards the presumption that Eastern thought is endemically irrational is faulty, and is often based on outdated scholarship and on familiarity with only a narrow range of oriental texts. Sinologists, for example, are now agreed that 'there is much more rational discourse in [Chinese philosophy] than used to be supposed', and that the analysis of Chinese texts and concepts 'has revealed that most of the ancient Chinese thinkers are very much more rational than they used to look' (Graham 1989: xi and 71).[24]

QUIETISM

The charge of irrationalism is often associated with the accusation of *quietism*.[25] Put simply: without clear, objective, rationally founded beliefs, all ethical standards collapse and give way to an aimless indifferentism, or even nihilism, where one value is as good as another, and nothing is in the final analysis worth striving for. This is reinforced by the common perception that meditation and yoga practices are 'selfish' and lead in the direction of a total withdrawal from reality and entry ultimately into something like a catatonic trance; 'an ethic for the retired', as Don Cupitt ironically observed (1992: 148). Moreover, it is commonly believed that many aspects of Eastern thought are pessimistic and life-denying, forms of 'other-worldly asceticism' in Max Weber's phrase, by contrast with the supposed life-affirming, yea-saying characteristics of the West.

Considerations of this kind have frequently been used to discredit orientalism. R. C. Zaehner, for example, speaks of *Mahāyāna* Buddhism as 'steeped in pessimism and passive mysticism' which, while it may satisfy some individuals briefly, 'cannot be integrated into modern society' (1963: 185). In similar tones Hendrik Kraemer speaks of the influence of the East as 'negativistic', tending to sap the moral and social dynamism of the West (1960: 229), and the psychologist

John Rowan suspects that the West's interest in Eastern ideas might lead to 'quietism and retreatism in political terms' (1976: 25). The doctrine of *karma* along with the related concept of reincarnation is sometimes seen as encouraging a fatalistic attitude to life and the view that present ills need not be confronted since they are but passing moments in the endless turning of the wheel of rebirth. Similarly the central Taoist concept of *wu-wei* (literally 'non-action') is also often seen as promoting an attitude of unconcern towards the demands of worldly existence, and a reluctance to confront social evils. Such perceptions are reinforced by an impression that Eastern religions are not strong on moral prescriptions, and that historically they have been lacking in a well-developed political or social awareness. For example, Zen has sometimes been seen as being characterised by a kind of moral void, whose antinomian outlook helped to make possible, if not actively to encourage, the perpetration of Japanese war crimes in World War II.[26]

It could be argued that all of this represents a misunderstanding of Eastern ethical attitudes and practices, the perpetuation of a nineteenth-century myth that has polarised in people's minds the dynamic, world-affirming West with the enervating, life-denying East. Recent studies have tended to show that this sort of myth, and the perception of Eastern religions as socially indifferent, involves a systematic misrepresentation. Trevor Ling has insisted that 'Buddhism is not, as so many Westerners have imagined, a private cult of escape from the real world. . . . Buddhism could never be a "private" salvation . . . by its very nature its concerns were with the *public* world' (1973: 122 and 140); and Ken Jones documents in detail the active role that Buddhism has played in the social and political life of various Asian communities from the time of the Emperor Asoka, and argues that the Buddhist diagnosis of the human condition supports a socially activist ethic, and contributes to vital contemporary moral issues (1989: passim). Furthermore W. T. de Bary has claimed that traditional Confucianism was far more socially radical, anti-conservative, and challenging to imperial policies than has standardly been supposed in the West (in Lee 1991: 352); and Arthur Wright points to the Confucian-inspired support in the Sung Dynasty for works of charity such as public clinics and homes for the aged and infirm (see Wright 1971: 94). On the other hand scholars such as Richard Gombrich have argued that, whatever Buddhism's social role may have been or may have become, the Buddha himself taught a doctrine of personal salvation, not of social reform (see Gombrich 1988: 30); and Christopher Ives, while insisting that 'Zen does contain significant sources for a social ethic', on which he proceeds to speculate in detail (1992: 2 and Chapter 6), goes further and argues that traditionally Zen has offered no social ethic of its own, and that 'Historically, monastic Zen has not studied, analysed, or responded self-critically to the full range of suffering in the social world' (ibid.: 104).

In response to such views it must first of all be borne in mind that in many cases the lure of the Orient has lain precisely in its apparent power to counterbalance what is perceived as the excessively active and extraverted attitudes prevalent in Western culture. At many points in our historical survey we came across a desire to use the East as a critique of a certain unbalanced aspect of Western culture, not in order to destroy the latter but to bring it to wholeness, as it were. Jung argued that 'in the West, the outer man gained the ascendency to such an extent that he was alienated from his innermost being' (1978: 121), and even more pointed is Ives' insistence that 'Given the chaotic attempts to win and to dominate others, perhaps what the [Western] world needs most are monasteries and quietistic saints who do nothing in the normal activist sense' (1992: 110).

Furthermore, just as in the case of the reason/unreason dichotomy discussed above, the active/passive contrast carries a heavy ideological weight. The West has often seen itself as dynamic, capable, and masculine, by contrast with the passive, accepting, feminine attitude of the East, and has always been ready to vaunt its own activist, social-directed morality as inherently superior to the East's supposedly inner-directed one. As with the previous argument, the confrontation between East and West is beginning to be fruitful in so far as it provokes fundamental questions about the underlying ethical assumptions of the West, and about the nature of morality itself. The concept of *wu-wei*, for example, has proved difficult for Westerners to make sense of, for the ideal of non-action, especially in the face of known evils or dangers, is contrary to an instinctive moral activism in the West. But as many commentators point out, this term does not imply moral indifference but rather a highly moral demand to work in harmony with rather than in conflict with nature, to act in a selfless and non-manipulative manner, an ideal which is an important counterbalance to the typically Western model of self-assertion and personal success.

But before we allow ourselves to be carried back into the seductive language of global polarities, it is worth recalling that orientalism has in fact often been sharply focused on moral and social issues in ways which could be described as activist, even as radical or revolutionary. In the course of our historical narrative we have noticed several examples of this practical perspective: in the interest of the *philosophes* in Confucianist moral and political teachings, in the geopolitical outlook of 'universalist' thinkers ranging from Leibniz to Northrop, and in the pursuit of East–West dialogue by Christian theologians and philosophers committed to the furtherance of greater harmony and peace between hitherto warring cultures. Furthermore, as we noted in Chapter 9, the practice of meditation, which has often been seen in the West as encouraging a passive attitude to life, helping to distract us from rather than to confront the 'real' issues of life, is increasingly seen to have 'nothing to do with escaping this world by getting into trance states or "altered states of consciousness"' (Hayward 1987: 189), leading, not to 'some mystical state where visions of unearthly bliss unfold, but a series of responses to the question: how am I to live in this world?' (Batchelor and Brown 1992: 34).

Moreover, in the past few decades Buddhism, Taoism, and Hinduism have all in various ways been drawn into a number of central moral and social debates as stimulants rather than as tranquillisers, and as catalysts in the formulation of new social and political norms rather than as paths of retreat from contemporary problems. Significant in this regard is the part which Buddhism has played, especially in America, in the peace movement since the late 1970s when Robert Aitken founded the international Buddhist Peace Fellowship, an influential movement which has in fact become an umbrella organisation for a variety of kinds of social activism. Amongst the latter is the International Network of Engaged Buddhists which took shape in the late 1980s. This movement was inspired originally by the Vietnamese Buddhist monk Thich Nhat Hanh who became prominent in the anti-war movement in the 1960s and who through his editorship of the journal *Vietnamese Buddhism* campaigned for the engagement of Buddhism with social and political issues.[27] Moving to the other side of the Atlantic, the Welsh philosopher Ken Jones, who is secretary of the UK Network of Engaged Buddhists, has sought to emphasise the role that Eastern ideas have begun to play in Western moral discourse by underlining the strong identification of Theravada Buddhism with national struggles against colonialism in the East, and by arguing that 'the Buddhist revolutionary analysis of the human condition does carry social implications, and [that] the latter are immensely more radical than anything imaginable within the secular mentality' (1989: 199). Another writer who has been involved in the movement for Socially Engaged Buddhism is Joanna Macy who makes use of Buddhist ideas to help formulate an alternative ethic and an alternative conception of power. Having studied Buddhism with refugee Tibetan monks in India, and worked with the Sarvodaya movement in Sri Lanka in which Buddhist principles guide a programme of social renewal, she urges that, contrary to the 'patriarchal, hierarchical construction of reality' endemic in the Western tradition, which encourages attitudes of domination and control, Buddhism rests on a linear, reciprocal conception of 'dependent co-arising' which encourages an attitude of 'power-with, where beings mutually affect and mutually enhance each other' (in Eppsteiner 1985: 172). One further example of the East's involvement in twentieth-century political argument must be given, namely that of Mahatma Gandhi, whose views, though inspired in part by Western thinkers such as Thoreau, Ruskin, and Tolstoy, transposed ancient Hindu religious ideas and the Jain teaching of *ahimsā* into a political and social philosophy that helped to propel India towards independence. His religious-based philosophy proved a major catalyst in revolutions against colonialism, racism, and violence, and his importance in twentieth-century politics is difficult to overestimate.[28]

Feminism represents yet another link between Eastern ideas and contemporary social issues. On the face of it, feminist concerns may seem remote from the wisdom traditions of the East which are deeply embedded in traditionally patriarchal societies. Furthermore, there is a growing body of critical literature in recent years that has drawn attention to the relationship between imperial rule and gender politics, and has attempted to demonstrate the complicity of orientalism in oppressive gender discourse. In spite of this, however, there are many signs of a developing recognition of the relevance of oriental traditions to issues about gender, and of a belief that the feminist agenda can be illuminated by oriental ideas. These latter are drawn on explicitly to help uncover the shortcomings of Western social and moral ideas and practices, such as a patriarchal, rule-based, deontological conception of morality; and to help articulate techniques of self-awareness and self-criticism which can be especially important for feminist *praxis*. Buddhism in particular is seen by a growing number of feminists as their most significant Eastern ally, finding in it both the tenderness of compassion and mutual concern, and also the toughness of psychological and ideological analysis. The American historian of religion Rita M. Gross, for example, views as 'auspicious' the 'combination of the gentleness of Buddhism and the strength of feminism, to join the vision of Buddhism with the vision of feminism' (1986, 2: 74). While acknowledging the chasm that lies between traditional Buddhist practices and modern feminist concerns, she draws attention to ways in which the two may be seen to converge, and to senses in which 'Buddhism supplements and goes beyond feminism' (ibid.: 44), for example the rootedness of both movements in human experience rather than in theory, and their rigorous and uncompromising confrontation with conventional attitudes. The particular value of Buddhism to the construction of the feminist agenda lies, she believes, in its power to lay bare the psychological basis of the human situation, in its rigorous analysis of the question of human suffering, and in its critique of fixed ideological beliefs and essentialist views about human nature. The links between a feminist outlook and Buddhist notions have also been elaborated by other thinkers in recent years, including J. Powers and D. Curtin who argue that a 'Buddhist/feminist conversation could engender fruitful new directions for a women-oriented ethics of compassion, love, and caring', directions which offer an appealing alternative to Kantian prescriptivism and to utilitarian calculus of pleasure, both of which 'represent typically universalizing, masculine patterns of moral thinking' (1994: 13 and 7). Such ideals are increasingly being seen by feminist thinkers to 'give birth to a profoundly humane and creative worldview' (Boucher 1988: 23).[29]

None of this is to deny that orientalism may in some instances have proved to be a haven for the world-weary and the life-denying. It may also have offered to some a way of retreat from all things modern, from ideas such as those embodied in science, democracy, and progress. But it is important to counterbalance this with the recognition that orientalist endeavours have from the eighteenth century onwards often been directed towards goals which overlap with and support in certain respects the Enlightenment/modernist project, goals such as the eradication of narrow feudal attitudes and barriers, and the critique of indigenous religious and cultural traditions, and at the same time have refined and propagated the virtues of compassion, tolerance, non-violence, and humility. Orientalism has certainly opened the way for many who wish to tread the path to personal growth and spiritual fulfilment, a path which often conflicts with the extraverted demands and values of the modern world. But this is only a part of the picture which is extraordinarily rich and varied, and which has stimulated the mind and conscience of the West in so many different and fruitful ways.[30]

POWER

Discussion of the political and ethical significance of orientalism inevitably leads us back to the issue of power which was addressed in Chapter 2 in relation to Said's critique of orientalism. The final question we need to raise in this chapter, then, is whether the historical exposition of the middle sections of this book has succeeded in providing an alternative to the Saidian thesis that orientalism represents a discourse of power and domination over the East which reflects, supports, and justifies Western colonial oppression in Asia.

It is possible to dispense straight away with the notion that in any simple and straightforward way orientalism has constituted a buttress for apparatuses of colonial power: indeed, this simplistic view was never part of the argument of Edward Said, who disclaimed any accusation that orientalism was 'representative and expressive of some "Western" imperialist plot to hold down the "oriental" world' (1985: 12). Arguably the missionary logic associated with the proselytising work of the Christian churches in Asia has had a symbiotic bond with the interests of Western imperialism, and indeed some of the Asian delegates at the 1893 World's Parliament of Religions criticised the Christian missionary work on the grounds of its complicity in the strategies of Western colonial expansion and domination (see Seager 1995: 53 and 73–7). The activities that we have embraced within the term 'orientalism' fall for the most part into a very different category, for orientalism has often confronted and challenged colonising interests, even sought at times to destabilise and subvert them. It is important, though, when dealing with historically complex matters, not to oversimplify, for there are some obvious exceptions. We have noted how the influential evolutionary historicism that came out of Hegel's writings tended to confine India and China to a position of inherent inferiority, and there is no doubt that orientalism served the needs of empire by providing information for imperial civil servants – 'the necessary furniture of empire', as Lord Curzon described it.[31] But it is also important to recall from earlier chapters how the endeavours of orientalists, whether at a philosophical or scholarly level, often ran contrary in many respects to the needs of empire, and often challenged the ideological assumptions of the imperial powers, such as belief in the inherent superiority of Western culture and of Christianity. The early scholarly work of Jones and his colleagues, to take an important historical example, was certainly encouraged by the British authorities as an adjunct to the process of colonisation, but the motivations of these scholars and the cultural consequences of their work go far beyond this official sponsorship; Jones, for example, saw his translation work as addressing fundamentally moral needs, and was considerably more influential amongst the German Romantics than amongst his fellow-countrymen.[32] Civil servants who 'went native' by taking too close and sympathetic an interest in indigenous beliefs and practices were often seen as a danger to the imperial power, and the authorities of the Indian Raj were deeply suspicious of movements which identified with the indigenous culture, as for example in the case of the Theosophical Society which was placed under the surveillance of the British secret police. If Christianity was a central, if sometimes unconscious, factor in the buttressing of imperial aims, then orientalism was often a means for levering it from its pedestal.

Nevertheless, the theme of power and domination may be modulated into a less obvious key, without thereby denying that orientalism, like any other form of knowledge, is shaped by the interests of the knower. Here we need to take note again of the obvious mixture of motives evinced by orientalist scholars through the centuries and the variety of uses and misuses for which their work has been exploited, some of which we have investigated. And here too we need to go beyond Gadamer whose hermeneutical approach, as his critics have pointed out, is too closely identified with consciously contrived meaning, and shows insufficient awareness of the underlying layers of political interest and ideological manipulation, in brief of the relationship between knowledge and power. It may be the case that the role of orientalist discourse within the broad historical sweep of Western global hegemony is to be found, not in any direct support for the aims of empire but in a more subtle, but nonetheless palpable, cultural realm, namely in the desire to appropriate and control Eastern ideas within a Western conceptual framework, or, to put it more portentously, within the world-ordering rationality or universalising project of the European Enlightenment. Orientalism on this view may be seen as an expression of what Said has described as 'a kind of intellectual authority over the Orient within Western culture' (1985: 19), as functioning in relation to the discourse of European power as a way not of reinforcing the exercise of any literal control over subjugated peoples, but rather of creating a unified régime of knowledge about the East which enables the latter to be intellectually and culturally subsumed under Western interests. In other words what we may be dealing with here is a form of cultural or intellectual hegemony, which is historically related to Western global political and economic goals, and which has empowered the West to assimilate foreign cultural traditions within its own intellectual parameters, but which at the same time cannot be identified with or comprehended exclusively in relation to purely political and economic factors.

This way of interpreting orientalism is on the face of it much more persuasive than the one which somewhat reductively associates it with political and economic power, and which 'ends up referring the whole structure of colonial discourse back to a single monolithic originating intention' (Tiffin and Lawson 1994: 20). But here a certain amount of finesse is called for, and two qualifications must be entered. In the first place the history of orientalism shows that its polemical impetus is often directed inwards rather than outwards, and its strategies of appropriation are often connected more with power struggles within rather than beyond Western borders. A good example of this is the idea of 'universalism' which we associated with such names as Moore and Radhakrishnan, or the ideal of the 'perennial philosophy' of thinkers such as Huxley and Guénon. Arguably, these orientalist strategies could be seen as appropriating Eastern cultural products for the benefit of a manifestly Western project, a commodification of Eastern traditions for Western consumption. But at the same time it must be recalled that universalising projects such as these were often subversive and counter-cultural within the Western context, designed to confront indigenous Western religious and philosophical assumptions and practices with a radical alternative, and in this sense they are expressive of ruptures within the West itself. And while projects such as universalism are effectively ways of subsuming Eastern systems of thought under the 'intellectual authority' of Western categories and for purposes that flow from specifically Western aspirations, they are nevertheless premised on a belief that Eastern contributions to these projects have an inherent excellence that Western sources lack.

A second point that needs to be emphasised is that in many cases orientalism has been associated, not with the obliteration of indigenous Eastern cultures – a procedure all too evident elsewhere in the history of Western colonialism – but with their revivification and re-empowerment, that it has played a part in the revival and revoicing of Eastern traditions such as Hinduism, Zen, and Confucianism within their indigenous locales, in the encouragement of Asian scholars to explore their own traditions, and in the recovery of forms of knowledge which were atrophying and might otherwise have been lost. A good example is the role played by Western translations of the *Bhagavad Gītā* in the resurgence of Hinduism over the past 100 years or so, its wide dissemination having made a powerful impact not only on purely spiritual or intellectual matters but also on the growth and articulation of nationalist resistance to British rule.[33] Another, related, example is the Theosophical Society which, though seeking to beatify the ancient perennial wisdom of India, nevertheless gave strong encouragement to contemporary indigenous voices, such as those of Anagarika Dharmapala, Gandhi, and Krishnamurti, who played important roles in the re-energising and reformulation of ancient traditions. On a broader front, we should also recall once again the impact made by orientalism on what has become known as the 'Hindu Renaissance' when, as the historian David Ludden points out, 'from Rammohan Roy . . . to Nehru and beyond, orientalism as a body of knowledge informed the discourse of India's nationhood', and argues that orientalism became 'a body of knowledge to be deployed against European supremacy' (in Breckenridge and van der Veer 1993: 269 and 272).[34] A further example is offered by the work of Joseph Needham which, though in one sense arising out of a primarily Western problematic within the historiography of science, has proved both an important facilitative factor amongst Chinese scholars, and, in the view of the Australian philosopher Arran Gare, 'far from being complicit in Western imperialism, has contributed in at least a small way to the liberation of China from Western domination' (1995: 324).

Some might object that the work of scholars such as Needham, with their strategies for encompassing Chinese intellectual history within their own historicist enterprises, must still be seen as a form of arrogant Western condescension whereby orientals, having failed to conserve their own cultures, have lost any right to them; as one critic puts it: 'The Orientalist would henceforth speak for the Oriental through a lineage of scholarship whose task was to represent the Orient because the Orient was incapable of representing itself' (Lopez 1994: 39). As we noted earlier, some critics have argued, further, that it was the *classical* civilisations of the East which orientalism glorified, leading to the perception of modern Asia as in decline and hence requiring the West to speak on its behalf. However, the growth of orientalism has been linked with colonial expansion in much more intricate and subtle ways than such criticisms suggest, and recent scholarship has tended to emphasise the reciprocal nature of the relationship between coloniser and colonised.[35] Thus, for example, such criticisms do not give sufficient credit to the actual growth of knowledge of Asian intellectual and cultural histories brought about initially by Western scholars, or to the new ways of looking at the world which these endeavours entailed. Such endeavours may have been borne along on the back of the expansion of European military power and commerce and an accompanying suprematist historicism, but they have also, in the words of an Islamicist, 'helped to arouse a new kind of curiosity, a desire to study the infinite variety of the human and natural world, and to study it without fear, and with freedom from the kind of judgement which limits curiosity' (Hourani 1991), benefits which transcend Western borders and interests. Nor do these criticisms take adequate account of the extent to which Eastern scholars and intellectuals have themselves participated in orientalist enterprises. To be sure, as I argued at the end of Chapter 2, this involvement, along with the profound transformation of Eastern cultures that has occurred over the past few centuries, was provoked initially by external rather than by internal pressures, but the whole orientalist enterprise, from Matteo Ricci's debates with Chinese literati onwards, has involved a highly complex interaction between cultures which cannot be reduced to the imposition of power or of a 'master narrative' by the one over the other. It is not so much that orientalism has frequently been seen positively by oriental thinkers themselves, and welcomed as an inspiration towards their own cultural resurgence – though this is in fact often the case – but rather that they have themselves increasingly become involved, whether as critics or as enthusiasts, in the orientalist enterprise. From Vivekananda through Suzuki to the Dalai Lama there is a distinguished line of Eastern scholars who have both participated in and actively encouraged the orientalist pursuit, and who cannot simply be dismissed as victims of Western manipulation. Indeed the accusation of 'condescension' could be made against those who depict the East as a wholly passive recipient of orientalist attentions, and who urge that the huge body of knowledge concerning the Orient that has been its product is nothing but a Western construct, created in accordance with purely Western purposes and concepts. Though in certain important respects Asia finds itself in an historical context created by Europe, the view that its

involvement with orientalism has been one of pure passivity ignores the independence of Asian voices which have responded, argued, answered back, sometimes,
to be sure, lured into Westernising postures of oppression, but sometimes transforming these for their own liberating purposes.[36]

In general what emerges from this is that while issues of power and colonial
domination must certainly be factored into any account of orientalism, the latter
cannot be understood simply in terms of the West's power over the East. Critics
of orientalism in the West have often portrayed it in confrontational terms,
thereby perpetuating a Kiplingesque polarity which views the East and the West
in eternal enmity with one another. But while orientalism has undoubtedly been
in some respects a means by which the West has achieved a measure of control
over the intellectual and religious traditions of the East, the growth of orientalism has in other respects been marked by a growth in mutuality, in dialogue, in
knowledge, and in sympathy. Thus, while acknowledging the evident political
tensions and divergences of interest that have marked the relationship between
East and West, we must take account of the fact that the East has, first, increasingly acquired authority over its own cultural traditions as a result of its
encounter with the West, and second, that it has achieved power over the West
by becoming a counter to and critique of fundamental aspects of Western culture. As Jung put it:

> while we are turning upside down the material world of the East with our
> technical proficiency, the East with its psychic proficiency is throwing our spir-
> itual world into confusion . . . [and] while we are overpowering the Orient
> from without, it may be fastening its hold upon us from within.

(Jung 1961: 249)

Such issues can perhaps be better viewed in the light of the contemporary developments of orientalism, and these will be treated more fully in the final chapter.

Chapter 12

Orientalism and postmodernity

MODERNITY AND POSTMODERNITY

Where is orientalism now? Has it run its course? Are we now in a post-orientalist age, as some would have it, with cravings for the exotic 'other' finally extinguished with the end of empire and of modernity? The factors which produced orientalism – the opening up of Europe to a multiplicity of texts and contexts, and the expansion of Europe's power and consciousness to planetary dimensions – have undergone profound changes in recent years. The Western imperial remit has almost completely disappeared, and even the cultural and economic hegemony of the West is being challenged. The universalising aspirations of the Enlightenment period, which did so much to open the European mind to oriental philosophies, have given way to a fragmenting plurality and to the relativisation of world views; and the duality of East and West, which was a controlling myth of orientalism, has disintegrated under the combined force of cultural criticism and social transformation. The globalisation of culture, which has been emphasised by sociologists such as Anthony Giddens, has had the effect of shaping new forms of world interdependence which are not necessarily or uniformly Eurocentric, but which are shaped out of multiple overlapping identities. In the realm of intellectual exchange we experience now, as never before, a luxuriating hybridity of ideas and discursive practices which again are resistant to being squeezed into a dualistic mould of 'the West and the Rest'. Furthermore, these transformations are due not only to the West's own internal disruptions, but equally to the reassessment of its own identity by Europe's 'other', for, as the anthropologist James Clifford observes, 'Since 1950 Asians, Africans, Arab orientals, Pacific islanders, and Native Americans, have in a variety of ways asserted their independence from Western cultural and political hegemony and established a new multivocal field of intercultural discourse' (1988: 256).[1]

In the light of this assessment of our current condition, we must be left in some doubt as to the identity of the subject matter of this book at the present time. If the conditions that gave rise to it have passed, then orientalism might be expected to fade into history, a strange and exotic by-product of the modern

world, one which disappeared with the latter's passing. This presumption is partly fulfilled. Orientalism, as we have seen in Part III, has changed in recent years.
Its universalising aspirations have for the most part given way to a guarded pluralism, its epistemological confidence to a more modest, more self-critical
hermeneutical methodology, and its naïve idealism to greater resolution in
revealing its hidden and sometimes sinister motivations. Its tendency towards a
romanticisation of the Orient has been replaced to a large extent by a more
measured realism, with the East viewed, not as the site of some eternal, transcendent wisdom, but as a diverse and multi-layered set of cultural factors and
intellectual movements arising out of a variety of historical conditions.[2]
Furthermore, orientalism has been busily engaged in deconstructing the fabric of
its own discourse by calling into question the essentialist East–West polarity on
which it has often seemed to rest, and by investigating the social and political
conditions of its own production.

Nevertheless, there is plenty of evidence to suggest that, though transformed,
orientalism is alive and well, and indeed if anything it flourishes more vigorously
than ever, and wields an increasingly visible and significant influence on many
aspects of Western culture. Across a whole range of academic disciplines and
areas of public and personal interest the 'East' continues to be a notable focus of
interest and curiosity, and to provide a powerful source of cultural criticism and
inspiration.

This still-flourishing role betrays some intriguing connections with prominent
contemporary debates, for in many respects orientalism appears to be in league
with postmodernism. It could even be said that orientalism, with its encouragement of cultural pluralism and relativism, its questioning of some of the central
myths of modernity, its anti-Eurocentrism, and its advocacy of the valorisation
of excluded epistemologies and hidden histories, is postmodernist *avant la lettre*.
This appears to land us in a paradox: if orientalism was so closely associated
with modernity how can it also be associated with postmodernity? Are we not
thereby stretching to breaking point the idea, insisted upon earlier in this book,
that orientalism is entitled to be seen in terms of a single coherent narrative?
The answer to this must lie in the supposition that in certain crucial respects,
ones which are central to our present concerns, postmodernism is a continuation
of modernist discourse, or at any rate constitutes its late, if mature, manifestation. This is a view which, though clearly controversial, has won the support of a
number of writers in the field. David Harvey, for example, in his wide-ranging
inquiry into postmodernity, comes to the conclusion that 'there is much more
continuity than difference between the broad history of modernism and the
movement called postmodernism', and sees the latter as 'a particular kind of crisis within the former, one that emphasizes the fragmentary, the ephemeral, and
the chaotic' (1990: 116).[3] Clearly there are major differences as well. The rejection of grand narratives, of totalising world views, and absolute foundations,
along with emphasis on fracture, heterogeneity, and incommensurability, mark
out postmodernism from the modernist Enlightenment project. Nevertheless, as

I argued in Chapter 2, the very nature of this latter project, with its self-conscious reflexivity, and its scrupulosity in regard to truth, values, and goals, has tended to encourage rather than to quell the fires of Cartesian doubt, and it is these doubts, inflated to alarming proportions, and fanned by the tropes of play and irony, that have set alight the postmodern conflagration. From the time that the Jesuits went to China, Japan, and India in the sixteenth century, the East has come to represent a challenge to the intellectual uniqueness and even cultural identity of Europe, and provoked questions which in the contemporary cultural climate revolve round terms such as 'incommensurability' and 'relativism', and on the issues of 'rationality' and the 'universality of truth'. Contemporary restlessness concerning cultural identity, the validity of tradition, and the empowerment of repressed voices, which again can be seen as distinctively postmodernist, is inevitably brought into the foreground by orientalist concerns which in all sorts of ways help to clarify and focus these issues. Moreover, the challenge to modernist values represented by pluralism and relativism has been carried to the very heart of modernist values, namely its endemic humanism and its emphasis on the infinite value of the subject; here too orientalism has been able to bring new and often perplexing and disturbing perspectives to bear.

It will be useful to amplify and illustrate these points by examining briefly several concepts which are central to contemporary postmodernist debates and whose space is shared to some extent with orientalist preoccupations.

The first of these concepts is *pluralism* which, in this context, means the fragmentation of hitherto unified traditions and of the coherent beliefs and values that have derived from them. Its sources are manifold, and include social diversification and disintegration, the rise of political consciousness amongst hitherto marginalised groups, and philosophical scepticism about the universality of knowledge and values. Trade in oriental ideas over the past few centuries has clearly helped to open up the European mind and sympathies to viable world views at variance with its own, and, in the light of this, orientalism can be seen to have fostered from the start a pluralistic outlook and to have encouraged the recognition of the possibility of alternative ways of thinking, valuing, and acting. There have indeed been countervailing tendencies in the history of orientalism where plurality has been seen as a station on the way towards a loftier unity. But even here, as in the case of the early universalising strategies of the Hawaii East–West conferences, the net result has often been to demonstrate the inherent impossibility of the enterprise, and overall the upshot has been the emergence of a culture of mutual recognition rather than of mutual absorption. This pluralising tendency has also become increasingly evident within the emerging self-reflexiveness of orientalist discourse itself. Here the idea of the oriental 'other' as a unified and unchanging topos has given way to the view that the 'East' is but a poor cypher for an incredibly rich variety of cultural and intellectual phenomena. Consciously transcended is the notion that the East is to be treated as some eternal essence that can be contemplated from afar, like the heavenly bodies, and there has emerged a recognition of the West's own essentialising practices, and a much greater understanding of Asian teachings as being embedded in a variety of ongoing traditions which have their own historical dynamic.

Arguments concerning cultural pluralism have inevitably led to the issue of *representation* which in turn leads to related issues concerning authority and power, to questions such as 'Whose representations prevail, and why?', and 'Who has the authority to represent reality?', questions which come sharply into focus in the context of orientalism. In an increasingly explicit alliance with literary critical theory, and with feminist and black studies, this issue raises important questions about deeply embedded attitudes towards knowledge, encouraging sensitivity towards alternative histories and recalcitrant voices, and towards non-Western textual practices.[4] As we have seen throughout this book, orientalism has indeed for long been involved in challenging the dominant European epistemological order. It has frequently been involved in questioning the possibility of establishing universal, culture-neutral grounds on which to base knowledge claims and attestations of rationality. By drawing attention to alternative yet equally viable conceptual schemes, it has helped to call into question not only the specific values of modern European culture, but also the assumption that these values are epistemically fundamental and universally prescriptive, and to controvert the use of concepts such as rationality, individualism, and progress in judging other cultures. We have seen, too, that the currently favoured idea that our representations are in some sense *constructed*, and are systematically misleading in some radical sense, is a notion anticipated within many Eastern philosophies. What orientalists have discovered and exploited is a rich vein of Asian philosophical thinking which is concerned to 'deconstruct' all categories, thereby confronting us with the fabricated nature of all thinking. Taoism, for example, has been noted for its ironic scepticism of all linguistic and symbolic forms, and its persistent endeavour to undermine our attachment to words and concepts. The link between this approach and postmodernism has been especially underlined in the case of Buddhism, as represented in particular by Nāgārjuna and the *Mādhyamaka* school. As we noted in an earlier chapter, this school, with its emphasis on stripping away the culturally-formed inveiglements of language, and on the mind-formed sources of human experience, and with its dialectical method designed to demonstrate the contradictory nature of all philosophical positions, has been frequently cited in connection with the so-called 'linguistic turn' in recent critical and philosophical thinking, and with the deconstructive style associated with Nietzsche and Derrida.[5]

Nothing has proved more radically misleading, according to postmodernist thinking, than representations of the *self*, and one of the most telling and disturbing aspects of postmodernity is its decentring of the human subject, that most sacred of all Western icons. Here again the East, in the hands of orientalists, has proved to be able to offer a provocative external perspective, and the idea that the self is not given by nature but constructed, not stable and permanent but painfully fractured, is one which has drawn contemporary concerns close to traditional teachings of   Buddhism. Far more radically than either Derrida or

Lacan, the theologian David Tracy argues, 'the Buddhist way forces modern Westerners to confront our cultural and psychological notions of ego, self, and subject beyond the usual alternatives' (1990: 75). With its rooted essentialism, Western thought has traditionally tended to postulate human nature as a fixed essence that renders humans distinct from nature and from all other living beings, and to subscribe to a model of the self as a fundamentally permanent and stable seat of power and cognition. Much attention has been directed in recent discussions towards an alternative model offered by Taoism and Buddhism which insists that nothing is fixed and permanent, that all is in flux, most especially human beings themselves. Taoism, for example, with its rejection of the humanistic teachings of Confucianism, is already engaged in a process of decentring, calling into question the Confucian idea of the 'superior man' who finds the axis of his existence within himself in the unfolding of his essential humanity. Lao-tzu was opposed to the artificial conventions both of language and of the state, was radically hostile to anthropocentrism, and in placing becoming above being emphasises alterity and difference rather than identity and essence.[6] One of the most notable features of Zen, one which has attracted many Westerners, is its emphasis on the transient present, the small, the commonplace, the insignificant, on *this* feeling, *this* cloud, *this* sound, rather than on the timeless and the eternal, and on 'emptying out' in order to gain wisdom rather than on building and consolidating. The teaching of all Buddhist schools concerning radical impermanence carries with it the implication that the self is ever-changing, a series of momentary experiences which in turn are conditioned elements within the whole web of interacting phenomena, an idea known as 'dependent co-origination'. What this teaching denies is not the existence of consciousness, or even of *self*-consciousness, but rather the assumption that there is a permanent entity which lies behind consciousness and which is denoted by the personal pronoun.[7]

ORIENTALISM IN THE POSTCOLONIAL ERA

How then should orientalism be evaluated at the present time? In view of the association with the language of postmodernism through which all the discursive constructs of modernity are readily decomposed, can orientalism do anything other than reflect post-Enlightenment relativism and disillusionment? Can there ever be anything other than a distorting and manipulating orientalism, trading nostalgically on its own past, perhaps, but mortally wounded by the very deconstructive instruments that it has helped to forge? For reasons offered in the last chapter, a truly open-ended and impartial, enlightened dialogue, an orientalism without bias or prejudice, is surely impossible, even inconceivable. Nevertheless, there is evidence to suggest that orientalism continues to demonstrate the possibility of a productive inter-cultural exchange, albeit one which seems often one-sided and deficient when measured up against an ideal archetype. Even though the conditions of the encounter between Asia and Europe have changed drastically during the twentieth century, it nevertheless remains true that 'Europe still turns towards those non-European traditions which it tried to master [and] to enlist them as allies against developments initiated by itself' (Halbfass 1988: 440). Some see this as an ameliorative process in which bad habits of former times are being erased. The orientalist Maxime Rodinson, for example, believes that within his field of scholarship 'real progress has already been made where there is no longer a prior and wilful selection, manipulation or embellishment of . . . facts to suit a conscious ideological synthesis' (1988: 40); and Sheldon Pollock speaks of 'the current self-interrogations in our field' that have accompanied the disappearance of the 'traditional foundations and uses of Indology' (in Breckenridge and van der Veer 1993: 111). Edward Said himself, in what is sometimes seen as a major concession to humanistic values, believes that in a postcolonial period, with increasingly sophisticated scholarship and a growing 'critical consciousness', a post-orientalist epoch may arrive in which Westerners could approach the Orient without the encumbrance of former prejudices and distorting assumptions. Admitting the possibility of 'decolonizing' knowledge, he acknowledges that 'there is scholarship that is not as corrupt, or at least as blind to human reality' as the orientalism which he condemned (1985: 325).[8] There is evidence, in his view, that orientalism has begun to embark on the task of revealing and working with its own repressed historicity and biases, a task which Said himself announced in *Orientalism*.[9] Said was, of course, speaking of the Middle East, but similar considerations apply to Western discourse concerning the rest of Asia. Orientalism in this latter context is in many respects undergoing major changes which reflect a wider cultural metamorphosis in which there has been a remarkable world-wide multiplication of channels of communication and interaction, leading to the rejection of the old ideals of Western hegemony, and of its global pretensions, and the recognition of the claims of diversity and difference. Old boundaries are dissolving, and there are genuine attempts to bring about a 'fusion of horizons'. The earlier tendency to idealise the Orient is giving way to one which is able to be critical without being patronising, and can draw from the traditions of the East without fearing to be selective or critical. Eastern traditions have, in this way, been demystified and brought down from the incense-clouded heights in which orientalism has sometimes located them, and the preternatural halo of popular imagination has begun to be replaced by productive alliances with contemporary philosophical, social, and ecological concerns.

Inevitably this is a slow and uneven development in which the optimism of scholars such as Rodinson, Pollock, and Said must be set against the stubborn persistence of old Eurocentric attitudes, for a number of factors are clearly working in quite the opposite direction. Amongst the most obvious of these factors are the resurgence of nationalism after the end of the Cold War, the revival of extreme right-wing politics in Europe and America, and the ominous growth of religious fundamentalisms, a phenomenon which is now evident amongst Hindus and Buddhists as well as in the Abrahamic traditions. There is, furthermore, an ambivalence arising from the liberating energies of orientalist discourse itself. One of the consequences associated with the latter – though many other factors enter into the equation – is the increasingly aggressive assertion of multiple ethnocentric identities, which, though clearly in reaction against the process of Europeanisation, may turn out to be an almost deliberately formed mirror image of it, and to this extent orientalism may have encouraged the very divisiveness that it so often appears to have wished to transcend. As critics such as Sara Suleri have pointed out, the very 'alterism' (as she calls it) of some postcolonial discourse, aimed at the re-empowerment of the colonised 'other', tends to perpetuate 'the fallacy of the totality of otherness' and thereby reinforce the old binary essentialism of East and West (1992: 13). Moreover, the demand for recognition and respect by or on behalf of minority groups and interests has sometimes given rise to a new form of intolerance that goes under the popular title of 'political correctness'. The issues surrounding political correctness clearly go much wider than orientalism, but since the publication of Said's book in 1978, orientalism has often been associated with 'Third Worldism', namely an attitude of mind which encourages the West's sense of postcolonial guilt and self-contempt, its 'self-laceration for the crimes of colonization', as Ferenc Feher puts it, leading to 'the zeal of anti-ethnocentrism', a new 'political fundamentalism with a religious coloring' (in Deutsch 1991: 181). The attitude of self-recrimination encourages not only an exaggerated and unhelpful sense of the West's supposed degeneracy, but also an overly-elevated and a-historical vision of the East's moral and spiritual purity, a process in which old myths are demolished only to be replaced by new ones.

This paradoxical situation is connected with the fact that orientalism is often caught in a dialectical tension between the extremes of universalism and pluralism: it tends towards a universalistic outlook which transcends cultural boundaries and encourages an inter-cultural perspective, yet increasingly it also seeks to affirm local and regional differences and to nurture the unique particularity of cultures; globalisation and parochialisation thus appear as equal yet opposite allurements. Looked at in a wider perspective, this situation clearly reflects the tensions involved in all hermeneutical encounters, which typically circulate from the particular to the general and back again, a circularity which is not necessarily vicious. Such a process does indeed seem peculiarly apt for the needs of the contemporary world. Nationalist and ethnic aspirations are not necessarily intolerant and aggressively chauvinistic; globalism is not necessarily blind to local and regional demands. There is no reason why orientalism should not be able to point the way towards the mediation between these two positions. After all, the East–West dialogue has at one and the same time helped to recover and revive indigenous traditions, while at the same time opening up minds to wider and more universal sympathies. Readers do not need to be reminded that the world today abounds in conflict, and that the creation of communities of understanding, able to recognise the demands of both the universal and the particular, are urgently needed. An enlightened orientalism has an important contribution to make to the creation of such a community of understanding. Its history, however chequered, is one of attempted crossings of boundaries, of dialogues between remote cultures, of the sharing of horizons, and most especially of critical reflex-iveness. It has the capacity, at its best, to widen sympathies, enrich the imagina-tion, encourage openness and multiculturalism, and enhance toleration between peoples. It may even contribute to the attainment of a new world order, a prospect to which we return shortly.

The role of orientalism in educational curricula can be evaluated in the light of these considerations. In recent years some moves can be observed towards a greater willingness in the West to incorporate non-Western components within the curriculum, and to break out of the restrictive bounds of its traditional Eurocentrism. The growing presence of an element of oriental studies, whether at school or at university level, is evidence of a determination to combat narrow nationalistic outlooks, as well as giving a voice to views which hitherto have been silenced or marginalised. At one level this arises from the conviction of some academics that 'the understanding of our own Western civilization is distorted and incomplete unless it is seen in a global and not merely in a regional and parochial context' (Lewis 1993: 128), but at a more radical level by demanding a fairer treatment of non-Western texts and traditions it involves a challenge to the 'Western canon' along with its Eurocentric assumptions. As Solomon and Higgins have recently noted:

> there is a vigorous attempt in academia to combat ethnocentrism of the tradi-tional ('male, white, European') college curriculum and the implicit chauvin-ism (if not racism) it represents. In philosophy in particular, some administrations have all but mandated that as a field of study it should become increasingly conscious of and attentive to other philosophical traditions.
>
> (1993: xi)

This attentiveness to other voices and other traditions is a contribution, not to a new cultural melting pot, but rather to a multicultural mosaic which, by encour-aging us to transcend the limits of our acculturation and our inbred thought pat-terns, prevents us from falling into the trap of identifying our own provincial thinking with 'human reason' as such.[10]

Such ideals and aspirations are clearly not enough in themselves to transform an unjust and oppressive world or a world divided into mutually hostile factions and ethnic groupings, and we should beware of being seduced by a model of friendly dialogising which becomes a substitute for confronting social inequity and inter-cultural hostility. Nor is it part of my argument to claim that oriental-ism escapes entirely the grip of racism, of ethnocentricity, of exploitation, or of distortion; in one way or another all these faults and more have been document-ed at various points in this book. However, orientalism in its various guises and manifestations has, in spite of these deficiencies and limitations, served – and indeed continues to serve – as an important emancipatory force within Western civilisation, while at the same time playing an important role in the recovery and exploration of Eastern texts and teachings themselves. We have a right to be suspicious of the motives of orientalism, and to underline its shortcomings, but it does not follow from this that it is destitute of value or locked irretrievably in an imperialist past. The kind of either/or logic which pervades both racist and politically correct thinking needs precisely the tolerance, pluralism, and relativism that characterises orientalism at its best.

THE TRANSFORMATIONS OF ORIENTALISM

These modest conclusions, associated as they are with the sometimes depressingly sceptical spirit of postmodernism, may leave the reader, as they leave the writer, dissatisfied. The present world situation is urgent enough to demand, not merely the silencing of old oppressive voices, nor even just the advocacy of a tolerant plurality of new ones, of vital importance though these are. As the Australian philosopher Arran Gare provokingly argues, what is needed 'in the service of achieving greater mutual understanding between people . . . is not merely the subversion of Eurocentric narratives, but the construction of grander narratives beyond Eurocentric perspectives' (1995: 324). But does not the postmodernist trend lead, not only to a sense of disillusionment and disenchantment, but to the definitive abandonment of such inflated talk, indeed to the abandonment not only of 'grander narratives' but of any notion of universal, objective standards? The search for some supra-cultural, supra-historical receptacle of truth has been one of the besetting preoccupations of Western philosophy, and many have come to see its abandonment as a definitive break with the past.

There are deep philosophical issues here which cannot be addressed in the present context, but as we survey the various contemporary forms of orientalism we do in fact find evidence of affirmative outlooks and of ideas which bring into view constructive possibilities – if not 'grander narratives' – that point beyond the death of modernism but do not seek simply the rebirth of pre-modern world views.[11] Of course no new overarching synthesis is on offer, for it would be difficult to imagine at the present time, in the light of deconstructive strictures, any concerted return to an integral world view which welds together the insights of East and West into a single universal philosophy. Moreover the misuses of orientalism that we have discussed – such as its occasional alliances with racist and fascistic discourses – should encourage a degree of caution and vigilance, and foster a spirit of self-critical modesty in Western approaches to non-European traditions. Particular caution needs to be exercised with respect to eschatological anticipations of a new spiritually transformed age, a fateful idea which has a Judaeo-Christian pedigree but which has sometimes – as in the case of Blavatsky's theosophy – drawn support from Eastern sources. Nevertheless some auspicious conjectures may be seen to emerge from the critical ferment which has taken hold of orientalist discourse of late which need to be honoured and encouraged, and there are signs of intellectual initiatives which draw on premodern oriental sources without lapsing into the mythology of 'East is good, West is bad', or into believing that ancient Asian philosophies can cure all our modern and postmodern discontents. In Part III of this book I sketched some of the ways in which contemporary interests in oriental ideas were marking out new territories and opening up fresh possibilities, such as, for example, in the Buddhist–Christian dialogue and in the psychological investigations into consciousness, and I do not need to repeat these here. In this section I want to suggest in broad and speculative terms some of the ways in which the spirit of orientalism may be seen to have transmigrated, albeit in a disassembled form, into certain identifiable contemporary cultural and intellectual developments, and which constitute recognisable factors in the creative dynamic of contemporary thought. For convenience I identify four groups.

The first of these ways is connected with the growing number of Westerners who are adopting, albeit in an often transposed form, Eastern spiritual ideas and practices. Increasingly over the past few decades many people, either individually or within the compass of organisations, have deliberately adopted Eastern ways, ranging from the regular practice of meditation and yoga to a thoroughgoing religious commitment, often involving the adoption of a Zen or Tibetan Buddhist teacher. Now I want to suggest that what we are witnessing here may not simply be a further chapter in the old European story of cultural expropriation, or even the reversal of Christian proselytising of the East, but in some sense an historical evolution of the oriental traditions themselves. Buddhism is an obvious case in point. Throughout its long and complex Asian history it has been planted and transplanted in many fertile cultural and religious habitats, transforming and being transformed in the process, and bequeathing to us a picture of a living organism whose evolution is still ongoing. In the West at the present time Buddhism is undergoing conscious metamorphosis, one which may be analogous, as Kenneth Inada suggests, 'to what transpired in China and Japan . . . in creating their own respective brands of Buddhism' (in Callicott and Ames 1989: 233). We have already noted a manifestation of this kind of transformation in connection with the Buddhist–feminist dialogue, and a number of writers have reflected along these lines in recent years from a variety of standpoints. For example, Stephen Batchelor, who, before his return to England, spent many years as a Buddhist monk in India and Korea, has maintained that Buddhism is passing through a confusing but creative period of transition in its encounter with the West, and he goes on to offer some challenging speculations about the emergence of 'an existential, therapeutic, democratic, imaginative, anarchic, and *agnostic* Buddhism for the West' (1994: 274–7). In his view, adaptation 'is not so much an option as a matter of degree', pointing out that even the most conservative Tibetan Lamas or Sri Lankan *bhikkus* tend to adapt their teachings to the Western context (ibid.: 337). A good example of deliberate adaptation is to be found in The Western Buddhist Order, founded by an English monk with the adopted name of Sangharakshita who set out to create a Buddhist way adapted to Western cultural and social needs.[12] Placing the matter in broad historical context, the theologian David Tracy comments that 'The Western Buddhists have not merely rendered Buddhism a live option for many Westerners, but have subtly changed Buddhism itself as radically as the earlier classic shifts from India to Thailand, Tibet, China, and Japan once did' (Tracy 1990: 39).[13]

Moreover, there would seem to be room here for both progressive and conservative factions, for those on the one hand who perceive the need for an evolved Buddhism which reflects the needs of a postmodern world, and for those on the other hand who deem that the same situation requires the resolution and discipline to preserve ancient and hallowed traditions. Buddhism has always demonstrated the capacity to embrace both these needs and tendencies without having or choose definitively between them.

Taoism is another example of this trend, though one which as yet falls short of the popular profile and appeal of Buddhism. The absorption of aspects of Taoism by the West is undoubtedly aided by the fact that its indigenous traditions and institutions in the East have been severely curtailed. While it would seem unlikely that Taoism, with its deep roots in ancient Chinese culture, will achieve the status of a religion in the West, nevertheless there are aspects of this tradition, such as the practices of *t'ai chi ch'uan* and *feng shui*, and its symbiotic approach to the relationship between the human and the natural worlds, which have been eagerly embraced, transposed, and developed in the West. Martin Palmer has noted that in its journey to the West 'certain Taoist images and terms, insights and practices . . . are now entering a new manifestation [which] will bear little resemblance to the original faith', and while he regrets that Westerners lack the application needed to study historical Taoism in depth, he recognises the historical significance of this movement, viewing it in the light of earlier transformations in China itself (1991: 127–8).

Reference to Taoism points to a second constructive path for orientalism which can be summed up in the word 'ecological'. This development, which of course has important roots in the Western cultural traditions as well, involves not only a radical critique of modernist values and assumptions but also indications of a more productive and affirmative outlook. Indeed, some would argue that the ecological model, as a broad-ranging philosophy, offers the only viable way forward, not only in the West, but also in the global context. An interesting example of this sort of thinking is to be found in the work of the American political philosopher Charlene Spretnak, who in various ways has sought to integrate Eastern insights into a new secular spirituality which she calls 'ecological-postmodernism'. In elaborating this idea she identifies the outlines of a new wisdom tradition which moves beyond 'the failed aspects of modernity' but which draws on aspects of 'the very traditions that modernity has rejected with contempt', traditions which can now be seen to 'contain revelations of ecological communion and dynamic oneness' (1991: 19 and 23). While postmodernist critics gleefully strip away layers of cultural conceptualisation, they arrive at positions and offer perspectives which are in some respects central to the great wisdom traditions of the past, most especially those of the East. As Spretnak remarks: 'some of the most prominent deconstructive-postmodernist thinkers have begun to ask the sorts of questions that bring them to the threshold of the wisdom traditions'

(ibid.: 219), namely to the point where the conventions of speech and doctrine
are seen to be illusions that constrain and repress us.

This does not mean a tired retreat into outworn creeds, a lapse into some
mystical oblivion to evade present terrors, nor least of all a return to doctrinaire
fundamentalism, but rather a hermeneutical re-engagement with old ideas,
adapted and applied to the present condition, and implemented in an open-
ended and critical way. Following Spretnak, this new ecological postmodernist
view can be seen to embrace the following characteristics:

1 the concept of an immanent deity and of the sacredness of all things;
2 a sense of the universe as self-creative, and human life as in the process of
   self-actualising;
3 the overcoming of dualism by the embedding of the subject within a larger
   natural and interpersonal reality;
4 an anti-patriarchal sense of subjectivity and inner-directed wisdom;
5 an enhanced awareness of the body, its emotional, symbolic, and spiritual
   potential;
6 a clear recognition of the relativity of human discourse and the multiplicity of
   human texts;
7 a recognition of the endless flux and flow and the convoluted interweaving of
   things in the natural world; and
8 a suspicion of laws and rules in favour of compassion and mutual feeling, and
   the possibility of an ethical system which does not rest on the basis of transcendent sanctions and eternal principles.

This points to a third way for, where Spretnak wishes to go beyond deconstructive postmodernism by seeking to rediscover a sense of communion with reality
that transcends cultural constructions, there are others who claim to find within
the deconstructive practice itself a potential for spiritual awakening which has
fruitful connections with the 'wisdom traditions' of the East. The perceived tendencies of deconstructive postmodernism towards nihilism and the dissolution of
meaning might at first sight seem to forbid any such connections. To draw out
this unlikely affinity we need to look more closely at the concept of *shūnyatā*
(emptiness), and at the philosophy of the Buddhist thinker Nāgārjuna who, as we
noted earlier, is the subject of growing interest in the West. His philosophy,
which represents one of the most important developments within the *Mahāyāna*
tradition, offers a way of thinking which, in Western contexts where nothingness
is often associated with pessimism, dread and meaninglessness, may look like
calamitous nihilism. However, it is important to emphasise that the goal of
Nāgārjuna's 'deconstructive' method, *shūnyatā*, is a state which, by removing all
illusions, seems to open up rather than close down the possibility of a richer and
more authentic existence, and which is seen as offering the possibility of deliver-
ance from neurotic habits of mind. This key Buddhist concept does not imply a
denial that the world exists or that it is merely an illusion, but rather that there is
nothing besides fleeting appearances, and contrary to Western expectations does

not point to *angst* and nihilism but rather to liberating insights and a strategy of mental cure and spiritual growth. *Shūnyatā* is in effect an invitation to see that what exists cannot be squeezed into conventional linguistic categories with their tendency to hypostatise individuality, permanence, and essence, and thereby helps to release us from cramping obsessions and obstacles to enlightenment. In *Hīnayāna*, emptiness is only applied to persons, but in the *Mahāyāna* tradition all things are regarded as without essence, 'empty of a certain mode of being called "inherent existence", "objective existence", or "natural existence"' (Hopkins 1983: 9), all of which are superimposed on phenomena but which, through philosophical analysis, can be seen as illusory. Nāgārjuna taught this as a remedy for all dogmatic views, and as a way of liberation from *samsāra*, the cycle of rebirth, going even further and claiming that the concept of *shūnyatā* is itself empty and should not be clung to: 'Those who believe in *shūnyatā* are deemed incurable' (quoted in Hayward 1987: 282). All belief systems, including Buddhism itself, are illnesses to be cured.

This has proved to be an alluring concept to a number of contemporary thinkers in the West, and is being deployed in various ways to question prevailing categories and to open up new horizons.[14] Jeremy Hayward, for example, a scientist and a Buddhist teacher, sees *shūnyatā* not as a philosophical abstraction, nor even as a way of combating the residues of a mechanistic paradigm, but as involving a profound existential gestalt switch, 'a transformation of perception that is said to be like waking up from a dream', a realisation 'of the extraordinary and profound error that one has been making all one's life'. It is, he insists, 'an earth-shaking experience accompanied by great joy and relief as if an unimaginable burden had dropped, and to be the entry into a new way of conducting one's life' (1987: 211). A similar but more fully developed line of thinking has been offered by the theologian Don Cupitt. He sees pessimism as an endemic disorder of the age, one which is encouraged by postmodernist thinkers who emphasise the impermanence of all things, including our most inner selves, abandoning us to a world 'that is no longer a single cosmos, more a flux of interpretations, theories, perspectives, meanings, signs', and as a consequence 'we Westerners have thrust upon us an almost Buddhist sense of universal impermanence' (1992: 109–10). But in some ways it is much worse for us than for traditional Buddhists, he argues, for our Western intellectual and religious legacies, with their typical emphasis on permanence and substantiality, and their belief that underneath the flux of appearance lies 'an eternal intelligible order of Reason, with all the qualities the heart desires' (ibid.: 110), these 'logocentric' traditions leave us gaping in despair into a black hole once the comforting support of such beliefs has been dislodged. The problem has its source, therefore, in our deeply rooted expectations of comforting solutions which, in the contemporary world, are no longer forthcoming. The way beyond this painful dilemma, Cupitt believes, is to wean ourselves from the need for such comforts by facing the inescapability of their absence, and the *Mahāyāna* Buddhist tradition, with its 'admirably non-realist' philosophy, can help us to do this. It offers a diagnosis and 'cure' for the human situation which emphasises, first, the purely artificial nature of linguistic categories, second, the need to develop 'a deconstructive practice that works to undo all the opposition and alienation' so that they no longer hold us captive, and third, the attainment of 'a soul-healing glimpse' of the 'aboriginal, ineffable unity of all the opposites' (ibid.: 127). In a similar way, he notes, the thirteenth-century Japanese Zen Master Dōgen stressed the impermanence of all things, including our innermost self, urging us to 'give up grand cosmological aims and the realistic dogma', and pointing towards a peace of mind in which 'time-being abides in each moment and nothing is really arriving or going away' (ibid.: 129). This does not mean turning our backs on indigenous traditions, however, for Cupitt sees the importance of bringing together Buddhist and Christian traditions in a creative hermeneutic, rather than in the replacement of the one by the other. An anti-realism derived from these two traditions 'alone can make us self-less, emptied-out, free, and innocently creative' (ibid.: 163).[15]

If all this seems rather abstract, even esoteric, then as a final example we will return once more to orientalism's connections with the political realm and with some of the wide-ranging politico-economic transformations that are taking place at the present time. Some see the present time as a new axial age, not only one that is witnessing the end of the great universalising project associated with the European Enlightenment, but also one in which the global fulcrum may be passing from the West to Asia, and in which the dramatic shift of power from East to West which occurred in the Renaissance period is in the process of being reversed. The transposition of geopolitical focus from the Atlantic to the Pacific, the seemingly inexorable rise of the economies of Japan, Korea, Singapore, and Taiwan, the resurgence of China and India as world players, suggest that the great civilisations of the East are themselves in the process of a profound revitalisation, reflected, as we have already noted, in the self-conscious renewal of indigenous intellectual and spiritual traditions. The affirmation of 'Asian values' in countries such as Malaysia and Singapore, centring on the family, on national well-being, and on responsibility towards the community, in contrast with the Western ideals of democracy and human rights, is a potent manifestation of this transposition.

In this context the combination of globalism and pluralism that we have associated with orientalism has an important reflexive role to play, and indeed a number of scholars and critics are beginning to recognise the relevance of the long-standing East–West dialogue to the contemporary situation just outlined. Here the spotlight of interest is trained most conspicuously on Confucianism, a philosophy which is returning to fashionable attention after long neglect in the West, and whose relevance to current disputes echoes in interesting ways its involvement in European debates in an earlier age. As one historian somewhat summarily expresses it:

> Over the last decade or two Confucius has been dragged by the topknot into discussions of matters it would have been beneath his dignity as a junior

> member of the Zhou aristocracy to notice or talk about: trade [and] eco-
> nomic growth.
>
> (Jenner 1992: 169)

It is becoming apparent that a vigorous 'new Confucianism' debate is taking place in Western Pacific countries where Confucian moral teaching, with its emphasis on communality, is seen as offering an important critique of and alternative to Western individualism (see Lai 1995), and according to Judith Berling, Confucianism has 'taken on a new guise as a critical participant in the search for values and understandings of the human situation in the contemporary world' (in Lee 1991: 476). These recent developments provide an interesting new perspective on orientalism and its attempts to build a creative interface between the world views of Europe and Asia. One thinker who has seized upon the vital importance of this interface for critical reflection on the contemporary world is John Gray. The central task of this political philosopher's recent writings has been to find a way beyond the failed ideology of traditional liberalism and beyond the universalist ambitions of the Enlightenment project, a path which seeks to avoid the fundamentalisms of both left and right, but which can accommodate, even celebrate, a pluralist-inspired toleration of cultural diversity. What he is searching for is, in brief, a 'pluralistic régime of a peaceful *modus vivendi* among different cultural traditions, ways of life, and peoples', a politics in which the universalising project of Western cultures will be 'replaced by a willingness to share the earth with radically different cultures' (Gray 1995: 140 and 180). In contrast with Francis Fukuyama's triumphalist view that in the post-communist period Western institutions and political ideals will spread world-wide, he points, *inter alia*, to the emergence of the Asian 'tiger' economies, and the renewed debate, in both Asia and the West, about the comparative merits of the Confucian communalist and Western individualist philosophies. Factors such as these indicate, in his view, that the way forward is one which both acknowledges the passing of the Enlightenment project and also confronts the fact that 'political life is dominated by renascent particularisms, militant religions, and resurgent ethnicities' (ibid.: 2). What may emerge from a renewed encounter between East and West, he hopes, is not a 'clash of civilizations' (in Samuel Huntington's phrase) but a new form of 'agonistic liberalism' in which 'the rivalrous encounter of ideas and values' will form the basis for toleration and mutual co-existence (ibid.: 84). This calls for a break with the Western tradition which has tended to assert the ultimate harmony of values, and for a new form of toleration – 'radical toleration', he calls it – which demands, not merely the grudging acceptance of alien and incompatible ways of life but the ability to affirm that Western civilisation, even liberal democracy itself, 'is simply one set of cultural forms among others' (ibid.: 179). One might amplify Gray's diagnosis by insisting that what is required is not just the affirmation of difference but the readiness to submit this difference to the scrutiny of friendly and informed dialogue, the marking out of a democratic space in which not only is diversity celebrated but where there is also an inducement towards the critical and agonistic quest for common ground. The search for core ethical values amidst the recognition and respect for cultural diversity which characterised the centennial re-run of the 1893 World's Parliament of Religions offers an encouraging exemplification of this model.[16]

BEYOND ORIENTALISM?

What then, finally, does all this tell us of the ideals of dialogue, along with their humanistic-sounding corollaries of tolerance, mutual respect, and critical reflexiveness? What in the last analysis remains of orientalism as an agency of renewal and as a locus for the creative inter-cultural engagement of ideas? The master-myths of polarity and complementarity between East and West may be at last in the process of out-running their usefulness for all kinds of reasons, not least because the twin terms, East and West, have lost whatever coherent meaning they may once have had. Nevertheless, the foregoing examples, and perhaps the whole parade of encounters and debates that have been presented in this book, may encourage us to believe that orientalism is by no means consigned to history and that talk of dialogue, albeit no longer between anything recognisable as 'the two ends of the Old World', still has useful life left in it. What we are witnessing today is a pandemic transformation of ideas and institutions, led by a cultural and political energy which had its origins in the West, but which now extends world-wide in its scope and influence. The long historical process of planetary fusion, a process which was given a powerful stimulus 400 years ago at the time when Matteo Ricci was sending back his glowing reports of the Celestial Kingdom for eager European readers, is even today growing apace in all kinds of fields of intellectual, cultural, and political endeavour. Future historians may view this as marking the end of the ancient division of East and West, and the end of orientalism. On the other hand they may see it as the beginning of a new phase of orientalism – or whatever it might be called – in which this particular encounter of ideas is no longer an exclusively European enterprise, premised on peculiarly Western interests and historical precedents, and certainly no longer in any recognisable sense an imperialist one. It may even come to be seen as a contribution towards the building of a truly global hermeneutic, a new and momentous phase in the long conversation of humanity.

Notes

1 ORIENTATIONS: THE ISSUES

1 For further examples and discussion of such stereotypes, see Dawson 1967, Isaacs 1972, and Mackerras 1989.
2 See Gulick 1963 for an abundant sample of such polarities, and Rao 1939 which in many ways anticipates Said's work in its ruthless critique of the West's construction of the East–West duality.
3 J. Burnet's influential *Early Greek Philosophy* set the tone in this century with his insistence that 'the mysticism of the Upanishads and of Buddhism were of native growth and profoundly influenced philosophy, but were not themselves philosophy in any true sense of the word' (1908: 21). F. L. Baumer's widely-used survey of the modern Western intellectual tradition, *Modern European Thought*, makes only a passing reference to encounters with Eastern ideas, though the *Journal of the History of Ideas* has published a number of articles on the influence of Asian thought on the West.
4 There is a large and growing literature on the orientalism associated with Islam and the cultures of the Middle East, but which it is beyond the scope of this study to discuss. The following should be mentioned in so far as they have close links with the themes of the present book: Amin 1989, Hourani 1991, Huff 1993, Kabbani 1986, Lewis 1993, Rodinson 1988, Said 1985, and Turner 1994.
5 For a useful summary of the current state of the Saidian debate, see MacKenzie 1995, and Prakash 1995.
6 I shall use the traditional Wade–Giles romanisation of Chinese words, except where the Pinyin system is used in direct quotes, in view of the wide employment of the former in the texts examined.
7 This approach has often been associated with the work of A. O. Lovejoy who is usually seen as the founder of the discipline of the history of ideas.
8 Halbfass 1988 includes a detailed investigation of the influence of Western thought on Indian intellectual life from the early nineteenth century onwards.
9 Other examples of the explicit use of the hermeneutical approach in this context are to be found in Clarke 1994, Dilworth 1989, Gare 1995, Gestering 1986, Halbfass 1988, Maraldo 1986, Panikkar 1979a, Sharpe 1985, Solomon and Higgins 1993, and Zhang 1988 and 1992.
10 The situation appears to be much better in America and Australasia than in Europe.

2 ORIENTALISM: SOME CONJECTURES

1 Parallel attempts to rethink the role of non-European cultures in the formation of Western civilisation can be found in the work of Martin Bernal in relation to Egyptian and African sources (see Bernal 1987), and S. Amin in relation to Islam (see Amin 1989).

2 I am using the term 'Romanticism' here in its more popular and superficial sense. At another level, of course, Romanticism does not imply escape from immediate concerns, but can be seen as one way of engaging with them.

3 China's lack of curiosity towards the West has often been exaggerated. The scientific knowledge brought to China by the Jesuits in the seventeenth century was welcomed by a small group of Mandarins who eagerly studied astronomy, geometry, and mechanics, and as Leibniz noted in his Preface to *Novissima Sinica* the emperor K'ang-hsi, who ruled from 1661 to 1722, showed great interest in Western knowledge and studied mathematics, geometry, and astronomy extensively under the Jesuit Father Verbiest (see Gernet 1987: passim, Lach 1957: 72–4, and Pullapilly and Van Kley 1986: 27–43).

4 For discussion of this aspect of Said's thesis see Richardson 1990 which accuses Said of being 'light on empirical data', and of constructing an image of orientalism that arises more from anti-colonial ideology than from empirical evidence; a number of recent studies have sought to rectify this deficiency, good examples of this being found in Breckenridge and van der Veer 1993. Said's book has stirred up a whole sea of critical discussion and has provoked a meta-orientalist discourse that has gone well beyond its origins into the realms of, *inter alia*, colonial and postcolonial studies, area studies, and critical literary theory; amongst those relevant to the present discussion are: Ahmed 1992, Baker 1985, Breckenridge and van der Veer 1993, Clifford 1988, Faure 1993, Hourani 1991, Lewis 1993, Lowe 1991, MacKenzie 1995, Rodinson 1988, Turner 1994, and Young 1990. Moore-Gilbert 1986 argues against the view that Said's thesis can be applied to India. For some of Said's own recent reflections see Said 1993a, and his Afterword to the 1995 edition of *Orientalism*.

5 This conclusion may, of course, be philosophically plausible, and I will return to this question in a later chapter. Said has recently distanced himself from Foucault's all-pervasive use of 'power' (see Said 1993b: 24–5).

6 See Marshall and Williams 1982: 155ff. They emphasise the close connection between intellectual mapping and the imposition of Western power over Asia, though at the same time they are careful to deny that 'Western oriental scholarship became the handmaid of imperialism' (p. 156). They point out too that up to 1800 the British government had been very reluctant to don the colonial mantle.

7 For discussion of this argument see Sheldon Pollock in Breckenridge and van der Veer 1993: Chapter 3. Said speaks of Germany as having 'a kind of intellectual authority over the Orient' (1985: 19).

8 For a fuller discussion of these and related arguments see Lewis 1993: Chapters 6 and 7.

9 As MacKenzie points out, Said acknowledges that the Orient has been 'a means of regenerating the West . . . [and] has the capacity to become a tool of cultural revolution, a legitimising source of resistance to . . . western conventions', but fails to develop the point (1995: 10). The counter-cultural, counter-hegemonic role of orientalism has been observed by a number of other critics; see for example Tuck 1990: 8, and Young 1990: 140.

10 This view is to be found in Levenson 1967 which provides a selection of comparative writings on the topic of European expansion in the Renaissance period. For

accounts of Cheng Ho's expeditions see Boorstin 1983: Chapter 25, and Duyvendak 1949.

11 Here our inspiration will come from Joseph Needham who, echoing Max Weber's classic question concerning the European origins of capitalism, addressed a parallel problem, namely: why did modern science develop in Europe and not in China where conditions would seem to be more favourable for its emergence than in Europe? Following Wittfogel, Needham 1954 and 1969a argues that the tradition of a centralised bureacracy in China inhibited the growth of a merchant class and hence, by contrast with Europe in the post-Renaissance period, deprived it of conditions in which modern science could develop. For discussion of Needham's thesis see Bodde 1991, Huff 1993, and Sivin 1995. Sivin (ibid.: 62–6) claims that a scientific revolution did in fact take place in China in the seventeenth century comparable to that taking place in contemporary France.

12 This is the briefest of sketches of a complex historical period, interpretations of which have generated much dispute. For an account of the intellectual turmoil of the period see Hazard 1953, Jones 1965, and Popkin 1968.

13 See Beck 1992 and Giddens 1991. Not all sociologists would agree with this general approach. Norbert Elias, for example, has argued that modern life tends to become more rather than less regulated, and members of the Frankfurt School such as Marcuse and Habermas have emphasised the danger in modern society of conformity and of the mechanisation of human attitudes and conduct. On this whole question see Turner 1994: Chapters 12 and 13.

14 Popkin 1968 argues that scepticism was the foundational problem of modern Western philosophy.

3 CHINA CULT: THE AGE OF ENLIGHTENMENT

1 For an investigation into the links between Greek mystery religions and Hindu beliefs see Danielou and Hurry 1979.

2 On the possible links between Gnosticism and Indian religious thought see Halbfass 1988: 17–18, Radhakrishnan 1939: 126, Thundy 1993, and Welburn 1991.

3 On the relationship between neo-platonism and Indian thought see Halbfass 1988: 17 and Harris 1982.

4 For further studies of the East–West cultural encounters in the ancient and mediaeval worlds see Almond 1986, Garbe 1959, Gruber and Kersten 1995, Guénon 1945, Halbfass 1988, McEvilley 1982, Mackenzie 1928, Marlow 1954, Radhakrishnan 1939, Tarn 1938, West 1971, and Willson 1964.

5 For discussion of issues concerning the global expansion of European interests and power in this period see Cipolla 1965, and Levenson 1967.

6 Mungello argues that for some Jesuits the aim was not so much conversion as the amalgamation of Confucianism and Christianity (see 1977: Chapter 7).

7 For fuller accounts of the Jesuit missions to China and of the so-called 'rites controversy' see Dunne 1962, Faure 1993, Gernet 1987, Minamiki 1985, Mungello 1989, Ronan and Oh 1988, and Young 1983.

8 According to Jacobson 1969, David Hume should also be included in this list since certain of his most characteristic teachings – those concerning the self, experience, morality – were likely to have been influenced by oriental philosophies. The evidence offered is circumstantial rather than direct, however, and for further discussion see Betty 1971, Conze 1963, and Hoffman 1980.

9 It should be noted that 'The image of Muhammad as a wise, tolerant, unmystical, and undogmatic ruler became widespread in the period of the Enlightenment, and

it finds expression in writers as diverse as Goethe, Condorcet, and Voltaire' (Lewis 1993: 90). See also Rodinson 1988.

10 Neo-Confucianism emerged in China in the Sung dynasty (960–1279), integrating traditional Confucian teachings, which focused primarily on the political and moral orders, with some of the cosmological ideas of the Taoists and the spiritual teachings of the Buddhists. On the relationship between Enlightenment orientation and neo-Confucianism see Mungello 1977: 23–4. See Paper 1995: Chapter 1 for discussion of the long-term implications of the Jesuit-inspired views of Chinese religion.

11 On Malebranche's relationship with Chinese thought see Mungello 1980.

12 On Voltaire and Confucianism see Bailey 1992, Guy 1963, and Song 1989.

13 See Leibniz 1994 for a collection of his writings on China.

14 On this question see Cook and Rosemont 1981, Gare 1995: 320, Liu 1982, Mungello 1977: 15, and Needham 1956: 291–2 and 496–505.

15 On Leibniz, binary arithmetic, and the *I Ching*, see Mungello 1977: passim, and Needham 1956: 340–5. See also Roy 1972.

16 For further details of this affair see Lach 1953.

17 For discussion of the influence of the Chinese examination system on European political debates see Leites 1968, and Teng 1943.

18 For an account of the physiocrats' engagement with China, see Guy 1963: 341–59.

19 For a fuller discussion of the relationship between deism and orientalism see Halbfass 1988: Chapter 4. See also Leites 1968.

20 See also Allen 1958, R. C. Bald in Ching and Oxtoby 1992, Dawson 1967, Honour 1961, and Reichwein 1925. See Siren 1990: 80–3 for discussion of the dispute over the extent of Chinese influence on English garden design. On orientalism and the arts in general see MacKenzie 1995.

21 Nevertheless, recent work of Joseph Needham and others suggests that the exalted estimates of Chinese civilisation were in certain respects nearer to the truth than the negative views that came to prevail in the nineteenth century, and that China was not merely perceived to be but actually was in many respects superior to European civilisation in the Enlightenment period.

22 For further details and discussions of the sinophilism of the Enlightenment period see Appleton 1951 (deals with the Chinese vogue in England), Ching and Oxtoby 1992 (a selection of articles reprinted from the *Journal of the History of Ideas*), Dawson 1967, Edwardes 1971, Franke 1967, Lach 1977, Mackerras 1989, Marshall and Williams 1982, Maverick 1946 (includes a translation of Quesnay's *Le despotisme de la Chine*), Mungello 1979 (contains a review of the literature to date on the subject), Pinot 1932, Pullapilly and Van Kley 1986, Reichwein 1925, and Rowbotham 1945.

4 PASSAGE TO INDIA: THE AGE OF ROMANTICISM

1 For an account of Western attitudes towards China in the nineteenth century see Mackerras 1989: Chapter 4. There were some exceptions to the predominantly negative attitude, for example Johnson 1873, Meadows 1856, and Simon 1885, all of which contain favourable accounts of Chinese life and thought.

2 For criticism of the idea of an 'Oriental Renaissance' see Bernal 1987, and Said in his Foreword to Schwab 1984.

3 The Romantics were aware of the multiplicity of religions and mythologies in India, but they did not always make clear discriminations between them. Though many references to the Vedas appear in the literature of that period, the main interest of the philosophers was in the teachings of the Upanishads, and most specifically in the

Advaita (non-dual) *Vedānta* school of Shankara, according to which the soul, manifest reality, and God are identical.

4 For a fuller account of the contributions of Holwell and Dow see Marshall 1970: 4–8, and Schwab 1984: 149–51.

5 For a discussion of the relationship between the Oriental Renaissance and English Romantic literature, see Bearce 1961, Drew 1987, Leask 1992, Schwab 1984, and Winks and Rush 1990.

6 On Goethe's orientalism see Friedenthal 1965: 432–45 and 515.

7 For fuller accounts of the orientalist interests amongst the German Romantic philosophers see Dumoulin 1981, Halbfass 1988, Hulin 1979, Iyer 1965, Marshall 1970, Schwab 1984, and Willson 1964.

5 BUDDHIST PASSIONS: THE NINETEENTH CENTURY

1 On the influence of Chinese Taoism on Tolstoy's outlook see Bodde 1950.

2 For an analysis of the views of James Mill and the utilitarians on India see Stokes 1959.

3 See Inden 1990 which contains powerful a critique of European attitudes towards India in the nineteenth century. See Mackerras 1989 and Sawyer 1977 on Marx and the idea of the Asiatic mode of production, and Ahmad 1992 which contains an extended critique of Said's views on Marx and India. On China's supposed 'stagnation' see Dawson 1964: 14–18, Mackerras 1989: Chapter 7, and Qian 1985. The best known and most influential twentieth-century development of Marx's ideas on this question is to be found in Wittfogel 1957, which links despotism and the supposed stagnation of Chinese society with the need to control the great waterways of China.

4 A discussion of the the the ideological underpinnings of Rhys Davids' scholarship is offered by Charles Hallisey in Lopez 1995.

5 For a fuller study of the history of Buddhist scholarship in the West see de Jong 1974. For an intellectual biography of Max Müller see Chaudhuri 1974.

6 On the question of Schopenhauer's attitude towards *nirvāna*, see Welbon 1968: Chapter 5.

7 For a discussion of Schopenhauer's alleged pessimism, see Gerstering 1986. General discussions of Schopenhauer's relationship with Hindu and Buddhist thought can be found in Abelson 1993, Halbfass 1988, Magee 1987, and Schwab 1984.

8 On the Indo-European/Aryan myth, its origins and development in the nineteenth century, see Mallory 1989, Poliakov 1971, and Todorov 1993. On its implications for orientalism, see Halbfass 1988: 139–40, and Schwab 1984: 431–4. We will return to this issue in Chapter 11.

9 For a fuller discussion of Nietzsche's relation to Buddhism, see Frazier 1975, Mistry 1981, Parkes 1991, and Welbon 1968. The Parkes volume contains an especially rich collection of articles discussing questions both of influence and of affinity.

10 Summaries and discussions of such arguments are to be found in Almond 1988, Carus 1897, Garbe 1959, Kellogg 1885, Scott 1890, Thundy 1993, and Tweed 1992. The debate has continued, albeit spasmodically, up to the present day; see for example Gruber and Kersten 1995.

11 On this debate see Almond 1988 and Tweed 1992.

12 Other works from the same period which discuss the relationship between Christianity and Buddhism include: Aiken 1900, Bunsen 1880, Cushing 1907, Lillie 1887, and Saunders 1912. Almond 1988 and Tweed 1992 give excellent accounts of Buddhism in nineteenth-century Britain and America respectively. On Carus and

the East–West encounter see Fields 1986, Henderson 1993, Jackson 1968, and Tweed 1992.

13 For fuller details concerning the relationship between Eastern thought and the transcendentalist movement see Carpenter 1930, Christy 1932, Fields 1986, Jackson 1973, Riepe 1970, Schwab 1984, and Versluis 1991.

14 On this issue see Welbon 1968. A glowing account of Buddhism appeared in Jennings 1858, but this book was not fully cognisant of the work of contemporary French scholars.

15 It was not the first epic poem of its kind. A few years earlier Richard Philips had published *The Story of Gautama Buddha and his Creed*, but it did not achieve anything like the popularity of Arnold's work.

16 For further discussion of the Theosophical Society and its contribution to what Hendrik Kraemer calls the 'Eastern Invasion', see Campbell 1980, Fields 1986, Godwin 1994, Kraemer 1960, Riepe 1970, and Washington 1993. See Campbell 1980 and Sharpe 1985 for discussion of the influence of the Theosophical Society on Gandhi and the Indian independence movement. On the occult revival in the nineteenth century and its links with orientalism see Goodrick-Clarke 1992 and Webb 1976.

17 For further information about the World's Parliament of Religions see Barrows 1893, Braybrooke 1992, Fields 1986, Lancaster 1987, and Seager 1993. Küng and Kuschel 1993 contains a brief account of the Parliament, but is mainly concerned with the event held to mark its centenary. On this latter occasion the emphasis was on the serious practical problems currently facing the globe, and the outcome was a 'Declaration Toward a Global Ethic' which attempted to find common ground on issues such as world peace, social and economic injustice, and environmental degradation.

6 EAST–WEST ENCOUNTER IN THE TWENTIETH CENTURY

1 See Dumoulin 1976, Humphreys 1951, and Oliver 1979 for accounts of the development of Buddhism in England and Germany in the first half of the twentieth century.

2 For brief discussions of the history of Zen's impact on the West see Dumoulin 1976, Faure 1991, and Scharf 1993. Fields 1986, Prebish 1979, and Tworkov 1994 give more extended accounts from a purely American perspective.

3 Bishop 1993: 132. This book offers a comprehensive study of the way that Tibetan Buddhism has been encountered in the West. See also Lopez 1994 and 1995.

4 A definitive account of Taoism and the West has yet to be written, but the popularity of Capra's book, *The Tao of Physics*, is indicative of the widespread interest that it has elicited. Joseph Needham's writings have played a crucial role in demonstrating the importance of Taoism as a natural philosophy, and indications of the growing importance of Taoism at the present time are to be found in Cooper 1990, and Palmer 1991.

5 See for example Ajaya 1983 which makes use of Tantric philosophy in the construction of a psychotherapeutic system; and Scott 1983 which argues for the 'need to revive the science of the Chakras and set it in a context that Western science can assimilate' (1983: 229). Shaw 1994 engages with Tantric Buddhism from a feminist viewpoint.

6 For an examination of the link between imperialism and English literature in the nineteenth and twentieth centuries see Said 1993a, Suleri 1992, and Viswanathan 1989. For studies of the relationship between the East and English literature see

Greenberger 1969, and Gupta 1973. On Kipling's orientalism see Moore-Gilbert 1986.
7 Concerning Yeats' involvement with Eastern philosophies see Campbell 1980, Naito 1984, Ravindran 1990, Surette 1993, and Wilson 1982.
8 On the influence of Chinese literature on Pound and on modernism see Qian 1995. For a discussion of Pound's use of Chinese pictograms see Fields 1986: 163–6, and Zhang 1992: 23–6. On Fenellosa's influence on Pound and on orientalism in America see Chisholm 1963.
9 On Eliot's interest in Buddhism see McCarthy 1952, and Titmuss 1995. On his involvement with Hindu philosophy see Perl and Tuck 1985, and Sharpe 1985: 132–5.
10 On Kandinsky's interest in Eastern ideas see Long 1980, and on orientalist influence on the Bauhaus see Webb 1976: 423–4. The relationship between orientalism and the modern movement is discussed in Surette 1993 who argues that this relationship has often proved an embarrassment to commentators who have done it less than justice.
11 On Hesse's relation to Chinese culture see Hsia 1974.
12 The impact of Eastern ideas on the beat and hippie generations is examined in Fields 1986, Prebish 1979, and Roszak 1970. See also Watts 1959. On the Hari-Krishna cult in the West see Jackson 1994, and Stillson-Judah 1974.
13 See Palmer 1993: 38–9. For a critical discussion of New Age ideas from a Christian viewpoint see Perry 1992.
14 See Vyas 1970 for discussion of the role of the ideal of universalism in modern Indian thought. For a critical discussion of Radhakrishnan's thinking as a whole see Organ 1989. Radhakrishnan's syncretistic tendencies have been criticised by a number of Indian thinkers including Aurobindo and Coomaraswamy.
15 On Keyserling's life and his role in the propagation of Eastern ideas in the West see Hardy 1987, and Parkes 1934.
16 For an introduction to Brunton's writings see Godwin et al. 1990.
17 On this point see Kitagawa 1990: 11.

7 PHILOSOPHICAL ENCOUNTERS

1 For a discussion of Marxist attitudes to Eastern thought see Halbfass 1988: 137, which contains several bibliographical references on this subject.
2 Exceptions to the general lack of interest in the East among linguistic philosophers include Arthur Danto and Herbert Fingarette.
3 More recent exceptions include Cooper 1996, and Plott 1979.
4 Halbfass 1988: Chapter 9 offers an overview of the development of philosophical historiography in relation to Eastern traditions of thought.
5 For discussion of Stcherbatsky's thought see Murti 1955, Tuck 1990, and Welbon 1968.
6 See Bilimoria 1995 for an account of the development of comparative philosophy in Australasia.
7 For a discussion of Heidegger's views on dialogue and what he called 'planetary thinking' see Halbfass 1988: 167–70 and 441–2. On Heidegger's links with Asian thought see also Caputo 1986, Heine 1985, May 1996, Parkes 1987, and Steffney 1981.
8 Interest within Europe has been boosted by the foundation in 1993 of *The European Society for Asian Philosophy*. For a discussion of why, considering the long tradition of

specialist Oriental studies in France, there has been a virtual absence of interest in comparative studies in French philosophy in recent decades, see Droit 1989.

9 On Santayana and Buddhism see Michelson 1995.

10 For a discussion of the links between Buddhism and Whitehead's thinking, see Fredericks 1989, Jacobson 1983, Odin 1982, and Tracy 1990. *Philosophy East and West* devotes a whole issue, 15: 4, to Whitehead's relationship with oriental philosophies. See also Ingram 1995.

11 For fuller accounts of the Eastern influence on American thought and culture, see Fields 1986, Inada and Jacobson 1984, Jackson 1981, Prebish 1979, Riepe 1970, and Tweed 1992.

12 For discussion of Northrop's views see Inada and Jacobson 1992, Jones 1986, and Riepe 1970.

13 For another recent example of the universalist genre see Gangadean 1993. For a somewhat acerbic account of the Hawaii conferences see Organ 1989: 40–42.

14 Halbfass credits the Indian philosopher Brajendranath Seal with coining the phrase 'comparative philosophy' (1988: 423). Chapter 23 provides a useful survey of the history of the comparative method in relation to India.

15 Recent years have witnessed an exponential growth of writings in this area, mostly emanating from America, of which the following are representative examples: Bahm 1977, Betty 1971, Conze 1963, Coward 1990, Dilworth 1989, Gudmunsen 1977, Harris 1982, Heimann 1937, Heine 1985, Jacobson 1983, Katz 1981, Matilal and Shaw 1985, Moore 1968, Nakamura 1975, Organ 1975, Parkes 1991, Scharfstein 1978, Shaw 1987, Sprung 1954, Taber 1983, and Weiss 1954.

16 See Tuck 1990 which places Gudmunsen's Wittgensteinian interpretation of *Mādhyamaka* philosophy in its hermeneutical context. For further comparisons between Wittgenstein and Eastern philosophies see Thurman 1991, and Wienpahl 1979.

17 See for example Fredericks 1989 where Buddhism is used to illuminate Whitehead's process thought.

18 Spiegelberg draws close links between existentialism and the philosophy of Aurobindo in Chaudhuri and Spiegelberg 1960: 47–59. Links between Zen and existentialism are drawn by Ives (1992: 3), and Merton (1961: 233). Light 1987 maintains that there is a Japanese influence on the early development of Sartre's thinking.

19 For other Western attempts to 'rethink' Confucius, see Fingarette 1972, Neville 1994, and Rosemont and Schwartz 1979. Neville argues that Confucianism 'is now a world philosophy with all the intellectual responsibility this entails' (1994: 21). Some important recent discussions centre round the issue of Western individualism versus Confucian communalism, on which see Bockover 1991.

20 For further examples of this hermeneutical approach see Collins 1982, Kasulis 1993, Organ 1964, Parfitt 1984, and Raju and Castell 1968. Ames 1994 contains a useful collection of cross-cultural explorations of the concept of the person, and Levine 1994 offers a detailed analysis of the idea of pantheism which draws equally on Eastern and Western traditions.

21 For recent philosophical discussions of the question of communicating across cultural boundaries, see Allinson 1989, Larson and Deutsch 1988, Solomon and Higgins 1993, and Tuck 1990. The Epilogue to Halbfass 1988 raises questions about the prospects for a world-philosophy that spans the traditions of East and West. For a discussion of the philosophical problems involved in translating Eastern moral values into Western contexts see Danto 1976. I have used the term 'hermeneutical' in this section to characterise a reflexive and critical approach to orientalism, but there is a wider sense, following Gadamer, in which all understanding is hermeneutical.

8 RELIGIOUS DIALOGUE

1 Something of the extent and significance of these pluralistic developments is captured in Richardson 1985, and Wood 1988.
2 More recent examples of this genre include: Ching 1977, Otto 1957, Parrinder 1962, Smith 1981, Zaehner 1958. For a useful history of the study of comparative religion see Sharpe 1986.
3 Christopher Isherwood's *Vedānta for the Western World* comprises selections from this magazine. For discussions of Huxley's relation to *Vedānta* see Chakov 1981, and Eaton 1949.
4 In McDermott 1984: 22. See the journal *Studies in Comparative Religion* for articles by and on the ideas of Guénon and Schuon. The importance of the esoteric tradition for an understanding of the intellectual and cultural history of the West is emphasised in Faivre 1994.
5 For a more recent discussion of the relationship between Eckhart and Eastern mysticism see Potitella 1965.
6 On Buber's dialogue with Taoism see Herman 1996. See King 1989 on Teilhard's comparison between Eastern and Western mysticism. One of Teilhard's correspondents on this question was the French novelist and dramatist Romain Rolland whose thinking was impregnated with a universalist/mystical outlook, and who wrote biographies of Ramakrishna and Vivekananda.
7 See also Johanns 1932–3. The view that Christianity finds its fulfilment in Hinduism is to be found in Robinson 1979, and Halbfass discusses this issue in the context of Hindu strategies for including Christianity within a universalised *Vedānta*, though as he points out India remains within a Westernised world (1988: 370).
8 See Braybrooke 1992 and 1996 for accounts of the inter-faith dialogue between the two world wars.
9 The importance of Eliade in the inter-faith dialogue is emphasised in Tracy 1990. The analysis of the *Eranos* seminars in Webb 1976 places emphasis on their connection with the occultist and mystical interests of the period, but recognises at the same time their strong academic credentials.
10 See for example D'Costa 1986: 7–9, and Netland 1991: 9–27.
11 On Tillich's enthusiastic encounter with Eastern thought, see Abe 1966.
12 See Hick 1973: Chapter 9, and also Hick 1974, 1982, and 1993, and Hick and Knitter 1987.
13 See also Cobb 1982. For an interesting dialogue between Cobb and the Japanese philosopher Masao Abe, contemporary leader of the Kyoto school, see Cobb and Ives 1991. Since the death of Suzuki in 1966 Abe has become the chief exponent of Zen in the West, and the most prominent Japanese exponent of the Buddhist–Christian dialogue (see Abe 1995). On the role of the Kyoto school in the Buddhist–Christian dialogue see Kasulis 1982.
14 On the issue of relativism in this context see also Davis 1971.
15 For examples of such studies see Ching 1977, Lee 1991, and Yao 1996.
16 See also Barnes 1991, Déchenet 1960, and Johnston 1971, all Jesuit-authored works which examine the possibilities of integrating Eastern with Christian practices.
17 While on this Asian journey Thomas Merton died accidentally of electrocution in Bangkok where he was attending a conference of abbots from Christian monasteries in Asia. I was privileged to meet him in Singapore only a few days before he died, a meeting which was one of the initial steps in the journey that has led to the writing of this book.

9 PSYCHOLOGICAL INTERPRETATIONS

1 For a discussion of the relationship between Buddhism and cognitive psychology see Pickering 1995, and Varela *et al.* 1991.
2 For fuller details on Autogenic Training see Luthe 1969.
3 For further discussion of psychosynthesis see   Hardy 1987, and Pelletier and Garfield 1976.
4 On this point see Coward 1985: 98.
5 The introvert/extravert model has been developed in relation to the East/West complementarity in Abegg 1952, and Campbell 1973.
6 On the theory and practice of the mandala see Jung 1959, and Tucci 1969.
7 For discussions of Jung's encounter with Eastern ideas see Clarke 1994, Coward 1985, Jones 1979, Meckel and Moore 1992, Moacanin 1986, and Odajnyk 1993. Jones is especially critical of Jung's attempts to draw comparisons between Western psychology and Eastern spiritual teachings. Gomez (in Lopez 1995) holds that Eastern thought was more of a 'catalyst' for Jung than a direct influence (op. cit.: 205), and emphasises the ambivalence of Jung's attitude towards Eastern philosophies.
8 Some indication of what his Eastern journey meant for Laing is to be found in Mullan 1995.
9 See also Graham 1986. The influence of Zen and Taoism is very evident in Maslow 1973.
10 On this matter see Fagan and Shepherd 1972: 60–1, Sallis 1982, and Page and Chang 1989.
11 Further discussion of attempts to relate Western psychotherapy, mental health, and personal growth to Eastern philosophies can be found in Ajaya 1983, Brandon 1976, Claxton 1986, Crook and Fontana 1990, Epstein 1996, Goleman and Thurman 1991, Hayward 1987, Silva 1979, and Welwood 1979 and 1983.
12 For further studies of the psychological implications of meditation see Claxton 1986, Fontana 1992, Goleman 1989, Naranjo and Ornstein 1971, Pelletier 1985, Pelletier and Garfield 1976, Shapiro and Walsh 1984, Welwood 1979, West 1987, and Wilber *et al.* 1986.
13 See also Griffiths 1986 which discusses ASCs in the context of Eastern thought.

10 SCIENTIFIC AND ECOLOGICAL SPECULATIONS

1 Parallel attempts have been made recently by Buddhist philosophers in Sri Lanka to draw Buddhism and modern science close together; see Ling 1968: 416–17.
2 For an insight into Buddhism's role in recent Russian history see Snelling 1992a and 1992b.
3 On this point see Wilber 1985: 218.
4 Moore 1989: 173. This book gives a useful summary of the development of Schrödinger's philosophical ideas and of his debt to Indian philosophy.
5 On this last point see Gare 1995 which offers a defence of Needham's orientalism, and Jones 1981 which argues that Needham's thesis involves a distortion of Taoism whose goals are quite distinct from the empirical investigation of nature.
6 For critiques of Capra's views see Clifton and Regher 1989, Jones 1986, Polkinghorne 1986, and Sturch 1993. The latter two argue that Christianity is more compatible with modern science than Asian religions.
7 Other works which have developed the theme of a synthesis of East and West aris-

ing out of the new physics include Griffiths 1989, Hayward 1987, Margenau 1984, Riencourt 1981, Siu 1957, Talbot 1980, and Zukav 1979.

8 For a discussion of traditional Chinese medicine in relation to Western paradigms of health and sickness see Capra 1982: Chapter 10. For a discussion of the philosophical and historical background to Ayurvedic medicine see Heyn 1987.

9 We are concerned here more with what Arne Naess calls 'ecosophy' – philosophical ecology – than with the *science* of ecology, though the two are clearly connected.

10 They have also turned towards the belief systems of the indigenous peoples of North America and Australasia.

11 For a parallel view see Alexandrin 1978.

12 For similar themes see Titmuss 1995, and for collections of writings on this issue see Badiner 1990, and Callicott and Ames 1989.

13 For a recent critique of these and related ideas see Bookchin 1995 which views Eastern influence on recent Western thought as an unhealthy encouragement to mystification.

14 This view is to be found in, *inter alia*, the teachings of St Thomas Aquinas.

15 Hindus are traditionally vegetarian, but principle and practice in this regard vary amongst Buddhists. For a discussion of the Buddhist history of this issue see Ruegg 1980.

16 For a study of the dynamics of this debate and its present state see Callicott and Ames 1989. For a critical analysis of attempts to use Eastern ideas to assist in articulating an environmental philosophy see Rolston 1987, which appears in a special edition of *Philosophy East and West* devoted to this whole issue.

11 REFLECTIONS AND REORIENTATIONS

1 See for example Streng 1967 in which it is assumed that Indian thinkers speak the same philosophical language and address the same philosophical questions as their Western 'counterparts'.

2 The problem of self-referentiality has sometimes been observed in the case of Said's argument which on the face of it has no way of escaping the terms of its own critique; see for example Young 1990: 129–40.

3 On the controversies surrounding Gadamer's hermeneutics see Bleicher 1982, and Ormiston and Schrift 1990. For a critique of fashionable relativistic views in relation to East–West comparative studies see Griffiths 1986.

4 See Goody 1996 which argues that 'the major societies of Eurasia were fired in the same crucible' as the West (p. 226). See Hodgson 1993 which confronts the standard Eurocentric approach to world history.

5 Issues concerning the relativity of language and of conceptual schemes are discussed from an orientalist point of view in Scharfstein 1978: Chapter 1. The importance of linguistic and conceptual differences between Eastern and Western cultures is emphasised in Gernet 1987: 238–47.

6 See for example Deutsch 1991.

7 For a discussion of ideological and technical issues involved in the translation of Eastern texts see Figueira 1991.

8 For further examples and discussion see Cleary 1991: 3, Graham 1989: 258n, and MacIntyre in Deutsch 1991: 514. Richards 1932 is an early 'classic' discussion of the question of the conveyance of meaning from Eastern texts into Western languages, and related questions about differences of mentality.

9 On the question of the 'classical' prejudice in orientalism see Ahmad 1992: 163–8,

Dirks 1992: 9, and Rosane Rocher's comments in Breckenridge and van der Veer 1993: 225–6.

10 See for example Jones 1979 in which Jung is criticised for substituting his own theoretical constructs for Eastern religious concepts. A similar critique is offered by Luis Gomez in Lopez: 1995.

11 This process is not confined to Western thinkers. Scharf 1993 argues that Suzuki's teachings in the West concerning Zen involved a radical decontextualising of the Japanese tradition and its remoulding within a more 'suitable' form derived in part from the ideal of a 'Religion of Science' associated with Paul Carus and in part from the process of ideological reconstruction in the Meiji period, an example which indicates the complexity of the hermeneutical interchange between East and West. For a revised version of this article see Lopez 1995.

12 See Lopez 1995, where Buddhist scholarship is examined in the context of the ideologies of empire. The theme of the culturally conditioned nature of orientalist scholarship is central to debates in this field from Said's *Orientalism* onwards. See also Tuck 1990 which points out that Buddhist interpretation in Europe has inevitably been subject to changing trends and fashions and has evolved in parallel with major shifts in Western thought. Analytic/positivist assumptions are evident in the interpretation of Indian philosophy in Potter 1963.

13 A parallel hermeneutical approach has been offered by Alastair MacIntyre who emphasises the creative potential generated by the encounter between different intellectual traditions, sc. the Confucian and the Aristotelian (see Deutsch 1991).

14 Discussion of this issue is to be found in Huntington 1989, where attention is drawn to the different Western interpretative traditions in relation to the *Mādhyamaka* school, and also in Tuck 1990.

15 On racist attitudes towards India in the colonial period see Inden 1990, and Kiernan 1972.

16 This attitude is well documented in Almond 1988: Chapter 2.

17 For a different view of Schlegel on this question see Said 1985: 98–9. Herder himself did not subscribe to the belief in German national or racial supremacy.

18 On this whole question see Poliakov 1971, Schwab 1984, Todorov 1993, and Young 1990.

19 On the issues concerning the relationship between Heidegger and Jung respectively with the Nazis see Wolin 1991, and Maidenbaum and Martin 1991. On Jung's links with the Nazis see also Sklar 1977, and Webb 1976. On Ezra Pound's anti-semitic and fascist views see Casillo 1988, according to which Pound was hostile to Buddhists and Hindus whom he lumped in with Jews as being hostile to nature (see ibid.: 127 and 262).

20 There are interesting parallels here with the case of green ideas which were linked earlier in the century with both *völkisch* and Nazi thinking but which have in more recent times become dissociated from these ideologies.

21 For further discussion of these issues see Faivre 1994, Goodrick-Clarke 1992, Sklar 1977, and Webb 1976. It should be added that followers of Eastern religious paths were given no special treatment in Nazi Germany, and the persecution of the Christian churches in Germany in the 1930s was extended indiscriminately to the small band of Buddhists. It would be as absurd to condemn the whole of orientalism as it would be to dismiss the teachings of Jung and Heidegger *tout court* as irredeemably contaminated on account of their association – even on the worst interpretation – with Nazism.

22 For a discussion of the controversy between Koestler and Suzuki on the moral implications of Zen see Fader 1980, and Faure 1993.

23 For a similar argument see Webb 1976: 13.

24   See also Goody 1996 which offers a sustained argument against the belief that rationality is a unique possession of the West. His discussion of the role of the thinking of Max Weber in this context is especially relevent.

25   Quietism is a Christian heresy which holds that perfection is acquired through passivity and the practice of contemplation, leaving all salvific agency to God alone.

26   On the issue of the relationship between Zen and militarism/fascism within Japanese history see Dumoulin 1990, Faure 1993, Ingram and Streng 1986, Ives 1992, and Scharf 1993. See also the discussion between Abe and Cobb in Cobb and Ives 1991.

27   See Batchelor 1994: Chapter 21 for an account of the life and work of Thich Nhat Hanh and his influence on the movement for engaged Buddhism in the West. For a useful collection of writings on this subject, including two articles by Thich Nhat Hanh, see Eppsteiner 1985.

28   For discussion of Gandhi's influence on pacifist and ecological thinking see Naess 1965, and Spretnak 1991.

29   On the issue of gender and orientalism see Kabbani 1986, Prakash 1995, and Suleri 1992. Gross 1993 surveys the historical role of women in the history of Buddhism in Asia, as does Paul 1979. Boucher 1988, and Friedman 1987 help to document the wide extent and intensity of the current 'Buddhist/feminist conversation', and the mutual transformations that are taking place between these two movements in America. Shaw 1994 uses a study of women's historical role in Tantric Buddhism to rethink the role of women as sources of spiritual insight and power. Needham contrasts the 'masculine, hard, managing, domineering, even aggressive' outlook of Confucianism with the 'feminine, tolerant, yielding, permissive, mystical and receptive' attitudes of Taoism (1978, 1: 95). On related matters concerning Buddhist practice see Batchelor 1996.

30   For further discussion of these matters see Batchelor 1994, Batchelor and Brown 1992, Brandon 1976, and Eppsteiner 1985 which offer a variety of oriental perspectives on contemporary social issues and on 'engaged Buddhism'; Ives 1992 which speculates about a Zen-based concept of human rights that is not based on individualistic premises; Jones 1989, Keown 1995, and King 1992 which question the widely-held assumption that Buddhism has traditionally been socially inactive; Kraft 1992 which argues that Buddhist-inspired inner peace is a necessary complement to socio-political paths to peace; Macy 1985, and Snelling 1992b.

31   Another good example of cultural imperialism would be Macaulay's attempt to impose a purely British education system on the Indian élite in the mid-nineteenth century and a similar policy enacted thereafter in Ceylon. Breckenridge and van der Veer 1993 documents the extent to which orientalist knowledge was used in colonial adminstration.

32   Both Halbfass 1988: Chapter 4, and Rosane Rocher in Breckenridge and van der Veer 1993: Chapter 7 give useful indications of the mixture of motivational factors that entered into the scholarly activities of William Jones.

33   See Sharpe 1985: Chapters 5–6.

34   For an extended account of the 'Hindu Renaissance' see Nandy 1983.

35   See for example MacKenzie 1995: 11–12.

36   For a discussion of this from the point of view of a Japanese thinker, see Kitagawa 1990: 11–13. See Gernet 1987 for an account of the highly 'active' role of the Chinese literati in the period of Jesuit-led incursions into China. See Chuan-Ying Cheng's essay in Allinson 1989 which argues that Chinese thought can be further developed in Chinese terms, not destroyed, in the process of Westernisation, and that Western interest in the *I Ching* has played an important role in renewing the Chinese investigation into its own traditions.

12 ORIENTALISM AND POSTMODERNITY

1 A good example of this is the emergence of subaltern studies which represent an important attempt to investigate and liberate the voices of the hitherto dispossessed. See Guha and Chakravorty 1988 for a representative set of papers, and O'Hanlon 1988 for a critical analysis.

2 See for example Faure 1991 which opens up the social and ritualistic dimensions of Zen which have not normally featured in Western accounts; Gombrich 1988 for a socio-historical account of Theravada Buddhism; and Schipper 1993 for a study of Taoism in the context of traditional Chinese life. Breckenridge and van der Veer 1993, and Dirks 1992 contain a number of studies of the relationship between knowledge, power, and social factors within colonial and post-colonial contexts.

3 See also Beck 1992 in which fragmentation and contradiction are portrayed as fundamental features of the modernisation process, and where terms such as 'late modernity' and 'reflexive modernization' are preferred to 'postmodern'; also Giddens 1991 in which features associated with 'postmodernism' are construed as the late unfolding rather than the transcendence of modernity.

4 On the question of textuality in this connection see Maraldo 1986.

5 For a discussion of Nāgārjuna's relevance to contemporary Western philosophy see Scharfstein 1978: 276–84. For a discussion of his connection with the 'linguistic turn' see Gudmunsen 1977, and also Huntington 1989, and Loy 1987 which draw comparisons between deconstructionism and the *Mādhyamaka* philosophy. Jones 1986 links recent discussions of the conventional and constructed nature of language with both the *Theravāda* and the *Advaita Vedānta* traditions. Issues concerning scepticism and relativism in the writings of Chuang-tzu are discussed in Kjellberg and Ivanhoe 1996.

6 David Hall has also offered Confucianism, with its strong sense of the embodiment of the individual within the communal matrix, as a tool for critiquing the individualising and fragmenting forces of modernity (see Deutsch 1991: 59).

7 For a detailed analysis of the Buddhist 'no-self' doctrine see Collins 1982. Claxton 1994 sketches a decentred model of the self which draws on both recent psychological research and the mystical traditions of East and West, and argues that Buddhist techniques of mindfulness can be a powerful tool in freeing up the reified image we have of ourselves.

8 However, as Bryan Turner, amongst others, has pointed out, Said's adherence to a Foucauldian perspective necessarily results in a pessimistic conclusion since *all* discourse is subject to shifting power relationships, and hence orientalism can never free itself from political and economic interest (1994: 31–2 and 45–6). Aijaz Ahmad also accuses Said of inconsistency on this point (1992: 164), as does John MacKenzie (1995: 6).

9 For further discussion of this point see Said 1989, where he sees the discipline of anthropology, hitherto caught in the vice of imperialism, starting to tell a different story by critically examining its whole approach to the notion of 'culture'.

10 Developments in this field have been more in evidence in the USA and in Australasia (on the latter see Bilimoria 1995) than in Britain. The issues relating to multiculturalism in general and to the educational curriculum and the Western canon in particular have been subject to intense debate in recent years, especially in the USA, and the views that I have expressed are by no means universally accepted. On this and related questions see Foster and Herzog 1994, and Taylor 1992.

11 A useful distinction is developed in Griffin 1988 between a deconstructive or eliminative postmodernism on the one hand and a constructive or revisionary postmodernism on the other. The SUNY Series in Constructive Postmodern Thought, of

which David Griffin is editor, represents an attempt to move the postmodernist debate forward to more fertile ground, while at the same time acknowledging its critical achievements. Deep ecology is often cited as an example of a constructive or revisionary postmodern theory.

12 For an account of this Order see Batchelor 1994.
13 See also Cobb and Ives 1991: 3–4, Ives 1992: 2 and 101, and King 1994: 29. According to the theologian John Cobb, Christianity is undergoing a parallel transformation in its dialogue with Buddhism, and distinctions between Christianity and Buddhism are likely to become blurred (1982: 49–52). The mutual transformation of Buddhism and Christianity, rather than just mutual understanding, is emphasised in Abe 1995.
14 See also Huntington 1989: 26, Riencourt 1981: 172, and Cobb and Ives 1991: 32 and 61, all of which argue for the rejection of the nihilistic interpretation of *shūnyatā*. A similar rejection was expressed earlier in the work of Stcherbatsky (see Welbon 1968: 290). Links between Nāgārjuna and deconstruction are to be found in Loy 1988, Mabbett 1995, Magliola 1986, and Tracy 1990. On Nāgārjuna's philosophy itself see Kalupahana 1986, and Tuck 1990.
15 Mitchell 1991 represents another theologian's attempt to encourage a rapport between Christian spirituality and the Buddhist idea of emptiness, thereby leading towards a mutual transformation of the two traditions.
16 See Küng and Kuschel 1993 for a detailed account of this occasion and its final declaration. See also Zheng 1995 for an attempt to reconcile Confucian political ideas with liberal-democractic thinking. It would be a mistake, of course, to identify Confucianism as the sole ideological engine of economic progress in East Asia.

Bibliography

Abe, M. (1966) 'In Memory of Paul Tillich', *The Eastern Buddhist* (New Series), 1:2.
—— (1995) *Buddhism and the Interfaith Dialogue*, London: Macmillan.
Abegg, L. (1952) *The Mind of East-Asia*, London: Thames & Hudson.
Abelson, P. (1993) 'Schopenhauer and Buddhism', *Philosophy East and West*, 43:2.
Ahmad, A. (1992) *In Theory: Classes, Nations, Literatures*, London: Verso.
Ahmed, A. S. (1992) *Postmodernism and Islam: Predicament and Promise*, London: Routledge.
Aiken, C. F. (1900) *The Dhamma of Gotama Buddha and the Gospel of Jesus the Christ*, Boston, Mass.: Marlier.
Ajaya, S. (1983) *Psychotherapy East and West: A Unifying Paradigm*, Honesdale, Penn.: The Himalayan International Institute.
Alexandrin, G. (1978) 'Buddhist Economics: Demand and Decision-Making', *The Eastern Buddhist* (New Series), 11:2.
Allen, B. S. (1958) *Tides in English Taste (1619–1800): A Background for the Study of Literature*, Vol. 1, New York: Pageant.
Allinson, R. E. (ed.) (1989) *Understanding the Chinese Mind: The Philosophical Roots*, Oxford: Oxford University Press.
Almond, P. C. (1986) 'The Mediaeval West and Buddhism', *The Eastern Buddhist* (New Series), 19:2.
—— (1988) *The British Discovery of Buddhism*, Cambridge: Cambridge University Press.
Ames, R. (ed.) (1994) *Self as Person in Asian Theory and Practice*, Albany, NY: State University of New York Press.
Amin, S. (1989) *Eurocentrism*, New York: Monthly Review Press.
Angel, L. (1994) *Enlightenment East and West*, Albany, NY: State University of New York Press.
Appleton, W. (1951) *A Cycle of Cathay: the Chinese Vogue in England in the Seventeenth and Eighteenth Centuries*, New York: Columbia University Press.
Arendt, H. (1955) *Men in Dark Times*, New York: Harcourt Brace.
Arnold, E. (1884) *The Light of Asia*, New York: Crowell.
Assagioli, R. (1975) *Psychosynthesis: A Manual of Principles and Techniques*, Wellingborough: Turnstone Press.
Avalon, A. (see Woodroffe, J. G).
Badiner, A. H. (ed.) (1990) *Dharma Gaia: A Harvest of Essays in Buddhism and Ecology*, Berkeley, Cal.: Parallax.
Bahm, A. (1977) *Comparative Philosophy: Western, Indian and Chinese Philosophies Compared*, Albuquerque, NM: World Books.
Bailey, P. (1992) 'Voltaire and Confucius: French Attitudes towards China in the Early Twentieth Century', *History of European Ideas*, 14:6.
Baker, F. (ed.) (1985) *Europe and its Other*, Colchester: University of Essex Press.

Barnes, M. (1991) *God East and West*, London: SPCK.
Barrows, J. H. (ed.) (1893) *The World's Parliament of Religions*, 2 vols, Chicago: The Parliament Publishing Co.
Batchelor, M. (1996) *Walking on Lotus Flowers: Buddhist Women Living, Loving, and Meditating*, London: Thorsons.
Batchelor, M. and Brown, K. (eds) (1992) *Buddhism and Ecology*, London: Cassell.
Batchelor, S. (1994) *The Awakening of the West: The Encounter of Buddhism and Western Culture*, London: HarperCollins.
Baumer, F. L. (1977) *Modern European Thought: Continuity and Change in Ideas, 1600–1950*, New York: Macmillan.
Bearce, G. D. (1961) *British Attitudes towards India 1784–1858*, Oxford: Oxford University Press.
Beck, L. A. (1928) *The Story of Oriental Philosophy*, New York: Farrar & Rinehart.
Beck, U. (1992) *Risk Society: Towards a New Modernity*, London: Sage.
Benoit, H. (1955) *The Supreme Doctrine: Psychological Insights in Zen Thought*, London: Routledge.
Berger, P., Berger, B. and Kellner, H. (1974) *The Homeless Mind: Modernization and Consciousness*, Harmondsworth: Penguin.
Bernal, M. (1987) *Black Athena: The Afroasiatic Roots of Classical Civilization*, Vol. 1, London: Vintage.
Bernstein, R. J. (1983) *Beyond Objectivism and Relativism: Science, Hermeneutics and Praxis*, Oxford: Blackwell.
Berry, T. (1974) 'The Religious Life of Modern Man', *Philosophy East and West*, 24:2.
Betty, L. S. (1971) 'The Buddhist–Humean Parallels: Postmortem', *Philosophy East and West*, 21:2.
Bilimoria, P. (1995) 'Comparative and Asian Philosophy in Australia and New Zealand', *Philosophy East and West*, 45:2.
Billington, R. (1990) *East of Existentialism: The Tao of the West*, London: Unwin Hyman.
Bishop, P. (1993) *Dreams of Power: Tibetan Buddhism and the Western Imagination*, London: Athlone.
Bleicher, J. (1982) *The Hermeneutic Imagination*, London: Routledge.
Bockover, M. (ed.) (1991) *Rules, Rituals, and Responsibility*, La Salle, Ill.: Open Court.
Bodde, D. (1950) *Tolstoy and China*, Princeton, NJ: Princeton University Press.
—— (1991) *Chinese Thought, Science, and Society*, Honolulu: University Press of Hawaii.
Bohm, D. (1981) *Wholeness and the Implicate Order*, London: Routledge & Kegan Paul.
Bookchin, M. (1995) *Re-enchanting Humanity*, London: Cassell.
Boorstin, D. J. (1983) *The Discoverers*, London: Dent.
Boss, M. (1965) *A Psychiatrist Discovers India*, London: Wolf.
Boucher, S. (1988) *Turning the Wheel: American Women Creating the New Buddhism*, Boston, Mass.: Beacon.
Bouwsma, W. J. (1957) *Concordia Mundi: The Career and Thought of Guillaume Postel (1510–1581)*, Cambridge, Mass.: Harvard University Press.
Brandon, D. (1976) *Zen in the Art of Helping*, London: Routledge & Kegan Paul.
Braybrooke, M. (1992) *Pilgrimage of Hope: One Hundred Years of Global Interfaith Dialogue*, London: SCM.
Breckenridge, C. and van der Veer, P. (eds) (1993) *Orientalism and the Postcolonial Predicament*, Philadelphia, Penn.: University of Philadelphia Press.
—— (1996) *A Wider Vision: A History of the World Congress of Faiths*, Oxford: Oneworld.
Brockington, J. (1992) *Hinduism and Christianity*, London: Macmillan.
Brunton, P. (1970) *In Search of Secret India*, York Beach: Weiser.
Bunsen, E. de (1880) *The Angel-Messiah of Buddhists, Essenes, and Christians*, London: Longmans.

Burnet, J. (1908) *Early Greek Philosophy*, London: Black.

Burton, N., Hart, P. and Laughlin, J. (eds) (1974) *The Asian Journal of Thomas Merton*, London: Sheldon.

Burtt, E. A. (1955) 'What can Western Philosophy Learn from India?', *Philosophy East and West*, 3:2.

Callicott, J. B. and Ames, R. T. (eds) (1989) *Nature in Asian Thought: Essays in Environmental Philosophy*, New York: State University of New York Press.

Campbell, B. F. (1980) *Ancient Wisdom Revived: A History of the Theosophical Movement*, Berkeley, Cal.: University of California Press.

Campbell, J. (1973) *Oriental Mythology*, London: Souvenir.

Capra, F. (1976) *The Tao of Physics*, London: Fontana.

—— (1982) *The Turning Point*, London: Wildwood.

Caputo, J. (1986) *The Mystical Elements in Heidegger's Thought*, New York: Fordham University Press.

—— (1987) *Radical Hermeneutics: Repetition, Deconstruction, and the Hermeneutical Project*, Bloomington, Ind.: Indiana University Press.

Carpenter, F. I. (1930) *Emerson and Asia*, Cambridge, Mass.: Harvard University Press.

Carus, P. (1897) *Buddhism and its Christian Critics*, Chicago: Open Court.

—— (ed.) (1994) *The Gospel of Buddha*, Oxford: One World.

Casillo, R. (1988) *The Genealogy of Demons: Anti-Semitism, Fascism, and the Myth of Ezra Pound*, Evanston, Ill.: Northwestern University Press.

Chakov, B. L. (1981) *Aldous Huxley and Eastern Wisdom*, Atlantic Highlands, NJ: Humanities Press.

Chaudhuri, H. and Spiegelberg, F. (1960) *The Integral Philosophy of Sri Aurobindo: A Commemorative Symposium*, London: Allen & Unwin.

Chaudhuri, N. C. (1974) *Scholar Extraordinary: the Life of Professor the Rt Hon. Friedrich Max Müller, PC*, London: Chatto & Windus.

Ching, J. (1977) *Confucianism and Christianity: A Comparative Study*, Tokyo: Kodansha.

Ching, J. and Oxtoby, W. (eds) (1992) *Discovering China: European Interpretations in the Enlightenment*, Rochester, Mass.: University of Rochester Press.

Chisholm, L. W. (1963) *Fenellosa: The Far East and American Culture*, New Haven, Conn.: Yale University Press.

Christy, A. (1932) *The Orient in American Transcendentalism*, New York: Columbia University Press.

Cipolla, C. M. (1965) *Guns and Sails in the Early Phase of European Expansion, 1400–1700*, London: Collins.

Clark, S. (1977) *The Moral Status of Animals*, Oxford: Oxford University Press.

Clarke, J. F. (1871) *Ten Great Religions*, Boston, Mass.: Osgood.

Clarke, J. J. (1994) *Jung and Eastern Thought: A Dialogue with the Orient*, London: Routledge.

Claxton, G. (ed.) (1986) *Beyond Therapy: The Impact of Eastern Religions on Psychological Theory and Practice*, London: Wisdom.

—— (1994) *Noises from the Darkroom: The Science and Mystery of the Mind*, London: HarperCollins.

Cleary, T. (trans. and ed.) (1991) *The Secret of the Golden Flower*, San Francisco, Cal.: Harper & Row.

Clifford, J. (1988) *The Predicament of Culture: Twentieth-Century Ethnography, Literature, and Art*, Cambridge, Mass.: Harvard University Press.

Clifton, R. K. and Regher, M. G. (1989) 'Capra on Eastern Mysticism and Modern Physics: A Critique', *Science and Christian Belief*, 1:1.

Clooney, F. X. (1993) *Theology after Vedānta: An Experiment in Comparative Theology*, Albany, NY: State University of New York Press.

Cobb, J. B. (1980) 'Buddhism and Christianity as Complementary', *Eastern Buddhist* (New Series), 13:2.

—— (1982) *Beyond Dialogue: Towards a Mutual Transformation of Christianity and Buddhism*, Philadelphia, Penn.: Fortress.

Cobb, J. B. and Ives, C. (eds) (1991) *The Emptying God: A Buddhist-Jewish-Christian Conversation*, Maryknoll: Orbis.

Collins, S. (1982) *Selfless Persons: Imagery and Thought in Theravada Buddhism*, Cambridge: Cambridge University Press.

Collis, M. (1941) *The Great Within*, London: Faber & Faber.

Conze, E. (1963) 'Buddhist Philosophy and its European Parallels', *Philosophy East and West*, 13:1 and 2.

—— (1967) *Thirty Years of Buddhist Studies*, Oxford: Cassirer.

—— (1975) *Buddhism: Its Essence and Development*, New York: Harper & Row.

Cook, D. J. and Rosemont, H. (1981) 'The Pre-established Harmony Between Leibniz and Chinese Thought', *Journal of the History of Ideas*, 42:3.

Cooper, D. (1996) *World Philosophers: An Historical Introduction*, Oxford: Blackwell.

Cooper, J. C. (1990) *Taoism: the Way of the Mystic*, London: Mandala.

Coward, H. (1985) *Jung and Eastern Thought*, Albany, NY: State University of New York Press.

—— (1990) *Derrida and Indian Philosophy*, Albany, NY: State University of New York Press.

Cox, H. (1977) *Turning East: The Promise and the Peril of the New Orientalism*, New York: Simon & Schuster.

Critchley, S. (1995) 'Black Socrates? Questioning the Philosophical Tradition', *Radical Philosophy*, 69.

Crook, J. and Fontana, D. (eds) (1990) *Space in Mind: East–West Psychology and Contemporary Buddhism*, Shaftesbury: Element.

Cupitt, D. (1992) *The Time Being*, London: SCM.

Cushing, J. N. (1907) *Christ and Buddha*, Philadelphia, Penn.: American Buddhist Publications.

Danielou, A. and Hurry, K. F. (1979) *Shiva and Dionysus, the Religion of Nature and Eros*, New York: Inner Traditions International.

Danto, A. (1976) *Mysticism and Morality: Oriental Thought and Moral Philosophy*, Harmondsworth: Penguin.

Davids, C. A. F. Rhys (1914) *Buddhist Psychology: An Inquiry into the Analysis and Theory of Mind in Pali Literature*, London: Bell.

Davids, T. W. Rhys (1896) *Buddhism: Its History and Literature*, New York: Putnam.

Davies, M. (1990) *A Scientist Looks at Buddhism*, Sussex: Book Guild.

Davis, C. (1971) *Christ and the World Religions*, New York: Herder & Herder.

Dawson, R. (1964) *The Legacy of China*, Oxford: Clarendon Press.

—— (1967) *The Chinese Chameleon: An Analysis of European Conceptions of Chinese Civilization*, Oxford: Oxford University Press.

D'Costa, G. (1986) *Theology and Religious Pluralism: The Challenge of Other Religions*, Oxford: Blackwell.

Déchenet, J.-M. (1960) *Christian Yoga*, Tunbridge Wells: Search Press.

Deussen, P. (1894–1917) *Allgemeine Geschichte der Philosophie*, 7 vols, Leipzig: Brockhaus.

Deutsch, E. (1968) *Advaita Vedanta: A Philosophical Reconstruction*, Honolulu: East–West Center Press.

—— (ed.) (1991) *Culture and Modernity: East–West Philosophic Perspectives*, Honolulu: University Press of Hawaii.

Devall, B. and Sessions, G. (1985) *Deep Ecology*, Salt Lake City, Utah: Gibbs Smith.

Dickinson, G. Lowes (1914) *An Essay on the Civilizations of India, China and Japan*, London: Dent.

Dilworth, D. A. (1989) *Philosophy in World Perspective: A Comparative Hermeneutic of Major Theories*, New Haven, Conn.: Yale University Press.

Dirks, N. (ed.) (1992) *Colonialism and Culture*, Ann Arbor, Mich.: University of Michigan Press.

Drew, J. (1987) *India and the Romantic Imagination*, Oxford: Oxford University Press.

Droit, R.-P. (1989) *L'oubli de l'Inde: une amnésie philosophique*, Paris: Presses Universitaires de France.

Dumoulin, H. (1963) *History of Zen Buddhism*, London: Faber & Faber.

—— (1974) *Christianity Meets Buddhism*, La Salle, Ill.: Open Court.

—— (1976) *Buddhism in the Modern World*, London: Collier.

—— (1981) 'Buddhism and Nineteenth-Century German Philosophy', *Journal of the History of Ideas*, 42:3.

—— (1990) *Zen Buddhism in History*, 2 vols, New York: Macmillan.

Dunne, G. H. (1962) *Generation of Giants: The Story of the Jesuits in China*, London: Burns & Oates.

Duyvendak, J. J. (1949) *China's Discovery of Africa*, London: Probsthain.

Eaton, G. (1949) *The Richest Vein: Eastern Tradition and Modern Thought*, London: Faber & Faber.

Edkins, J. (1893) *Religion in China*, London: Kegan Paul.

Edmunds, A. J. (1908) *Buddhist and Christian Gospels*, Philadelphia, Penn.: Innes.

Edwardes, M. (1971) *East–West Passage: The Travel of Ideas, Arts and Inventions between Asia and the Western World*, London: Cassell.

Eliade, M. (1960) *Myths, Dreams and Mysteries*, New York: Harper & Row.

Emerson, R. W. (1978) *Essays*, London: Dent.

Eppsteiner, F. (ed.) (1985) *The Path of Compassion: Writings on Socially Engaged Buddhism*, Berkeley, Cal.: Parallax.

Epstein, M. (1996) *Thoughts Without a Thinker: Psychotherapy from a Buddhist Perspective*, London: Duckworth.

Evans-Wentz, W. Y. (trans. and ed.) (1960) *The Tibetan Book of the Dead*, London: Oxford University Press.

Fader, L. (1980) 'Arthur Koestler's Critique of D. T. Suzuki's Criticism of Zen', *The Eastern Buddhist* (New Series), 13:2.

Fagan, J. and Shepherd, I. J. (eds) (1972) *Gestalt Therapy Now: Theory, Techniques, Applications*, Harmondsworth: Penguin.

Faivre, A. (1994) *Access to Western Esotericism*, Albany, NY: State University of New York Press.

Farquar, J. (1930) *The Crown of Hinduism*, Oxford: Oxford University Press.

Faure, B. (1991) *The Rhetoric of Immediacy: A Cultural Critique of Chan/Zen Buddhism*, Princeton, NJ: Princeton University Press.

—— (1993) *Chan Insights and Oversights: An Epistemological Critique of the Chan Tradition*, Princeton, NJ: Princeton University Press.

Fields, R. (1986) *How the Swans Came to the Lake: A Narrative History of Buddhism in America*, Boston, Mass.: Shambhala.

Figueira, D. M. (1991) *Translating the Orient: The Reception of Sakuntala in Nineteenth-Century Europe*, Albany, NY: State University of New York Press.

Fingarette, H. (1972) *Confucius: The Secular as Sacred*, New York: Harper & Row.

Flew, A. G. N. (1971) *An Introduction to Western Philosophy: Ideas and Arguments from Plato to Sartre*, London: Thames & Hudson.

Fontana, D. (1992) *The Meditator's Handbook: A Comprehensive Guide to Eastern and Western Meditation Techniques*, Shaftesbury: Element.

Foster, L. and Herzog, P. (eds) (1994) *Defending Diversity: Contemporary Philosophical Perspectives on Pluralism and Multiculturalism*, Amherst, Mass.: University of Massachusetts Press.

Foucault, M. (1977) *Discipline and Punish: the Birth of the Prison*, London: Tavistock.

Fox, W. (1990) *Toward a Transpersonal Ecology: Developing New Foundations for Environmentalism*, Boston, Mass.: Shambhala.

Franke, W. (1967) *China and the West*, Oxford: Blackwell.

Frazier, A. M. (1975) 'A European Buddhism', *Philosophy East and West*, 15:2.

Fredericks, J. (1989) 'Cosmology and Metanoia: A Buddhist Path to Process Thought', *The Eastern Buddhist* (New Series), 22:1.

Friedenthal, R. (1965) *Goethe: His Life and Times*, London: Weidenfeld & Nicolson.

Friedman, L. (1987) *Meetings with Remarkable Women: Buddhist Teachers in America*, Boston, Mass.: Shambhala.

Friedman, M. (1976) 'Martin Buber and Asia', *Philosophy East and West*, 26:4.

Fromm, E. (1986) *Psychoanalysis and Zen Buddhism*, London: Mandala.

Fromm, E., Suzuki, D. T. and De Martino, R. (1960) *Zen Buddhism and Psychoanalysis*, New York: Harper & Row.

Gadamer, H.-G. (1975) *Truth and Method*, London: Sheed & Ward.

Gangadean, A. K. (1993) *Meditative Reason: Towards a Universal Grammar*, New York: Lang.

Garbe, R. (1959) *India and Christendom*, La Salle, Ill.: Open Court.

Gare, A. E. (1995) 'Understanding Oriental Cultures', *Philosophy East and West*, 45:3.

Garratt, G. T. (ed.) (1937) *The Legacy of India*, Oxford: Clarendon.

Gellner, E. (1992) *Postmodernism, Reason, and Religion*, London: Routledge.

Gernet, J. (1987) *China and the Christian Impact: A Conflict of Cultures*, Cambridge: Cambridge University Press.

Gerstering, J. (1986) *German Pessimism and Indian Philosophy: A Hermeneutic Reading*, Delhi: Ajanta.

Giddens, A. (1991) *The Consequences of Modernity*, Cambridge: Polity.

Goddard, D. (ed.) (1994) *A Buddhist Bible*, Boston, Mass.: Beacon Press.

Godwin, J. (1994) *The Theosophical Enlightenment*, Albany, NY: State University of New York Press.

Godwin, J. with Cash, P. and Smith, T. (eds) (1990) *Paul Brunton: Essential Readings*, Wellingborough: Crucible.

Goldman, A. and Sprinchorn, E. (eds) (1964) *Wagner on Music and Drama*, New York: Dutton.

Goleman, D. (1989) *The Meditative Mind*, Wellingborough: Crucible.

Goleman, D. and Thurman, R. A. F. (eds) (1991) *MindScience: An East–West Dialogue*, Boston, Mass.: Wisdom.

Gombrich, R. (1988) *Theravāda Buddhism: A Social History from Ancient Benares to Modern Colombo*, London: Routledge.

Goodrick-Clarke, N. (1992) *The Occult Roots of Nazism: Secret Aryan Cults and their Influence on Nazi Ideology*, London: Tauris.

Goody, J. (1996) *The East in the West*, Cambridge: Cambridge University Press.

Graham, A. C. (1989) *Disputers of Tao: Philosophical Argument in Ancient China*, La Salle, Ill.: Open Court.

Graham, H. (1986) *The Human Face of Psychology*, Milton Keynes: Open University Press.

Granet, M. (1934) *La pensée chinoise*, Paris: Albin Michel.

Gray, J. (1995) *Enlightenment's Wake: Politics and Culture at the Close of the Modern Age*, London: Routledge.

Greenberger, A. J. (1969) *The British Image of India: a Study in the Literature of Imperialism*, London: Oxford University Press.

Griffin, D. R. (ed.) (1988) *The Reenchantment of Science: Postmodern Proposals*, Albany, NY: State University of New York Press.

Griffiths, B. (1982) *The Marriage of East and West*, London: Collins.

—— (1989) *A New Vision of Reality: Western Science, Eastern Mysticism and Christian Faith*, London: Collins.

Griffiths, P. (1986) *On Being Mindless: Buddhist Meditation and the Mind–Body Problem*, La Salle, Ill.: Open Court.

Gross, R. M. (1986) 'Buddhism and Feminism: Towards their Mutual Transformation', *The Eastern Buddhist* (New Series), 19:1 and 19:2.

—— (1993) *Buddhism after Patriarchy: A Feminist History, Analysis, and Reconstruction of Buddhism*, Albany, NY: State University of New York Press.

Gruber, E. and Kersten, H. (1995) *The Original Jesus: The Buddhist Sources of Christianity*, Shaftesbury: Element.

Gudmunsen, C. (1977) *Wittgenstein and Buddhism*, London: Macmillan.

Guénon, R. (1941) *East and West*, London: Luzac.

—— (1945) *Introduction to the Study of Hindu Doctrines*, London: Luzac.

Guenther, H. (1989) *Buddhism in Western Perspective*, Berkeley, Cal.: Dharma Publishing.

Guha, R. and Chakravorty, G. (eds) (1988) *Selected Subaltern Studies*, New York: Oxford University Press.

Gulick, S. L. (1963) *The East and the West: A Study of their Psychic and Cultural Characteristics*, Rutland: Tuttle.

Gupta, B. K. (1973) *India in English Fiction, 1800–1980: Annotated Bibliography*, Metuchen, NJ: Scarecrow.

Guthrie, W. K. C. (1971) *A History of Greek Philosophy*, Vol. 2, London: Cambridge University Press.

Guy, B. (1963) *The French Image of China before and after Voltaire*, Geneva: Institut Musée Voltaire.

Haas, W. S. (1956) *The Destiny of Mind*, London: Faber & Faber.

Habermas, J. (1987) *The Philosophical Discourse of Modernity*, Oxford: Oxford University Press.

Halbfass, W. (1988) *India and Europe: An Essay in Understanding*, Albany, NY: State University of New York Press.

Hall, D. L. and Ames, R. T. (1987) *Thinking Through Confucius*, Albany, NY: State University of New York Press.

Hardy, J. (1987) *Psychology with a Soul: Psychosynthesis in Evolutionary Context*, London: Routledge.

Hardy, R. S. (1853) *A Manual of Buddhism, in its Modern Development*, London: Partridge & Oakley.

Harris, R. B. (ed.) (1982) *Neoplatonism and Indian Thought*, Norfolk: International Society for Neoplatonic Studies.

Hartshorne, C. (1970) *Creative Synthesis and Philosophic Method*, La Salle, Ill.: Open Court.

Harvey, D. (1990) *The Condition of Postmodernity: An Inquiry into the Conditions of Cultural Change*, Oxford: Blackwell.

Hayward, J. W. (1987) *Shifting Worlds, Changing Minds: Where the Sciences and Buddhism Meet*, Boston, Mass.: Shambhala.

Hazard, P. (1953) *The European Mind (1680–1715)*, London: Hollis & Carter.

Hegel, G. W. F. (1956) *The Philosophy of History*, New York: Dover.

Heidegger, M. (1971) *On the Way to Language*, New York: Harper & Row.

Heimann, B. (1937) *Indian and Western Philosophy: A Study in Contrasts*, London: Allen & Unwin.

Heine, S. (1985) *Existential and Ontological Dimensions of Time: Heidegger and Dogen*, Albany, NY: State University of New York Press.

Heisenberg, W. (1959) *Physics and Philosophy: The Revolution in Modern Science*, London: Allen & Unwin.

Henderson, H. (1993) *Catalyst for Controversy: Paul Carus of Open Court*, Chicago:University of Illinois Press.

Herman, J. R. (1996) *I and Tao: Martin Buber's Encounter with Chuang Tzu*, Albany, NY: State University of New York Press.

Herrigel, E. (1985) *Zen in the Art of Archéry*, London: Arkana.

Heyn, B. (1987) *Ayurvedic Medicine*, Wellingborough: Thorsons.

Hick, J. (1973) *God and the Universe of Faiths*, London: Macmillan.

—— (1974) *Truth and Dialogue in World Religions*, Philadelphia, Penn.: Westminster.

—— (1982) *God has Many Names*, Philadelphia, Penn.: Westminster.

—— (1993) *The Metaphor of God Incarnate: Christology in a Pluralistic Age*, London: SCM.

Hick, J. and Knitter, P. (eds) (1987) *The Myth of Christian Uniqueness*, Maryknoll: Orbis.

Hillman, J. (1975) *Revisioning Psychology*, New York: Harper & Row.

Hocking, W. E. (1956) *The Coming World Civilization*, London: Allen & Unwin.

Hodgson, M. G. (1993) *Rethinking World History*, Edmund Burke III (ed.), Cambridge: Cambridge University Press.

Hoffman, F. J. (1987) *Rationality and Mind in Early Buddhism*, Delhi: Motilal Banarsidass.

Hoffman, Y. (1980) *The Idea of Self East and West: A Comparison between Buddhist Philosophy and the Philosophy of David Hume*, Calcutta: Firma.

Honour, H. (1961) *Chinoiserie: the Vision of Cathay*, London: Murray.

Hopkins, J. (1983) *Meditation on Emptiness*, London: Wisdom.

Hourani, A. (1991) *Islam in European Thought*, Cambridge: Cambridge University Press.

Hsia, A. (1974) *Hermann Hesse und China*, Frankfurt: Suhrkamp.

Huff, T. (1993) *The Rise of Modern Science: Islam, China, and the West*, Cambridge: Cambridge University Press.

Hulin, M. (1979) *Hegel et l'Orient*, Paris: Vrin.

Hume, D. (1898) *Essays Moral, Political, and Literary*, London: Murray.

Humphreys, C. (1951) *Buddhism*, Harmondsworth: Penguin.

Huntington, C. W. with Wanchen, G. N. (1989) *The Emptiness of Emptiness: An Introduction to Early Mādhyamaka*, Honolulu: University Press of Hawaii.

Huntington, S. (1993) 'The Clash of Civilizations', *Foreign Affairs*, 72:3.

Husserl, E. (1970) *The Crisis of European Sciences and Transcendental Phenomenology*, Evanston, Ill.: Northwestern University Press.

Huxley, A. (1958) *The Perennial Philosophy*, London: Fontana.

Inada, K. K. and Jacobson, N. P. (eds) (1984) *Buddhism and American Thinkers*, Albany, NY: State University of New York Press.

—— (1992) 'Northropian Categories of Experience Revisited', *Journal of Chinese Philosophy*, 19:1.

Inden, R. (1990) *Imagining India*, Oxford: Blackwell.

Ingram, P. O. (1995) *A Modern Buddhist–Christian Dialogue: Two Universalistic Religions in Transformation*, Queenston: Mellon.

Ingram, P. O. and Streng, F. J. (eds) (1986) *Buddhist–Christian Dialogue: Mutual Renewal and Transformation*, Honolulu: University Press of Hawaii.

Isaacs, H. (1972) *Images of Asia: American Views of China and India*, New York: Random House.

Isherwood, C. (ed.) (1945) *Vedānta for the Western World*, Hollywood, Cal.: Marcel Rodd.

Ives, C. (1992) *Zen Awakening and Society*, London: Macmillan.

Iyer, R. (ed.) (1965) *The Glass Curtain between Asia and Europe: A Symposium on the Historical Encounters and Changing Attitudes of the Peoples of East and West*, London: Oxford University Press.

Jackson, C. T. (1968) 'The Meeting of East and West: The Case of Paul Carus', *Journal of the History of Ideas*, 29:1.

—— (1973) 'Oriental Ideas in American Thought', *Dictionary of the History of Ideas*, Vol. 3, New York: Charles Scribner's Sons.

—— (1981) *Oriental Religions and American Thought*, Westport, Conn.: Greenwood

—— (1994) *Vedānta for the West*, Bloomington, Ind.: Indiana University Press.

Jacobson, N. P. (1969) 'Oriental Influences in the Philosophy of David Hume', *Philosophy East and West*, 19:1.

—— (1981) *Understanding Buddhism*, Carbondale and Edwardsville, Ill.: Southern Illinois University Press.

—— (1983) *Buddhism and the Contemporary World: Change and Self-Correction*, Carbondale and Edwardsville, Ill.: Southern Illinois University Press.

James, W. (1902) *The Varieties of Religious Experience: A Study in Human Nature*, London: Longmans Green.

Jaspers, K. (1953) *The Origin and Goal of History*, New Haven, Conn.: Yale University Press.

—— (1962) *The Great Philosophers*, 2 vols, London: Rupert Hart-Davis.

Jenner, W. J. (1992) *The Tyranny of History: The Roots of China's Crisis*, Harmondsworth: Penguin.

Jennings, H. (1858) *The Indian Religions*, London: Newby.

Joad, C. E. M. (1933) *Counter-Attack from the East*, London: George Allen & Unwin.

Johanns, P. (1932–3) *Vers le Christ par le Vedānta*, 2 vols, Louvain: Vallabha.

Johansson, R. E. A. (1969) *The Psychology of Nirvana*, London: Allen & Unwin.

Johnson, L. E. (1991) *A Morally Deep World: An Essay on Moral Significance and Environmental Ethics*, Cambridge: Cambridge University Press.

Johnson, S. (1873) *Oriental Religions and Their Relation to Universal Religion*, Vol. 1, Boston, Mass.: Osgood.

Johnston, W. (1971) *Christian Zen: A Way of Meditation*, San Francisco, Cal.: Harper & Row.

—— (1981) *The Mirror Mind: Zen–Christian Dialogue*, New York: Fordham University Press.

Jones, K. (1989) *The Social Face of Buddhism: An Approach to Political and Social Activism*, London: Wisdom.

—— (1993) *Beyond Optimism: A Buddhist Political Ecology*, London: Carpenter.

Jones, R. F. (1965) *Ancients and Moderns*, Berkeley, Cal.: University of California Press.

Jones, R. H. (1979) 'Jung and Eastern Religious Traditions', *Religion*, 9:2.

—— (1981) 'Against Needham on Taoism', *Journal of Chinese Philosophy*, 8:2.

—— (1986) *Science and Mysticism: A Comparative Study of Western Natural Science, Theravāda Buddhism, and Advaita Vedānta*, Cranbury, NJ: Associated University Presses.

Jong, J. W. de (1974) 'A Brief History of Buddhist Studies in Europe and America', *The Eastern Buddhist*, 7:1 and 7:2.

Jung, C. G. (1959) *The Archetypes and the Collective Unconscious, Collected Works, Vol. 9i*, London: Routledge & Kegan Paul

—— (1961) *Modern Man in Search of a Soul*, London: Routledge & Kegan Paul.

—— (1977) *The Symbolic Life: Miscellaneous Writings, Collected Works, Vol. 18*, London: Routledge and Kegan Paul.

—— (1978) *Psychology and the East*, London: Routledge & Kegan Paul

—— (1983) *Memories, Dreams, Reflections*, London: Fontana.

—— (1985) *Synchronicity: An Acausal Connecting Principle*, London: Routledge & Kegan Paul

Kabbani, R. (1986) *Europe's Myth of Orient: Devise and Rule*, London: Macmillan.

Kalupahana, D. J. (1986) *Nāgārjuna: The Philosophy of the Middle Way*, Albany, NY: State University of New York Press.

—— (1987) *The Principles of Buddhist Psychology*, Albany, NY: State University of New York Press.

Kasulis, T. P. (1982) 'The Kyoto School and the West: Review and Evaluation', *The Eastern Buddhist* (New Series), 15:2.

—— (ed.) (1993) *Self as Body in Asian Theory and Practice*, Albany, NY: State University of New York Press.

Katz, N. (ed.) (1981) *Buddhist and Western Philosophy*, New Delhi: Sterling.

Katz, S. T. (ed.) (1978) *Mysticism and Philosophical Analysis*, New York: Oxford University Press.

Kellogg, S. H. (1885) *The Light of Asia and the Light of the World*, London: Macmillan.

Keown, D. (1995) *Buddhism and Bioethics*, London: Macmillan.

Kerouac, J. (1959) *The Dharma Bums*, New York: Viking.

Kiernan, V. G. (1972) *The Lords of Human Kind: European Attitudes towards the Outside World in the Imperial Age*, Harmondsworth: Penguin.

King, U. (1980) *Towards a New Mysticism: Teilhard de Chardin and Eastern Religions*, London: Collins.

—— (1989) *The Spirit of One Earth: Reflections on Teilhard de Chardin and Global Spirituality*, New York: Paragon.

King, W. L. (1963) *Buddhism and Christianity: Some Bridges of Understanding*, London: Allen & Unwin.

—— (1992) 'Is there a Buddhist Ethic for the Modern World?', *The Eastern Buddhist* (New Series), 25:2.

—— (1994) 'Engaged Buddhism: Past, Present, Future', *The Eastern Buddhist* (New Series), 27:2.

Kitagawa, J. M. (1990) *The Quest for Human Unity*, Philadelphia, Penn.: Fortress.

Kjellberg, P. and Ivanhoe, P. J. (eds) (1996) *Essays on Skepticism, Relativism, and Ethics in the Zhuangzi*, Albany, NY: State Unversity of New York Press.

Knitter, P. (1985) *No Other Name: A Critical Survey of Christian Attitudes toward the World Religions*, London: SCM.

Koestler, A. (1960) *The Lotus and the Robot*, London: Hutchinson.

Kraemer, H. (1960) *World Cultures and World Religions: the Coming Dialogue*, London: Lutterworth.

Kraft, K. (ed.) (1992) *Inner Peace, World Peace: Essays in Buddhism and Non-Violence*, Albany, NY: State University of New York Press.

Küng, H. (ed.) (1987) *Christianity and the World Religions: Paths of Dialogue with Islam, Hinduism and Buddhism*, London: Collins.

Küng, H. and Ching, J. (1987) *Christianity and Chinese Religions*, New York: Doubleday.

Küng, H. and Kuschel, K.-J. (eds) (1993) *A Global Ethic: The Declaration of the Parliament of the World's Religions*, London: SCM.

Küng, H. and Moltmann, J. (eds) (1986) *Christianity Among World Religions*, Edinburgh: Clark.

Lach, D. F. (1953) 'The Sinophilism of Christian Wolff', *Journal of the History of Ideas*, 14:4.

—— (1957) *Preface to Leibniz' Novissima Sinica*, Honolulu: University Press of Hawaii.

—— (1970) *Asia in the Making of Europe*, Chicago: University of Chicago Press.

—— (1977) *Asia in the Making of Europe*, Vol. 2, Bk 2, Chicago: University of Chicago Press.

Lai, K. L. (1995) 'Confucian Moral Thinking', *Philosophy East and West*, 45:2.

Lancaster, C. (1987) *The Incredible World's Parliament of Religions*, Fontwell: Centaur.

Larson, G. J. and Deutsch, E. (eds) (1988) *Interpreting Across Boundaries: New Essays in Comparative Philosophy*, Princeton, NJ: Princeton University Press.

Leask, N. (1992) *British Romantic Writers and the East: Anxieties of Empire*, Cambridge: Cambridge University Press.

Le Bris, M. (1981) *Romantics and Romanticism*, Geneva: Skira.

Lee, P. K. (1991) (ed.) *Confucian–Christian Encounters in Historical and Contemporary Perspective*, New York: Mellen.

Leibniz, G. W. (1994) *Writings on China*, Introduction and translation by D. J. Cook and H. Rosemont (eds), La Salle, Ill.: Open Court.

Leites, E. (1968) 'Confucianism in Eighteenth-Century England: Natural Morality and Social Reform', *Philosophy East and West*, 18:2.

Levenson, J. R. (ed.) (1967) *European Expansion and the Counter-Example of Asia*, Englewood Cliffs, NJ: Prentice-Hall.

Levine, M. M. (1992) 'The Use and Abuse of *Black Athena*', *The American Historical Review*, 97:2.

Levine, M. P. (1994) *Pantheism: A Non-Theistic Concept of Deity*, London: Routledge.

Lewis, B. (1993) *Islam and the West*, Oxford: Oxford University Press.

Light, S. (1987) *Shuzo Kuki and Jean-Paul Sartre*, Carbondale and Edwardsville, Ill.: South Illinois University Press.

Lillie, A. (1887) *Buddhism in Christendom, or Jesus the Essene*, London: Kegan Paul.

Ling, T. (1968) *A History of Religion East and West*, London: Macmillan.

—— (1973) *The Buddha: Buddhist Civilization in India and Ceylon*, London: Temple Smith.

Liu, M.-W. (1982) 'The Harmonious Universe of Fa-tsang and Leibniz: a Comparative Study', *Philosophy East and West*, 32: 1.

Long, R.-S. W. (1980) *Kandinsky: The Development of an Abstract Style*, Oxford: Clarendon Press.

Lopez, D. S. (1994) 'New Age Orientalism: The Case of Tibet', *Tricycle*, 3:3.

—— (ed.) (1995) *Curators of the Buddha: The Study of Buddhism under Colonialism*, Chicago: University of Chicago Press.

Lopez, D. S. and Rockefeller, S. C. (eds) (1987) *The Christ and the Bodhisattva*, Albany, NY: State University of New York Press.

Lovejoy, A. O. (1948) *Essays in the History of Ideas*, Baltimore, MD: Johns Hopkins University Press.

Lowe, L. (1991) *Critical Terrains: French and British Orientalisms*, Ithaca, NY: Cornell University Press.

Loy, D. (1987) 'The Clôture of Deconstruction: A Mahāyāna Critique of Derrida', *International Philosophical Quarterly*, 27:1.

—— (1988) *Non-Duality: A Study in Comparative Philosophy*, New Haven, Conn.: Yale University Press.

Luthe, W. (1969) *Autogenic Therapy*, New York: Grune & Stratton.

Lyon, D. (1994) *Postmodernity*, Milton Keynes: Open University Press.

Mabbett, I. W. (1995) 'Nāgārjuna and Deconstruction', *Philosophy East and West*, 45:2.

McCarthy, H. E. (1952) 'T. S. Eliot and Buddhism', *Philosophy East and West*, 2:1.

McDermott, R. A. (ed.) (1984) *The Essential Steiner: Basic Writings of Rudolf Steiner*, San Francisco, Cal.: Harper & Row.

McEvilley, T. (1982) 'Pyrrhonism and Madhyamika', *Philosophy East and West*, 32:1.

Mackenzie, D. A. (1928) *Buddhism in Pre-Christian Britain*, London: Blackie.

MacKenzie, J. M. (1995) *Orientalism: History, Theory and the Arts*, Manchester: Manchester University Press.

Mackerras, C. (1989) *Western Images of China*, Hong Kong: Oxford University Press.

McKinney, J. P. (1953) 'Can East Meet West?', *Philosophy East and West*, 3:3.

Macy, J. (1985) *Dharma Development: Religion as Resource in Sarvodaya Self-Help*, West Hartford, Conn.: Kumarian Press.

—— (1991) *World as Lover, World as Self*, Berkeley, Cal.: Parallax.

Magee, B. (1987) *The Philosophy of Schopenhauer*, Oxford: Clarendon.

Magliola, R. (1986) *Derrida on the Mind*, West Lafayette, Ohio: Purdue University Press.

Maidenbaum, A. and Martin, S. (eds) (1991) *Lingering Shadows: Jungians, Freudians, and Anti-Semitism*, Boston, Mass.: Shambhala.

Mallory, J. P. (1989) *In Search of Indo-European Language, Archaeology, and Myth*, London: Thames & Hudson.

Maraldo, J. C. (1986) 'Hermeneutics and Historicity in the Study of Buddhism', *The Eastern Buddhist* (New Series), 9:1 .

Margenau, H. (1984) *The Miracle of Existence*, Woodbridge: Ox Bow.

Marks, J. and Ames, R. T. (eds) (1995) *Emotions in Asian Thought: A Dialogue in Comparative Philosophy*, Albany, NY: State University of New York Press.

Marlow, A. N. (1954) 'Hinduism and Buddhism in Greek Philosophy', *Philosophy East and West*, 4:1.

Marshall, P. J. (ed.) (1970) *The British Discovery of Hinduism in the Eighteenth Century*, Cambridge: Cambridge University Press.

Marshall, P. J. and Williams, G. (1982) *The Great Map of Mankind: British Perceptions of the World in the Age of Enlightenment*, London: Dent.

Maslow, A. (1973) *The Farther Reaches of Human Nature*, Harmondsworth: Penguin.

Masson-Oursel, P. (1926) *Comparative Philosophy*, New York: Harcourt Brace.

Matilal, B. K. and Shaw, J. L. (1985) *Analytical Philosophy in Comparative Perspective*, Dordrecht: Reidel.

Maverick, L. A. (1946) *China, A Model for Europe*, San Antonio, Tex.: Anderson.

May, Rollo (1958) *Existence*, New York: Basic Books.

May, Reinhard (1996) *Heidegger's Hidden Sources: East-Asian Influences on his Work*, trans. and with a complementary essay by G. Parkes, London: Routledge.

Meadows, T. T. (1856) *The Chinese and their Rebellions Viewed in Connection with their Natural Philosophy, Ethics, Legislature, and Administration*, London: Smith, Elder.

Meckel, D. J. and Moore, R. L. (eds) (1992) *Self-Liberation: The Jung/Buddhist Dialogue*, New York: Paulist Press.

Mehta, J. L. (1985) *India and the West: The Problem of Understanding*, Chico: Scholars Press.

Merleau-Ponty, M. (1964) *Signs*, Evanston, Ill.: Northwestern University Press.

Merton, T. (1961) *Mystics and Zen Masters*, New York: Delta.

Michelson, J. M. (1995) 'The Place of Buddhism in Santayana's Moral Philosophy', *Asian Philosophy*, 5:1.

Mill, J. (1858) *The History of British India*, London: Madden.

Mill, J. S. (1977) 'On Liberty', *The Collected Works of John Stuart Mill*, Vol. 23, Toronto: University of Toronto Press.

Minamiki, G. (1985) *The Chinese Rites Controversy from its Beginning to Modern Times*, Chicago: Loyola University Press.

Mistry, F. (1981) *Nietzsche and Buddhism: A Prolegomena to a Comparative Study*, Berlin: de Gruyter.

Mitchell, D. (1991) *Spirituality and Emptiness: The Dynamics of Spiritual Life in Buddhism and Christianity*, New York: Paulist Press.

Moacanin, R. (1986) *Jung's Psychology and Tibetan Buddhism: Western and Eastern Paths to the Heart*, London: Wisdom.

Monier-Williams, M. (1889) *Buddhism, in its Connexion with Brahmanism and Hinduism, and its Contrast with Christianity*, London: Murray.

Montaigne, M. E. de (1958) *Essays*, J. M. Cohen (ed.), London: Penguin.

Moore, C. A. (ed.) (1946) *Philosophy East and West*, Princeton, NJ: Princeton University Press.

—— (1949) *The Second East–West Philosophers' Conference: A Preliminary Report*, Honolulu: University Press of Hawaii.

—— (ed.) (1951) *Essays in East–West Philosophy*, Honolulu: University Press of Hawaii.

—— (ed.) (1967) *The Japanese Mind: Essentials of Japanese Philosophy and Culture*, Honolulu: University Press of Hawaii.

—— (ed.) (1968) *The Status of the Individual East and West*, Honolulu: University Press of Hawaii.

Moore, W. (1989) *Schrödinger: Life and Thought*, Cambridge: Cambridge University Press.

Moore-Gilbert, B. J. (1986) *Kipling's 'Orientalism'*, London: Croom Helm.

Mosse, G. L. (1981) *The Crisis of German Ideology: Intellectual Origins of the Third Reich*, New York: Schocken.

Mullan, B. (1995) *Mad to be Normal: Conversations with R. D. Laing*, London: Free Association.

Müller, F. Max (1879) *Sacred Books of the East*, Vol. 1, Oxford: Oxford University Press.

—— (1893) *Introduction to the Science of Religion*, London: Longmans Green.

Mungello, D. (1977) *Leibniz and Confucianism: The Search for Accord*, Honolulu: University Press of Hawaii.

—— (1978) 'Sinological Torque: the Influence of Cultural Preoccupations on Seventeenth-Century Interpretations of Confucianism', *Philosophy East and West*, 28:2.

—— (1979) 'Some Recent Studies on the Confluence of Chinese and Western Intellectual History', *Journal of the History of Ideas*, 40:4.

—— (1980) 'Malebranche and Chinese Philosophy', *Journal of the History of Ideas*, 41:4.

—— (1989) *Curious Land: Jesuit Accommodation and the Origins of Sinology*, Honolulu: University Press of Hawaii.

Murti, T. R. (1955) *The Central Philosophy of Buddhism: A Study of the Madhyamika System*, London: George Allen & Unwin.

Musil, R. (1953–65) *The Man Without Qualities*, London: Secker & Warburg.

Naess, A. (1965) *Gandhi and the Nuclear Age*, Tolowa: Bedminster.

Naess, A. and Hannay, A. (eds) (1972) *Invitation to Chinese Philosophy*, Oslo: Universitetsforlaget.

Naito, S. (1984) *Yeats and Zen*, Kyoto: Yamaguchi.

Nakamura, H. (1975) *A Comparative History of Ideas*, London: Routledge & Kegan Paul

Nandy, A. (1983) *The Intimate Enemy: Loss and Recovery of Self under Colonialism*, Delhi: Oxford University Press.

Naranjo, C. and Ornstein, R. E. (1971) *On The Psychology of Meditation*, New York: Viking.

Nash, R. F. (1967) *Wilderness and the American Mind*, New Haven, Conn.: Yale University Press.

—— (1989) *The Rights of Nature: A History of Environmental Ethics*, Madison, Wis.: University of Wisconsin Press.

Nasr, S. H. (1990) *Man and Nature: The Spiritual Crisis of Modern Man*, London: Unwin Hyman.

Needham, J. (1954) *Science and Civilization in China*, Vol. 1, Cambridge: Cambridge University Press.

—— (1956) *Science and Civilization in China*, Vol. 2, Cambridge: Cambridge University Press.

—— (1969a) *The Grand Titration: Science and Society East and West*, London: George Allen & Unwin.

—— (1969b) *Within Four Seas: Dialogue between East and West*, London: George Allen & Unwin.

—— (1978) *The Shorter Science and Civilization in China: An Abridgement of Joseph Needham's Original Text*, 2 vols, Cambridge University Press, Cambridge (see Ronan, C. A. 1978).

—— (1979) *Three Masks of Tao: A Chinese Corrective for Maleness, Monarchy and Militarism in Theology*, London: Teilhard Centre for the Future of Man.

Needleman, J. (1972) *The New Religions*, Harmondsworth: Penguin.

Netland, H. A. (1991) *Dissonant Voices: Religious Pluralism and the Question of Truth*, Grand Rapids: Eerdmans.

Neville, R. C. (1994) 'Confucianism as a World Philosophy', *Journal of Chinese Philosophy*, 21:1.

Nietzsche, F. (1968a) *Twilight of the Idols*, and *The Anti-Christ*, Harmondsworth: Penguin.

—— (1968b) *The Will to Power*, New York: Vintage.

—— (1974) *The Gay Science*, New York: Viking.

—— (1979) *Ecce Homo*, Harmondsworth: Penguin.

Norris, C. (1993) *The Truth About Postmodernism*, Oxford: Blackwell.

Northrop, F. S. C. (1946) *The Meeting of East and West*, New York: Macmillan.

Nozick, R. (1981) *Philosophical Explanations*, Oxford: Clarendon.

Odajnyk, V. W. (1993) *Gathering the Light: A Psychology of Meditation*, Boston, Mass.: Shambhala.

Odin, S. (1982) *Process Metaphysics and Hua-Yen Buddhism*, Albany, NY: State University of New York Press.

O'Hanlon, R. (1988) 'Recovering the Subject: *Subaltern Studies* and Histories of Resistance in Colonial Asia', *Modern Asian Studies*, 22:1.

Oliver, I. P. (1979) *Buddhism in Britain*, London: Rider.

Organ, T. W. (1964) *The Self in Indian Philosophy*, The Hague: Mouton.

—— (1975) *Western Approaches to Eastern Philosophy*, Athens, Ohio: Ohio University Press.

—— (1987a) *Philosophy and the Self: East and West*, London: Associated University Presses.

—— (1987b) *Third Eye Philosophy: Essays in East–West Thought*, Athens, Ohio: Ohio University Press.

—— (1989) *Radhakrishnan and the Ways of Oneness of East and West*, Athens, Ohio: Ohio University Press.

Ormiston, G. and Schrift, A. (eds) (1990) *The Hermeneutical Tradition from Ast to Ricoeur*, Albany, NY: State University of New York Press.

Ornstein, R. E. (ed.) (1974) *The Nature of Human Consciousness*, New York: Viking.

—— (1977) *The Psychology of Consciousness*, New York: Harcourt Brace.

Otto, R. (1957) *Mysticism East and West: A Comparative Analysis of the Nature of Mysticism*, New York: Meridian.

Page, R. C. and Chang, R. (1989) 'A Comparison of Gestalt Therapy and Zen Buddhist Concepts of Awareness', *Psychologia*, 32:1.

Palmer, M. (1991) *The Elements of Taoism*, Shaftesbury: Element.

—— (1993) *Coming of Age: An Exploration of Christianity and the New Age*, London: Thorsons.

Panikkar, R. (1978) *The Intrareligious Dialogue*, New York: Paulist Press.

—— (1979a) *Myth, Faith, and Hermeneutics*, New York: Paulist Press.

—— (1979b) 'The Myth of Pluralism in the Tower of Babel: a Meditation on Non-Violence', *Cross-Currents*, 29.

Paper, J. (1995) *The Spirits are Drunk: Comparative Approaches to Chinese Religion*, Albany, NY: State University of New York Press.

Parfitt, D. (1984) *Reasons and Persons*, Oxford: Clarendon.

Parkes, G. (ed.) (1987) *Heidegger and Asian Thought*, Honolulu: University Press of Hawaii.

—— (ed.) (1991) *Nietzsche and Asian Thought*, Chicago: University of Chicago Press.

Parkes, M. G. (1934) *An Introduction to Keyserling*, London: Jonathan Cape.

Parrinder, G. (1962) *Comparative Religion*, London: Sheldon.

—— (1964) *The Christian Debate: Light from the East*, London: Gollancz.

Paul, D. Y. (1979) *Women in Buddhism: Images of Feminism in Mahāyāna Buddhism*, Berkeley, Cal.: Asian Humanities Press.

Peiris, W. (1970) *Edwin Arnold: Brief Account of his Life and Contribution to Buddhism*, Kandy: Buddhist Publication Society.

Pelletier, K. R. (1985) *Toward a Science of Consciousness*, Berkeley, Cal.: Celestial Arts.

Pelletier, K. R. and Garfield, C. (1976) *Consciousness East and West*, New York: Harper & Row.

Perl, J. M. and Tuck, A. P. (1985) 'The Hidden Advantage of Tradition: On the Significance of T. S. Eliot's Indic Studies', *Philosophy East and West*, 35:2.

Perry, M. (1992) *Gods Within: A Critical Guide to the New Age*, London: SPCK.

Pickering, J. (1995) 'Buddhism and Cognitivism: A Postmodern Appraisal', *Asian Philosophy*, 5:1.

Pinot, V. (1932) *La Chine et la formation de l'esprit philosophique en France (1640–1740)*, Paris: Guenther.

Plott, J. C. *et al.* (eds) (1979) *Global History of Philosophy*, 5 vols, Delhi: Motilal Banarsidass.

Poliakov, L. (1971) *The Aryan Myth: A History of Racist and Nationalist Ideas in Europe*, London: Heinemann.

Polkinghorne, J. (1986) *One World: The Interaction of Science and Theology*, London: SPCK.

Popkin, R. H. (1968) *The History of Skepticism from Erasmus to Descartes*, New York: Harper & Row.

Porkert, M. (1982) *Chinese Medicine*, New York: Holt.

Potitella, J. (1965) 'Meister Eckhart and Eastern Wisdom', *Philosophy East and West*, 15:2.

Potter, K. (1963) *Presuppositions of India's Philosophies*, Englewood Cliffs, NJ: Prentice-Hall.

Powers, J. and Curtin, D. (1994) 'Mothering: Moral Cultivation in Buddhist and Feminist Ethics', *Philosophy East and West*, 44:1.

Prakash, G. (1995) '*Orientalism* Now', *History and Theory*, 34:3.

Pratt, J. B. (1928) *Pilgrimage of Buddhism and a Buddhist Pilgrimage*, New York: Macmillan.

Prebish, C. S. (1979) *American Buddhism*, North Scituate, Mass.: Duxbury.

Prigogine, I. and Stengers, I. (1984) *Order out of Chaos: Man's New Dialogue with Nature*, London: Fontana.

Prime, R. (1992) *Hinduism and Ecology: Seeds of Truth*, London: Cassell.

Pullapilly, C. K. and Van Kley, E. J. (eds) (1986) *Asia and the West: Encounters and Exchanges from the Age of Exploration*, Notre Dame: Cross Roads.

Qian, Wen-yuan (1985) *The Great Inertia: Science and Stagnation in Traditional China*, London: Croom Helm.

Qian, Zhaoming (1995) *Orientalism and Modernism: The Legacy of China in Pound and Williams*, Durham: Duke University Press.

Radhakrishnan, S. (1939) *Eastern Religions and Western Thought*, Oxford: Oxford University Press.

Raju, P. T. and Castell, A. (eds) (1968) *East–West Studies on the Problem of the Self*, The Hague: Martinus Nijhoff,

Rao, P. K. (1939) *East versus West: A Denial of Contrasts*, London: George Allen & Unwin.

Ravindran, S. (1990) *W. B. Yeats and the Indian Tradition*, Delhi: Konark.

Reichwein, A. (1925) *China and Europe: Intellectual and Artistic Contacts in the Eighteenth Century*, London: Kegan Paul.

Reynolds, J. (trans. and ed.) (1989) *Self-Liberation through Seeing with Naked Awareness*, Barrytown: Station Hill.

Richards, I. A. (1932) *Mencius on the Mind: Experiments in Multiple Definition*, London: Kegan Paul.

Richardson, A. (1985) *East Comes West*, New York: The Pilgrim Press.

Richardson, M. (1990) 'Enough Said', *Anthropology Today*, 6:4.

Riencourt, A. de (1981) *The Eye of Shiva: Eastern Mysticism and Science*, New York: Morrow.

Riepe, D. (1970) *The Philosophy of India and its Impact on American Thought*, Springfield: Thomas.

Robinson, J. (1979) *Truth is Two-Eyed*, London: SCM.

Rodinson, M. (1988) *Europe and the Mystique of Islam*, London: Tauris.

Rolland, R. (1930) *Prophets of the New India*, London: Cassell.

Rolston, H. (1987) 'Can the East Help the West to Value Nature?', *Philosophy East and West*, 37:2.

Ronan, C. A. (1978) *The Shorter Science and Civilization in China: An Abridgement of Joseph Needham's Original Text*, 2 vols, Cambridge: Cambridge University Press (see Needham, J. 1978).

Ronan, C. E. and Oh, B. B. (eds) (1988) *East Meets West: The Jesuits in China (1582–1773)*, Chicago: Loyola University Press.

Ropp, P. S. (ed.) (1990) *Heritage of China: Contemporary Perspectives on Chinese Civilization*, Berkeley, Cal.: University of California Press.

Rorty, R. (1992) 'A Pragmatist View of Rationality and Cultural Difference', *Philosophy East and West*, 42:4.

Rosemont, H. and Schwartz, B. I. (eds) (1979) 'Studies in Classical Chinese Thought', *Journal of the American Academy of Religion*, 47:3.

Roszak, T. (1970) *The Making of the Counter-Culture*, London: Faber & Faber.

Rougemont, D. de (1963) *The Meaning of Europe*, London: Sidgwick & Jackson.

Rouner, L. S. (ed.) (1984) *Religious Pluralism*, Notre Dame: University of Notre Dame Press.

Rowan, J. (1976) *Ordinary Ecstasy: Humanistic Psychology in Action*, London: Routledge & Kegan Paul

Rowbotham, A. H. (1945) 'The Impact of Confucianism on Seventeenth-Century Europe', *The Far Eastern Quarterly*, 4:5.

Roy, O. (1972) *Leibniz et la Chine*, Paris: Vrin.

Ruegg, D. S. (1980) 'Ahimsa and Vegetarianism in the History of Buddhism', in S. Balasooriya *et al.* (eds) *Buddhist Studies in Honour of Walpola Rahula*, London: Fraser.

Saher, P. J. (1969) *Eastern Wisdom and Western Thought*, London: Allen & Unwin.

Said, E. (1985) *Orientalism*, Harmondsworth: Penguin
—— (1989) 'Representing the Colonized: Anthropology's Interlocutors', *Critical Inquiry*, 15:2.
—— (1993a) *Culture and Imperialism*, London: Chatto & Windus.
—— (1993b) 'Orientalism and After: An Interview with Edward Said', *Radical Philosophy*, 63.
—— (1995) *Orientalism* (with a new Afterword), Harmondsworth: Penguin.

Saint-Hilaire, J. B. (1895) *The Buddha and his Religion*, London: Routledge.

Sallis, J. (1982) 'Meditation and Self-Actualization: A Theoretical Comparison', *Psychologia*, 25:1.

Saunders, K. J. (1912) *Buddhist Ideals: A Study in Comparative Religion*, Calcutta: YMCA.

Sawyer, M. (1977) *Marxism and the Question of the Asiatic Mode of Production*, The Hague: Martinus Nijhoff.

Scharf, R. H. (1993) 'The Zen of Japanese Nationalism', *History of Religions*, 33:1.

Scharfstein, B.-A., Alon, I., Biderman, S., Daor, D. and Hoffmann, Y. (1978) *Philosophy East/Philosophy West: A Critical Comparison of Indian, Chinese, Islamic, and European Philosophy*, Oxford: Blackwell.

Schipper, K. (1993) *Taoist Body*, Berkeley, Cal.: University of California Press.

Schmitz, O. A. H. (1923) *Psychoanalyse und Yoga*, Darmstadt: Reichl.

Schopenhauer, A. (1969) *The World as Will and Representation*, 3 vols, New York: Dover.
—— (1974a) *On the Fourfold Root of the Principle of Sufficient Reason*, La Salle, Ill.: Open Court.
—— (1974b) *Parerga and Paralipomena*, 2 vols, Oxford: Clarendon.

Schrag, C. (1970) 'Heidegger on Repetition and Historical Understanding', *Philosophy East and West*, 20:3.

Schrödinger, E. (1969) *What is Life?: Mind and Matter*, London: Cambridge University Press.

Schultz, J. H. (1934) *Das Autogene Training*, Leipzig: Thieme.

Schumacher, E. F. (1974) *Small is Beautiful*, London: Abacus.

Schuon, F. (1984) *The Transcendental Unity of Religions*, Wheaton: Quest.

Schurmann, F. and Schell, O. (eds) (1967) *Imperial China: The Eighteenth and Nineteenth Centuries*, London: Penguin.

Schwab, R. (1984) *The Oriental Renaissance: Europe's Rediscovery of India and the East 1680–1880*, New York: Columbia University Press.

Schweitzer, A. (1936) *Indian Thought and its Development*, Boston, Mass.: Beacon.

Scott, A. (1890) *Buddhism and Christianity: a Parallel and a Contrast*, Edinburgh: Douglas.

Scott, M. (1983) *Kundalini in the Physical World*, London: Routledge & Kegan Paul.

Seager, R. H. (ed.) (1993) *The Dawn of Religious Pluralism: Voices from the World's Parliament of Religions, 1893*, La Salle, Ill.: Open Court.

—— (1995) *The World's Parliament of Religions: The East/West Encounter, Chicago, 1893*, Bloomington, Ind.: Indiana University Press.

Shapiro, D. H. and Walsh, R. N. (eds) (1984) *Meditation: Classic and Contemporary Perspectives*, New York: Aldine.

Sharpe, E. J. (1985) *The Universal Gītā: Western Images of the Bhagavad Gītā*, La Salle, Ill.: Open Court.

—— (1986) *Comparative Religion: A History*, London: Duckworth.

Shaw, M. (1987) 'William James and Yogacara Philosophy: A Comparative Inquiry', *Philosophy East and West*, 37:3.

—— (1994) *Passionate Enlightenment: Women in Tantric Buddhism*, Princeton, NJ: Princeton University Press.

Silk, J. A. (1994) 'The Victorian Creation of Buddhism', *Journal of Indian Philosophy*, 22:2.

Silva, P. de (1979) *An Introduction to Buddhist Psychology*, London: Macmillan.

Simon, E. (1885) *La cité chinoise*, Paris: Nouvelle Revue.

Siren, O. (1990) *China and the Gardens of Europe in the Eighteenth Century*, Washington, DC: Dumbarton Oaks Research Library.

Siu, R. G. H. (1957) *The Tao of Science: An Essay on Western Knowledge and Eastern Wisdom*, London: Chapman & Hall.

Sivin, N. (ed.) (1995) *Science in Ancient China: Researches and Reflections*, Aldershot: Variorum.

Sklar, D. (1977) *The Nazis and the Occult*, New York: Dorset.

Smart, N. (1981) *Beyond Ideology: Religion and the Future of Western Civilization*, London: Collins.

—— (1992) *Buddhism and Christianity: Rivals and Allies*, London: Macmillan.

Smith, E. F. (1930) *Prophets of the New India*, London: Cassell.

Smith, J. H. (1972) 'Tao Now: An Ecological Testament', in I. G. Barbour (ed.) *Earth Must be Fair: Reflections on Ethics, Religion, and Ecology*, Englewood Cliffs, NJ: Prentice-Hall.

Smith, J. R. (1994) 'Nishitani and Nietzsche on the Selfless Self', *Asian Philosophy*, 4:2.

Smith, W. C. (1981) *Towards a World Theology: Faith and the Comparative Study of Religion*, London: Macmillan.

Snelling, J. (1992a) *Buddhism in Russia*, Shaftesbury: Element.

—— (ed.) (1992b) *Sharpham Miscellany: Essays in Spirituality and Ecology*, Totnes: Sharpham Trust.

Solomon, R. C. and Higgins, K. M. (eds) (1993) *From Africa to Zen: An Invitation to World Philosophy*, Lanham: Rowman & Littlefield.

Song, Shun-ching (1989) *Voltaire et la Chine*, Aix-en-Provence: Publications Université de Provence.

Spretnak, C. (1991) *States of Grace: The Recovery of Meaning in the Postmodern Age*, San Francisco, Cal.: HarperCollins.

Sprung, M. (ed.) (1978) *The Question of Being: East–West Perspectives*, Philadelphia, Penn.: Pennsylvania State University Press.

Stcherbatsky, Th. (1958) *Buddhist Logic*, 'S-Gravenhage: Mouton.

—— (1968) *The Conception of the Buddhist Nirvāna*, Varanasi: Bharatiya Vidya Prakashan.

Steffney, J. (1981) 'Mind and Metaphysics in Heidegger and Zen Buddhism', *The Eastern Buddhist* (New Series), 14:1.

Stillson-Judah, J. (1974) *Hare Krishna and the Counter-Culture*, New York: John Wiley.

Stokes, E. (1959) *The English Utilitarians and India*, Oxford: Clarendon.

Streng, F. (1967) *Emptiness: A Study of Religious Meaning*, Nashville, Tenn.: Abingdon.

Sturch, R. L. (1993) 'Quantum Interpretations of the Christian World-Views', *Science and Christian Belief*, 5:2.

Suleri, S. (1992) *The Rhetoric of English India*, Chicago: University of Chicago Press.

Surette, L. (1993) *The Birth of Modernism: Ezra Pound, T. S. Eliot, W. B. Yeats and the Occult*, Montreal: McGill-Queen's University Press.

Swidler, L., Cobb, J. B., Knitter, P. F. and Hellwig, M. K. (1990) *Death or Dialogue: From the Age of Monologue to the Age of Dialogue*, London: SCM.

Taber, J. A. (1983) *Transformation Philosophy: A Study of Sankara, Fichte, and Heidegger*, Honolulu: University Press of Hawaii.

Talbot, M. (1980) *Mysticism and the New Physics*, New York: Bantam.

Tarn, W. (1938) *The Greeks in Bactria and India*, Cambridge: Cambridge University Press.

Tart, C. T. (ed.) (1975) *Transpersonal Psychologies*, New York: Harper & Row.

Taylor, C. (1992) 'The Politics of Recognition', in A. Gutman, C. Taylor, S. Wolf, S. Rockefeller and M. Walzer (eds) *Multiculturalism and the Politics of Recognition*, Princeton, NJ: Princeton University Press.

Teilhard de Chardin, P. (1958) *The Phenomenon of Man*, London: Collins.

Temple, R. (1991) *The Genius of China: 3000 Years of Scientific Discovery and Inventions*, London: Prion.

Teng, Ssu-Yü (1943) 'Chinese Influence on the Western Examination System', *Harvard Journal of Asiatic Studies*, 7:2.

Thoreau, H. D. (1961) *A Writer's Journal*, London: Heinemann.

Thundy, Z. P. (1993) *Buddha and Christ*, Leiden: Brill.

Thurman, R. A. (1991) *The Central Philosophies of Tibet*, Princeton, NJ: Princeton University Press.

Tiffin, C. and Lawson, A. (eds) (1994) *De-Scribing Empire: Post-colonialism and Textuality*, London: Routledge.

Tillich, P. (1963) *Christianity and the Encounter of World Religions*, New York: Columbia University Press.

Titmuss, C. (1995) *The Green Buddha*, Totnes: Insight.

Todorov, T. (1993) *On Human Diversity: Nationalism, Racism, and Exoticism in French Thought*, Cambridge, Mass.: Harvard University Press.

Townsend, M. (1905) *Asia and Europe*, London: Constable.

Toynbee, A. (1948) *Civilization on Trial*, London: Oxford University Press.

Tracy, D. (1990) *Dialogue with the Other: The Inter-Religious Dialogue*, Louvain: Peters.

Tucci, G. (1969) *The Theory and Practice of the Mandala*, London: Rider.

Tuck, A. P. (1990) *Comparative Philosophy and the Philosophy of Scholarship: On the Western Interpretation of Nāgārjuna*, New York: Oxford University Press.

Turner, B. S. (1994) *Orientalism, Postmodernism, and Globalism*, London: Routledge.

Tweed, T. A. (1992) *The American Encounter with Buddhism 1844–1912*, Bloomington, Ind.: Indiana University Press.

Tworkov, H. (1994) *Zen in America*, New York: Kodansha.

Varela, F. J., Thompson, E. and Rosch, E. (1991) *The Embodied Mind: Cognitive Science and Human Experience*, Cambridge, Mass.: MIT Press.

Versluis, A. (1991) 'From Transcendentalism to Universal Religion: Samuel Johnson's Orientalism', *American Transcendental Quarterly*, 5:2.

—— (1993) *American Transcendentalism and Asian Religions*, New York: Oxford University Press.

Viswanathan, G. (1989) *Masters of Conquest: Literary Study and British Rule in India*, New York: Columbia University Press.

Voltaire, F.-M. A. (1963) *Essai sur les moeurs*, Paris: Garnier.

Vyas, R. N. (1970) *The Universalistic Thought of India: From the Rigveda to Radhakrishnan*, Bombay: Lalvani.

Ward, B. (1957) *The Interplay of East and West: Elements of Contrast and Cooperation*, London: George Allen & Unwin.

Washington, P. (1993) *Madame Blavatsky's Baboon: Theosophy and the Emergence of the Western Guru*, London: Secker & Warburg.

Watts, A. (1959) *Beat Zen, Square Zen, and Zen*, San Francisco, Cal.: City Light.

—— (1973) *Psychotherapy East and West*, Harmondsworth: Penguin.

Webb, J. (1976) *The Occult Establishment*, La Salle, Ill.: Open Court.

Weber, M. (1951) *The Religion of China: Confucianism and Taoism*, New York: The Free Press.

—— (1958) *The Religion of India: The Sociology of Hinduism and Buddhism*, New York: The Free Press.

Wehr, G. (1987) *Jung: A Biography*, Boston, Mass.: Shambhala.

Weiss, P. (1954) 'The Gita, East and West', *Philosophy East and West*, 4:3.

Welbon, G. (1968) *The Buddhist Nirvāna and its Western Interpreters*, Chicago: University of Chicago Press.

Welburn, A. (1991) *The Beginnings of Christianity: Essene Mystery, Gnostic Revelation, and Christian Vision*, Edinburgh: Floris.

Welwood, J. (ed.) (1979) *The Meeting of the Ways: Explorations in East/West Psychology*, New York: Schocken.

—— (ed.) (1983) *Awakening the Heart: East/West Approaches to Psychotherapy and the Healing Relationship*, Boston, Mass.: Shambhala.

West, M. A. (ed.) (1987) *The Psychology of Meditation*, Oxford: Clarendon.

West, M. L. (1971) *Early Greek Philosophy and the Orient*, Oxford: Clarendon Press.

Whorf, B. L. (1956) *Language, Thought and Reality: Selected Writings*, Cambridge, Mass.: MIT Press.

Wienpahl, P. (1979) 'Eastern Buddhism and Wittgenstein's Philosophical Investigations', *The Eastern Buddhist* (New Series), 12:2.

Wilber, K. (ed.) (1985) *The Holographic Paradigm and Other Paradoxes*, Boston, Mass.: Shambhala.

Wilber, K., Engler, J. and Brown, D. P. (eds) (1986) *Transformations of Consciousness: Conventional and Contemplative Perspectives and Developments*, Boston: Shambhala.

Williams, S. W. (1883) *The Middle Kingdom*, 2 vols, New York: Scribner's.

Willson, A. L. (1964) *A Mythical Image: The Ideal of India in German Romanticism*, Durham, NC: Duke University Press.

Wilson, B. (1982) ' "From Mirror after Mirror": Yeats and Eastern Thought', *Comparative Literature*, 34:1.

Winks, R. W. and Rush, J. R. (eds) (1990) *Asia in Western Fiction*, Manchester: Manchester University Press.

Wittfogel, K. A. (1957) *Oriental Despotism: A Comparative Study of Absolute Power*, New Haven, Conn.: Yale University Press.

Wolin, R. (ed.) (1991) *The Heidegger Controversy*, New York: Columbia University Press.

Wood, R. C. (1988) 'British Churches Encounter the Challenge of Pluralism', *The Christian Century*, 19.

Woodroffe, J. G. (alias Arthur Avalon) (1919) *The Serpent Power*, Calcutta: Ganesh.

—— (1966) *The World as Power*, Madras: Ganesh.

Wright, A. F. (1971) *Buddhism in Chinese History*, Stanford, Cal.: Stanford University Press.

Wright, B. (1957) *Interpreter of Buddhism: Sir Edwin Arnold*, New York: Bookman Associates.

Yao, X. (1996) *Confucianism and Christianity*, Brighton: Academic Press.

Yeats, W. B. (1961) *Essays and Introductions*, London: Macmillan.

Young, G. M. (ed.) (1952) *Th. B. Macaulay: Prose and Poetry*, London: Hart-Davis.

Young, J. D. (1983) *Confucianism and Christianity: The First Encounter*, Hong Kong: Hong Kong University Press.

Young, R. (1990) *White Mythologies: Writing History and the West*, London: Routledge.

Zaehner, R. C. (1958) *At Sundry Times: An Essay in the Comparison of Religions*, London: Faber & Faber.

—— (1963) *Matter and Spirit: Their Convergence in Eastern Religions, Marx, and Teilhard de Chardin*, New York: Harper & Row.

—— (1970) *Concordant Discord: The Interdependence of Faiths*, Oxford: Clarendon Press.

—— (1974) *Our Savage God*, London: Collins.

Zhang Longzi (1988) 'The Myth of the Other: China in the Eyes of the West', *Critical Inquiry*, 15:1.

—— (1992) *The Tao and the Logos: Literary Hermeneutics, East and West*, Durham, NC: Duke University Press.

Zheng, C. (1995) *A Comparison between Western and Chinese Political Ideas*, New York: Mellen.

Zimmer, H. (1951) *Philosophies of India*, Princeton, NJ: Princeton University Press.

Zukav, G. (1979) *The Dancing Wu Li Masters: An Overview of the New Physics*, London: Fontana.

Index